TRAINING FOR WESTERN HORSE AND RIDER

By
J'Wayne McArthur

"The Outside of a Horse is Good for the Inside of the Man."

—Will Rogers

I

FIRST EDITION 1976
SECOND EDITION 1979
THIRD EDITION 1986
FOURTH EDITION 1988
FIFTH EDITION 1992

Copies available by writing to:
J'WAYNE McARTHUR
ADVS Department
Utah State University
Logan, Utah 84322-4815

Printed by

Keith W. Watkins and Sons, Inc.
Providence, Utah 84332

ISBN 0-89832-003-8

ACKNOWLEDGEMENTS

Horsemen have been writing down their ideas about horses and horsemanship for well over 2350 years. This insight into the history of horsemanship literature leaves me feeling quite inadequate for this task.

Without the help of many good horsemen and women, as well as top researchers and veterinarians, this book would not have been possible. Their information and critiques have helped refine some of the information to its present state.

Special thanks go out to all the students that have put up with me and my strict rules and procedures. As a result of these experiences in teaching, I have developed a method of working around the horse and riding him that puts the safety of the rider and the horse in first priority. I hope the students have found comfort in getting through the class safely.

Working with horses and students, one never knows when something unexpected will happen and someone will be hurt. It may be you and it may be tomorrow, but by learning the right procedures, that chance is reduced immeasurably.

Thanks to Holly Benson for posing for many of the pictures. I also appreciate the help of my advanced students, Erik Chustz and Shane Getz, for their assistance in the photo sessions for the training portion of this book. I owe a special thanks to Stephan W. Guymon for the help with photography, word processing and proof reading.

Carol Hinshaw and Jess Faupell have been of great help in doing much of the riding I should have been doing while I was writing instead. Their help in teaching the beginning students has helped to keep me partially sane.

None of the pictures in this book could have been possible without the cooperation and patience of the fine horses used. There were many takes and retakes of pictures. I'm sure they wondered why they were doing all the things they did just for a picture.

In all my writing I get so mentally involved day and night that I'm not very attentive to others and their needs. I wish to thank my beautiful wife, Jolene, for putting up with me all these years.

J'Wayne McArthur

INTRODUCTION

Saddle horses and ponies play an important part in the recreation of Americans today, even more than they did yesterday, but less than they will tomorrow. Spectators watch rodeos, races, and horse shows (registered, youth, and open) in ever increasing numbers. Some of these spectators have other direct contacts with horses, some do not.

Ranch horses are still used in the management and production of beef and sheep in America. These horses must have special training to handle their specific role, as do most other horses. Surveys show, however, that most American horses are used for personal enjoyment and for recreational riding.

Many books have been written about how to handle and ride a horse, but few, if any, have described the step-by-step details discussed in this handbook. Based on sixteen years of teaching Western Horsemanship at Utah State University, each step that is discussed includes safety considerations that were derived through trial - and sometimes error. The procedures have repeatedly proven their worth in safety and in instructional effectiveness in the teaching of over twenty-five hundred students.

Some readers of this material may say, "Well, that's not the way I do it and I have made out fine." This may be true. There are many ways of doing everything discussed. Few horse trainers agree on methods. Some are almost opposite in their opinions and procedures and still get similar results, but this material is based on proven methods with the safety of horse and rider as the main objective. One truism is universally valid, however: horses learn through repetition of stimuli. In a class, insisting that all students handle their horses in a similar manner helps minimize the chance of horses reacting adversely to change. My intent has been to develop a handbook that can be used in various group training situations or by individuals. I have, therefore, gone into substantial detail and made liberal use of graphics to reinforce the text. Both riders and their horses are referred to with masculine pronouns for the sake of simplification - not to imply male superiority.

It is best for a beginner to follow a proven method until he has a background adequate to evaluate other books and training tips he might come across. Comparing methods without first having a background can cause confusion and compound the problems of learning to ride. The same is true with care and training of your horse. Don't be led astray by each person that has once owned a horse and now has all the answers for your problems.

Table of Contents

CHAPTER ONE
The Horse

Parts of the Horse

Before you can hope to be called a horseman, you must know a great deal about the horse. A good place to start is with the memorization of the parts of the horse. Much of the following material (and virtually all books about horses and riding) use certain terms that you must be familiar with if you want to understand the instructions. Study the diagram below and become familiar with the terms used.

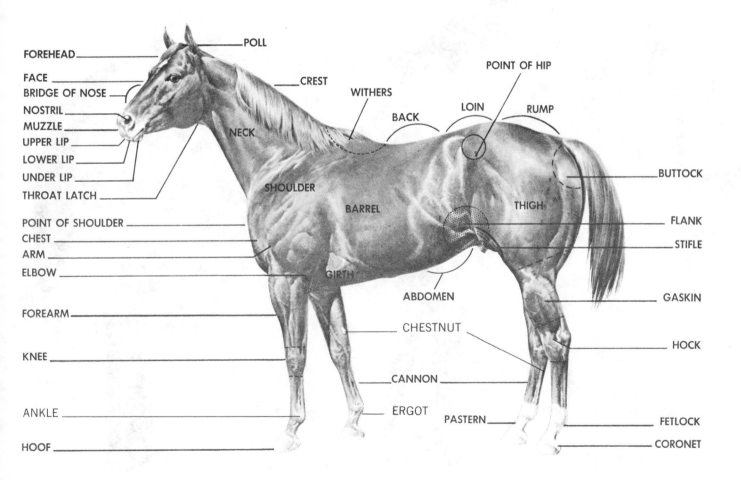

Parts of the Horse

1

Horse Colors

Some horsemen have no real preference for specific horse colors. Their saying is: "I've never ridden a good horse with a bad color." Other people have a special color in mind when they shop for a horse. Whether or not you care about it, you should be able to identify a horse by its color. If you're sent to fetch the bay in a big pen of horses and you bring back a sorrel, you may have to ride him, whatever his training.

The mane, tail and legs are also known as "points" and that term will be used hereafter. White markings on the face or legs do not have a bearing on the basic color designation of the horse. Horse colors can be broken down according to black or red points.

Black Points - - Black mane, tail, legs

2

Black Points

Horses with black points can be categorized as follows:

Black: True black all over with no brown hairs.

Brown: Almost black in appearance and always has black points, but brown hairs may be present on muzzle and head, as well as on flanks and shoulders. In some seasons a brown horse can closely resemble a true black.

Bay: Always has black points with a uniform body color of brown to red. In some seasons the dark bay looks like a brown.

Buckskin: A dilution of the bay. It can range in color from a dark cream to a light yellow, but will always have black points. It may also have a dark dorsal stripe and may have dark zebra or horizontal striping on the legs. In some seasons the dark buckskin may look like a bay.

Grulla: A dilution of black or dark brown. The hair is a uniform mouse color over the body with black points and generally a dorsal stripe. It may have zebra striping on the legs.

Gray: Born blue or almost black, these horses steadily turn lighter as more and more white hairs come into the coat. By age eight or ten these horses may appear almost white. Many people confuse this gray-white horse with a pure white horse. By looking closely, one can distinguish white leg and/or face markings on gray horses. Their skin will be black and their eyes dark brown.

In the dapple, the darker spots embossed in the coat generally occur between the horse's second and fifth year. They may totally disappear as the white color increases.

A young gray with a lot of black in his coat is called a steel gray. When only small specks of black are present, he is called a flea-bitten gray, and when more white shows, he is called a silver gray.

Black (Blue) Roan: Black horse with white hairs intermingled. The blue roan and the gray are sometimes confused. Both have whitehairs intermingled with black, but the gray continues to gain more white, while the roan will hold his color after he is a year or two old. The roan will have a black or dark head while a gray becomes white on his muzzle and head early in life. The blue roan maintains his black points.

Bay or Brown (Strawberry) Roan: Reddish brown hair intermingled with white on the body. The head will be reddish brown and the points are black. The color will not change appreciably throughout life.

Perlino: Off-white or pearl, with blue eyes. The mane and tail generally appear rust colored on the tips. The legs may also be rust in color. The perlino represents a heavy dilution of bay. It really doesn't have black points, but is directly related to the black mane and tail horses.

This color is also known as type B Albino, which is not a true albino.

Red to Cream Points

The horses with red or flaxen mane and tail can be categorized as follows:

Chestnut: From liver brown to dark red in color. The liver brown color is sometimes confused with brown. The liver brown chestnut, however, will have no black on his body. A chestnut may have a flaxen-colored mane and tail.

Sorrel: The lighter red coat colors are called sorrel and are combined with red to flaxen (cream to white) manes and tails.

Red Dun: Lighter than the sorrel, with darker red points than the body color. Generally, a red dorsal stripe will be present. These horses may have zebra stripes around legs.

Palomino: Cream to yellow-brown with near white mane and tail.

Chestnut or Sorrel (Red) Roan: The color is sorrel or chestnut, with white hairs intermingled in the coat. The head and legs will generally be darker red than the body.

Cremello: A dilution of chestnut called type A Albino. The body is off-white or cream with lighter mane and tail. The eyes are blue and the skin pink.

Albino (White): Clear white color with light brown eyes and pink skin.

Two other color patterns also exist, but both are simply superimposed over any one of the previously mentioned colors except albino. These are Appaloosa and pinto (paint).

Appaloosa

Eight color patterns are classified as Appaloosa. Many variations and combinations of these eight can occur, however.

1. **Blanket**: Refers to a horse that has a solid white area, normally over, but not limited to, the hip area (with a contrasting base color).

2. **Blanket with Spots**: Refers to a horse with a white area, normally over, but not limited to, the hips with dark spots located within the white. The spots are usually the same color as the base color of the horse (chestnut spots on a chestnut horse, black spots on a black horse, bay spots on a bay horse). However, a horse may also have more than one color of spots.

3. **Leopard**: A white horse having dark spots over the entire body, including legs, neck and head.

4. **Roan**: Refers to an Appaloosa roan pattern (e.g. a mixture of white and dark hairs), and may have a lighter area on the forehead, over the back, loin, and hips with darker areas on the frontal bones of the face, legs, stifle, above the eye, point of hip and behind the elbow. (Must have Appaloosa characteristics to receive regular papers.)

5. **Roan Blanket**:Refers to a horse that has a mixture of white and dark hairs over a portion of the body, normally over, but not limited to, the hip area.

Sclera of the Eye,
Particolored Skin

Vertical-striped hoof

6. **Roan Blanket with Spots**: Refers to a mixture of white and dark hairs over a portion of the body with white and/or dark spots within the roan area.
7. **Spots**: Refers to a horse with white or dark spots over a portion of its body or over the entire body.
8. **Solid**: Refers to a horse that has a base color such as chestnut, bay, etc. and has no contrasting color in the form of an Appaloosa coat pattern.

Other distinguishing characteristics of Appaloosas are vertical stripes of black and white on the hoof, a white sclera (or ring) encircling the eye, and particolored or mottled skin.

Pinto

Two basic color patterns are recognized.
1. **Tobiano:**
    A.   Predominant body color may be dark or white.
    B.   Head marked like a solid-colored horse; may have blaze, stripe, star or snip.
    C.   All four legs will be white, at least below the hocks and knees.
    D.   Spots are usually regular and distinct, often coming in oval or round patterns that extend down over the neck and chest, giving the appearance of a shield.
    E.   A dark color usually covers one or both flanks.
2. **Overo**:
    A.   Predominant body color may be dark or white.
    B.   White does not cross the back between the withers and the tail.
    C.   One or more legs will generally be dark and often all four legs are dark color.
    D.   Head markings are often bald-faced, apron (white over lower half of face) or even bonnet-faced (white over upper half of face).
    E.   Irregular, scattered, and/or splashy white markings on body, often referred to as calico patterns.
    F.   Tail is usually one color.

It should be kept in mind that there are always exceptions to these general rules. Two color designations can also be noted. Piebald refers to a black and white pinto. Skewbald describes a pinto that is white and any color other than black. These colors can appear on either tobiano or overo patterns.

Tobiano

Overo

Markings

Sometimes it is not enough just to designate a horse by color. For example, when there are four bays in a corral, facial or leg markings may then help identify exactly which bay you are talking about.

Facial Markings

Facial markings are defined as follows (see the following page for illustrations):

Spot: A few white hairs in the center of the forehead.
Star: A small, clearly defined area of white hairs on the forehead.
Snip: A small patch of white which runs over the muzzle, often to the lips.
Stripe: A long, narrow band of white from the forehead down toward the muzzle.
Race: Similar to a stripe but veers off to one side.
Blaze: A broader, more open stripe of white running from the forehead down to the nasal peak.
Bald Face: One which has white over most of the flat surface of the face, often extending out around the eyes and possibly to the upper lip and around the nostrils.

The star, stripe, and snip can be combined as a star and snip, a stripe and snip, or a star and stripe.

Leg Markings

Leg markings can be defined simply as:

Stockings: White from the hoof up to the knee or above.
Boots: White from the hoof up past the pastern but not to the knee. There are other more specific names for these lower markings, but they are so infrequently used that unless identification for registration is needed, the more common terminology is adequate.

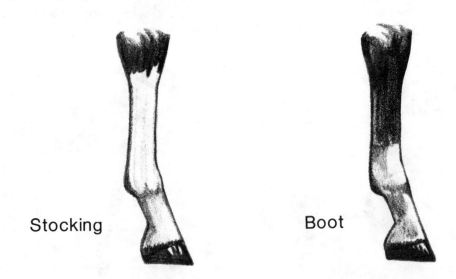

Stocking   Boot

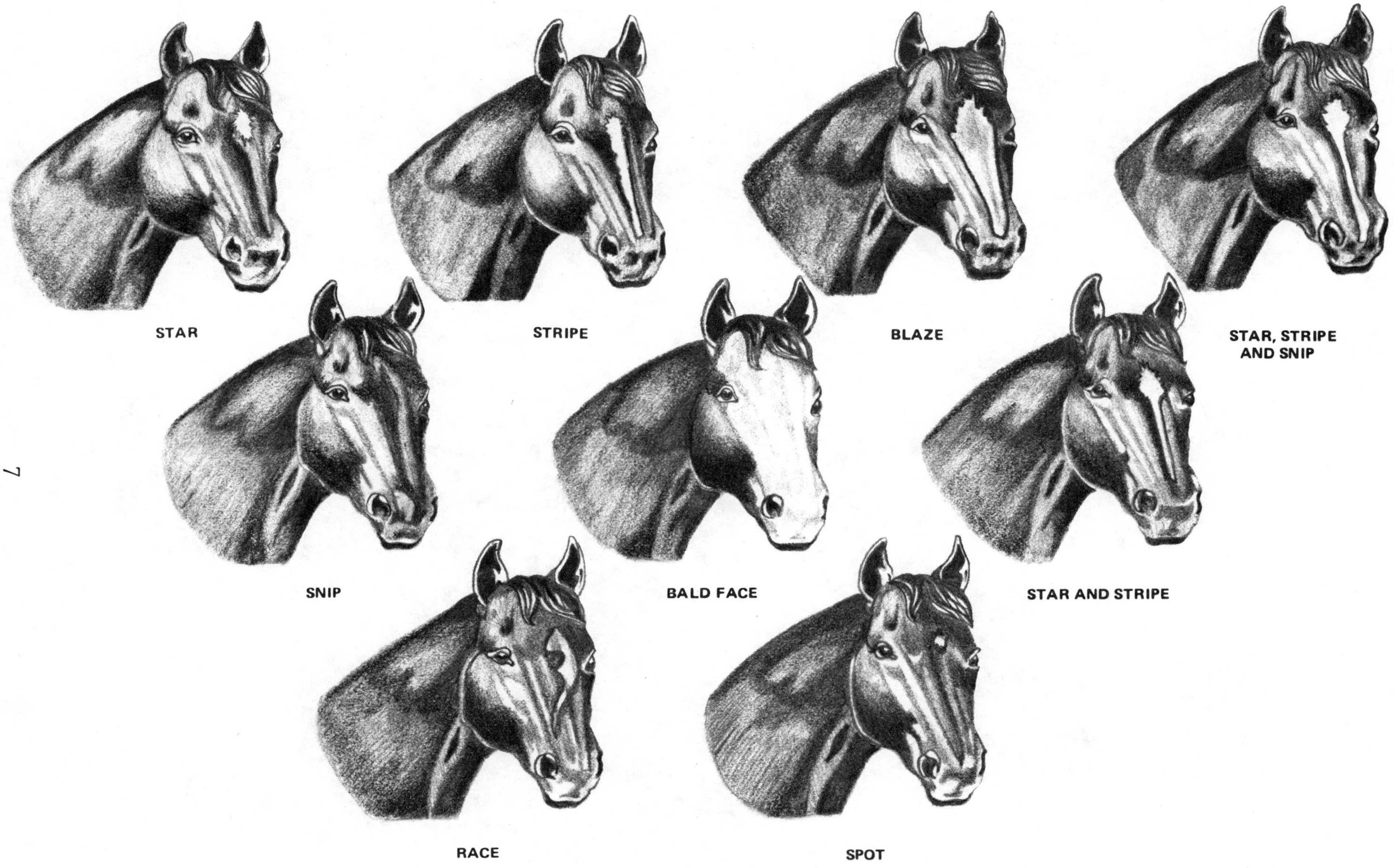

STAR, STRIPE
AND SNIP

STAR AND STRIPE

BLAZE

SPOT

STRIPE

BALD FACE

RACE

STAR

SNIP

Facial Markings

7

CHAPTER TWO
Horse Evolution, Domestication and Breeds

The Evolution of the Horse

Today we look around and see the cars, boats, trains and airplanes, but where would we be if we hadn't had the use of the horse to bring us from the dawn of history to the advent of the motorized vehicle? We would probably be back in caves or huts with very little social evolution.

It was the horse and his cousins that provided the transportation, broke the ground for farming, built the roads and railroads that brought this industrial nation into its own. It's too bad the cars and trucks that took the place of the horse don't have horse sense. You never saw horses run head on and crash, did you?

Just where did these horses come from anyway? The horse of today is a descendant of a small, primitive, five-toed animal. He was no larger than a fox. Scientists named him Eohippus. Eo is the word for "dawn" and hippus is the word for "horse" in Greek. The Eohippus was found in North America along the base of the newly created Rocky Mountains.

As the semi-tropical climate changed, the Eohippus had to travel further for food and graze grass instead of browsing leaves. The neck elongated, the outer two side toes drew up, the next two toes shortened, thinned and reposed into splint hooves. The center toe developed into one strong hoof.

The size of the Eohippus had also changed. By the Ice Age and the dawn of man the horse had evolved to the Equus state, or the horse was similar in size and structure to the present horse.

During a number of stages of development, the ancestors to the horse migrated or were displaced to Europe but did not endure and evolve, but rather became extinct. Only in North and South America did the horse find an environment conducive to his development.

Some time during the Ice Age, the horse "Equus" migrated to all continents except for Australia. This migration took place over the land and ice bridges between North America and Asia.

After the evolution of the horse and the development of man, the two became travelers on the same trail through history. At first it was a one sided trail with the horse being hunted for food. In Solutree, France, the bones of over 40,000 horses were found outside the settlement which existed 25,000 years ago.

The hunting of horses for food is one good explanation for the disappearance of the horse on the American Continent 8,000 years ago. This would be long before the estimated domestication of the horses in the old world, which took place between 4500 and 2500 B.C. By 1000 B.C., the domestication of the horse had spread throughout Europe to Asia and North Africa. The horse was introduced into the Olympic Games in about 1400 B.C. and has been a continuous participant up to the present.

Hot blooded horses evolved in the hot climates. These horses had a thinner skin with short hair. They had more sweat glands in the skin to help maintain body temperature. The Arabian is the prime example of the hot blood. These horses had one less vertebra than the cold bloods, prior to their crossing.

Cold blood horses evolved in the cold areas of Europe. To protect them from the cold, they had a thicker skin and longer hair. Their legs were feathered with long hair to keep them warm in the snow. These horses had fewer sweat glands which helped keep the heat in. The draft horse and the heavy boned, long haired ponies are examples of the cold bloods. These horses are also known for their mild temperament.

When the hot blood Arabians were crossed with the European cold bloods, a cross bred was developed. This horse had many of the hot blood characteristics but carried the larger frame with the increased number of vertebrae and a less attractive, larger head.

Cortez brought horses into Mexico in 1519. Coronado rode horses from California through Arizona to Kansas in 1540. DeSoto landed in Florida and rode horses through the Southeast in 1541. It was the missionaries who brought large numbers of horses to the American Continent. In Santa Fe, New Mexico, a mission was set up in 1594. This was where the Plains Indians got their start of horse stock in 1600. By 1700, horses were as far north as Utah and east to the Missouri Valley. The Ute, Apache and Kiowa Tribes were the first to put horses to extensive use. The Nez Perce had horses to use around 1730. By 1750, horses were in use by the Indians clear into Canada.

1750 to 1875 was the Golden Age of the Plains Indians. With the horse to carry them and their possessions, they could follow the roving buffalo herds throughout the good weather months. They could also raid the enemy's horse herds at greater distances in shorter periods of time. This Golden Age pushed into 1886, the year when virtually the last buffalo was killed by white hunters.

During the Golden Age and even beyond, the horse was used as a medium of exchange. A warrior's wealth was measured in the number of horses he owned. To some degree this is still true with the different tribes, such as the Navajo on the large Navajo reservations. All the older males claim ownership of many horses. Usually these horses run loose on the desert in a semi-wild state. Often these horses are claimed by more than one person. It is the idea of ownership, not the actual function of ownership, that is important.

It would take a number of years for a tribe to convert to a horse culture after they once obtained them. Some older members never obtained or used horses, but rather they walked until they died.

Possibly they did not change because of the fear of riding these wild beasts. The first introduction to the horse would have been very life threatening for the Indian. Many Indians were injured or even killed trying to tame these animals.

They say this is why some Indians were so mean. Riding a Pinto or Appaloosa for any distance would make anyone fighting mad. The number of Indians decreased shortly after obtaining the horse. This also has been blamed on the taming of these wild mustangs. Most Indian children learned to ride by about five years of age. Many of these youth grew up to be fine horsemen. They practiced with their horses until they could make them move or stop on verbal commands. They also taught the horse to turn with leg pressure so they could have their hands free for buffalo hunting and warring.

The Indians mounted their ponies from the right side because being right handed it was easier to grab the mane in the right hand and swing on.

A warrior often painted his favorite war horse with the same colors and patterns he used for his own face and body. He would do this at the same time he painted himself.

Breeds

Arabians

Historians do not all agree on the origin of the Arabian horse. They are not sure just when the Arabian inhabited Arabia or just when they were domesticated. The preponderance of evidence favors the belief that the foundation stock of the Arabian horse was obtained many centuries following equine domestication from Egyptians or the Libyan tribes of northern Africa. There is no question, however, that the Arabs have been breeding and selecting for improved stock for 2,000 years or more.

It is believed by some historians that the Barb horse of North Africa (the Barbary States) were ancestors of the Arabian. Others believe the Arabians were ancestors of the Barb. At any rate the Arabian, Barb, and Turkmere horses all were developed in this general area. Almost all the hot-blooded horses of the world can be traced to these ancestors.

The Arabian possesses an anatomical difference in comparison with other breeds, having one less lumbar (back) vertebra and one or two fewer vertebrae in the tail. The Arabian breed is noted for the proud carriage of the head on a long, graceful neck. He has a long sloping shoulder, well sprung ribs, a high well-set tail, all on a small frame.

In Arabia and adjacent states, the Arabian horse was used, and still is for that matter, for war and basic transportation for the nomadic tribes.

The desert warriors preferred to ride a mare to battle. "Banat er Rih" he called her, which in Arabic means "Daughter of the Wind". That is how she traveled, a quick gust when the enemy pursued, a steady flowing pace when no one threatened.

Mile after mile and day after day this little horse carried her master. She did this on sparse rations. No matter how meager the rations, however, her master saw that her thirst was quenched. On the march, he carried an animal hide to make into a water container especially for her, and at night he milked his camel and gave the fresh, foaming milk to the mare. She bedded down in the tent with the family.

I doubt that the desert men regarded their horses as pets. Rather they depended on them to warn them of enemies and to carry them swiftly and safely to battle. A good mare was a prized possession and was seldom for sale. She was better than gold or silver in the master's purse. She was wealth, freedom and power. She was life itself. To sell her was unworthy; to give her away was a princely act.

You may wonder why they preferred mares to male horses. It may be found in the fact that the practice of gelding was not in use. All male Arabians were stallions and many were more than the riders wanted to handle.

An Arabian chieftain jealously guarded his mares. He bred them only to the noblest stallions so that the pedigree of the foal became sacred. When a foal was several months old, it was given a camel as a nursemare. The big clumsy creature adopted the nimble little one whole heartedly, screaming in worried tones if it strayed, snorting softly when it came near. She refused to move from camp unless the foal accompanied her.

To judge the qualities of an Arab horse, the desert men would study the head first. Were the eyes set low and wide apart? Were they large, dark and fiery in excitement? The ears they desired were pointed inward as if each point were a magnet for the other. Each ear came to a prick point. The face was wedge shaped, wide at the forehead, tapering to a muzzle so fine the creature might sip water from a tea cup. The forehead hollowed out like the surface of a saucer. This was the head of a royal bred Arabian.

Color was of no great concern. Chestnut or bay, nutmeg brown or iron gray were all good. Under the hair, however, the skin had to be jet black for protection against the rays of the sun.

As for size, even the smallest Arabians were considered big enough. Warriors of all eras rode them into battle. George Washington's Arabian charger, Magnolia, was delicately made, but she was big enough to carry him through his fiercest campaigns. Napolean's desert stallion, Marengo, bore him on his long retreat from Moscow.

The storytellers relate the Prophet Mohammed would tolerate only the most obedient mares for his campaigns. To test them, he trained them to come to the call of the bugle. He penned a hundred mares and withheld water for days. He then opened the gate to the spring. All the horses burst for the water. Almost there, the horses heard the notes of the war bugle. Only five mares halted. These were chosen by the Prophet to mother the race.

From the time of Mohammed, the Arabian horse has influenced the formation of much of the saddle horse population. One of its most important roles was as base stock for the development of many other lines. The Arabian was obtained by Spain, France and England and crossed with the cold blood lines that were in existence in those areas. Soon many fine new lines were in existence: the Thoroughbred, the Welsh Pony, the Lipizzan.

In America, the Arabian was used in the development of the American Saddler, Tennessee Walker, and Morgan. The Appaloosa and the Paint have been upgraded by the infusion of Arabian blood. Even the Quarter Horse owes much to the Arabian. The Thoroughbreds imported from England were products of the Arabian crosses. These Thoroughbreds were crossed with the Indian ponies of the southeast to get the Quarter Miler used in the Colonial States. In the west the Quarter Miler was crossed with the Mustangs, which was a Spanish Barb, to develop the illustrious American Quarter Horse.

Today, the Arabian Horse Registry of America has over 170,000 Arabians registered for over 60,000 owners. They register approximately 20,000 purebred Arabian foals and transfer ownership on about 27,000 Arabians annually.

All sires must be blood typed prior to registration of their offspring. The blood types are permanently filed so that if a question of a horse's identity arises at any time, blood typing can be used in an investigation. A certain percentage of foals are blood typed each year to spot-check breeders. The breed has been kept pure for centuries and the goal is for that to continue for centuries more.

If it were not for the fine headed little Arabians, we would not have the breeds we so fiercely protect as purebred lines today. Many times we put down the Arabian in the process of elevating our breed. Maybe we should all take another look, even another position, and thank this stout hearted little animal for its pure lines and intelligent mind which it brought to our other breeds.

Thoroughbred

Three extraordinary horses were imported into England around 1690. The first was known as the Byerly turk. Some say he was one of the spoils of war. Some say his forebears were Arabians while others say Barb.

What is known is that he was ridden by Captain Byerly in King William's War in Ireland. Returning to England, he sired many famous race horses. In his fourth generation of progeny was a horse named Herod, one of the foundation sires of the Thoroughbred.

Next to arrive in England was a horse known as the Darley Arabian. He was a bay horse of about fifteen hands, which was large for an Arabian in those days. This horse was discovered in Syria by Thomas Darley, a traveling merchant.

One of the Darley Arabian's great-great-grandsons, named Eclipse, dimmed the brightness of every other race horse of his time. He was never beaten. In all fairness, Darley's Arabian cannot be given full credit for the speed of Eclipse. On his mother's side he was closer to the Godalphin Arabian, the third of the Near East trio.

The Godalphin Arabian was a little stallion who sired big. His clear bay coat was ticked with gold. He was a royal gift from the Sultan of Morocco to the boy King of France, but the horse's smallness made him the laughing stock of the noblemen. The horse was later sold to a merchant for a wood cart horse. He was bought by a Quaker who shipped him to England and there he became a favorite stallion of the Earl of Godalphin. This stallion never raced yet his name is found in the pedigree of nearly all race horses today.

In his second generation of offspring, Matchem was produced. To these three, Matchem, Herod and Eclipse, every living Thoroughbred traces its direct male lines.

On the dam side were many refined mares sired by war horses of the knights. These dams gave the Thoroughbreds their size and much of their muscle development. The Arabian and Barb brought the refinement, slender neck, refined bone, and heart.

Samuel Riddle, owner of Man O' War, was quoted as saying, "Thoroughbreds have an extra quality greater than speed." He called it heart. "Thoroughbreds don't cry," he would say.

There was War Admiral, who often limped painfully in his stall. Let the bugle sound and he would walk square and strong to the post and then fight like a gamecock to win.

Assault stepped on a sharp stake, injuring his foot so badly it was malformed the rest of his life. A horse with less heart would have favored it, but he kept testing it, using it, and he became a Triple Crown winner. He was known as the horse that ran on three legs and a heart.

Black Gold, a middle-aged horse trying for a come back, broke his leg in the final furlong but drove on to finish his race just the same.

Dark Secret ruptured a tendon a sixteenth of a mile from the finish in the Gold Cup Race. This forced him to put his weight onto his good front foot, which he shattered a step before the finish line. Yet he crossed it to win the race.

Now you see why they say Thoroughbreds don't cry. This same heart shows up in the crosses of the Thoroughbred lines in many of our present breeds. When you ride a horse with heart you are well mounted. When the horse doesn't have this heart, he might as well be pulling a wood cart.

Morgan

It all happened in 1789. George Washington was elected President of the United States and Justin Morgan obtained a colt.

Justin Morgan was a frail singing master. He took students to tutor, in and around Randolph, Vermont. In the fall of that year, Master Morgan walked to West Springfield, Massachusetts, a considerable distance, to collect a debt from a farmer. Farmer Beane did not have money sufficient to pay the school teacher, so he offered him a big sturdy colt and a smaller fine boned colt as payment.

That was all Justin needed, two more mouths to feed, but it looked like this was all he could get from the farmer. He accepted the colts and led them back to Vermont.

He planned the sale of these two colts all the way home. On arrival he was able to sell the big strong colt, but no one wanted the smaller one. Justin ended up raising the colt to maturity and then leased him out to a farmer.

His new master worked Figure, the name Justin gave him, hard pulling stumps and clearing fields. At the end of each day, he was as upheaded and prancy as he had been at the start of the day.

Because of his athletic ability and strength, he soon became known all over Vermont as the fastest trotting and running horse as well as the hardest pulling horse in the area.

When the singing master died, his name was given to the little horse. Justin Morgan, he was called. His offspring were to become known as Morgans.

There were mares of many types bred to this stallion, thus we have Morgans of many types. There are heavier, large-boned Morgans and smaller, light-boned horses.

There was a strange thing about his descendants. Whether they were brown, bay or black, they all had the same round barrel, the same closely coupled body, the same full neck, and the same compact look. What was more, they had the same eagerness to go.

These all-purpose horses helped the pioneers open the frontier and worked on both sides of the war. General Phil Sheridan rode a black Morgan named Rienzi on his famous twenty mile dash to rally his troops. The Vermont cavalry, more commonly called the Green Mountain Boys, was also mounted on Morgan horses.

Comanche, the lone survivor of the Battle of Little Big Horn, was a Morgan. Many of the Cavalry horses came from the breed of the Morgan stallion. In 1907, the U.S. Government developed the U.S. Morgan Horse Farm, which was dedicated to the preservation and development of the Morgan horse at Weybridge, Vermont.

The Morgan was designated the "Bicentennial Horse" in 1976. This all started with a little bay colt that no one wanted. The parentage of this little colt was of unknown background, yet this colt was the only horse known to found a breed. Justin Morgan was the only man to have a breed named after him.

The American Morgan Horse Association, Inc. (AMHA) was organized in 1907. Its goal is to maintain and promote the Morgan horse. The breed has grown from less than 1,000 head in 1950 to 10,000 in 1983. The Association projects the breed to number 20,000 by 1990.

Each year we see more and more Morgan enthusiasts in the Intermountain West. Possibly the breed will meet the Association's expectations.

American Quarter Horse

Although the Quarter Horse is considered the supreme cow pony, it did not originate in the vast cattle country of the West. Rather, its origins were among the colonial seaboard settlements of the Carolinas and especially the Tidewater section of Virginia in the eighteenth century. When the colonists first moved into this territory they found there a small, extremely hardy breed of horse known as "Chickasaws" running wild. The Spanish Conquistadores brought the first modern horses to the New World. These horses, like the Mustangs of the western plains, were descendants of the Spanish horses, who can be traced back to the desert Arabian. The Chickasaws were in actuality ponies — inbreeding and lack of forage had reduced their size. They had developed a thick hide both for warmth and protection from flies. They were swift and agile, always on the alert for predators.

As the colonists settled in and began to clear the land, they imported blooded horses from England for pleasure and sport. Oval racing was not practical in the thick forests, so they invented a new type of racing. Two parallel paths were cleared through the forest, about a quarter of a mile each in length, on which two horses raced at a time, one on each path. Hence the name "quarter pather racing."

The colonists soon discovered that the horses most suited to this kind of racing, which required no staying power but only the ability to start fast, and go at top speed for a very brief period, was neither the little native Chickasaw, nor the longlegged Thoroughbred, but rather the offspring resulting from the Thoroughbred/Chickasaw cross.

One of the three Foundation Sires of the English Thoroughbred was the Godalphin Barb. He sired a racehorse called English Janis, who in turn sired a horse named Little Janis out of a Chickasaw mare. Little Janis was small in stature, not over 14.2 hands. He was a bright chestnut, very compact and well formed, but his muscles were quite different from those of the ordinary race horse. Instead of being long and flat they were bunchy and bulging. He had tremendous heart and in spite of his short legs, was speedy enough to race successfully and win.

Janis was a most unusual stallion and an exceedingly pre-potent one. One reason why Arabian blood is used to improve other breeds is because it not only introduces Arabian characteristics but seems to bring out and improve the best in the original stock. This was true with Janis. When he was put to Thoroughbred stock, the offspring made wonderful records on the race track. When he was put to the little native Chickasaws the ability to start, stop, turn quickly, and run short distances at speed were greatly improved. Through Janis a particularly speedy, hardy good-looking line of Quarter Milers was produced.

After the American Revolution and with the growth of large plantations, quarter mile racing gave way to the longer distances. The need for pleasure horses on the plantations brought about the Tennessee Walkers and high stepping saddlers. The speedy little Quarter Miler might have been neglected or even forgotten if he had not been swept along in the westward march of the pioneers. These horses pulled wagons, drove stock and carried the pioneers to their new frontiers.

As the settlers began raising cattle, they had need of a sturdy, intelligent, swift, hardy horse. By crossing the Quarter Milers to the southwest mustangs, they developed an offspring that encompassed all these attributes. The Quarter Horse stepped into his role as if by inspired design.

Ranchers and cowboys soon discovered that the compactness of the Quarter Horse enabled him to turn quickly and stop short. His large, rounded hindquarters gave him plenty of drive and thrust for surefire starts. His even temperament made him the cowboy's closest companion. So the little quarter racer found his true vocation and came into his own.

Three outstanding stallions are in the pages of equine history as being the most important in the development of the Quarter Horse. The first is Copperbottom (1828-1860). He was the son of the Thoroughbred Sir Archy and through his dam, traced back to Janis. The second was another descendant of Sir Archy named Shiloh (1840-1869). Finally, and most popular of all, came Steel Dust (1845-1874).

The mating of Shiloh to a daughter of Steel Dust produced another fine sire, with the plain name of Billy (1860-1886). The family that Billy founded figures in the pedigree of many modern Quarter Horses. Billy and Steel Dust were among the first to stand in the state of Texas.

One of the most active breeders interested primarily in improving the stock horse was Captain Richard King, founder of the King Ranch in Texas. King began by mating the native horses with imported Thoroughbreds. This was successful to some extent, since it improved the fineness of the native horse and increased its size.

The Klebergs, who took over the King Ranch, found that too much Thoroughbred blood produced horses that were too nervous to work cattle, too delicate and thin skinned to live off the country, and too leggy to negotiate the sudden stops, starts and turns that were ever so necessary. The time had come to find another sire, preferably of Quarter Horse strain, and with his help produce the ideal stock horse.

In 1916, they bought a stallion of Quarter Horse breeding called Old Sorrel. With hopes that he would be able to pass along his intelligence and ability to future generations, they bred him as a start to fifty mares, all with at least a quarter Thoroughbred blood and many with as much as half. An outstanding son, Solis, was then mated to one of Old Sorrel's daughters. The result was most promising, and the experiment continued by mating Solis to forty of his half-sisters, most of whom were from the same band of halfbred and quarterbred Thoroughbred mares.

Of all the sons of Old Sorrel, Solis proved most pre-potent and was the only one with strong enough genes to stand up to a program of line and close inbreeding that was undertaken in order to perpetuate the blood of Old Sorrel. The most outstanding son of Solis is Wimpy P-1.

Wimpy is known to all as the foremost and first foundation sire of the modern American Quarter Horse. It was he that was chosen to receive the registration number one when the American Quarter Horse Association was formed in 1940.

Quarter Horse Racing

Quarter Horse racing is not a western phenomena. The quarter mile races were quite prevalent in the southeast and coastal states before they were states.

A circular mile track was hard to come by, but a quarter mile straight away could be found most anywhere. Many towns had street names for the races they hosted. Some were just called Race Street.

For this reason the horses with fast bursts of speed that could be maintained for a quarter mile were in demand. These horses were the progenitors of the modern Quarter Horse.

The formation of the American Quarter Horse Association in 1940 brought greater emphasis to the quarter mile races. After World War II the race enthusiasm really took off.

16

Thoroughbred racing was also flourishing strong at this time. Many people enjoyed the longer distances run by the Thoroughbred. They felt the Thoroughbred was truly a faster horse with more heart.

In August of 1947, a matched race was set up between a Thoroughbred, Fair Truckle, then current world record holder for three quarters of a mile, and the Quarter Horse, Barbara B., then current world record holder for one quarter of a mile. The race was staged at Hollywood Park in Inglewood, California, with a stake of $50,000 put up by the owners of the respective runners.

Because the distance was supposedly best suited to the Quarter Horse, the start was designed to equalize the two contenders by favoring the Thoroughbred with a flagged or running start to which he was accustomed. Therefore, the gates were set forty-five feet behind the starting line of a quarter mile race. Arrangements were made to time the race in two ways from the gate to the finish and from forty-five feet in front of the gate to the finish. This arrangement was to serve as an accurate check on the controversial difference between the standing start of the Quarter Horse and a running start of the Thoroughbred.

Fair Truckle was the first from the gates surprisingly, but Barbara B. was abreast of him within ten yards. Fifty yards from the gate she had a substantial lead and continued to widen her margin. At the wire Barbara B. had a two length advantage. Officially clocked by the four watches, the time was 22.5 seconds from a standing start and 21.6 seconds by the Thoroughbred system.

No matter how you clocked it, the Quarter Horse won handily. This should have set the doubters to rest but new generations of race enthusiasts still ponder this comparison.

The Quarter Horse Racing Association boasts of the richest race in the world. The All American Futurity on Labor Day each year offers a purse of $2.5 million, with the winning horse and owner taking home a cool $1 million. This is more than the combined winner's purse for Thoroughbred racing's Triple Crown.

Today there are over one hundred tracks conducting Quarter Horse races. In 1983, there was in excess of $60 million paid out in winnings at these tracks.

Today the Quarter Horse record for 440 yards is 21.02 seconds from a standing start. This is equivalent to an average speed of forty-six miles per hour.

If you wish to lay a bet down on one of these races you must go to a state that permits pari-mutuel wagering. Under pari-mutuel betting you are betting against other betters. The race track acts as an agent, or stake holder, deducting a percentage for its commission. The track has no interest in which horses win or lose, and thus, has no interest in fixing races.

When you buy a $2.00 ticket on a horse, you are, in effect, buying one share in the horse's performance in that race. If few people bet on the horse you bet on, his odds will increase. If, however, many people bet on your favorite his odds will be small. All the money wagered on win bets goes into a pool. Then the entire pool of win bets must be divided among the holders of winning tickets. If there were few betters the horse will be a long shot and possibly pay 30 to 1 or for a $2 bet you would receive $60 back.

An outstanding favorite will sometimes return as little as $2.10 for a $2.00 wager. This return is the least return permitted at pari-mutuel races. The pay-off for place (second place) or show (third place) is determined by first dividing the pool into two parts in the case of the place pool and three parts in the show pool. Then this is divided among the holders of winning show and place tickets on the horses involved.

So, when you bet to win, you collect only if your horse finishes first. When you bet to place, you collect only if your horse finishes first or second, thus the two parts of the pool. When you bet to show you are betting that your horse will finish first, second or third. You collect if your horse places in any one of these positions, thus the three parts to the pool.

Now you know so much about pari-mutuel racing all you need to do is learn to pick the winner.

One way to pick your horse is to look at his previous track record. His speed index (SI) will be a helpful guide.

First check to see if he has a Register of Merit (ROM). The AQHA Register of Merit is awarded to any horse officially rated with a speed index of eighty or higher at a standard distance, with a minimum carried weight of 116 pounds.

There are seven approved distances in Quarter Horse racing. A Register of Merit can be earned at any of these distances if they run a speed index twenty or less points below the recognized track record or on a new track that much below the minimum track record set by the AQHA.

If a track's record time for a distance is less than the minimum track records set up by the AQHA, then the minimum track record will be used to calculate speed indexes for that track.

When a new track is set up, the minimum track record will be used to calculate speed indexes the first year. If, in that year, track records exceed the minimum, the next year the new track record will be used to calculate the speed index.

A speed index point varies according to the distance of the race. At 220 yards, two one-hundredths of a second (0.02) equals one speed index point. The minimum track record equals 12.0 seconds for 220 yards, thus, a horse running a 220 yard race in 12.0 seconds would receive a speed index of 100. If he ran the race in 12.40 seconds, he would get a speed index of 80 (12.00 minus 12.40 would equal a minus 0.40 which would be divided by 0.02 and would equal a minus 20).

Example of Register of Merit times for seven distances.

Distance	Yards	220	250	300	330	350	400	440
Minimum track record	Sec	12.00	13.40	15.60	17.00	17.90	20.20	22.10
Speed Index = 100	Sec	12.00	13.40	15.60	17.00	17.90	20.20	22.10
Speed Index = 80	Sec	12.40	13.80	16.20	17.60	18.60	21.00	22.90
Speed Index one point =	Sec	.02	.02	.03	.03	.035	.04	.04

If a horse ran faster than the track record (100 speed index), then the horse would receive a speed index higher than 100. Assume a horse ran a 440 yard race in 22.02 seconds, then he would have a speed index of 102 (22.10 minus 22.02 would equal 0.08 which when divided by 0.04 would equal a positive 2). This record speed would then be used as the track record the next year and would be equal to 100 on that track's index.

Speed indexes from 70 to 79 are given the A classification, 80 to 89 are AA, 90 to 99 are AAA and 100 and above are AAA+, sometimes called top AAA.

Cow Cutting Yesterday and Today

In the beginning, a cutting contest was a test for cow horses working under range conditions. The first recorded cutting event where money was offered as a purse was held in 1898. It was called the Cowboy Reunion. The location was Haskell, Texas. Eleven horses competed for a $150 purse. Sam Grove won it on a twenty year old horse named Hub.

In 1946 the National Cutting Horse Association became an official organization. Their goal was to preserve the cutter's Western heritage and to strive for continuing refinement in the contest area.

At first there were no rules to go by except that a cutting would pit one horse against one cow. Each ranch that hosted a cutting established its own contest rules. In some cases it meant cutting as many cattle as possible out of a herd within a five-minute limit. Or it called for a horseman to cut calves marked with specific color only, while another instructed each cowboy to cut his calves and drive each into an enclosure.

The early cutting horses were heavy boned and bulgy muscled. Poco Bueno was a good example of this early cutting horse. In his day the horses would stop and turn so hard it would pop a rider right out of the saddle. That's when they started holding the horn. Some say today's horse would break a bone stopping and turning that hard.

Others say the input of horses like Doc Bar made the cutting horse turn faster with less hard, body rocking jolts. Today the Doc O Leanas, crosses of Doc Bar and Poco Bueno daughters, can move so smooth and free with such speed that they have time to spare.

The old style horse would stop after a turn and wait for the cow to move. The turnback men stayed back out of the way and only worked if a cow ran towards them. These new horses can move quicker so they are being tested harder by the turnback men pushing the cow towards the horse cutting. This makes the cow try harder to get past the cutter.

The new trainers are training for flash as well as ability. If the cow stops, the cutting horse still moves from side to side with nervous anticipation. The audience likes this, thus the judges have been giving more credit for it.

On the ranch a horse had to work all day rather than two and one-half minutes. If he was that keyed up all day, he would be totally exhausted long before the yearlings were cut out. A ranch horse never has a turnback man trying to defeat his purpose. The ranch horse may cut fifty or more head before he gets a rest. Some horses on the ranch will cut as many as one hundred fifty head at one time. All he would have to do is move the animal to the outside of the herd once his rider showed him which one to move. This may only require a walk or trot. Once on the outside, a herd holder would pick the animal up and move it to the herd being cut into.

Today's horse enters the herd like a sly fox, his head carried low and his ears moving like radar. He will be guided to the cow desired and then he takes over, moving the cow out and away from the herd.

Once the cow turns, it is eyeball to eyeball as the horse makes every move with precision and grace. If you close your eyes and listen, you hear nothing more than cattle shuffling. This horse remains silent, so quiet he barely shakes a hair as he moves. Today's cutting horse is a phenomenal athlete. Some question if he could stand the hard ranch work, others feel he can.

It's nice to see a real cutting horse work, but on the other hand it is hard to watch an unexperienced cow cutter handle the reins for two and one-half minutes. The beginning horse is so nervous he seldom knows there is a cow in the arena. If a trainer never gives his horse a chance to think for himself, he will never know if the horse has any cow in him. This is the biggest fault most young trainers make. If a horse hasn't the cow horse breeding, he will be less likely to be interested in cutting cows. If you are interested in cutting, buy a horse with a pedigree that says he should have a good chance to do the job.

The raising and training of cutting horses is possibly the fastest growing segment of the horse industry. Once you have ridden one you are hooked for life. You can see a horse work because he enjoys it and knows how. You don't have to hire a jockey to ride him. You're up and feeling the movement of every muscle as the horse explodes gracefully from side to side.

The breed bills for top cutting horse stallions may exceed $20,000. The stakes are high with $1.25 million in purse money. There are also good local cutting horse stallions to breed to for $2,000 or less. The local jackpot cuttings are open to any newcomer for a small entry fee. Many counties have cuttings in conjunction with their fairs.

Standardbreds

When Indian trails through the wilds of America were widened out into roads, wagons were built and men began to drive as well as to ride their horses.

Picture a young pioneer family in their go-to-meeting wagon driving proudly down the road. Father hears hoofbeats coming up fast. He clucks to his horse, slaps the lines, and suddenly it's a race.

Instead of running, these horses are trotting hard and fast. The opposite front and back feet reach out then land while the other opposite pair are in flight.

"Go Papa, go!" the children are shouting while mother is holding on for all her worth, yelling for this foolishness to cease. The race is on until Papa leaves his competition in the dust, just in time to slow up and drive in quiet and presentable for the gathering church go-ers.

From the friendly brushes on the road, America's own sport of harness racing was born. Our Eastern forefathers created a breed expressly for trotter racing. In and around Orange County, New York, the farmers and businessmen found the fastest stock came from the lineage of Rysdyk's Hambletonian, so they bred their mares to this fine trotter. About ninety-nine percent of the Standardbreds presently registered trace their lineage to Hambletonian.

Rysdyk's Hambletonian carried the blood of the Darley Arabian. This line was also known for running speed so it was surprising to also find the trotting characteristic here.

Upon Hambletonian's death, trotter-horse admirers founded a club and their rules were as American in spirit as their sport itself. Performance, not lineage, was the standard that counted. If a horse could trot the mile in two and a half minutes or better, he could be registered. This new breed was named Standardbred because each horse had been bred to a standard of speed.

Presently, the registration of Standardbreds is restricted to those horses sired by registered sires and dams. Just over 12,000 Standardbreds are registered each year.

The record for one-mile tracks for trotters is 1:54 4/5, set in 1969. The pacer's record for the mile is 1:52.0, set in 1971.

Pacers differ from trotters in that they move both legs on the same side in unison. This generally requires a harness around the front and back legs on each side that encourages the movement of both legs on the same side to move in unison. These horses are also Standardbreds.

It is interesting to note that pacers bred to pacers produce pacers. Trotters bred to pacers generally produce pacers, and trotters bred to trotters seldom produce pacers. Pacers, therefore, must be the dominant characteristic.

Today, eight of nine races on the pari-mutuel tracks will be pacers. There are still some classic races for trotters written.

American Saddle Horse

The popularity of the American Saddle Horse did not occur until the Civil War and thereafter, even though the breed began about the turn of the Twentieth Century. The Thoroughbred stallion, Denmark, was the most important horse in the development of this breed. Morgan, Arabian, Canadian Pacer and American Trotter horses were all used in conjunction with Denmark to develop this breed.

A famous family line of Saddlers is the Chief family, which traces to Mambrino Chief, a trotter. He in turn can be traced to the Thoroughbred Messenger, imported in 1788.

The Confederate armies of Generals Morgan and Forrest were mounted almost entirely on American Saddlebreds. General Grant generously ordered that all Confederates could keep their horses. He knew most of these horses were privately owned by the soldiers in the first place.

These horses were taken back to the southern states and further developed. With the St. Louis Fair in 1866 came a need for show horses and these Saddlebred horses fit the bill.

In 1891, a group of Saddlebred breeders met and formed the National Saddle Horse Breeders Association with a stud book and offspring registry. There were twenty-six men from eleven states elected as officers and directors of the new association. This was the first horse registry in the United States. Gaines Denmark, a son of Denmark, was in the pedigree of sixty percent of the horses in the first stud book. Denmark was thus given the first number in the stud book to designate his importance to the breed. This was the Thoroughbred Denmark.

Rex McDonald, a son of Rex Denmark, defeated his sire in the Saddle Stallion class to start a show career which spanned twelve years. He was defeated only three times.

In Kentucky in 1900, a colt of Trotting blood, going back to Justin Morgan and Messenger was foaled. This was Bourbon King, a fine gaited show stallion. After winning the Grand Championship at the Kentucky State Fair as a three-year-old, he was retired to stud.

Living to the ripe old age of thirty, Bourbon King became the great progenitor of the Chief family of Saddle Horses. When the Denmarks and Chiefs were crossed, the resulting offspring became today's modern American Saddlebred Horses.

The average height of these modern horses is 15 to 16 hands with many going 17 hands. They weigh from 1,000 to well over 1200 pounds.

The colors vary from bay, brown, black, chestnut, gray to roan. The dark colors are preferred, while large white markings are avoided.

The Saddlebreds can be three or five gaited. The basic three gaits are walk, trot and canter. These are natural gaits for horses. The two unnatural gaits are the pace or running walk and the rack. These are taught by the trainer. The trainer also sets the tail and develops the head carriage. Because of the stylish appearance of this breed, they are known as the peacock of the horse world.

Tennesse Walking Horse

The Tennessee Walking Horse developed naturally out of the needs of the people in the Middle Basin of Tennessee. Plantations stretched as far as the eye could see. The plantation owners wanted a horse that could cover country so they could be in more places in a day. They wanted one with comfortable gaits, with a springiness that would not jolt the rider.

As pioneers settled the Middle Basin of Tennessee, they brought with them fine saddle horses from surrounding territories. The Thoroughbred, Morgan and Standardbreds were of primary notice. In 1885, Maggie Marshall, a great-great-granddaughter of Justin Morgan, had a fine son by a great-great-grandson of Rysdyk's Hambletonian. Now Maggie was a famed trotter, so everyone expected her foal Black Allen to be a great trotter too.

Black Allen did not want to be restricted by his mother's trotting gait. He wanted to pace and pace he did. So in disgrace, he was traded into the back country of Tennessee.

Out of this back country pacing mares kept producing horses with such great ability that people started to take notice of their sire Black Allen. One of his famous sons, Roan Allen, was reportedly able to trot in harness and win, then do five gaits and win, then return and win the walking classes. Thus, Black Allen F-1 was almost as important to the Tennessee Walking Horse development as Justin Morgan was to the Morgan's development.

The Tennessee Walking Horse breed registry describes the breed as follows:

The Tennessee Walking horse is the only horse in the world which is capable of naturally overstriding. When performing the running walk, a good show horse of the breed will overstride; that is, he will place the back hoof ahead of the print of his

21

forehoof. Some of the great Tennessee Walking Horses have been known to overstride fifty inches or more. The flat-foot walk is the slowest of the three gaits and is a diagonally opposed movement of the feet. It is a bold, even gait and is gentle on the rider. The natural gait is the running walk. A bit faster than the flat foot walk, this gait is smooth and gentle and combines the nod of the head with each step. The fastest of his gaits is the rocking-chair canter, or refined gallop. It is a high, bounding elastic movement.

The running walk, however, is the normal gait of the Walking Horse, and he enters into it with animation. His head nods in time with his feet. His ears swing and sometimes he snaps his teeth so loud they click like castanets as he moves.

The running walk is actually a variation of the trot. Diagonal legs work almost in unison, the left forehoof touching the ground an instant earlier than the right hind. The hind foot comes forward and oversteps well beyond the right front hoofprint. This overstep can be from eighteen to over fifty inches. The greater the overstride the faster and smoother the action.

The walking horse can maintain this fast running walk, traveling six to eight miles per hour for several hours at a time. They are said to be able to walk a hole in the wind.

Walking horses are solid in color but during the 1940's and 1950's the gray and roan were in vogue. The darker colors are more preferred today. These horses can have white markings.

The Tennessee Walking Horse Breeder's and Exhibitor's Association was formed in 1935. This was an open registry for many years. Thus, there are horses with blood lines to every other American breed in their registry.

There are about 215,000 horses registered as Tennessee Walking Horses today. About 7,000 head are registered annually.

Albino

The American Albino horse is probably the most misunderstood breed one can think of. The breed association was founded in 1937 at Naper, Nebraska. Caleb and Ruth Thompson, owners of the White Horse Ranch, used the sire Old King, who was milk-white in color with pink skin and brown eyes as the foundation sire. They bred him to Morgan mares to obtain albino offspring. They started their breeding program in 1918.

To separate the dominant white from the diluted cream colored horses, the American Albino Association formed a separate registry in 1970. This Association was known as the Cream Horse Registry. In 1980 the American Albino Association changed its name to White Horse Registry.

To understand the white versus the cream colored horses one must understand the genetic makeup of these color patterns. The gene for white (W) is dominant and covers up all other color genes. The pure white individual (WW) has never been observed. It would appear as pink eyed as the white albino rabbit if it were possible. The hair would be white, the skin pink.

It is thought that this individual (WW) in horses dies early in embryonic life. Therefore, all albinos in horses are (Ww). These individuals do not breed true because the (w) gene permits the expression of all other color genes when the (W) is not present.

When the (W) white gene is present it will hide the other genes' color. Thus the individual will be white regardless of the other color genes present.

Horses can also have dilution genes. This does not necessarily hide the expression of the other genes, but it does dilute other colors. One dilution gene makes a sorrel or chestnut color into a palomino. Two dilution genes makes the individual a creamy white, cremello or type A albino. Thus, two of these genes have more of a dilution effect than one.

A bay with one dilution gene will be a buckskin. With two dilution genes, the color is cream with rust tips on the mane and tail. These are also known as perlino, or type B albino.

Dominant white is not a dilution such as cremello or perlino. The presence of the dominant white gene (W) causes the hair and skin to possess no pigment, but the eyes are colored. Thus it also is a pseudo or false albino. This is the horse registered as the White Horse. The cremello and perlino are registered as Cream Horses.

The White Horse can have eyes with blue, brown, or hazel pigment. The skin is pink and the hair is clear white. The cremello will have blue eyes and perlinos will have hazel to dark eyes.

There are no conformation standards for either the White or Cream Horse Registry because they are color registries. All sizes and types are accepted. There have only been 2,500 registered since 1937.

It is interesting to note that most breeds of horses have white or cream horse colors. There are, however, only two known in the Thoroughbred breed, one in Kentucky and one in France. Both of these were born in 1963.

The albino colored horses may have sunburn problems because of the pink skin. They may also have problems with weeping eyes due to the bright light reflecting off the white hair and pink skin. The use of eye shadow around the eyes, such as that used by football players, can reduce this problem.

Buckskin

The buckskin horse coat color is possibly the basic color pattern in the pre-historic equine. This is evident when one observes the Tarpan, a wild horse of central Europe which exhibits this color exclusively.

The American Buckskin Registry Association, Inc., founded in 1963, and the International Buckskin Horse Association, founded in 1971, both register buckskin colored horses. Their description of the variations in the color are very similar.

Basically these Associations define the colors as follows:

Buckskin : The body coat of the buckskin is predominately a shade of yellow, ranging from gold to nearly brown. Points (mane, tail and legs) are black or dark brown. On the true buckskin the dorsal stripe, shoulder stripe and barring on the legs are always present. However, the dorsal stripe is not necessary for registration of the buckskin.

Dun : The dun differs from the "buckskin" only in the respect that the body color is of a lighter shade.

Grulla : Smokey blue or mouse colored, with black points. The grulla (grew-yah) has no white hair mixed in with darker hair, as is seen in the roan or grey. The name "grulla" comes from the Spanish, meaning "blue crane". Grulla hair is solid mousy blue or slate color.

Red Dun : The red dun is just that - red. Body coat may vary from a yellow-tan to a nearly flesh color. Points are dark red. Dorsal stripe must be present.

The grulla, red dun and dun must have the dorsal stripe to be eligible for registration. The dorsal stripe is not a requirement for the buckskin.

The buckskin would signify the presence of one partially dominant dilution gene accompanying a pair of bay genes. If there were two dilution genes present, the coat color would be perlino (type B albino) or cream with rust mane and tail.

The dun would signify the presence of one dominant dilution gene accompanying a pair of bay genes.

The grulla would signify the presence of one dominant dilution gene accompanying a pair of black or brown genes.

The red dun would signify the presence of one partially dominant dilution gene with no mane and tail dilution gene accompanying a pair of chestnut or sorrel genes. If there were two dilution genes present, the coat color would be cremello (type A albino) or cream.

From this one can see that the Tarpan horse must not have the partially dominant gene in its line. If it did there would be perlinos and cremellos in the population.

The Tarpan horse has the dun or grulla color with the dorsal stripe. These colors must breed quite true, while the buckskin is much less repetitive.

The buckskin in America most likely traces back to the Spanish Buckskin or Sorraia and the Norwegian Dun. These were crossed with Barb and Arabian horses in Spain. Prior to the exploration of the Americas, Spain was the center of fine horse breeding. Many of their lines exhibited the buckskin and grulla colors.

Today the buckskin colors can be found in most breeds of horses. It is very popular, bringing a premium at most sales. Of the estimated 5,000 head of registered buckskins in both Associations, many are cross registered in another breed.

Because these two Associations are based on color, a horse can be registered in the tentative registry until a stallion has sired twelve foals which are registered, or a mare has three foals which are registered. Then they are advanced to the permanent registry.

Foals obtain appendix papers until they qualify in color to obtain tentative registration. If both parents of a foal are in the permanent registration, the foal will obtain permanent registration when they qualify on color. Geldings with this color are eligible to go directly to the permanent registration.

There are some shows and contests sponsored by the two associations. The color is sought after but the breed associations have had limited growth.

Palomino

The fabled beautiful golden horses with silver manes and tails were ridden by the earliest emperors of China. The great Greek warrior, Achilles, rode with his two super horses, Balios and Xanthos, who were "yellow as gold, swifter than storm wind".

This golden horse appears in ancient tapestries and paintings of Europe and Asia. In Japan and China, the horse has been known prior to history being recorded. The exact origin of the golden horse is not recorded but the horse with the golden color was known far and wide.

In Spain the golden horse, when honored, was called Golden Isabella after Queen Isabella, or in plain talk he was known as Caballo de Oro - horse of gold.

It is believed the golden horse was first introduced into America in the fifteenth century. The earliest ranch for breeding the golden horse was owned by Zacatecas, a Mexican. These horses were introduced to the United States by Spanish settlers of California. Some of the golden horses became wild in California where they roamed in an area known as "the pigeon loft" or "Palomino" in Spanish.

A palomino has a body color near that of an newly minted U.S. gold coin and the mane and tail are white. The skin is dark, except under white markings. The eyes are dark or hazel. White markings are permitted on the legs to the knees or hocks and on the face. If more white markings are present the presumption is pinto blood. Horses with excessive white markings or albino characteristics cannot be registered as Palominos.

Breeders of these colorful horses were searching for gold, but many times found an albino foal at the end of the rainbow. Because of the genetic inconsistency in breeding palominos, only about half the matings designed to create palominos actually do. Even in his disappointment, a breeder knows why he keeps prospecting for the gold. He is looking for a sire that will be able to color his offspring with that precious gold.

The Palomino Horse Breeders of America was founded in 1936. It was apparent that there were Palominos registered as other major breeds, therefore, provisions were made to double register these horses. Today a registered Quarter Horse or American Saddle Bred may also be a registered Palomino if its color is golden.

There are stock, pleasure and parade type Palominos. They are different in conformation but the same in color.

Probably the most famous of all Palominos was Trigger. You all remember whose horse he was? Roy Rogers, of course. This horse made every young horse lover see gold. We all wanted a horse that could stand on his hind feet and paw as we waved goodbye and rode off into the golden sunset on our golden horse.

Pinto and Paint

It's no wonder the American Indian prized the spotted horse. They are very colorful and eye catching. The words paint, pinto and spotted horse are virtually synonymous, but are used by different organizations to describe the same colored horse. Pinto comes from the Spanish word "pintado", an adjective meaning painted or mottled, and the verb "pintar", which means to paint, color or dapple.

There are two color groups all pintos fall in. They are piebald, which is black and white, and skewbald, which is white and any other color than black. You have all heard poems and songs with the word piebald used, that is if you are old enough to have heard the old cowboy songs. How many of you really knew what that piebald was?

The spotted horses have two color patterns. The overo pattern is the recessive pattern and is less in number. These horses have no white crossing the back from the withers to the tail. The tail will be dark and one color. They usually will have one or more dark legs and the head is often bald, apron, or bonnet faced or solid with no white markings. The white markings are irregular or splashed in appearance. The amount of white or dark color does not play a part in determining patterns.

The tobiano pattern is usually designated by four white feet, white crossing the back between the withers and the tail head and a normal head color with normal facial markings. Body spots are large and regular shaped and one or both flanks are usually dark.

Thus, a horse with just a couple of spots will always be an overo. If there is a question in your mind always use the rule of no white over the back for an overo as the hard and fast rule. All other rules may or may not hold true. It is not a cut and dry order of things. Mother Nature just does not work that way. Many overos will have four white legs and some tobianos will have abnormal face markings.

It is believed by some that spots were the original markings of prehistoric horses. This was thought to be a camouflage similar to the zebra and giraffe. This theory could be questioned because the wild horses of Asia are grulla and buckskin colored. The Bible refers to spotted horses, and there are cave drawings dating back to early B.C. depicting these horses, showing they were some of the early patterns to exist in horse colors. Many hundreds of years later the Arabs began domesticating and cross breeding horses to improve their stock. Arabian stallions were bred to the pinto colored horses producing beautiful hot-blooded animals. Paintings and artifacts place the pinto-colored horse in early Egypt, India, China and Tibet. He was also known to have been used by the Romans in the days of the great Empire. After the fall of the Roman Empire little was recorded about the pinto until the Middle Ages when the Germans began experimentally breeding to produce the color patterns.

Vases dating from the 3rd century B.C. prove the pinto's presence in Spain. The Spaniards brought the Spanish Barb and Andelusian with them in 1492. Included were horses with the pinto color. Cortez had two of the pinto horses on his ship when he landed in Mexico in 1519. The Spaniards, fearing an Indian uprising, issued an edict that Indians could not own or ride any horse. Nevertheless, the Indians managed to build up herds of horses by stealing, trading or raiding.

The Indians were not versed in horse husbandry so they let the mares and stallions run together and never gelded any horse. Soon the Indian horses were inbred and small. This is the pinto that had to be used in the 1950's to try to improve and standardize a breed.

In 1956, the Pinto Horse Association of America Inc. was founded. The horses registered in this association could be almost any breed as long as they had the pinto color. Some pinto color fanciers wanted more quality in their horses so they set up the American Paint Horse Association in 1965. All horses must be sired by a stallion with a registration number in the APHA, the American Quarter Horse Association, or the Jockey Club of New York to be eligible for registration in this association. There is an appendix registry for animals under two years of age with unregistered dams. There is also a breed stock registry for solid-color foals from registered sires and dams.

In 1935, there was an association set up in Iowa for the spotted horse. This was renamed the Morocco Spotted Horse Cooperative Association of America. This association did not remain active for long. It was reactivated in 1971, but is not a very viable association number wise.

Today many of the Paint horses are as fine of specimens of horse flesh as can be seen in any other breed. Still, there are many small Paints that are throw backs from the Indian ponies.

If you are interested in raising Paints, be sure to study the market, because some colors and some patterns bring higher prices. A person could lose his shirt by investing with inadequate knowledge. There is, however, money to be made in this breed, because it is growing and has a bright future.

Appaloosa

The earliest record of spotted horses, marked like our present day Appaloosas, comes from a cave wall in southwestern France. This drawing of two spotted horses was done by cavemen in the upper Paleolithic period which was between eight thousand and twenty thousand years before Christ.

A vase from Mycenae of the fourteenth century B.C. shows men driving chariots pulled by horses with spots. On the walls of an Egyptian noble's tomb of the early fifteenth century B.C. is painted a harvest scene which includes a chariot with a prancing spotted horse.

During the T'ang Dynasty, 618 A.D. to 906 A.D., decorated statuettes of horses with spotted bodies were buried with their masters. Even as late as the Ming Dynasty (1368-1637 A.D.) the spotted horses appeared on Chinese art.

From the number of scrolls and paintings showing spotted horses, it is obvious they were quite common in China for many centuries. Tamarlane and his Mongol hordes in Persia rode the spotted horse in their plundering.

Further artistic evidence shows that the spotted horses were well-known throughout Europe during the Middle Ages. The Spaniards used a number of these spotted horses for expeditions to foreign lands.

During the 1500's, spotted horses were landed on the American Continent. Then during the 1600's many shipments to Mexico included spotted horses.

The spread of the horses northward was made by the Plains Indians. By about 1730 the Nez Perce had obtained them.

When Lewis and Clark passed through the Nez Perce country, in the corners of Washington, Oregon and northern Idaho, they recorded that the horses found with these people looked like the English Thoroughbred found on the East coast. They had recorded how small and of poor quality the horses of the Plains Indians were.

What happened to this fine Thoroughbred looking horse they had seen? Let's look at the history of the Nez Perce for this answer.

Old Chief Joseph asked for missionaries to be sent to his people because of his like for the Lewis and Clark Expedition's contact. He was the first Nez Perce to be baptized. This was accomplished in 1836.

After twenty-seven years as a Christian, Chief Joseph became very upset over broken treaties and the fighting among the Catholic and Protestant missionaries for converts.

In 1863 he went before his people and tore up his New Testament and declared he was going to follow his Fathers' ways from that time on. There were fifty-five families that followed him. These people were known as the non-treaty Nez Perce because they would not sign the treaty giving away their land, now that gold had been discovered on it.

Those Nez Perce Chiefs staying with the Christian religion were then very willing to sign the treaty to give Chief Joseph's land away. The Government treated the treaty as if it was binding on all Nez Perce and proceeded to move miners and farmers onto Chief Joseph's lands.

The Nez Perce were not a warring tribe. They loved the peace and quiet of their secluded area and wanted it to stay that way. Old Chief Joseph disputed the treaties and defied the Government until his death in 1871.

Young Chief Joseph became the leader of his people. He and his brother Ollikut tried diligently to retain their tribe's lands but to no avail. They were ordered to move to the reservation peacefully or be rounded up forcefully and placed on it.

On May 15, 1877, Chief Joseph was notified he had until June 15th to get to the reservation. He was to trade the million acres of land and the thousands of horses and cattle the tribe had for twenty acres and a team per family.

Because he was peace loving and did not want to fight the white soldiers, he finally agreed. This meant rounding up cattle and horses over a million acres of rangeland in less than a month. Many animals were left on the range when they started for the reservation.

The Snake River was in their path to the reservation. This meant they must cross it in its highest waters. Using buffalo hide boats they ferried all the people and their goods across the river with no accidents. Getting the horses and cattle across was another matter. Once they had their stock across they found they had lost nine hundred mature horses, all the colts and calves, and a large portion of the cattle. Many of these older animals saved themselves downstream, but they were lost to the tribe.

That evening a couple of young braves got mad and ran off and killed an old farmer who had killed the father of one of the braves. When they returned with their story, Chief Joseph knew it would mean war.

Turning east, Chief Joseph took his group on a run to reach Sitting Bull in Canada. Sitting Bull was in exile after killing Custer. Crazy Horse had been shot in a guardhouse about this same time.

After traveling 1600 miles over tough terrain with all their animals and belongings, and in doing so fighting five different armies in nine battles, Chief Joseph had his people within fifty miles of the Canadian border. In the Bear Paw Mountains of Montana the small tattered band of Indians were attacked by a large army. They were surrounded and captured but not before many were killed.

The surrender was based on the Indians being sent back to the Idaho reservation. The spotted horse was to accompany them.

Within a very short time they were loaded on barges and shipped to the Oklahoma Territory. Not being used to this humid climate and the diseases there, many became sick and died.

Chief Joseph was permitted two trips to Washington, D.C. to plead with two Presidents for his people's freedom to Idaho. In 1899, Joseph and his people who had survived the Oklahoma Territory ordeal were shipped back to the Lapwaoi Reservation in northern Idaho.

The spotted horses, however, were sold throughout the midwest and northwest in 1877. The Government knew the Indians would be more controllable without this horse that had out distanced five armies for 1600 miles.

Because the Appaloosa horse was so scattered, there was little chance to maintain the conformation or color that the Nez Perce had spent almost one hundred fifty years developing. These horses were bred to draft horses and Plains Indian ponies. They soon lost their color and conformation. The genes for the spotted color were hidden deep in the many horses of the Plains.

In 1938 a few white ranchers decided to try to bring this breed back. They had to search for horses with spotted horse characteristics. The white sclera around the eye, the mottled skin and the striped hoof were all tell-tale signs of the presence of the spotted gene.

They found these characteristics in draft type horses, ponies and all other conformations. From these they had to inbreed until more color started to appear. They brought back the color through these genes but the conformation was never restored. This is why we saw all the big headed and coarse conformationed Appaloosas during the 1940's and 1950's. It took years of upgrading to improve the horses to an eye pleasing conformation.

Over the past forty years the Appaloosa has been judged on the same basis as the Quarter Horse. Therefore, to win, an Appaloosa had to look like a Quarter Horse.

Today the Appaloosa is a Quarter Horse with spots. Even the spots are not required since the last rules on color were changed.

One day we will wonder why we bothered to bring the spotted horse back if the Association is going to let the color fade into anonymity.

Shetland Pony

When the Romans conquered the British Isles they began exploring the North Sea. Here they discovered a group of islands they named Ultima Thule, or the edge of the world. These islands were about two hundred miles north of Scotland and three hundred fifty miles south of the Artic Circle. The Norse settled these islands about 850 A.D.. They called them the Shetland Islands, which meant Highland Islands. They were islands that had rough rocky coasts which were barren and wind swept. Upon the highlands, three hundred feet above sea level, were thin layers of soil that supported coarse grass.

The islands were claimed by Denmark until 1468 when Christian I pledged the Shetland Islands as dowry of his daughter Margaret. She was betrothed to James III of Scotland. Thus, the islands became the property of the Scottish crown. In the late 1800's the inhabitants of the islands still resembled the Danish people - they had little like for the Scottish government. These island people all spoke the English language in a more pure form than the Scottish.

The Shetland Islands consist of about one hundred and twenty islands or islets, the whole area of which is about five hundred square miles. Only a few of these islands are inhabited.

There is very little temperature variation, ranging from an average of thirty-nine degrees in the winter months to an average of fifty-three degrees in the summer. Rainfall is not excessive but the air is usually filled with salt water moisture. The chill factor and humidity makes below freezing temperatures very severe. The daylight hours are similar to those in Alaska, long summer days with no darkness, to winters with only five or six hours of daylight.

Inhabiting the islands, when the Norse arrived, were many shaggy miniature draft horses. They were no more than ten hands high (forty inches) and were very hearty animals. They had to be to survive the harsh winters and sparse feed on the islands.

The basic colors of the native herds were black, brown or bay. The pinto color also flourished on the islands.

The Norse were primarily fishermen. The women farmed and hauled peat for their fires. They found the wild ponies were easily domesticated for use in hauling the heavy peat.   They were good to pull plows or wagons called "traps". These ponies were also good to ride. They could carry a man all over the island and back in a day. The horses were not the only undersized animals on the island. The cattle measured about thirty-five inches to the shoulder when mature. The Cheviot and black face sheep were also undersized.

The draft type ponies were soon exported to England to work in the coal mines. The Sheltie, as he was called in England, had a life of bleak drudgery. Once mature, he was taken into the mine to pull loads of coal down deep in the mine. Some of the mine ponies never, in all their lives, came up for a breath of clean, fresh air. They had to breath the coal dust and hot stuffy air day in and day out.

This went on for many years. Once electricity was harnessed it pulled the coal out of the mines. At last the Shelties were free of their bondage.

What could be done with all the Shelties now that they were not needed for draft work? Markets in America, France, Germany and Spain for children's ponies soon developed. Many buyers came to the islands to buy and ship these miniature draft horses abroad.

The American Shetland Pony Club was organized in 1888. It was the second horse breed association to be formed in America. The Sheltie made a very good playmate for a child. They were loveable and affectionate. These ponies were very big barrelled and stubby legged, making them slow and plodding.

During the 1930's the demand for luxuries was almost non-existent. The American Shetland Pony Club was in a depression too. To increase revenue they permitted registration of many questionable horses at $5.00 each. This brought an influx of Welsh Mountain Pony and Hackney blood into the Shetland. Soon the horse industry was on the mend and prices were looking up. By 1950, the Shetland had become an investment program for the rich and middle class American horse fancier.

Through questionable registry, more Welsh and Hackney blood was brought in and the Shetland had lines of high stepping, fine boned harness horses. The silver dapple ponies started to show up about this time. These became the rage.

During the 1950's the demand for Shetlands was so good that they were selling in the six digit figures. Then, in 1962 and 1963, the bottom dropped out of the Shetland market. Many investors lost their fortunes overnight on these little horses.

Today there are two divisions of the Shetland breed. The A division is for those Shetlands with a registered Shetland sire and dam. The B division is for cross breeds of registered Hackney or Welsh ancestry.

Shetlands are used for pulling contests at fairs today. These stocky miniature draft horses are descendants of the Sheltie. The show and fine harness Shetlands are surely infused with Welsh or Hackney blood to have such refinement. By far the largest number of these ponies are used as babysitters for children.

Today the Shetland can be obtained quite reasonably and maintained at a small cost compared to a full size horse. They are still hearty, easy keepers. A ditch bank can keep one fat all summer and a small amount of hay will carry him through the winter. This is much more than their ancestors had, coarse grass in the highlands in summer and the washed up sticky sea weed in winter.

In 1972 the ASPC opened a registry for miniature horses, thirty-four inches or less at maturity. There are many breeders of these miniature ponies.

Welsh Mountain Pony

There is a fineness about the Welsh Mountain Pony. A kind of nobility in his being, as if he knows that in his veins flows the blood of the noble Arabian. It shows in the refinement of his head, in his dished face, his small clean muzzle, even in his color. Never is there a piebald or a skewbald marked pony among the true Welsh Mountain Ponies. There are bay, brown or chestnut, with grays predominant, just as in the Arabs.

At first thought, one would wonder how the blood of the horse of the desert found its way into the Welsh Mountains. Then as one researches the facts it becomes clear. In faraway times the Romans invaded Wales. Was it not likely they had brought with them the spoils of their campaigns in Africa? For the Arabians were the desert ponies that satisfied the Romans' eye for beauty and their need for quick flight and durability.

The Romans occupied Wales for four hundred years. During this time they imported more and more Arabian horses. These horses mingled with the native wild herds of small ponies. Their offspring became pack ponies for Romans, but they did not look like pack ponies at all. They had the elegant form of the Arabian. They were also fleet of foot like the Arabian. In truth, they were diminutive Arabians.

The Welsh Mountain pony increased in numbers until they were competing for the sparse feed available in the lower grazing grounds. This created a conflict in the eyes of the royalty as well as the peasants.

They were hunted and tracked down by the sheep herders, who looked upon them as thieves of the sparse grasses belonging to their sheep. Once captured the horses were killed and eaten. Packs of dogs also found the pony to be a delicacy. This found favor with the sheep herders because it meant fewer sheep would be killed by these dogs and it also saved the valuable feed.

King Henry VIII, with a gesture of his jeweled hands, decreed that "little horses and nags of small stature must be eliminated from the common grazing grounds". As a result, many ponies were killed, with the blessing of this law, while others fled into the mountains. Here they found a quiet tableland high above the grazing grounds. Although the rocky soil furnished scanty vegetation, the air was clean and clear and sparkling cold water ran down the mountainside.

Yet even here they were attacked. Now winter was their enemy - biting cold, howling wind and spitting hail and sleet. By sneaking down into the valleys, they found food enough to make it through the winters.

Hardship strengthens and so it was with the ponies. Those that survived developed hoofs as flinty as the rocks they climbed. Their muscles were like spring steel and their heart and lungs were strong and durable.

The Welsh pony withstood its enemies. These enemies made the pony stronger, hardier, wiser and above all they preserved the purity of his blood.

Today the ponies still live high up on the tablelands. They possess the same beautiful styles and nobility that they did when the Romans left.

Perhaps the ponies of Wales are like the Welsh people who, in a changing world, cling steadfastly to their ancient language and customs. They are like them in another respect too. On the Welsh coat of arms a motto describes the people. The words of the motto are Ich-Dien, "I serve". Every Welshman who understands pony character insists that Ich-Dien describes the mountain pony, too. He serves his master well.

Draft Horses

Sometimes both a man and horse have strong sense of determination, and when they put their minds and muscle to the same load, it moves.

Horse pulling contests at county fairs are as old as kerosene lamps, and like the lamp, they often cause a good deal of smoke. Many pulling contests in the early days ended in fist fights over who really had the best team. Soon more sophisticated pulling sleds were designed so the teams had equal opportunity to prove their moving power.

Draft horses have been popular with fair go-ers since their import to America. There are five major breeds of draft horses in the United States today. They are the Belgian, Clydesdale, Percheron, Shire and Suffolk. These are all descendants of the "Great Horse", or the horse the knights in armor of the Middle Ages rode. These breeds are all named after the area in Northern Europe in which they were developed.

The Percheron is the only one of the draft horses that may have had an infusion of Arab, or hot blood, in its ancestry. The Percheron was the most popular breed of draft horse at the turn of the century. They were a big breed yet active and light on their feet. They were generally blacks or grays. They had little feathering or hair about the fetlocks.

The Belgian was first imported to the United States in 1886 but did not become a prominent breed until the early 1900's. These horses are generally bay, chestnut or roan. Many Belgians have flaxen manes and tails. There are presently more Belgians registered each year than any other draft breed.

Everyone knows about the Clydesdale. These horses are the ones that pull the Budweiser wagon in the Utah "Days of '47" parade each year. They have extensive white markings such as white legs and face. They have feathered, or haired legs to their knees and hocks. The Clydesdale is lighter in weight than the other breeds yet it is a taller horse. The bones of these horses are cleaner and flatter than other breeds. Many people feel these horses are more nervous and temperamental than the other breeds. They were not as popular on the farms as the Belgian and Percheron.

The Shire is the biggest, broadest horse in the world. He will weigh a ton or more at maturity. The Shire has a heavily feathered leg extending about half way to the knee and hock. There are few Shires in the United States compared to other breeds.

The Suffolk breed was developed primarily for farm work. Their color is dusty chestnut or sorrel. This breed has little, if any, white markings. They are small for a draft horse and for this reason were not very popular in the United States. Only ten or so are registered each year.

As you can see, the Belgian, Percheron and Clydesdale are the most important draft breeds in the United States. Because of the pulling contests the Belgian and Percheron have held their own over the years. The past ten years have seen many more of these horses being used in the timber both in the Northwest and Northeast. Many timbering firms are cutting costs by using these sturdy, hardworking helpers.

Recently the Clydesdales have had a real big push with the commercials on television and the personal appearances of the Budweiser teams. Breeders are popping up all over and the price of

31

these horses have shot up. If you have plenty of pasture and hay you might consider raising these docile, friendly beasts. You don't even have to be a rider, just a good manager, to turn a profit.

Mules

The least loved and most ridiculed member of the equine family is the mule. His name has been linked so often with such adjectives as lazy, vicious and stubborn that few people have any fondness for the unfortunate hybrid.

By crossing a mare with a donkey, the mule is produced. When the mare is a big draft mare a draft mule is produced. These weigh from 1200 to 1600 pounds and stand 16 to 17 1/2 hands high. Sugar mules were the plantation mules of the south. They weighed from 1150 to 1300 pounds and stood 16 to 17 hands high. Farm mules were of less quality and were thinner and plainer than draft mules. Cotton mules were still smaller, less quality animals. They were used for cultivating the cotton.

Pack mules are thick, blocky and have strong loins and backs. These mules vary in size. They are used for packing in areas of hazardous terrain.

The mule is usually sterile, both male and female. There have been cases of mule fertility, but they are so few as to be irrelevant. The male mule is gelded nevertheless for reasons of tractability.

The mule is not to be confused with the heny or jennet, which is the offspring of a stallion and a jenny or female donkey. This animal is not as widely used as the mule as it is smaller, less hardy, has a thinner coat and is less patient.

The mule's history is more illustrious than his present status. Mules were reported being used as far back as the nineteenth century B. C. The early kings of Israel rode mules to battle. The mule even has a biblical-type legend connected to him. The legend tells of Joseph choosing a mule to bring the Holy Family to Bethlehem. On the trip the mule kicked Joseph and the kind man promptly cursed the mule saying the mule would never have children to love.

The mule was first introduced into the United States by George Washington. The king of Spain presented the President with two jacks in 1787. Both George Washington and Henry Clay popularized the mule. The ugly new half horse was soon the main power source for the South.

Washington made popular an animal who probably wore thin his welcome countless times. The animal has many quirks that show he has brains but he is sometimes annoying and many times destructive.

He will balk if treated unfairly, overloaded, or if he doesn't think the trail is safe. He dislikes walking in water or on ice. He will never back up unless trained to do so because he wants to see where he is going. A mule would just as soon kick a dog to death as look at him. It is said a mule remembers people who are cruel to him and will patiently wait his time for revenge. Many old packers learned about this trait the hard way.

If one can overlook the mule's slight idiosyncrasies, he will find an animal with many advantages. The mule is very sensible and takes care of himself. He will not overeat or drink when hot and seldom founders. He can subsist on less food than the horse and carry more weight for his size. Generally he will not panic when in wire or other bad situations.

The Army started using mules in 1850. They were used extensively in the Civil War. As one general stated, "The Civil War could not have been carried out to any conclusion without the mule."

The Army used mules during the Indian wars. Without them they would have been much less effective.

Thirty thousand mules were used in World War I. The rain and the mud stopped everything but the hardy pack mules. With ammunition and supplies they went with the troops into battle after battle. They were used to transport wounded from the front lines to the aid station in the rear.

The mule does have his followers today also. The American Mule Association was formed by a group of the most enthusiastic devotees. Mules are actively registered through this organization. Although the mule is sterile, registering the animal encourages breeders to breed from the best stock of horses and to carefully record the mating.

There are shows and races sponsored through the American Mule Association. One such program is the Mule Days Celebration at Bishop, California. Bishop residents proudly boast the largest working mule population in the West. Their Mule Days celebration draws entries from many states. Events such as barrel racing, calf roping, reining, relays and races are undertaken strictly by mules and their riders. The main attractions are classes such as the model pack mule, matched pairs and the working pack train class. If you would like an interesting and exciting day take in the Mule Days at Bishop.

CHAPTER THREE
Selection and
Costs of Horse and Equipment

If there is a chance you may purchase a horse, or even if you already own one, you may want to know more about selection, price and cost factors to consider, equipment that will be needed, and the proper care of a horse. Many horse buyers purchase a horse with only the initial purchase price in mind. They don't calculate how much it will cost to properly maintain the horse, let alone buy equipment that will be needed to enjoy him.

Those with ample money, but no idea of what to buy, often go to a local tack shop and let someone who may not be a horseman sell them what everyone else has been buying. Many times the equipment does not fit the rider, let alone the horse.

It is important that you know what you want in a horse and equipment before you go shopping. Don't let a fast-talking salesman or horse trader sell you something you are going to be unhappy with. Once you have made your choices, only proper care will allow you to enjoy them for many years.

The Horse

In selecting a horse, the factors that must be considered include:
1. What will the horse be used for?
   a. Pleasure
   b. Showing
   c. Ranch
   d. Rodeos
   e. Racing
2. How many people will be using the horse and what experience has each had?
3. How much money do you have to spend?

Once you have answered these questions in detail and determined the costs and obligations involved in owning a horse, then you can look at the alternatives available to you.

If you need a ranch horse, he must be willing and able to work stock and have an easy-going disposition so you can concentrate on your work rather than staying on. A stock-working horse needs to have strong bones, good muscling, and stamina to endure a long, hard day's work.

For a rodeo horse you need all of the above, plus speed that will take you to a calf or steer in record time. A western show horse needs many of these same qualities to compete in the varied events in a horse show today.

The race horse owner wants speed. The ideal race horse has good conformation and eye appeal, as well as speed. Many race horses retire from the track to become show, rodeo, ranch and pleasure horses.

Some race horse breeders are not concerned with conformation or eye appeal as long as the horse is fast. Some horses that can and do run well do not have eye appeal or ideal conformations. Crooked legs and buck knees are common faults seen in horses bred to run. These animals, however, generally break down and become unsound early in life. If they have run exceptionally fast, some people still breed to them and thus perpetuate these faults.

Show horses used in hunter and jumper classes need special abilities to clear the high barriers.

The high-stepping English saddle type horses have inherited qualities that set them apart from other horses.

The pleasure horse is by far the most numerous of all horses in the United States today. This horse can fit any of the above descriptions. The only prerequisite is that he be a pleasure for his owner to ride. Some riders like gentle, plodding horses, while others like high-spirited, active horses. Some see beauty in arched necks and high, flowing tails, while others like roached manes and short tails. Picking a pleasure horse can be likened to picking a wife. First, you must have one you can live with, and second you must desire her for what she is. Because of the wide variance in human tastes, almost every horse finds a home.

The next consideration is what breed to buy. Some people are very narrow-minded and think only their favorite breed has good conformation, ability and eye appeal. No breed has a corner on these qualities. Therefore, after determining how you want to use your horse, you should investigate the different breeds of horses trained for these attributes. A stock, western show or rodeo horse may be an Arabian, Appaloosa, Morgan, Paint, Thoroughbred or Quarter Horse. Some other breeds, such as Buckskin and Palomino, that can be cross registered as Quarter Horses, or even a mixed breed, should also be considered. A pleasure horse can be any breed or may be a mixture of breeds and still be a pleasure to his owner. The point is that a prospective horseman should look for certain qualities in an individual animal rather than at the publicized qualities of a breed.

One universally necessary characteristic, however, is good conformation. Specific beauty and function requirements can vary from breed to breed, but straight legs and sound bodies are basic to all breeds.

Starting at the bottom, a horse should have sound hooves with no vertical cracks or excessive horizontal lines. Looked at from the side, the front leg of a horse standing squarely should sit directly under the shoulder, with hoof, pastern and shoulder showing the same angle or slope.

Looked at from the front, the front leg should again sit directly under the shoulders. If the legs are set too close or too far apart relative to the chest, the horse will have problems of weight distribution and generally will have crooked legs because of it.

Now look at the back legs. From a side view, the cannon bone should be on a vertical line with the rump. Many horses are sickle-hocked. Some horsemen profess a desire for horses that are a little sickle-hocked to use as reining horses because they believe such horses can get their hind feet under them. A sickle-hocked horse, however, must carry more weight than normal at his hocks, and many sickle-hocked horses go unsound as a curb or thickness of the plantar ligament causes enlargements at the back of the hocks.

Looked at from the rear, a horse's hind legs should be set straight under the hip. A straight line dropped from the hip should divide the hock, cannon and hoof in two equal parts. Many horses are cow-hocked. This is a turning in of the hock, which rotates the hooves out. Such a fault may cause one back foot to interfere with the other as the horse travels. Some horses are bowlegged in back. This also causes the horse to travel poorly, but usually does not cause interfering.

As we move up the horse, we want a long, backward-sloping shoulder blade, rather than a steep or straight shoulder. The steep shoulder is associated with a choppy, rough ride. A long hip and short back imply more strength for carrying a rider. The rump, or croup, should slope down gradually. A horse that drops off steeply in the rump is said to have a goose rump. For endurance the horse needs depth of chest and well-sprung ribs. These two features allow for adequate heart and lung capacity.

The neck should be relatively long (but in balance with the rest of the body) with adequate thickness. This gives the horse balance and ease of movement. Some horses have a heavy crest to the neck which overbalances the front end. The converse can also occur where the horse is low or ewe-necked. This can produce high-headed horses.

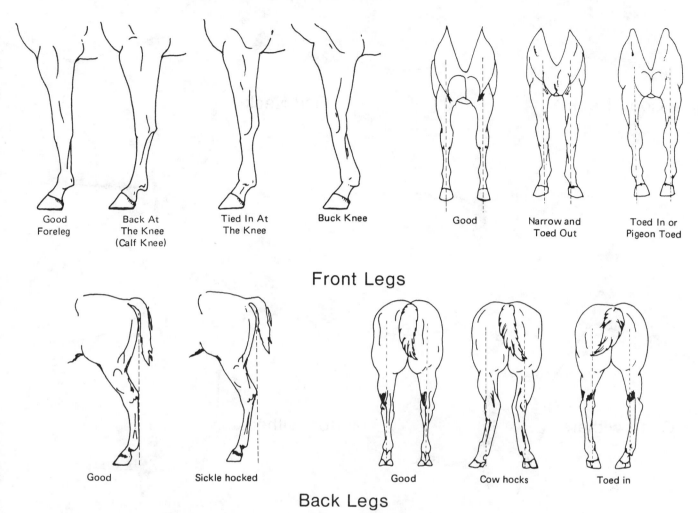

| Good Foreleg | Back At The Knee (Calf Knee) | Tied In At The Knee | Buck Knee | | Good | Narrow and Toed Out | Toed In or Pigeon Toed |

Front Legs

| Good | Sickle hocked | | Good | Cow hocks | Toed in |

Back Legs

The withers are the highest point of the horse's body. To measure a horse's height, start at the bottom of the front hoof and measure to the highest point of the withers (see illustration). This is converted to hands. A hand is four inches. Horses measuring fifty-eight inches are said to be 14½ hands high. The withers should be prominent and refined. Low, fat, coarse withers are called mutton withers. The saddle will not stay in place on a horse with mutton withers.

A large head can overbalance the front end of the horse. The saddle horse should have a relatively small, refined head that is in proportion to his body. The nose should be straight or slightly dished. Some horses have a heavy or Roman nose. This is not only unsightly, but can reduce the range of vision of the horse.

The eyes should be wide set, large and bright. Some horsemen judge the horse's disposition from the set of the eye. Horses with small, deep-set eyes, called pig-eyes, are said to be mean and unpredictable. Much of this characterization can be explained by the fact that such an eye set drastically reduces the horse's range of vision, thus causing the horse more than average concern over noise and movement that he cannot see adequately.

The face should be moderate in length, with nostrils that are mobile and large for adequate air intake.

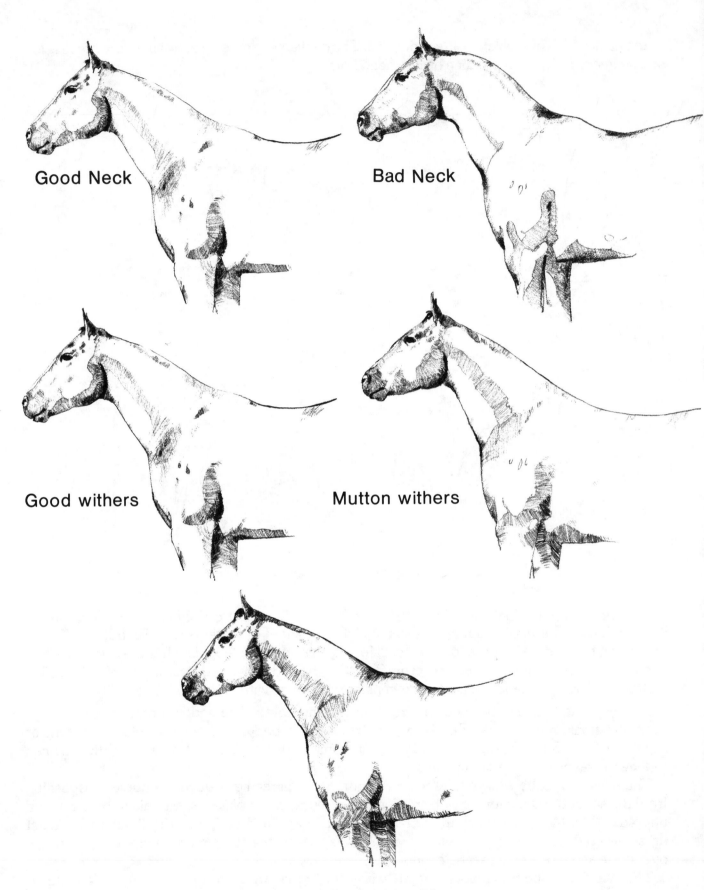

Good Neck

Bad Neck

Good withers

Mutton withers

Thin, overprominent withers

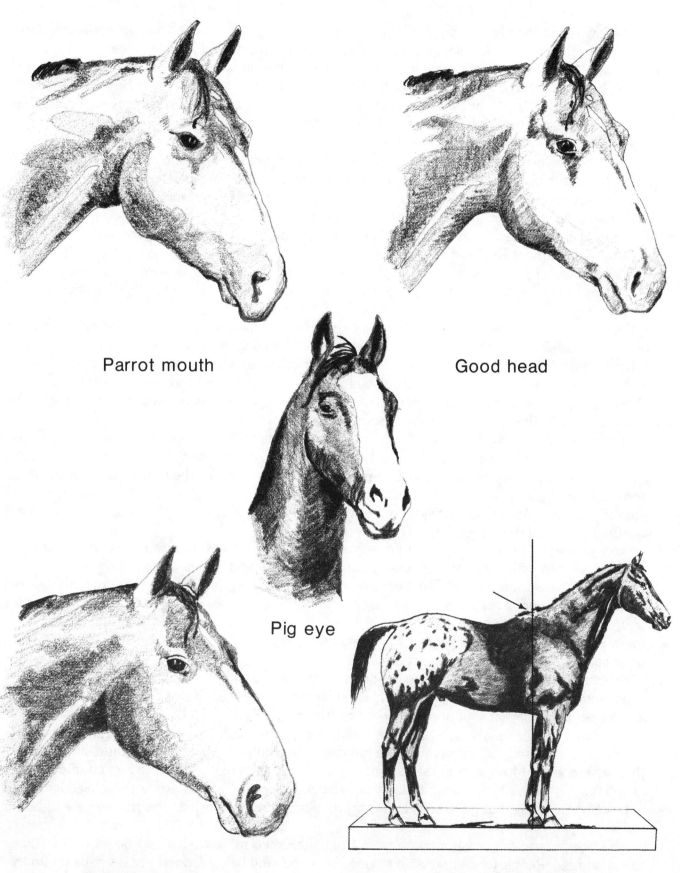

Parrot mouth

Good head

Pig eye

Roman nose

Horse Measurement

The jaw tends to indicate masculinity and femininity in the horse. Stallions generally develop a heavy, muscular jaw, while geldings and mares have less muscling over the jawbone.

All of these characteristics must be blended together in a way that creates balance and functional soundness. From this blending comes the eye appeal of the horse. Some horses have color that draws the eye, but the prospective buyer must realize that color is only skin deep. The wise horseman knows that a good horse doesn't have a bad color. Or, it doesn't matter what color a horse is if he is broke well and works well.

Some horses are natural sliders and spinners while others tend to be front end stoppers, with little ability to pivot smoothly. By watching colts running loose in a pen, one can soon pick the sliders. Watch also to see the length of stride. A horse with a long, sloping shoulder should have a long over-step at a walk. This is measured from the point where his front foot left the ground to the point where his back foot sits down. A horse that can barely reach the front foot mark will be choppy in movement and hard to ride.

Smoothness of travel, or way of going, can also be seen. Observe the horse at a walk, trot and lope. The horse you want should move free or flow through the air rather than bounce up and down.

Disposition is another characteristic you can observe. Does the horse seem at ease, or is he tense with eyes ablaze? You want life in a horse, but not enough to take yours out of you.

Many horse traders take advantage of the beginner's inadequate knowledge of conformation and overzealous interest in superficial eye appeal. Blaze faces and stocking legs also are characteristics many beginners fall for. A lot of bad conformation can be hidden behind color. Fat is another factor that can hide a lot of inferior conformation.

For these reasons, the beginner should learn as much as possible about conformation and true quality before attempting to purchase a horse. A beginner with access to a learned horseman should try to take him along as a consultant. It is you who will pay for the horse, so make sure that your money buys what will give you long-term satisfaction, not just momentary pride of possession. In making your decision, remember that it costs just as much to feed and care for a worthless nag as it does a good horse.

Now that you are able to sort out poor-quality, unsound horses, you must reconsider the use you are going to make of whatever horse you ultimately buy and who is going to ride him.

If you are a beginner, or if children or beginners will be riding the horse, pick a horse that is well trained and settled in his ways. A horse from nine to twenty years old can be the best choice for your needs. Horses that are still sound at nine years of age will most likely continue sound for many more years. Some horses at thirty years of age are still being ridden by children. The key is good care and a sound horse to start with.

An intermediate rider may want to concentrate on five to eight year old horses. This age horse can be quite settled and yet is able to be trained for the use desired. If you don't ride a horse of this age properly, he may go sour or develop bad habits.

An advanced rider has more options. A well-trained six to twelve-year-old is a good choice if the rider wants a horse ready to perform the job desired without any problems. Others like to break their own horses. Most colts are started at two or three years of age. For the first couple of years of riding, any horse is still learning and unpredictable. Some riders enjoy the challenge of an unpredictable horse, but generally cannot accomplish as much work as the rider on a well-broke horse.

Any age person may wish to raise foals from their own mares. This can be as rewarding as riding a horse. People who are unable to ride but who enjoy being around horses have found this aspect of horses very rewarding.

The age breakdowns mentioned above are only general guides, for some three-year-olds are quieter and easier to get along with than are some fifteen year old horses. The point is, if you want a beginning rider or child to have an enjoyable experience, get an older dependable horse that will not create fears in the rider. It is much better to buy a slow horse and keep him until the rider has mastered his speed, then sell him and buy one with more aggressive characteristics and more speed. Countless horse owners have become afraid of their poorly chosen horses and have sold them and the equipment prematurely. If they had purchased the proper horse, they might have conquered their fears and have an enjoyable pastime.

Once you know the type and age of horse you want, you are ready to look at what is for sale. The general rule is that you will want one that costs much more than you can afford. At this point you learn that you may have to live with some conformation faults if you are going to stay within your budget. Few horses are perfectly straight-legged. A few deficiencies in that area may be more than offset by some strong features elsewhere. The negatives must be evaluated as to whether they detract from the horse's ability to function. Nature has a way of enabling animals to adapt effectively to some conformational deficiencies. Under light use, some horses in this category can be as adequate as a perfect horse. They also can be bought at a much lower price than the perfect physical specimen.

Horses vary in price from a low "dog meat" level to millions of dollars. Breeding animals generally are worth much more than geldings because of their productive potential. A good gelding can, however, be worth more than a mediocre stallion or brood mare. There are many mediocre stallions and mares around that would be better used for riding than as breeding stock. A slight alteration in a stallion by a veterinarian can make a good gelding.

A grade, or unregistered, saddle horse will cost from $400 to $900. A registered horse will run from $500 to $1,500. Some saddle horses that have proven themselves may cost from $1,500 to $25,000.

A weanling foal can generally be bought more cheaply than a broke horse of the same quality. You must remember that a weaner, right off his mother, usually looks fat and shiny and will be worth more than at any other time until he is two and started. Yearlings are in a gangly, awkward-looking stage and usually can be bought cheap compared to foals. Unstarted two-year-olds are also generally cheap. But keep in mind that colts have to be fed until they are old enough to be broke. Then you have the cost of breaking them and the risk of their getting hurt before they are broke.

Horses can generally be bought at a cheaper price in the fall or winter than they can in the spring or early summer. If the cost of feeding the horse until he will be used is less than the added cost if you buy in the season of use, you can save by buying early. Many times, however, the feed costs exceed the savings. Don't be afraid to shop around, but if you see one within your budget that appeals to you and fits your needs, buy him, because the perfect horse is hard to find.

A horse sale is made when the buyer and seller agree upon a price. Don't let the owner make you a part of selling the horse by asking you what you will give him for his horse. Always make him put a price on his own stock. You may be willing to pay $2,000 for his horse and if you tell him that, he will sell it to you. But if you let him price it, he may be willing to take $1,500 for the horse.

Even when a seller places a price on the horse, assume that is the most he expects to get out of the horse, then you may be able to bargain for less. If you are rich it may not matter, but in today's economy most of us need to buy as cheaply as we can. You can always try the coin flip. If the man asks $1,500 for his horse and you are willing to pay $1,500 but would like him a little cheaper just tell the owner you will flip him for $1,400 or $1,500. Get your coin out even if he isn't too anxious.

Go ahead and flip while he is complaining then ask him to call it. Everyone has some sporting blood and most will call it even though they don't want to take less.

If this happens to you when you are selling horses always say you will flip for $1,400 or $1,600 but not $1,400 or $1,500 because only one person can win. By using $1,400 or $1,600 you will usually scare the buyer into taking the $1,500 because he surely doesn't want to pay more than the $1,500 he can buy the horse for.

Never start tearing down a man's horse to try to get him to sell cheaper. You may ask him about this point or that weakness, but don't be an arrogant fool or he may not sell you the horse at all. If the horse is way over-priced or unsound, just thank him for showing you the horse and tell him it's not quite what you had in mind; then leave friends.

One way to surely get taken is to let the seller know you really want to buy a horse and you don't know what you're doing. Many sellers have few scruples. The premise is "buyer beware". For this reason you should learn to be a good judge of horse flesh and know unsoundnesses and weaknesses.

A good habit to get into is always mouth the horse to check his age. Then check his papers for a confirmation of age and color markings.

The seller may say this is a registered horse and he is smooth-mouthed, so you assume the best if the horse looks good. You buy him with the promise of having the papers mailed to you. When you get the papers a week later, after your check has cleared the bank, you find the horse is eighteen instead of the ten-year-old you were hoping it would be.

If you are not a capable judge of horses, then get the advice of someone that is. Not all those that claim to be good judges of horses really are. You should find someone that is known for his knowledge and honesty. Some people in the business have many connections and will get a kickback for selling a friend's horse to you. If necessary, you may need to pay a consultant fee to a top horseman to assist you. This is especially true if you are going into a new line of the horse industry and you are going to invest a large sum of money.

Be sure to get a brand inspection, a bill of sale with any guarantees written out, and a vet inspection. You don't want to get stuck with a stolen horse. You want proof of sale and agreements. You may miss something the vet will pick up. This may save you buying an infertile stallion, a barren mare or an unsound gelding.

Going to an auction to buy is more dangerous than selling at an auction. If you are a beginner, the auction is not the place to start. There are many ways you can get taken, but most of all you just beat yourself by not being able to judge fast and think faster.

If you do know your horses, then an auction may be a good place to buy. Always inspect the sale horses carefully and pick the ones you may be interested in. Mark them in your book, then try to find out as much about the horse as you can. Ask the owner questions about his horse's breeding, temperament, health and previous training. You can learn a lot this way. You learn to read through people and you can tell if he needs to sell or if he is wanting to get rid of him. If the owner is never around to answer questions, you may want to think twice about that horse.

Some of the better sales have a veterinarian inspect the horses and they tell you anything they found. It is always best to look good for yourself anyway.

After you have looked the sale horses over and picked out a half dozen or so that might fit your needs, compare them to see which ones you would pay the most for and the ones you think should be bought for less. Once the sale starts, don't be afraid to buy your first horse if he comes in and is selling in your price range. If you wait, you may find the others selling for more than you thought. You must be able to make quick decisions and then be able to live with those decisions. If you have the money, you may want to buy a couple of these horses and then pick the best one, and resell the other.

Even the professional horse buyers get taken part of the time, but the joking theory is if you lose a little on each horse, you just make it up on volume.

When you're bidding, never make it obvious you want the horse badly. Many times the owner will bid you up a few hundred dollars because he knows you are planning to take that one home.

The best policy is don't ever start bidding until the bidding slows down and you can see the upper end of the price. All you do by bidding early is drive the price up on the horse you want. If the auctioneer isn't going too fast, always pause for a few seconds before your next bid to make the other buyer think you might drop it on him the next bid. If he really doesn't know if he wants it, he will stop bidding, but if he knows you are bidding fast and furious he will stay in a couple more times.

Few people can judge fast, think faster and make money on horses. One principle to remember is never gamble with more than you can afford to lose.

To make money on horses is an art. You must know the market and economic principles that apply. You must be a good judge of horses and people and, last but not least, you must be a gambler at heart.

Marketing Horses

Whenever you speak of buying, selling or trading horses you are dealing with economic principles. To make money marketing horses you should know these economic principles and use them to your best advantage.

1. Time utility: It is hard to sell a horse during the winter months, or off season, when no one else has need of or feed for an extra horse. Yet at certain time periods horses are in high demand. You must learn when to have your horses ready to sell or when to buy cheap.
2. Place utility: You may not be able to sell a horse in your local area. It is important to know the areas where there is a shortage of horses for the existing demand and where the surpluses are.
3. Form utility: The condition a horse is in when you try to buy or sell plays a large part in the price. A horse may be a real athlete but if he is not conditioned and groomed, he looks just like any other horse. Buy when they are in their working clothes then fit them up and sell in their Sunday best.
4. Function utility: What can a horse do for his owner? Some can just eat. Learn to distinguish what this or that horse may be best at, then train him, or have him trained for that function. There are sales for performance horses, yearlings, brood mares and then there are general sales. Plan far ahead to move your horses into select markets.

A young horse will look its best right off the mare so this is an ideal time to sell your production. If you don't, you will have to feed them through the weaner and yearling stages which is the most gangly stage in their life. Few people want an unbroke two-year-old so you end up feeding your colt until he is at least started into the bit. You now have developed a marketable product, assuming he didn't get cut up or develop crooked legs. Then there is always a chance of spoiling him when he is started. Now evaluate your added cost and returns. You will find that if you make the same total profit after the added two years or so you are lucky. You might have made more by selling him as a weaner or even selling him at one month of age with a four-month-old delivery date.

If you are going to sell at a sale, be sure it is well advertised and has had high average prices in the past. Know how to protect your consignment by a minimum price, a bid back or a no sale at the end of the bidding. If he goes too cheaply and he is a good horse, take him home and try another day or another way.

If there are some high quality horses in the sale, it will draw more buyers. If you go to a high quality sale and your horse is in the upper half of the horses as far as quality, you should do well; but if your horse is going to be in the bottom fourth, you may be better off going to a sale with less quality so your horse will be in the top half of the sale horses. That is why you can buy the bottom horses out of a registered sale and take them to a grade sale or cow sale and have them bring more money.

Where do you want your horse to be in a sale? Should he be first or last or somewhere in between? Never be the first horse. This is usually the best buy of the sale so try to steal this one. Everyone else is going to sit back and see how they are selling before they start buying. In a big sale many times the first half of the sale is a little low, then they start buying because they know there are not too many more left to buy.

In a futurity sale the last place horse is many times a good place to be if you don't have a top horse. This will be the buyer's last chance to buy and the auctioneers know it is the last horse so they take just a few minutes more than they did with the one right before the last.

If you hit a cold sale and have a horse you don't want to take home, you should have your horse ready for the sale and let him go for what he brings, but then buy back the horse that isn't in shape for this sale and buy him cheap. Then prepare him for the next sale. That way you don't take a loss, you just make a trade on the same cold sale. If it is a high sale, don't buy back unless you can find some that have not been prepared properly for that sale.

Right now brood mares and foals, as well as unbroke horses, are selling quite cheap. Well broke horses are bringing a premium because there are so few good ones on the market. If you are tired of sitting through one hundred head of horses to see fifteen good broke horses, you may want to go to a performance sale.

Just What Does It Take To Make A Champion

What makes a horse a champion? Is it his parentage, his conformation, his feeding and care, his training, or his desire? The breeder may look to his parentage and say that this played the major roll in his success. The scientist may look at his conformation and say he could measure scientifically all the parts of the horse and relate each to performance. Feed manufacturers like to make the point that without proper feeding, the horse will never reach his potential.

The trainer would say that there would be no champion if it wasn't for his care and training. Without training, the top quality horse would just be another hay burner.

A horse's innate desire to please, to perform and to compete is a quality that cannot be predicted. It is an unknown in every horse no matter how great the other four components are controlled and developed.

The parentage is important, but how accurate can it be evaluated? An offspring acquires fifty percent from each of its parents. By the time you reach the grandparents, you only have twenty-five percent of any specific grandparent's genes in the offspring.

When you realize a horse has a total of 64 chromosomes, 32 from its sire and 32 from its dam with many genes on each chromosome, it is easy to see all the combinations that could exist among the offspring of any two parents. If a parent has a homogenous pair of genes, or both genes for a specific characteristic are similar, such as BB for black color, all the offspring will receive a B from that parent. If the other parent is also BB, all the offspring will receive a B from that parent and be BB or pure black. If, however, the parents are heterogeneous or if each has Bb genes, then

44

the offspring from three matings could all be different because four matings could result in one BB, two Bb, and one bb.

It is difficult to know if a mare or stallion is homogenous for any one pair of genes. The characteristics exhibited by an offspring may be the best possible combination of two parents, the worst, or anywhere in between.

You may have an individual that is 15 hands tall and weighs 1,150 pounds with superb muscling. This could be the result of two similar parents. Thus, the offspring would possibly be more true at producing these qualities in its offspring when bred to a similar mate.

Or, it could be the result of a 13 1/2 hand 900 pound mare and a 16 1/2 hand 1,350 pound sire. This offspring could have all the high qualities yet would probably produce erratically in terms of size and quality.

It is more important to look at uniformity in ancestry than to measure or put all the emphasis on the individuals you are thinking of breeding together.

It is fun to research a horse's pedigree back until you run out of pedigree information. Sometimes you get up to ten generations. Is this really meaningful? Most researchers feel that beyond great-grandparents the influence is so small, such as 6 1/4 percent from each great-great-grandparent on the average, that it is of little use in evaluating the potential of the individual being evaluated.

If you are picking a sire or dam, study parentage individuality and progeny performance records. Some matings of apparently near perfect horses can produce inferior offspring while other similar mares could be bred to that stallion and produce exceptional offspring.

If you get an exceptional foal out of a given mating, use that mating over and over as long as you are having good results. You can shop around and may never find a combination that equals what you have.

What about measuring specific areas of the body? Some researchers have seventeen, others up to thirty-two, specific measurements they take. From these measurements they feel they can evaluate the individual's potential for speed. They also use these measurements to run through computers to pick the proper mate for a given horse.

This is all computed on an individual basis. Think back to that 15 hand 1,150 pound horse that could have been produced from a lopsided mating. This individual could measure perfectly but have no offspring that could run a lick.

This method can only work for groups of horses that are very true breeders. That would be hard to come by.

Others prefer measuring the balance of the horses. They feel a horse that is in balance, one part to another, will perform better than a horse that is heavy in the front end or long and over done in the rear end. They are not worried about how long a given bone is, but rather how that area of the anatomy blends and balances with the rest of the body.

Here again you are just looking at one individual so there cannot be a lot of conclusions drawn about what his progeny will look like. You may, however, be able to tell more about the individual's potential as an athlete.

Feed can make the difference of a horse becoming a plug or a champion. A balanced diet, proper worming, and external care can make a large difference in the manifestation of hereditary qualities. A horse can be 16 hands and weigh 1,250 pounds. His full brother can be 15 hands and 1,000 pounds. If you provide the best environment you can, your horse will be able to meet his potential. If you limit his feed during the growth years or use poor quality feeds, you will prevent your horse from meeting his potential.

If everything is in line up to this point, you can pick a trainer that is inadequate in knowledge or desire and you will not see the full potential in your horse. To be a good trainer, you have to almost live with your horse. You have to know when they don't feel well or when they are sore. You have to know the horse's personality and know how to get the most out of horses with each type of personality.

After you have done everything for the horse with that perfect body, you must rely on that horse's desire to please, to perform and to compete. This can be affected by heredity and environment. It is the composite of all that the horse is, its "heart". How do you estimate or predict such a nondescript factor?

When it comes right down to it, is there any one factor that can be used as the indicator of potential? Without a total understanding of genetics, conformation, feeding, care, training and desire you are going to have a hard time producing champions with any degree of success.

Equipment

Halter

The first piece of equipment needed is a good stout halter and lead rope. Halters come in leather, cotton and nylon. Each has drawbacks. Leather is quite expensive. Cotton is cheaper but will shrink and cut into the horse's head when wet. Leather and cotton both wear out and break. Nylon will stretch unless doubled. The round nylon halters come unclamped when horses pull back. The most functional equipment for the money is the doubled and stitched flat nylon halter. This is very strong and more reliable than the leather or cotton. A soft nylon rope eight to ten feet long, with a heavy snap in one end, makes a good lead rope. Cotton is not as strong, but will not burn your hands. It will be satisfactory. Do not use hard twist ropes because they will pull tight and be difficult to untie. This halter and rope will cost from $12 to $20.

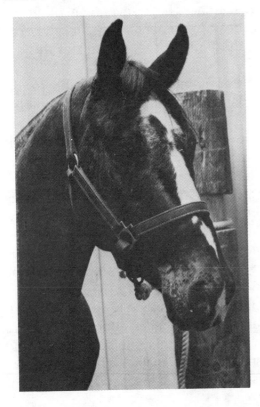

Leather

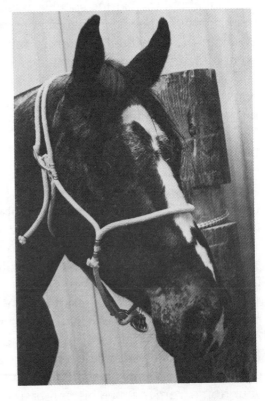

Cotton (or round nylon)

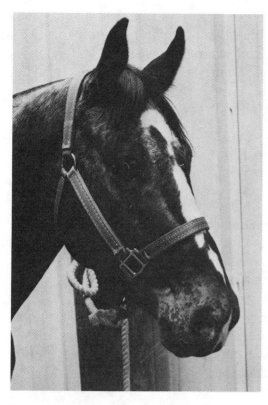

Flat nylon

Grooming Equipment

You will need many small items to keep your horse clean and neat. There are many types and makes to choose from, but the main thing is to try to buy materials that are built to last and then take good enough care of them so they do.

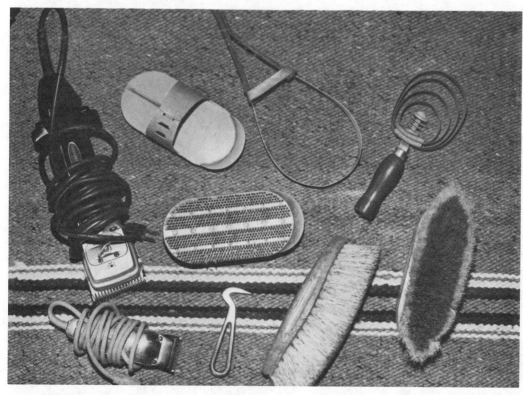

Grooming equipment

47

First you need two curry combs, one metal and one rubber. Next you will need a soft bristle brush and a hard bristle brush. A hoof pick should be available when needed. It is handy to carry a hoof pick on the saddle when riding, because you never know when you will need one. A sweat scraper always comes in handy when you wash your horse. Fly sprays are also very helpful in the fly seasons.

Other pieces of useful, but nonessential equipment, can be purchased if you desire, but the above basics can be obtained for from $10 to $20.

Bridle

The entire bridle above the bit is called the headstall. The chin strap is usually sold as part of the headstall. Headstalls are made in many styles. The main ones used are the single ear, the brow band, and the split ear. The split ear usually does not have a throat latch and in some instances could be unsafe because a horse might rub it off. Headstalls of all styles can be bought in either leather or nylon and are priced from $6 to $30. Show headstalls are much more expensive.

The importance of the bit is often overlooked when buying a bridle. Many stores sell nice leather or nylon headstalls equipped with a 50-cent bit like those on this page. If you buy such a bridle, replace the bit with one that is functional for your horse. Horses differ in jaw and mouth widths. This necessitates making different width bits. Before purchasing a bit, try a few different ones in your horse's mouth to determine what width bit is needed.

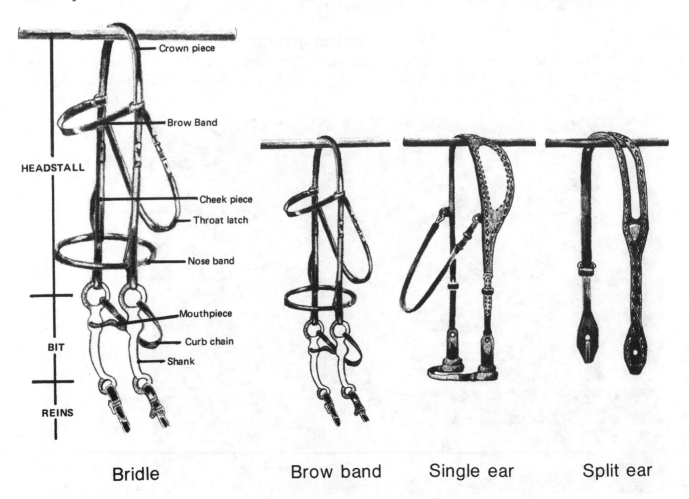

Crown piece
Brow Band
HEADSTALL
Cheek piece
Throat latch
Nose band
Mouthpiece
BIT
Curb chain
Shank
REINS

Bridle   Brow band   Single ear   Split ear

The Function and Selection of the Bit

In order to understand the function of a bit and select the proper bit for your horse, you must analyze the anatomy of the horse's mouth. The bit works on the gum bars, tongue, lips and palate (roof of the mouth) inside the mouth. It also can apply pressure to the curb groove under the chin and the nerves in the back of the poll (behind the ears).

When you look closely at a horse's mouth you will find that the fat tongue sits above the bars on the jaw bone. The palate is concave and the farther back in the mouth you look the more concave the area.

Horses with shallow mouths, or lips that are short to the corners, will carry the bit more forward where the lower jaw holds the tongue higher and the palate will be less concave and easier to come into contact with a high mouth piece in a bit.

Those horses with big deep mouths will hold the bit farther back into the mouth. The tongue will not be as high and the palate will be higher at that point of the mouth. By logic, this would tell you that the shallow mouthed horse would be much more sensitive to the bit than the deep mouthed horse.

Some horses have a dry mouth. Guys have hard calloused hands while girls have soft tender hands. The lotion keeps the girl's hands soft, while the dry working condition causes men's hands to be calloused and hard. Compare this to dry and moist mouths in horses. If the mouth is moist and soft it will be more sensitive. If it is calloused and dry it will not respond easily.

Copper on the mouth piece will make the horse salivate more, keeping the mouth moist and soft. Some horses will have enough moisture without the copper. If a copper bit is used these horses slobber all over.

A mouth piece that will rust is called a sweet steel. The horse seems to like the taste of this bit much more than stainless steel. Most good silver bits will have a sweet steel mouth piece. Some will have a little copper inlaid in the steel.

If the horse does get dry and calloused on the bars, a smaller diameter mouth piece can be used. The smaller the diameter the more pounds of pressure will be placed on a smaller area of the bars. This will make the mouth more sensitive by working on the bars in a smaller area. If this does not do the job then a twisted wire snaffle bit can be used for more abrasive action on the bars to make them more sensitive.

A snaffle bit is one that is connected in the mouth piece in one or even two places. As the reins are pulled back, the center of the bit arches up providing more tongue relief. It will rest in a slight arch over the tongue, resting lightly on the bars and tongue.

There are two distinct types of snaffles, the ring snaffle with no curb action and the shank snaffle that uses the action of the curb strap.

Most horses are started in a type of ring snaffle because it is a direct bit. When you want to go left you pull on the left rein. This puts pressure in the corner of the left side of the mouth but the major pressure is put on the lips on the right side. This pressure is at the point where the mouth piece attaches to the ring.

Some snaffles have finger or side bar extensions up and down from the ring. This puts more contact pressure area on the right side as you pull on the left. This helps the horse get the signal a little plainer.

Set the snaffle bit in the horse's mouth a little loose. Let it hang a quarter of an inch from the corner of his mouth. Just let him walk around and learn to carry it. Once he has found a comfortable spot to hold it, you can take the headstall up so the bit will rest in that place. This will usually be right at the corner of the horse's mouth.

The round ring, dee ring and egg butt snaffles all have their place. The ring snaffle usually has large rings on the sides of the mouth piece. These restrict the bit from pulling through the mouth. The chin strap on a snaffle will also prevent the bit from pulling through the mouth. It has no other function. Ring snaffles can vary from a very small diameter mouth piece to a large one. This bit is thought of as a Western snaffle.

The dee ring is used for race horses. It is balanced for a horse with his nose stretched out in a running position. This bit is working off the corners of the lips rather than the bars. If you look at a picture of a race horse you will see that the nose is extended and the line of the reins come from the corners of the mouth to the rider's hands. The race horse takes hold of the bit and runs into the pressure. Some even take the bit in their teeth, if they have a deep mouth. Because of this pressure, some dee rings have rubber covered mouth pieces to increase the contact area and make the bit less severe for young horses.

The egg butt snaffle is generally thought of as an English bit. It is egg shaped on the rings and has a thicker mouth piece. This distributes the pressure over a wide area of the bars. English riders tend to want more collection in their horses and ride with more mouth contact than Western riders. This bit works well to start colts because it is less severe. Both English and Western riders want their horses to have their nose tucked when traveling. The English prefer it perpendicular to the ground while the Western head set is more natural. Both of these head sets, however, enable the rider to work a snaffle off the bars of the mouth rather than the corners.

Snaffle Bits

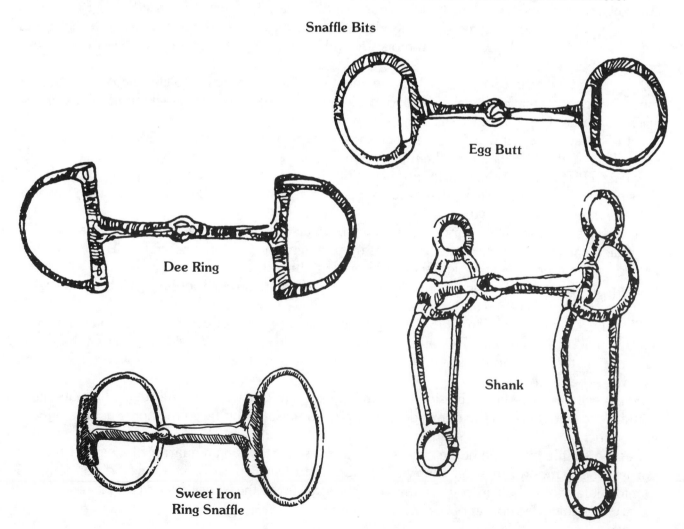

Egg Butt

Dee Ring

Shank

Sweet Iron
Ring Snaffle

50

Once the horse is turning easily on the direct pull, then the squaw rein is introduced. This puts the outside rein of a turn against the neck without pressure on that side of the bit. This gives the horse a sensation on the neck that will become a cue to turn the horse without the direct pull. The trick is never to put pressure on the outside rein or you end up pulling on both reins, which confuses the horse. You must use your hands properly to teach a horse to neck rein. A rider must realize that he has a responsibility not to injure the bars of the mouth by jerking on the bit.

As soon as the horse is moving away from the indirect rein or neck rein you can go to the shank snaffle. One with shanks that curve back a couple inches on a 2:1 ratio below shank to above shank would be a good choice. Some have a rein attachment behind the mouth piece as well as at the end of the shanks.

By placing four reins on this bit you can assist the horse to turn with a slight direct pull on the upper rein as you neck rein. When you stop the horse you use the lower reins for the curb chain action. This is a good transition bit that enables the horse to get use to the curb action without scaring him.

One thing to remember, never pull a curb bit in a direct side pull. This will drive the upper bit into the horse's molar teeth and make him fight the pressure. A slight back inside rein pull is okay if necessary but be sure it is not creating pressure. It is just a helpful cue.

If the horse won't turn on a neck rein in a curb bit it means you have too much bit on him. You need to drop back to a snaffle and teach him to neck rein on cue before you can use the curb.

The shape and length of the shanks of the bit play a very crucial role in the function of a bit. Most bits will have a 3:1 ratio. This means there will be three times the length below the mouth piece to the rein ring, to that length above the mouth piece where the chin strap connects. That above the mouth piece will generally measure 1 1/8 inch to 1 1/4 inch from the bar to where the chin strap hole starts. The longer this distance the more signal time a bit gives. The shorter, the quicker pressure is applied to the mouth. A bit with less than 1 1/8 inch length from the bar to the start of the chin strap hole will cause the bit to pinch the corner of the lip against the bit.

It's best to have a separate hole on the ring for the chin strap to attach. This also helps to prevent the bit from pinching the horse's lip as it is a quarter inch further from the mouth piece. The shorter shank bits will only have a ratio of 2:1. This means there will be two times the length below the mouth piece as above it. This also gives a quicker contact with the mouth than would one with the 3:1 ratio. Take a 3:1 ratio bit and a 2:1 and pull on the reins. You will see that the 3:1 rein ring hole will have to move farther to create the same amount of pressure. This gives a little longer cue for the horse to work on. Anything over a 3:1 ratio is too long but it does create more leverage if you like to pull hard. That's why you see them on mechanical hackamore bits.

The curve of the shank also varies the speed of the communication. A bit that is straight from the top ring to the rein ring will be held in the mouth so that the slightest touch of the reins will be felt immediately. Grazing or cutting bits are curved back a couple inches or more. As the horse balances this bit in his mouth he will hold it so that a pull on the reins will move the bit a half inch before the bit starts to take hold. This gives the horse more time to get prepared for the bit cue. It is a pre-cue that tells the horse something is going to be asked of him and he has time to focus his attention so as to respond to the cue.

A loose shank bit has this same benefit. It is slower to put pressure on the jaw. That is why a loose shank snaffle with a two inch shank curve back and a 2:1 ratio is a good choice. The long shank is too slow with too much leverage.

You will find that a bit with a 3:1 ratio, a high inverted "U" port (curvatures of mouth piece) and a swept back shank will create a more natural head set than most other bits.

Many of the cheaper bridles are sold with a bit that encompasses all the poor qualities a bit can have. They are less than 1 1/8 inch from the chin strap opening to the mouth piece. Thus, they pinch the lip against the mouth piece. They have straight shanks that provide immediate contact and they have solid sides so there is no cushion in the pull.

Many people like aluminum bits because they are light. This light bit tends to bounce around more in the horse's mouth because it is light. The horse won't take a hold of it and keep it in place as well as a heavier bit. Some horses, however, work well with aluminum bits.

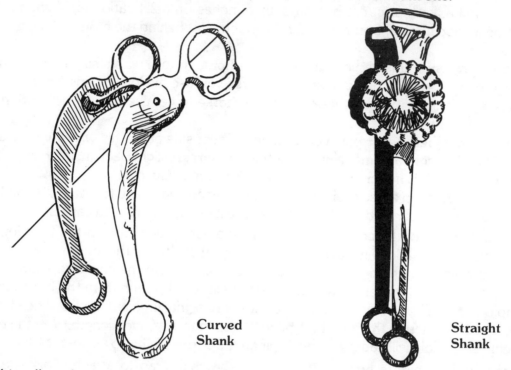

Curved Shank

Straight Shank

Curb bits all work on a vise principle. When you pull the reins, the chin strap causes a vise action against the bit causing curb groove and bar pressure. It also causes the bit to move higher in the mouth and causes a vise action from the corners of the lips to the poll or back of the head.

A true horseman would not need to bring the strong vise action of these leverages into play. You could get what you wanted out of the horse by a small cue pressure on the bit. This would be the result of the previous training in less severe bits.

If a horseman applies these vise pressures to the extreme, he is going to cause the horse to rebel out of fear and pain. When a horse won't respond properly with light pressure in a curb bit you need to go back to basic training with a milder bit.

A curb bit must sit properly in the horse's mouth. If it is too loose it may bang on the bit teeth. If too tight, it always has pressure on the corners of the lips and may even bump the molars.

Let the horse find a comfortable place to hold the bit by allowing it to sit a little lower than desired. The horse will pick it up with his mouth and carry it where it is most comfortable. Once you see where he likes it, adjust the headstall so that it is where the bit rides. This will generally be where the corner of the mouth has one wrinkle in it. Some horses will like it a little higher so you have to be flexible.

The straight bar mouth piece in a curb bit is one of the more severe bits. This is because the big fat tongue has to take all the pressure of this bit. The tongue is more sensitive than the bars. When the straight bar is pulled to the point of making contact with the bars, it finds the bars very sensitive because they have so little bit contact. Only finished horses can handle such a bit.

The half breed and spade also have a straight bar on the bottom and would fall into the severe category. With the half breed's high mouth piece and the spoon attached on the spade, these bits become potentially more severe.

Moving from the straight bar to a mullen mouth piece, with a gentle curve from one side to the other, you are getting a little tongue relief. The sweetwater mouth piece has even more tongue relief. This bit offers a straight bar, one inch over the gum bars, with a long wide low curve over the tongue.

The low-port mouth piece provides wider bar contact with a narrower low curve for tongue relief. This is still quite severe because it is working on the tongue as well as the bars.

There are medium and high port mouth pieces that provide more tongue relief and are the least severe of all the curb bits. They provide tongue relief without palate pressure. Try these for most of your curb bit horses.

Bits like the Mona Lisa, Salinas, San Joaquin and Las Cruces all have little or no tongue relief with an extension into the palate that will put pressure on the palate when pulled. The half breed bit works off the tongue and the palate. It is not as potentially severe as the spade, which has a spoon up into the palate. These bits were not designed for severity but rather head set and finger tip control. The Spanish in the Southwest used a snaffle to start their horses then moved to a hackamore during the time the horse was shedding his four year old teeth and until he had his bit teeth developed at five.

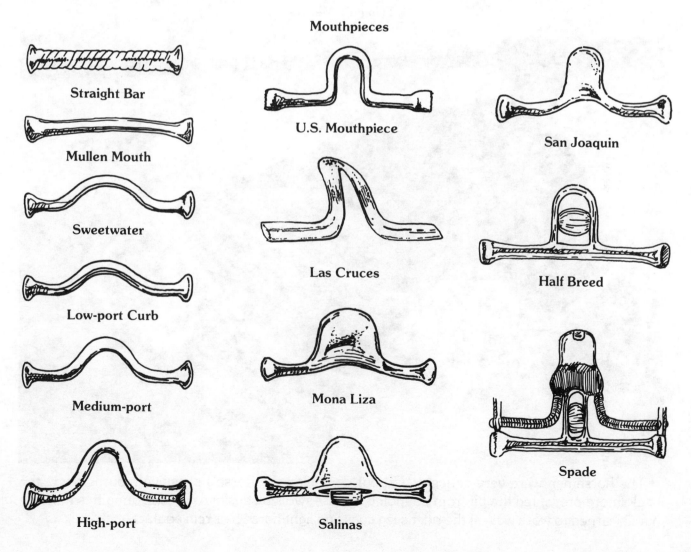

Mouthpieces

Straight Bar

Mullen Mouth

Sweetwater

Low-port Curb

Medium-port

High-port

U.S. Mouthpiece

Las Cruces

Mona Liza

Salinas

San Joaquin

Half Breed

Spade

53

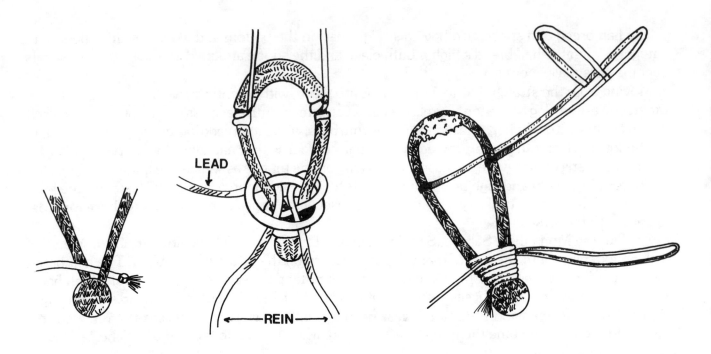

Tying the Mecate

The horsemen were very concerned about damaging the horse's sensitive mouth. Using the hackamore prevented the bit from pounding against swollen sensitive gums. During this time the horse learned to work well off the rider's leg cues and light horse hair rein contact.

The hackamore is made up of a bosal or braided rawhide round nose band. It has a light headstall called a hanger to hold it on a horse's head. The training hackamore will have a fiadore knot and a hackamore heel knot as well as a cheek tie knot, all made out of fifteen feet of cotton sack cord. These knots are specialized knots used on the hackamore. Few horsemen today know how to tie them.

The bosal, or nose band, is measured by its diameter. The bosal can be as small as 3/8 inch to 1 1/4 inch diameter. For most uses a 1/2 inch or 5/8 inch diameter bosal is quite adequate.

The bosal nose opening is about twelve to fourteen inches long. This also varies, but the diameter, length and shape of the bosal all play a part in how functional it is.

The heel knot provides the weight to hold the bosal off the jaw bones. This is the balance weight and must be allowed to function. Some riders tie the cheek knot so tight that it pulls the bosal up to horizontal, when it should be on a forty-five degree angle from the horizontal.

The reins can be of many types but usually are of braided horse hair. This type of rein is called a mecate (McCarty). The horse hair is prickly and will prickle the horse in the neck to make him more sensitive to the rein. For this reason, the first mecate used is made of tail hair because it is stiffer and will irritate the horse's neck more. As the horse learns to respond, a mecate made of mane hair will be used. This is much softer, yet still with a slight irritation.

The theory was to start a colt at three in a snaffle and ride him through his third year with this bit. Then, during his fourth and fifth years, as he was shedding his corner incisor teeth and getting his bit teeth he was put into the hackamore. The hackamore took all the pressure out of the mouth so the tender gums would not be irritated.

To use a hackamore properly, it must fit properly. The bosal should set up on the nose bone possibly six to eight inches from the nostril. The heel knot at the back of the bosal should have enough weight to hang down and away from the jaw.

A hackamore with a rawhide core is best. Most of them made today have metal cable cores. The leather is braided over the basic core.

Soak the bosal until it softens. Then place it over a coffee can and tie it tight. When it dries it will be round instead of long oval. This will fit the shape of the horse's nose much better. If the bosal is not rounded it will irritate the cheeks. The molar teeth are directly under that cheek and will cut into the inside of the cheek if the bosal is too narrow.

Start tying the mecate at the heel knot and wrap it forward until you come to the round of the bosal. Take one tie on the right side then go around the neck and back to the left side. Make another tie off and leave the excess for a tie line. This will put the pull of the rein right next to the jaw, not down by the heel knot.

Using a hackamore requires lower hands. The pressure should be placed on the nose bone as the reins are pulled. If the hands are high the heel knot is pulled up, putting the pressure on the jaw bones. Once the jaw bones are sore the horse's nose will go up when the bosal touches the tender jaw bones.

Starting a colt in a hackamore can cause a lot of problems because it is easy for a scared horse to run through the hackamore. The rider will usually jerk and pull, which scares the colt more and you have a runaway.

If you start the colt in the snaffle and get him handling well, with a good headset, you have no problem moving into the hackamore.

Remember, you are not trying to sore the horse's jaw or his nose. If you are using a heavy bosal you may want to pad it with black electrician tape to make it less severe. A horse that is sore is too worried about being hurt to listen to what you are telling him. He may work out of fear but he won't learn much. You want your horse to enjoy what he is doing and do it because he enjoys doing it.

Horses with head problems in a bit are very nervous and always worried about being hurt. Putting a hackamore on the horse will generally relax him within fifteen minutes riding. This is the advantage of the hackamore. It gives the horse a sense of well being. It will cause him to feel freer, yet he will still be able to be controlled with proper hands. Once the horse is relaxed, he will listen closer to cues you give him. He will be able to concentrate on the finer points of riding.

To move out of the hackamore, the top trainers use a curb, half breed or spade bit under the hackamore. The horse learns to carry the bit without having any communication through it. Once the horse is carrying it well, not mouthing the bit or gaping the mouth, then the reins on the bit are used.

The spoon at the top of a spade bit created a suction against the roof of the horse's mouth and in this position could be held perfectly still. By changing the angle of the spoon different head sets could be created.

Once the rider took hold of the reins on the spade bit the horse responded from movements of one quarter to one half inch of the hand. Any greater movement was considered cruel horse handling to the competent spade bit man.

Today some novice horsemen use the spade for horses they cannot control. If he doesn't stop, just tear his head off. That is just what a spade spoon does. The palate can be ripped up and the tongue cut severely by such hard handed unschooled riders.

If a horse does not respond, it is because he has not been trained properly to respond, or he is afraid of the rider's hand and panics. Always go to a softer bit and re-train him to respond out of understanding rather than force and fear.

Another piece of equipment that functions similar to a hackamore is a side pull. This side pull has no mouth piece. It works totally off of the nose.

The side pull nose band can be made of a round metal bar or a piece of nylon lariat rope. The reins connect to the nose band on each side. Thus, the name side pull was used. (see picture, page 57).

The side pull can be used in the place of the ring snaffle or the hackamore. When riding with a side pull always use a running mortingale.

This piece of equipment can be one of the most valuable tools for training you can have. They are not readily available in the tack stores so you may want to write to this author to obtain one. They are reasonably priced and ready for shipment. Also available are proper length running mortingales.

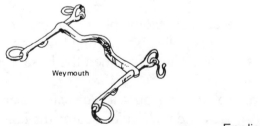
Weymouth

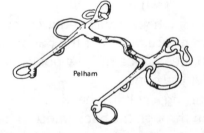
Pelham

English bits

The Pelham and Weymouth bits are primarily designed for English-style riders, but some are used for training Western horses.

The cost of a bit can run from $2 for the 50-cent bit to $50 for a fine stainless steel bit. Some silver show bits can cost upwards of $300. Be sure to find out what type of bit the previous owner used and observe how well the horse worked with it. Possibly you will want the same kind.

Reins come in many styles and shapes. The most common reins used on ranches and for pleasure are the split reins. These two separate reins, six to eight feet long, can be made out of leather, cotton, mohair or nylon. Some are flat while others are braided round. The flat leather reins are the most commonly seen. Flat braided cotton, mohair, or nylon reins work well on training bridles because they are easy to hold on to.

Ropers, barrel racers and goat tiers like the round rein that hooks on to the bit on one side, then runs over the horse's neck and down to the other side of the bit. These cannot be dropped when getting off the horse fast for a tie. They are also easy to slide the hand along for turning around barrels.

Some show horse riders prefer a romal and popper. This consists of a roping type rein with a whip attached where it is held. These are generally braided and relatively expensive. Reins will cost from $7 to $40. Some show romals will cost upwards of $100.

Split Reins

Round Reins

Romal and Popper

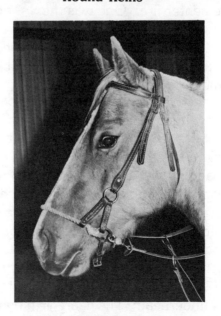

Rope Side Pull

Saddle

The biggest problem of riding properly is the poor fit of the saddle. If the saddle is too big, you bounce from one end to the other. If it is too small, it shakes your teeth out taking every movement, with no give.

How can you pick a saddle that will do the job if you do not really know much about their construction and different styles? Usually the salesman knows less than you do about what will fit your needs or your horse's back.

In picking a saddle, the type of horse to be ridden, the type of riding to be done, and your build must all be considered. An Arabian has a shorter back and thus, needs a shorter saddle. An American Saddler, Tennessee Walker and Thoroughbred usually will need a saddle with narrower bars and a high gullet. The Quarter Horse needs a semi or full Quarter Horse tree depending on how his withers are developed. If he has prominent withers, get a semi Quarter Horse tree, but if he is quite round backed get a full Quarter Horse tree.

Remember, the tree is the wooden portion that is covered with rawhide which is underneath the outer leather. This tree can also be made of Rawlide or other man-made synthetics that make the saddle lighter in weight. Some man-made synthetic trees have longer guarantees than the rawhide tree.

The bars are the two sides that lie against the horse's back. These should distribute the weight of the rider evenly over the back. They should, therefore, be on an angle that will allow the flat portion of the bar to have the greatest amount of contact with the horse's back, so one edge does not take all the weight and cut into the back of the horse.

From the tree is suspended the rigging or dee ring, to which are attached the front and back cinches. The early Spanish saddle had only one cinch attached to the extreme front of the tree. When the cowboy found this saddle was inadequate for roping, because the back of the saddle kept coming up, a back cinch was installed. This was called a full double rig.

The back cinch caused some colts to buck; while the forward cinch sat the saddle back too far for riding bucking horses. The bronc rider soon developed a saddle with the cinch in the middle of the tree. This was called a center fire. Three variations were later developed from the full double and the center fire. One was the 3/4 rig, which was halfway between a full double and a center fire. This could be made in a single or double rig. The 7/8 was halfway between the 3/4 and the double and the 5/8 was halfway between the 3/4 and the center fire. Some saddles have a rig which can be adjusted from a full double to a 7/8 or a 3/4 by changing the latigo and right billet attachment.

If your horse's withers tie into his back further back than normal, you will want to use a full double rig. If, however, he has low withers that tie in up closer to the shoulder, then a 3/4 rig may be best. Set the saddle on and wiggle it around a little until it finds a place to rest. Now feel under the bars to see if the horse's back is curving where the saddle curves. Be sure not to use too much padding or your saddle won't stay in place. Some of the big heavy Kodel pads will not let you keep your saddle in the right place. Try a one inch pad and double blanket; that is usually adequate. Too much padding will cause the saddle to be top heavy and make it hard for the horse to balance the rider on his back. In roping, thick pads puts the horn too far away from the horse's back and the jerk is hard for the horse to handle.

The cinch should be just behind the front leg. Too many people want to set the saddle too far back. If the cinch is around the belly it puts pressure on the horse's ribs that have no structural support underneath. The heart girth right behind the front legs has cartilage that supports the ribs and holds the pressure of the cinch.

Saddle

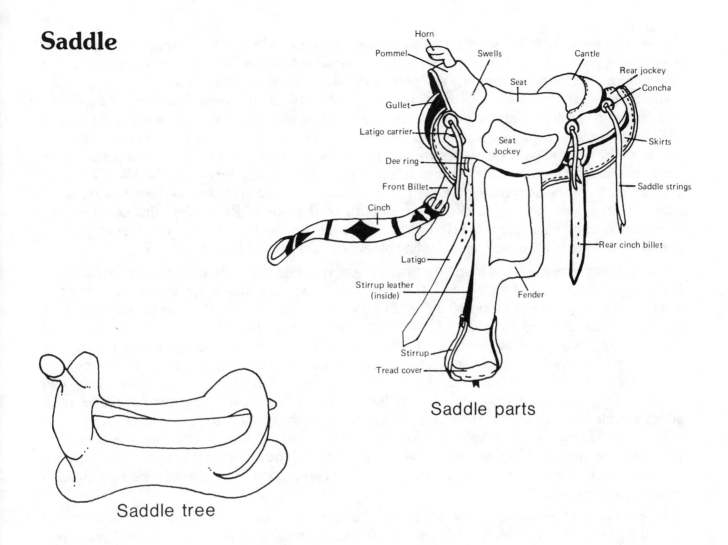

Saddle parts

Horn
Pommel
Swells
Seat
Cantle
Rear jockey
Concha
Gullet
Seat Jockey
Skirts
Latigo carrier
Dee ring
Front Billet
Saddle strings
Cinch
Latigo
Rear cinch billet
Stirrup leather (inside)
Fender
Stirrup
Tread cover

Saddle tree

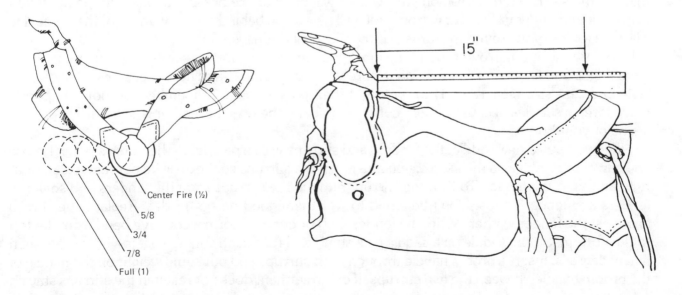

Dee ring settings

Center Fire (½)
5/8
3/4
7/8
Full (1)

Seat measurement

15"

Now to fit the rider to the saddle. The saddle seat is measured from the front of the cantle to the back of the pommel just below the horn. Seats for adults vary in length from twelve inches to seventeen inches, depending on the size of the rider through the pelvis and rear end.

Another factor that must be considered is the style of saddle needed or liked. The roping saddle, for example, has a low profile with very small swells. These saddles are usually bought slightly longer than the average, for quick exits. If you watch a roper, you will see he stands up or moves to the front of his saddle when roping. This puts the rider over the center of equilibrium on the horse making it easier for the horse to carry the weight. If you ride a long saddle and put all your weight in the back of the saddle, the horse will get sore over the kidneys so you need to buy a saddle that will set you up over the equilibrium of the horse. Remember the horse carries sixty-two to sixty-five percent of his weight on his front feet, so don't get in the center of his back and think you are in balance. Think of riding bareback, where would you be sitting?

The old time Wyoming and Montana cowboy liked a saddle known as the Fremont Form Fitter. It ranged from eleven to fourteen inches in seat length, with a cantle seven inches or higher and swells that wrapped back around the thighs of the rider. They bought them to fit snug, so when, not if, the horse bucked, they had a better chance to ride him. Today's saddle maker lengthened the seat and straightened out the swells so they point straight east and west. This saddle was then made with a low back and big horn. They really could not have made it much worse. To reach the swells, you must lift your thighs up three or four inches and in doing so you always lose your stirrups. This is the poorest choice in saddles, yet possibly sixty-five to seventy percent of all saddles made are of this type. If you keep on buying them, they will keep on making them.

Pick a saddle with swells coming out low from the tree so your thighs will be close when your feet are in the stirrups. Choose a saddle with a seat that sits you closer to the front. If you guys will all pull up your pants and sit on your crotch instead of your pockets, you won't need a sixteen or seventeen inch seat.

Before you buy a saddle, sit in it and adjust the stirrups up to fit you. Look down at your foot over your knee. While sitting straight up you should just be able to see the very tip of your boot. Your heel should be directly under your shoulders. There should be about two inches from your thigh to the swells. In this position your weight will be over the horse's equilibrium point. If you lean back and put your feet out in front, you will always be behind the movement of the horse. He will have to drag you around the turns and that hurts his kidneys.

If you are tall and narrow through the hips, you can ride a shorter seat than someone that has large thighs and is broader behind. Make sure you try a number of different saddles. Decide on a style and seat size (see Table 1) for you and then go shopping. Remember, do not buy poorly made foreign saddles because of their construction and the way the leather is tanned. They won't fit you or your horse.

When you buy a new saddle, the fenders and stirrups will lie parallel to the horse's body. Before you can comfortably use the saddle, you must turn the stirrups so they will be perpendicular, or at right angles to the horse. To turn the stirrup, remove the stirrups from the fenders and soak the fenders and fender straps. Don't be afraid to wet them good on both sides. Replace the stirrup and twist the fender leather. Make the fender arch or curve to form a concave bend from the top to the bottom. Sit the saddle on a saddle tree stand and turn each stirrup so it is a little more than ninety degrees. Insert a broom handle through both stirrups and put some weight on the middle of the broom handle between the two stirrups. If one treatment does not result in the stirrups staying turned at the ninety degree angle, give it a second treatment. You may want to store the saddle with the broom handle holding the stirrup if you do not ride very often.

When cleaning saddles or other leather goods use a high grade tallow saddle soap with a few drops of water and a sponge to work up suds. Rub this into the leather and let it set for an hour. Wipe off the leather to remove the dirt and grime that has been lifted out of the leather.

Leather New is a good product to put on for a finishing coat. This is liquid glycerine saddle soap. If the saddle isn't too dirty this may be all you will need to use.

Lexol is another glyceride base cleaner and preservative that will do a good job of cleaning and protecting the leather. You don't want to use a product that will dry the leather or leave a shine on the surface.

Neatsfoot oil may not be a good choice for your leather goods. Mold and mildew may form on leather covered with this product. It may also accelerate the rotting of the thread the leather is sewn with.

Remember use only talcum powder on the latigo. Do not oil this strap or it will be hard to tighten, the oil will make it stick to itself and not slide around the dee rings.

Working talcum powder into a new saddle will help reduce the squeeking. Some people say to wet the saddle to reduce the squeaks. This will dry the leather out. Work in a glyceride product as often as you can to get the leather soft and pliable.

The decoration put into the leather of a saddle affects the price. There are saddles made with rough out leather, smooth side out with no decorations or with decorations (carving or stamping) on the skirts and corners of the fenders, or carved all over. The plain saddle costs less, for the same quality. If a saddle is carved under your legs, it may irritate your legs. So if you want the carving, go for less carving on the seat jockey and the fender.

Prices of saddles vary, but the competition is strong enough that you will find each brand with comparable saddles at about the same price. Handmade saddles start at about $800 to $1,000 for the basic no-frill saddle and go up depending on carving and silver. Look for a good used saddle

TABLE 1: SADDLE SEAT SIZE

| Rider's Height (Feet & Inches) | Rider's Weight (Pounds) | Saddle Type | | | |
		Roping	Cutting	Barrell	Pleasure
Female					
5' & Under	89 or less	13	14	13	12½-14
5'1" - 5'6"	90-110	14	14½	14	13-14½
5'5" - 5'8"	100-120	14½	15	14	14-15
5'7" - 5'10"	110-130	15½	15	14½	14-15
5'10" & Over	120 & Over	15½	15½	15	15-16
Male					
5' & Under	99 or Less	13½	14		13-14
5'1" - 5'6"	100-130	14½	14		13-14½
5'5" - 5'8"	120-160	15	15		14-15
5'7" - 5'10"	150-180	16	15½		15-16
5'9" - 6'2"	170-200	17	16		15½-17
6' & Over	200 & Over	17½	17		16½-18

If you weigh more for your height go to the next line down.
If you weigh less for your height go to the next line up.

61

that is already broke in, if you do not need a show saddle. Just make sure it's not broken down. The leather in the older saddles, if taken care of, could be superior to a new one of lower quality.

One way to save money is to buy used equipment. Many times you can save up to half the "new" cost. Horse owners come and go. When they go they have to take a large depreciation on their equipment. Some just want to get rid of it as fast as they can because they had a bad experience with their horse. Don't let that someone be you.

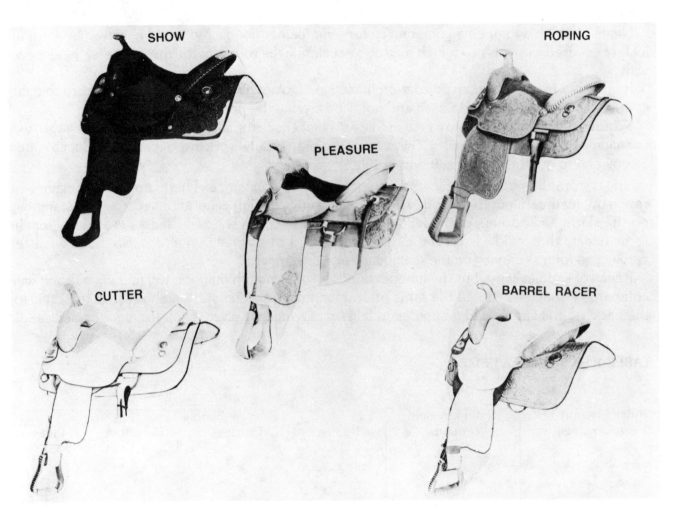

Saddle Styles

Pad and Blanket

Under the saddle you will need a pad and blanket. These come in all shapes and types of material. Pick a pad that is relatively thick, but soft. The cost can run from $9 to $30. The blanket will be either 30' x 30' or 30' x 60' and doubled. The cost ranges from $8 to $50, depending on the material and if it is handwoven.

Storing Tack

Once you have invested upwards of $500 in equipment, how can you make the various pieces last? The first thing to remember is always put your equipment in a dry rodent-proof storage shed. Mice will use pieces of blankets and pads for nests. They also find cinches quite tasty. Dogs, too,

Saddle rack or "tree"

Proper tack storage

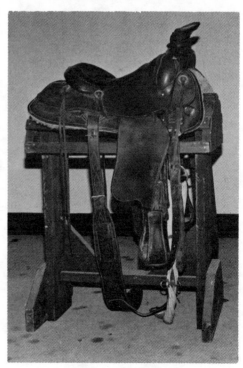

may chew, but their preference is for the leather. Colts and calves love to chew the saddle strings and reins. It only takes a few minutes of chewing to ruin your saddle, bridle, pad and blankets.

It is best to make a saddle rack, or "tree", as it is called. This tree should provide a solid rest that spreads the skirts and holds the saddle's shape. Laying the saddle on its side causes the skirts to roll up and crack. Hanging them from the ceiling is better than this, but is not as good as a tree.

Put the pads and blanket upside down on the top of the saddle. This will allow them to dry out. A rubber bucket makes a nice place for grooming equipment storage. Be sure to hang your bridle and halter by the top of their headstalls so they will be straight for the next use.

Table 2. Costs of Owning and Maintaining a horse and equipment in 1979.

		Range[1] (dollars)		Average[2] (dollars)	Your Cost[3] (dollars)
Fixed costs (one time)					
Horse		600	2000	1500	
Halter and Rope		12	15	14	
Grooming Equipment		8	15	12	
Bridle		30	70	50	
Saddle		150	1000	600	
	TOTAL	800	3100	2176	
Optional Fixed Costs					
Horse Trailer		1000	4000	2500	
Pickup		3000	16,000	10,000	
Annual Costs					
Feed and Supplements		200	500	350	
Housing and Corrals		100	500	240	
Vet Service and Supplies		20	100	50	
Shoeing and Trimming		45	90	60	
Tack Repair		10	50	30	
Training		0	400	100	
Transportation		10	200	75	
	TOTAL	385	1840	905	

[1] Range represents a realistic expenditure that will provide adequately for the needs of the horse and his maintenance. Many people spend in excess of the upper range because of high-cost metropolitan areas or just wasteful spending.

[2] The average horse owner could quite adequately own and maintain a horse and equipment for this cost.

[3] Find out the average cost in your area and calculate your potential costs before buying a horse.

CHAPTER FOUR
Care of the Horse

A horse needs to be properly fed and periodically wormed. His feet need shoeing or trimming. Sufficient exercise is essential and in some areas, adequate shelter must be provided. The wild horse of one hundred years ago did all of these things for himself. Today, even the wild horse needs human help because of fences, lack of water and overgrazing.

A domestic horse confined to a small corral must rely on his owner to satisfy all of these needs. If any one of them is neglected, the horse may become nonfunctional. This is true with the possible exception of adequate shelter, for a horse can endure a lot of heat and cold and still survive.

Feeding

The horse uses what he eats for: (a) body maintenance, (b) growth, (c) reproduction, (d) work, and (e) putting on fat. Each horse you own may have a different use pattern, but each will need some certain amount of feed for maintenance. Therefore, when possible, each horse should be fed as an individual, or at least horses of the same age should be fed together.

The amount of feed needed and its make-up will be governed by the age, weight and use of the horse. But all horses need: (a) good energy sources, such as carbohydrates and fats, (b) proteins, (c) vitamins, (d) minerals, and (e) water.

Energy nutrients are required to power the movement of muscles in walking, breathing, contracting the digestive system, and many other muscular reactions. From this use heat is produced for body warmth. The main energy nutrients are carbohydrates. Sugar and starches are simple carbohydrates that are easy to digest and have an outstanding energy value. Grains, such as oats, barley and corn are high in sugar and starch. Fats, such as soybean oil and linseed oil, are also used by the animal to provide energy and heat. The energy in fats is 2.25 times more concentrated than in carbohydrates. Energy consumed beyond the immediate needs of the horse is converted to body fat for future energy reserves.

Protein provides the material to make new body tissues. Feed protein is digested in the intestine into amino acids. The amino acids are absorbed into the bloodstream and are transported to the various tissues of the body where they may be recombined into new body proteins as required. Most feeds contain some protein but not all the protein in a feed can be utilized by the horse. Since the protein content is estimated from the nitrogen content of a feed and not all of the nitrogen is from protein, the result is called crude protein. Amino acids provided beyond the needs of tissue will be converted to fat and used for energy.

Horses also need small amounts of vitamins. A mature horse can apparently obtain these vitamins from either the feed or by synthesizing them in the intestine, with the exception of A and D. Green pasture forage and good quality, green-looking hay are the best sources of vitamin A. Vitamin D can be produced in the skin, when the sun's rays are available. Sun-cured hay also contains vitamin D. If the horse is to be confined inside a building with little green forage, then a supplement containing vitamins A and D should be fed.

A well-balanced ration generally will contain an adequate amount of minerals. This is especially true for trace minerals. In some areas of the country, however, specific minerals are lacking in

feeds grown on mineral deficient soils. Mineral deficiencies in feeds can be determined by chemical analysis.

When checking a ration for its mineral contents, you must be sure to have more calcium than phosphorous. If the phosphorus exceeds the calcium it will restrict proper use of the calcium. These two minerals are needed for proper bone and tooth formation and when lacking can cause irreparable damage in a horse of any age. Most forages contain adequate phosphorus (about 0.2 and 0.5%) but energy feeds and protein supplements contain much more phosphorus than calcium. When they become a major part of the ration, calcium may be deficient. Alfalfa hay is a rich source of calcium (1.2%) and will balance the deficiency. Otherwise a calcium supplement will be needed.

Sodium chloride, or salt, is also necessary in the horse's ration. The more a horse is worked, the more salt he will need because a pound of sweat contains about two grams of salt. Salt should constitute about 1/2 to 1 percent (by weight) of the ration. It can be fed with the ration or can be available to the horse at all times so he can balance his own needs. It is good to have plain salt and a mineral block available to the horse so if he needs salt, he can get it without increasing his intake of trace minerals.

Water makes up a large portion of the body weight of a horse. Blood consists largely of water. Water is necessary for most chemical reactions in the body. A horse can live longer without food than without water. If a constant supply of water is not available to the horse, he should be supplied with fifteen to twenty gallons of fresh water each day. In the winter he may drink less, but in the summer he may drink more. Make sure he has all he wants to drink.

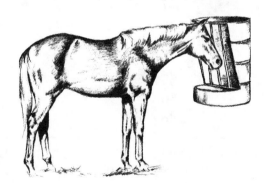 

Digestible Energy

The dry matter of most animal feeds is about 90% to 95% organic matter. Organic matter provides the chemical energy required by the horse much like energy we get from coal, oil and gas to heat our homes. The horse has only that part of the chemical energy of the feed that is digested and absorbed into the blood, available for its use. The energy value of a feed can be expressed as a percentage of the total energy that is digestible (digestible energy, %) or digestible energy as megacalories (Mcal) per unit or weight.

Forages and roughages are comparatively high in fiber and, therefore, lower in digestible energy. Forages are those plants grown and harvested particularly for livestock feed such as alfalfa, clovers and grasses. Forage plants can also be grazed directly by the horse. When adequate forage is available in a pasture the horse will select a higher quality diet than when fed harvested forage because it eats the plant from the top down. Roughages are crop residues and by-products such as straws, corn stover, corn cobs, seed hulls, etc. They are not only low in digestible energy and of low preference by horses, but the undigestible residues take up space in the digestive tract and restrict the intake of digestible energy from higher quality feeds. This feature can be used as an advantage to control feed intake.

Selecting Horse Hay

The stage at which green roughage is cut or grazed has a direct bearing on the feed value it will have. Late cut hays are not as nutritious and are lower in protein than early cut hays as can be seen in the example in Table 3.

Some horsemen do not like to feed horses alfalfa hay. Instead they prefer Timothy or other grass hays. One must remember that the farmer will generally cut grasses later than the buyers would like in order to obtain a greater yield. Cool season grass only yields one significant cutting a year. The more mature hay will probably be the same price per ton.

Table 3.

Stage of Growth	Protein (Percent)	Digestible Energy (Percent)
Timothy Hay		
Prehead	10.2	49
Early Head	9.0	47
Head	7.6	44
Alfalfa Hay		
Prebloom	18.7	55
Midbloom	17.1	50
Fullbloom	13.2	48

In feeding horses for the riding program at Utah State University, alfalfa hay has been used from all three cuttings and in some years fed as the only hay. No complications were observed and the horses were in fine flesh under continuous work. First and third cutting did produce looser feces. This still did not affect the horses' use. Research has shown that horses consistently prefer alfalfa hay and will eat about fifteen percent more than grass hay if allowed to eat all they want[1]. The extra feed intake allows for more rapid passage of feed through the digestive tract[2] and absorption of water may not be so complete. It may be compared to a beef cow on grass hay versus a dairy cow on alfalfa and silage. Does the soft fecal waste cause any problems for the dairy cow, or does it just allow the eating of more digestible energy for milk production? Alfalfa hay also contains an abundance of calcium and other minerals to balance the mineral needs of the horse where grass hays may be barely adequate in calcium.

The age of the hay, since it was harvested, should also be considered. The longer the hay is stored the lower its carotene or pro-vitamin A content[3]. Last year's hay may be cheaper but you may lose quality in the deal. Vitamin A can be added in a feed supplement if the price justifies the purchase of the older hay.

When buying hay look for the leafiness of the hay in the bale. It should have over twenty-five percent leaves to be considered adequate for a horse feed. The alfalfa hay need not be as high in quality as dairy cows require for high milk production. Color is another important quality to look for. Bleached hay can be reduced up to ninety percent in pro-vitamin A. Rain damaged hay will contain less digestible energy and will look bleached. The leaves will be browner and dry and the hay will have a tobacco smell. Moldy hay often contains toxins that are unsafe for the horse. Generally the horse will not eat the moldy hay unless that is all it has left to eat. Always remove moldy hay from any hay being fed.

Growing plants are always rich in vitamin A or carotene. This is lost rapidly when the crop is made into hay and put in storage. Hay rich in green color and leafy may still be rich in carotene. These are some typical losses in carotene: Fresh cut hay considered as 100 percent of carotene.

When dried and stored in barn - 42 percent of carotene.

After six months in barn - 11 percent carotene.

After one year in barn - 9 percent of carotene.

Alfalfa will have up to one hundred percent more carotene than other hays put up in equal quality. Vitamin A is most important in the field of fertility, reproduction, growth and milk production where greater amounts are needed than for mere maintenance.

Comparing Value of Horse Feeds

In order to more successfully pick your feed, you need to know how one feed compares with another. Table 4 compares the digestible energy and protein content of feeds. It also shows the relative value for supplying energy, and the relative value of energy feed and protein supplements within class of feed. It suggests limits on the percentage of the feed stuff that can be used in the horse diet.

When buying hay for horses you should consider its feeding value as well as the price for other hays available to purchase. The relative feeding value of forages and roughages is compared in Table 4 to that of a good quality alfalfa hay (mid-bloom) having about fifty percent digestible energy for horses and about fifteen percent protein. With alfalfa as the standard (1.00), oat hay has a relative value of about 0.90 while oat straw has only 0.76 as much digestible energy as alfalfa hay. In other words, the digestible energy of about eleven pounds of oat hay could be replaced with ten pounds of alfalfa hay. It is not always possible to make a substitution. For example, the horse may not have the capacity or appetite to eat twenty-six pounds of oat straw to match the digestible energy in twenty pounds of alfalfa hay (20 - divided by 0.76 = 26.3). Barley hay and even barley straw may be undesirable to feed horses. The beards tend to lodge along the gum next to the teeth and create sores.

A horse owner should pick his hay on quality first. However price is an important factor. By using the relative value from Table 4, a hay buyer can determine how much each hay is worth in feed value. Assume alfalfa hay (mid-bloom) is selling for $60 a ton. Oat hay with 0.90 the digestible energy of alfalfa hay is worth about $54 per ton ($60 x .90 = $54), while meadow hay would only be worth $49.20 a ton. If alfalfa can be purchased for $60 or less, it is a better buy for the nutrient supplied than meadow hay at $42 a ton.

Hay is usually the best buy in horse feed. At $50 a ton, alfalfa hay costs 2 1/2 cents a pound; at $60 it costs 3 cents a pound. Oat grain at $7 per hundred weight costs 7 cents a pound and at $8 it costs 8 cents a pound. Alfalfa hay contains about fifty percent digestible energy while oat grain contains about seventy-two percent digestible energy. As you substitute oat grain to supplement the digestible energy of alfalfa hay, less total feed is needed to meet the maintenance energy requirements. This would be alright except the horse craves a given amount of dry matter, or total feed, to comfortably fill its digestive tract. As you substitute grain in the ration you also create a

Table 4. Digestible Energy, Protein Content, Relative Feeding Value, and Feeding Limits of Some Common Feeds for Horses

Feeds (arranged by class)	International Feed No.	Dry Matter[1] (%)	Digestible Energy (DE) as fed[2] (%)	(Mcal/lb)	Crude Protein (%)	Relative Value Comparisons[3] to alfalfa hay	within feed class	Feeding Limits[4] (% of diet)
Forages								
Alfalfa hay, sun cured								
early bloom	1-00-059	90	53	.988	16.5	1.06	1.06	100
mid bloom	1-00-063	89	50	.935	15.0	1.00	1.00	100
full bloom	1-00-068	89	48	.882	13.5	.96	.96	100
Bermudagrass, hay	1-00-716	91	43	.808	8.5	.86	.86	100
Bluegrass, Kentucky, hay	1-00-776	90	47	.898	10.5	.94	.94	100
Bromegrass, hay	1-00-888	90	42	.845	10.0	.84	.84	100
Canarygrass, Reed, hay	1-01-104	91	43	.882	10.5	.86	.86	100
Clover, red, hay	1-01-415	89	50	.939	14.0	1.00	1.00	100
Meadow hay	1-03-181	90	41	.816	6.5	.82	.82	100
Oat hay	1-03-280	90	45	.845	8.0	.90	.90	100
Orchardgrass, hay	1-03-438	89	42	.845	8.5	.84	.84	100
Prairie, midwest, hay	1-03-191	90	42	.845	6.0	.84	.84	100
Timothy hay	1-04-883	88	44	.808	7.5	.88	.88	100
Roughages								
Barley straw	1-00-498	90	36	.665	3.5	.72	.72	70
Corn cobs, ground	1-02-782	90	34	.555	2.5	.68	.68	70
Corn stover	1-02-776	89	37	.735	5.0	.74	.74	75
Oat straw	1-03-283	92	38	.735	4.0	.76	.76	80
Wheat straw	1-05-175	89	35	.612	3.5	.70	.70	70
Energy Feeds								
Barley grain	4-00-549	89	78-83	1.47	12.0	1.57	1.08	30
Citrus pulp, dried	4-01-237	90	67	1.22	6.2	1.30	.90	30
Corn ears (corn & cob), ground	4-02-849	87	72	1.33	8.0	1.42	.98	35
Corn grain	4-02-985	88	84	1.50	9.8	1.61	1.16	25
Corn, oil		100	98	4.00	0.0	4.27	2.94	10
Molasses, sugarcane	4-04-696	75		1.33	3.0	1.42	.98	5
Oat, grain	4-03-309	89	72	1.36	12.2	1.45	1.00	40
Sorghum grain	4-04-383	90	77	1.44	11.3	1.54	1.06	30
Wheat bran	4-05-190	89	65	1.20	15.3	1.28	.88	30
Wheat grain, soft white	4-05-337	89	84	1.56	10.3	1.67	1.15	20
Protein Supplements								
Cottonseed meal	5-01-621	91	72	1.35	41.0	1.44	.92	10
Flax seed meal, solv. extd. (linseed meal)	5-02-048	91	69	1.24	35.0	1.33	.79	12
Milk, skimmed, dehy.	5-01-175	94	90	1.65	32.4	1.76	.85	15
Peanut meal, solv. extd.	5-03-650	92	81	1.50	48.2	1.60	1.02	10
Soybean meal, solv. extd.	5-04-604	90	80	1.47	45.8	1.57	1.00	10
Sunflower seeds w/o hulls meal, solv. extd.	5-04-739	92	70	1.27	45.3	1.36	.95	10

[1] The dry matter of air dry feeds can vary from 86 to 94% between extremely humid and dry climates. Dry feeds with less than 86% dry matter are in danger of molding.

[2] Digestible energy is shown as a percentage for convenience of comparing value of feeds. Digestible energy expressed as mega calories (Mcal) per pound is for the convenience of feeders that purchase and weigh out feeds in the English system commonly used in the United States. Multiply Mcal/lb by 2.2 to convert to the international unit of Mcal/kg. The nutrient composition of feed was supplied by the International Feedstuffs Institute, Utah State University.

[3] Relative value of all feeds is compared with alfalfa hay, midbloom, as the standard. Comparisons among energy feeds are made with oat grain as the standard. Comparisons among protein supplements are made with soybean meal as the standard.

[4] Maximum permissible part of the diet to be supplied by this ingredient or class of feed. When more than one feed of the feed class is used the limits are reduced proportionally.

need for a bulky feed to fill the space. A roughage feed such as bright, clean straw can be offered to satisfy the dry matter requirement.

Pasture can be a relatively inexpensive substitute for hay. It must be a large pasture that can be rotated in its use. Cattle one year and horses the next will reduce the internal parasite problem because the larva crawl up the grass petals and the cows harvest them, thus, the pasture is more free of parasites the following year. Plants in a small pasture that is heavily grazed will be short and covered with manure which harbors internal parasites. It is cheaper to feed hay than to use an inadequate pasture. Using parasite infested pastures is possibly the greatest error made by people feeding horses.

Estimating the Hay Ration

A bale of hay may weigh from forty to one hundred pounds, depending on the variety, condition and dryness of hay, and tightness and size of the bale (wire-tied bales are usually heavier than string-tied bales). When hay is purchased the average weight per bale should be calculated from the weight of the load and number of bales on the load. There will be some shrinkage as the hay dries in the stack due to extra moisture at the time of baling. The bales you feed may weigh less than the bales purchased. From the average weight of a bale it is easy to estimate the portion of a bale you need each day for each horse. For example, if the bales average sixty pounds and you want to feed your horse twenty pounds per day, you should not feed more than one third of a bale per day.

Pick your hay wisely. Do your horse and yourself a favor by knowing what hay to buy and what it is worth.

Energy Feeds

Energy feeds are low in fiber and high in digestible nutrients. The cereal grains fall into this class as does wheat bran, molasses and oil. Energy feeds are included in the diet when the energy requirement cannot be supplied by forage alone, because of the limited capacity of the horse. Oat grain is the most popular single grain for horses. It is the safest of all grains for horses because it is bulky, does not pack easily, and it will not cause colic unless eaten in great quantities. Wheat bran and dried citrus pulp are similar to oat grain as energy feeds and are relatively safe to feed.

Table 4 shows the relative value of the more common energy feeds. Digestible energy and protein content can vary greatly with the conditions under which it was grown, harvested, and stored. Figures used in this table are averages.

When buying grain be sure the kernels are full and dry. Off colored grain could be moldy. It should smell clean. Buy grain by the pound (weight) not the bushel (volume). This will reduce the problem of heavy grain versus light grain which could cost you up to twenty percent more for the nutrients if purchased at the same price [1].

As can be seen in Table 4, oat grain is not the highest value for energy feed, but among the lowest. Because of the safety of feeding these energy feeds, they have been most popular. Oat grain is often more costly than any of the other grains. By feeding horses individually, a person can use rolled corn and barley grain in place of the oat grain to reduce costs. One must make sure the digestible energy concentration (Mcal/lb) of the diet and the ration of pounds per day does not exceed capacity of the horse's digestive system. The feeding limits of Table 4 are given to avoid colic and founder from excessive consumption of energy feeds. Replacing part of the energy feed with hay, which is usually cheaper, will also help reduce feed costs.

Wheat bran is a bulky, highly palatable, medium protein, medium energy feed. Because of its laxative effect on horses it should not be used as the only energy feed. Citrus pulp has similar feed value and may be a more economical feed in some areas.

When buying feeds, the market price reflects both comparative feeding value and the shipping and handling costs. Feeds that are not grown in your area will usually cost more for the value received due to freight costs. The relative feeding value for the feeds can aid in comparing prices. If oat grain and barley grain were both selling for $5 a hundred weight, barley would be the best buy. Don't be afraid to substitute as long as feeding limits in Table 4 are observed.

When feeding grain you can estimate the weight by volume measurements as shown in Table 5. The same volume of corn and wheat grain is about twice as heavy as oat grain and a pound of oat grain contains much less digestible energy. To determine the quality of grain you are feeding, weigh a quart or bushel measure of it and compare that weight to the values in Table 5. Barley grain and corn also contain more digestible energy than oat grain (about 72% for oats, 78% for barley and 84% for corn) so you must feed less of these grains to supply the energy provided by the same weight of oat grain.

Table 5. A Guide for Measuring Digestible Energy by the Volume of Grain

Grain	Approximate wt. per bushel[1] (32 qt.)	Wt. per quart	DE per lb.	De per quart
	lb.	lb.	Mcal	Mcal
Wheat grain	58-60[1]	1.85	1.56	2.9
Wheat grain rolled	52	1.62	1.60	2.6
Corn grain	52-56	1.75	1.50	2.6
Corn grain cracked	58	1.81	1.54	2.8
Barley grain	40-50	1.25-1.50	1.46	1.8-2.2
Barley grain rolled	32-40	1.00-1.25	1.48	1.5-1.8
Oat grain	27-38	.85-1.20	1.32	1.1-1.6
Oat grain rolled	24-32	.75-1.00	1.36	1.0-1.4

[1] This weight per volume of grains varies with (1) size and shape of seeds of particles. (2) portion of fibrous seed coating or chaff, and (3) amount of water contained in the grain. These factors determine the quality or grade of the particular lot of grain.

Protein Supplements

Linseed oil meal is well-known for adding lustre or bloom to the hair coat. It is, therefore, used to feed show horses. It is more popular as a protein supplement for horses than soybean oil meal even though linseed oil meal is lower in protein content, protein quality and digestible energy. The solvent extraction process used today leaves very little oil in the meal so any advantage of linseed oil meal is doubtful. If the effect of linseed oil is desired the oil can be added to the energy feed mixture.

Cottonseed meal is of lesser importance as a protein supplement for horses. Like linseed meal, it has a low quality protein and contains more non-digestible matter than soybean meal.

When buying protein supplements to be used for young growing horses or lactating mares, you should compare the cost of each pound of protein. The quality of protein in the supplement should also be considered. Milk protein (dried skimmed milk) is the highest quality. Soybean meal, peanut meal and sunflower meal also supply quality protein (Table 4.)

Protein supplements also supply about the same amount of digestible energy as the energy feeds. As protein supplements are added to a diet or ration, the percentage of energy feeds in the formula should be reduced accordingly to avoid feeding a diet that will be harmful to the horse. Feeding protein in excess of the animal's requirements is both uneconomical and wasteful.

Feed supplements formulated for dairy and beef cattle, with non-protein nitrogen supplements (urea, etc.), should not be fed to horses[4].

Feeding Requirements

To totally balance a horse's ration you must consider many things such as total air dry feed, digestible energy, protein, minerals and vitamins. Table 6 is organized to show the digestible energy requirement for riding horses of (1) various body weights (2) performing various intensities of activity for (3) various lengths of time[5]. The amount of air dry feed that the horse can comfortably eat to perform this activity is also shown. Activity or energy expenditure increases appetite for feed. The horse can compensate for energy demands by eating some what more of the same diet used for maintenance. However, the bulk density (weight per volume, lb/qt), and the digestibility of the diet also limit the amount that can be consumed by a particular horse. More digestible feeds fill less space in the digestive tract because they are digested more rapidly with less residue thus allowing for more feed to be consumed.

Horses involved in a regular activity should be fed a diet to include the energy requirement of maintenance and the activity. The intensity, regularity and duration of the activity often requires more energy than the horse can consume from a diet of hay alone. Energy feeds must be substituted for forages and roughages in the diet to meet the energy requirements. The substitution should be made gradually, over several days to allow the digestive system to adapt to a diet with more digestible energy. Energy concentrations compatible with the level of activity are suggested in Table 6.

The amount of daily feed (ration) required to meet the energy requirements can be calculated with the information from Tables 4 and 6. The energy required for maintenance plus the level of activity of the horse is taken from Table 4 in units of megacalories (Mcal) per day. The amount of air dry feed (lb/day) that the horse can consume to supply this energy and the appropriate energy density of the diet (Mcal/lb) suggest the feed or combination of feeds that could be used to meet the energy requirements of the horse. Go to Table 4 to find the digestible energy supplied by a pound of the feed you intend to use. Start with the forage you plan to feed. Multiply the amount of feed from Table 6) by the digestible energy content of the air dry feed (from Table 4) to determine the energy provided. Compare the energy provided to the energy requirement (from Table 6).

For example, a 1,000 pound horse is ridden about four hours per day with an average activity close to level 2 (slow trotting, some cantering). The energy requirement is found in Table 6 to be about 24.3 Mcal per day. Table 6 also shows this horse can comfortably consume seventeen to twenty-four pounds of air dry feed depending on the energy density (0.9 to 1.1 Mcal/lb).

If alfalfa hay, mid-bloom, alone were fed (0.935 Mcal/lb of hay) and the horse consumed twenty-four pounds it would only get 22.4 Mcal digestible energy (24 lbs. x 0.935 Mcal/lb). This is 1.9 Mcal less than the requirement (24.3 - 22.4 = 1.9). If it is desired to feed a ration closer to the requirement, an energy feed can replace part of the hay.

Suppose we choose barley grain as the energy feed to use. Barley grain supplies about 1.47 Mcal digestible energy per pound. The difference between the alfalfa hay (.935 Mcal/lb) and barley grain is about .54 Mcal digestible energy per pound (1.47 minus .935 = .54). Therefore, if we want to keep the feed intake the same we can replace part of the alfalfa hay with barley grain and as we do so the digestible energy of the ration will increase by 0.54 Mcal/lb of substitution. Since the alfalfa hay alone is 1.9 Mcal short of energy, it would take three and one-half pounds of barley grain to replace three and one-half pounds of alfalfa hay to meet the energy requirement (1.9 - divided by .54 = 3.5).

A mature horse can eat dry hay at the rate of about 2.2 to 2.5 percent of its own body weight each day (not allowing for waste). This means a 900 pound horse could consume twenty-two and one-half pounds of hay each day and a 1100 pound horse could consume twenty-seven pounds of hay. If fed only hay over a time period the horse can increase its capacity by about ten percent more, however, the extra weight and girth would be undesirable for a horse in competition.

The same 900 pound horse may only require fifteen pounds of alfalfa hay for a maintenance diet. After eating the fifteen pounds he may still be hungry so high quality clean straw can be used as a filler.

If the horse is to be ridden two hours a day at light activity he will need more than maintenance digestible energy. If the activity becomes more strenuous during those two hours, still more digestible energy will be required. Riding four or six hours requires much more digestible energy. During moderate activity the horse transports fat as fatty acids to the muscles for energy[6].

The figures in Table 6 tend to exceed the limits of the horse to consume feed and energy as time and intensity of work increases (shaded area of Table 6). Under some levels of work a horse cannot possibly eat enough feed to supply the needed amount of energy. Therefore, he draws more intensively upon his body fat for the needed energy. This is only possible for short periods that are followed with rest and adequate feed to restore body fat.

The cowboys on the big cattle ranches used this principle by having a string of six horses - one for each working day. One day of work required more energy than the horse could acquire from night pasture so he was given six days to get energy built up for the one-day-a-week ride.

The race horse must use the readily available energy sources already in the muscle tissue for the short period of maximum effort. Body fat cannot be mobilized quick enough to supply these immediate demands. These performance horses must be properly maintained and highly trained, to increase muscle coordination, oxygen capacity and energy reserves. The diet and feed intake are regulated to improve performance without adding fat or other unnecessary weight.

A mature 1,000 pound horse (average size of riding horse) being used two hours daily requires about twenty-one pounds of alfalfa hay a day. An additional ten percent may be needed to allow for waste from hay dropped on the ground by the horse or horse feeder. Depending on your mangers and timing of feeding you can arrive at an approximate waste factor to use. Some owners only feed once a day. There will be less waste feeding smaller quantities more often. A feed manger designed to prevent the horse from pulling hay flakes out, and which will not allow the horse to get its head into the feeder to throw hay around, can reduce waste.

Many horsemen feel they need to feed grain to any horse they are riding and some even feed grain to the idle horse. This is a waste of feed and a waste of money. A feeding of half alfalfa hay and half grass hay will be adequate for most pleasure horses. The bigger the horse, the more alfalfa you will need to feed. If the horse will be used four hours, add grain to his ration. If you don't ride it four hours the next week, reduce the ration to maintenance. Many times the level of activity will exceed the horse's daily digestible energy intake but if it will only be for a day or so, do

Table 6. Energy Requirements for Horses for Various Activities and Times

Activity Level	Weight of Horse (lb.)	Daily Feed[1] (air dry basis) (lb.)	Digestible Energy Concentration of Diet (Mcal/lb.)	Maintenance[2] (Mcal/day)	Per Hr. Activity (Mcal)	Daily Energy Required[3]			
						Maintenance plus Activity for Hr. Indicated			
						1 Hr. (Mcal)	2 Hr. (Mcal)	4 Hr. (Mcal)	6 Hr. (Mcal)
1. Walking	800	15 to 20	0.9 to 1.0	12.9	.18	13.1	13.3	13.6	14.0
	900	16 to 21		14.1	.20	14.3	14.5	14.9	15.3
	1000	17 to 22		15.2	.23	15.4	15.7	16.1	16.6
	1100	18 to 23		16.4	.25	16.6	16.9	17.4	17.9
2. Slow trotting, some cantering	800	15 to 22	0.9 to 1.1	12.9	1.81	14.7	16.5	20.1	23.8
	900	16 to 23		14.1	2.04	16.1	18.2	22.3	26.3
	1000	17 to 24		15.2	2.27	17.5	19.7	24.3	28.8
	1100	18 to 25		16.4	2.50	18.9	21.4	26.4	31.4
3. Fast trotting, cantering, some jumping	800	15 to 24	1.0 to 1.1	12.9	4.54	17.4	22.0	31.0	40.1
	900	16 to 26		14.1	5.10	19.2	24.3	34.5	44.7
	1000	17 to 27		15.2	5.67	20.9	26.5	37.9	49.2
	1100	18 to 28		16.4	6.24	22.6	28.9	41.3	53.8
4. Cantering, galloping, jumping	800	15 to 24	1.1 to 1.2	12.9	8.34	21.2	29.6	46.3	63.0
	900	16 to 26		14.1	9.39	23.5	32.9	51.7	70.4
	1000	17 to 27		15.2	10.43	25.6	36.1	56.9	77.8
	1100	18 to 28		16.4	11.48	27.9	39.4	62.3	85.3
5. Strenuous effort[4] (racing and other maximum effort activities)	800	15 to 22	1.1 to 1.25	12.9	14.15	27.1	41.2	69.5	97.8
	900	16 to 23		14.1	15.92	30.0	45.9	77.8	109.6
	1000	17 to 24		15.2	17.69	32.9	50.6	86.0	121.3
	1100	18 to 25		16.4	19.46	35.8	55.3	94.2	133.2

[1] Daily air dry feed intake can vary with level of activity. As activity increases the appetite for feed can increase up to the limit of the digestive tract.

[2] The minimum level of energy required to maintain weight on a stabled horse.

[3] The upper limits of feed intake and safe digestible energy concentration of the diet limit the energy intake to about two times the maintenance requirement. The shaded area of the table indicates activities requiring more energy than the horse can comfortably consumer in one day. Energy for activity was calculated from requirements determined by Hintz et al. (1971) as presented in the NRC horse publication (NRC 1978).

[4] The energy demand is so intense that the only short periods of activity can be endured.

like the old cowboys and just give the horse a rest rather than keeping it on the ration designed for higher activity.

Environmental stress is another factor often neglected when feeding the horse. Hot and cold temperatures and the addition of solar radiation, humidity, wind, rain or snow can make it difficult for the horse to maintain its body temperature in the normal zone. The horse will need increasingly more energy (ten to fifty percent more) as the chill factor goes below and beyond freezing temperature[9]. The feeder may observe the horse's appetite increasing as winter temperatures arrive. Horses fed in open pastures of extremely cold temperatures will need better quality feed to provide the energy needs, otherwise body tissues will be depleted. Young horses will stop growing under extreme cold stress. The problem is more critical with the smaller body size as more heat is lost per unit of body weight.

Heat also increases energy requirements as the body organs try to keep the body cool. Heat stress, however, decreases the appetite so energy intake cannot be increased unless more acceptable feed is offered. The main concern during heat stress is that shade, water and salt be readily available. When horses are stabled they will also require ventilation. Under cool temperatures a stabled horse will drink water equal to about three times the weight of the dry feed intake[10].   Activity increases water requirements for cooling the body, and activity during hot weather can cause serious salt and water depletion.

Horses of the same size may have energy requirements some what above and below those shown in Table 6. A nervous horse will require more energy for walking the fence all day while a docile horse will stand still or lay down and sleep part of the day requiring less energy. Remember to watch your horse for signs of over or under feeding and make adjustments in the ration. Most feeding problems with horses are due to an inadequate use of common horse sense.

Do's of Horse Feeding

1. Know the approximate weight and age of each animal and feed each horse in proportion to size, weight, condition and nutrient needs.
2. Feed each horse as an individual when possible to insure proper intake of feed. Each horse is different; learn the likes and peculiarities of each.
3. Have a regular feeding time and feed twice a day.
4. Feed hay and grain in clean feeders.
5. Develop a sensible ration.
6. Make increases in the digestible energy concentration of the ration gradually over a few days to avoid upsetting the horse's digestive system.
7. Have fresh water available at all times or about three pounds of clean, fresh water a day for each pound of dry feed (about seven and one-half gallons for a horse eating twenty pounds of feed). Additional water (up to twenty gallons total) may be required to replace perspiration losses to cool the body in hot weather and during exercise.
8. Provide free access to both plain and mineral salt in summer. Just mineral salt is adequate for winter.
9. Give the horse proper exercise and get him in physical condition for extended exercise.
10. Check incisor teeth for loose baby teeth. If found, pull them out.
11. Make certain that the horse's molar teeth are not sharp. If they are, have them floated.
12. Worm mature horses spring and fall. Younger horses may need to be wormed as often as every two months.

Don'ts of Horse Feeding

1. Never feed moldy, musty, dusty or frozen feed.
2. Don't water a hot horse or feed a hot horse energy feeds.
3. Don't work a horse hard right after feeding of energy feeds or after excessive water consumption.
4. Don't overfeed, or horses will get fat and sassy.
5. Don't feed out of your hand. The horse may start nibbling or biting.

Watch your horse for signs of over or under feeding. If the horse is putting on too much weight, the composition of the diet should be adjusted or the amount cut down. If the horse shows signs of losing weight, ribs showing, stomach drawn up and coarse hair coat, additional feed or higher quality feed should be provided. If the horse does not start to pick up, you should call the veterinarian. The vet will probably need to float the teeth and/or worm your horse to promote intake and utilization of feed. A healthy horse is much cheaper to feed than one full of parasites or a mouth full of sharp teeth.

Remember, regular grooming and adequate exercise plus sensible feeding make for a well-conditioned horse.

Parasites

Over one hundred fifty differed kinds of internal parasites of the horse have been identified. Almost all horses harbor some form of parasite in their bodies. Only a few of these, however, cause serious damage.

Parasites live off the horse by draining nutrients out of the horse's system. It is not the intent of the parasite to kill the horse, for this would be committing suicide. Nevertheless, in some cases the horse actually dies as a direct or indirect result of internal parasites. More often, however, they cause the horse to be unthrifty, to have colic and/or anemia, to lose ambition and performance abilities, and to be dull and listless. A dry, rough hair coat and incomplete shedding are also telltales signs of internal parasites. Because the horse has to eat more than he needs to feed the worms, his belly may be enlarged and yet ribs may show.

Strongyles

Of the internal parasites, strongyles are the most damaging and destructive to the horse. Strongyles are classified as either small or large. The large strongyles are also known as bloodworms. These blood-loving parasites sometimes reach two inches in length and live mainly in the cecum and large intestine. They can severely damage their host's intestines and blood vessels.

Eggs of both large and small strongyles are passed in the horse's manure. These eggs develop into larvae. They then go through two moults, crawl into the grass and leaves and are taken into the horse's mouth as he eats. After entering the intestine, they penetrate to the bloodstream and migrate to the liver, heart and lungs, destroying healthy tissue along the way. They eventually attach themselves to the great mesentery artery or its branches.

As the bloodworms become firmly entrenched in these vessels, the vessel wall weakens from the burden and sac-like pouches develop. The pouches fill with blood that cannot circulate. Clots of blood break away from the sac, becoming floating chunks that are carried to smaller arteries to lodge and impede the blood supply to the intended area. Occasionally a vessel may be completely plugged, thereby causing death of the tissue or organ deprived of the blood. It is believed that most cases of colic result from the disturbances of the bloodstream by these worms.

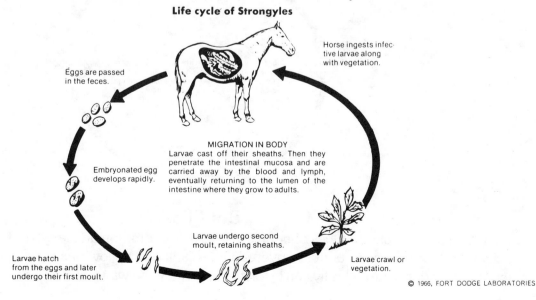

Life cycle of Strongyles

Eggs are passed in the feces.

Horse ingests infective larvae along with vegetation.

MIGRATION IN BODY
Larvae cast off their sheaths. Then they penetrate the intestinal mucosa and are carried away by the blood and lymph, eventually returning to the lumen of the intestine where they grow to adults.

Embryonated egg develops rapidly.

Larvae undergo second moult, retaining sheaths.

Larvae crawl or vegetation.

Larvae hatch from the eggs and later undergo their first moult.

If the sac of blood ruptures when enlarged it can result in hemorrhage and death of the horse. If clots lodge in a vessel in the leg, the leg can be affected by impaired circulation. It will be evidenced as unexplained lameness.

One of the most destructive stages of the large bloodworm, Strongylus vulgaris, is the arterial larvae stage. These deadly larvae migrate for up to six months in the walls of the horse's blood vessels. They feed on plugs of blood and intestinal mucosa as they damage vessel walls.

The favorite site of the large bloodworm larvae is the vital cranial mesentery artery. This is the artery through which ninety to ninety-five percent of the horse's blood passes on the way to the intestines and hind legs. Here they spend two to four months damaging the vessels and causing blood clots which can break off, clog the artery and cut off the flow of blood.

Ascarids

The ascarid, or common roundworm, often grows to the diameter of a lead pencil and can be eight to fifteen inches in length. Ascarids live in the small intestine, sometimes in large numbers. Fortunately, ascarids are seldom a problem in horses older than four to five years. Foals may become exposed soon after birth, in which case the worms will be mature when the foal is two to three months old.

Due to the large size of the adult worm and the great numbers that may be involved, the intestine of even adult horses may become partially, or even completely, obstructed with a mass of these creatures. Colic would be the expected result, and in a case of complete obstruction, death can occur.

Ascarid eggs are passed out in the manure. Within about ten days, under favorable conditions, the embryo develops. The horse will pick up the embryonic eggs as he eats contaminated food. The swallowed eggs hatch in the intestine. Larvae burrow into the wall of the bloodstream. From here they pass through the heart to the lungs. Larvae escape from the lung capillaries into the jaw. From there they migrate up the trachea and are swallowed, traveling to the small intestine. They then grow to maturity in the small intestine.

Life cycle of Ascarids

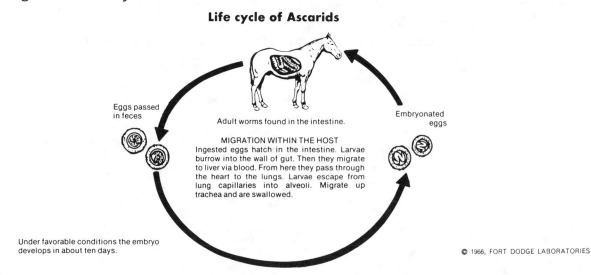

Eggs passed in feces

Adult worms found in the intestine.

Embryonated eggs

MIGRATION WITHIN THE HOST
Ingested eggs hatch in the intestine. Larvae burrow into the wall of gut. Then they migrate to liver via blood. From here they pass through the heart to the lungs. Larvae escape from lung capillaries into alveoli. Migrate up trachea and are swallowed.

Under favorable conditions the embryo develops in about ten days.

Bot Flies

There are three separate types of bot flies. The most common and largest of the three is about the size of a honey bee. Its body is covered with black and yellow hairs. In appearance it looks much like the honey bee. This fly can be distinguished by the way it curls its posterior up under it.

The female hovers about the horse, then darts in and attaches an egg on the leg, chest, side or flank. One fly can produce as many as five hundred eggs. In about seven days, the eggs are ready to hatch. They can remain unhatched for two or three months. When the horse licks or bites its hair, the eggs are stimulated from friction, moisture and the heat of the horse's mouth and will hatch. The newly hatched larvae are taken into the horse's mouth where they burrow into the tongue. They continue to burrow for three to four weeks then pass into the animal's stomach where they attach themselves and remain until mature.

The larvae will develop to a mature state in ten or eleven months. They then pass out of the animal with the feces. After a few days in the manure the pupal stage begins. The pupae burrows into the ground and forms a hard outer protective coating. This stage can last from fifteen to seventy days. At the end of this stage the fly emerges and mates. Then another life cycle begins.

The adult flies do not feed. Their sole purpose in the life cycle is to reproduce. They live from a few days to three weeks.

The throat bot is smaller than the common bot, but they are faster in flight. This fly hovers in front of the horse, darting up to the hair under the jaws and throat. They cement one to four eggs to hair during each attack. They keep this up until they have deposited all their eggs on some horse. This can also be up to five hundred eggs.

These eggs do not require moisture or friction to hatch. In about six days they hatch from body warmth. Newly hatched larvae crawl into the animal's mouth. Usually they lodge in the pockets between the molars. In twenty to thirty days, larvae pass from the mouth into the stomach. They travel to the forward end of the small intestine and attach themselves until they mature in ten or eleven months. They then are passed out in the manure.

The nose bot is the smallest of the flies, but is most rapid in flight. This fly deposits its eggs on the horse's lip hairs, usually along the front of the upper and lower lips. One female will lay about one hundred sixty eggs. Moisture is necessary for hatching, which occurs in about two days.

Newly hatched larvae burrow through the lips to the inside of the lips just in front of the teeth. Here they remain for six weeks or more.

Larvae then pass to various parts of the stomach and attach themselves to the stomach lining. The greatest number attach near the stomach exit.

Mature larvae release their attachment in the stomach, pass to the rectum and attach again. They remain here two or three days then release and drop to the ground.

The rectum attachment may cause irritation and tail rubbing. We may think the horse has pinworms and treat for that, when in reality it is the larvae of this bot.

The bot flies are annoying to the horse. Many times a horse will act up when being saddled or ridden because of the attacks of these flies. The bot larvae produces a severe irritation as they burrow into the animal's tongue, gums or lips. The horse will rub his mouth and nose on his legs or the fence trying to relieve the irritation.

Once the bot larvae reach the stomach they attach themselves with spiny mouth hooks. These attachments cause inflammation, which interferes with digestion. Even after a horse is wormed there may be ulcerated areas left on the stomach walls.

Infested animals often suffer from colic or other gastric disturbances. The degree of damage done by the feeding of larvae is roughly in proportion to the number present. Several hundred larvae may be found in one animal; more than one thousand have been found in the stomach of one colt.

Even if your horse looks fat and healthy, he is still infected with bot larvae. No horse can be totally isolated from the bot fly. Every horse has many eggs on them. The darker horses attract the most flies.

You can always wait until the first killing frost in the fall and worm him for bots. That's what the books tell you. Or, you can take some preventative measures. Keeping the manure cleaned out and hauled away will help. Fly sprays may also be helpful but are not totally effective. Fly bait will be of no value against the bot fly because they do not eat during their life cycle. Their only purpose in life is to lay their two hundred to five hundred eggs on the horse. This will perpetuate their kind.

If you want to make a fortune just find a chemical to dissolve the glue the fly uses to attach her eggs, or a way to effectively break the life cycle.

Many remedies have been used, such as warm water baths to hatch the larvae, sandpapering the legs and scraping the eggs with a knife. All these may be helpful but all have their drawbacks. The water may hatch some but will not do a complete job. Sandpapering the legs is a long tedious job and many eggs are missed. Using a knife is the most effective but there is a chance of cutting the horse or yourself. Always use a round ended knife, never use a sharp pointed one.

Next time try a pumice rock or "grill brick" like they clean grills with in restaurants. You can buy these at restaurant supply houses. Most medium size communities will have one. If not, go to the restaurant and get a piece of one of theirs. It doesn't take a large piece to do the job. Just hold it in your hand and rub in the direction of the hair. This will remove those eggs with little effort in a short time.

If you would remove the bot eggs a couple times a week, you could almost eliminate the problem. Do it, don't just think about it.

Remember, dark horses attract more bot flies. That doesn't mean the white legs don't have any on them. You have to look close, but you can find them if you do.

Life cycle of Bots

Horse licks legs. Friction and moisture from tongue hatch eggs. Young larvae taken into mouth on tougue—burrow into mucosa for 3-4 weeks—pass to stomach.

Bot fly attaches eggs to hair on legs. Ready to hatch in 7-14 days.

Larvae in stomach. (10-12 months)

Common bot fly active in summer.

Larvae pass out with feces in spring.

Pupal stage in loose earth or dry manure 3-5 weeks.

ENTIRE CYCLE REQUIRES A YEAR

Pinworms

The pinworm is seen around the rectum and in the droppings. These worms irritate the horses, causing them to rub their tail and rump against anything they can scratch against. These parasites are the least harmful of those discussed, but the loss of tail hair and irritability detract from the horse's looks and performance.

The female pinworm deposits eggs on and around the rectum. The embryo develops in about two days. As the horse rubs, the embryonic eggs drop off and contaminate the litter. Horses eat food and litter off the ground and the eggs are ingested. Larvae hatch in the intestines to grow to adults. The adult worms are found in the large intestine and cecum.

Life cycle of Pinworms

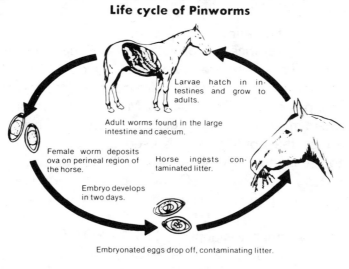

Larvae hatch in intestines and grow to adults.

Adult worms found in the large intestine and caecum.

Female worm deposits ova on perineal region of the horse.

Horse ingests contaminated litter.

Embryo develops in two days.

Embryonated eggs drop off, contaminating litter.

Worming Treatment

Obtain the advice of a competent horse veterinarian about worming treatments for your area. The most common time to worm mature horses is spring and fall. The spring worming is to kill strongyles, ascarids and pinworms. The fall worming should take place after the first hard killing frost. This freeze will kill the bot fly. The fall worming should kill all the internal parasites including bot larvae.

You only kill those worms in the digestive system when you worm. Any that are in migration will not be affected by the worming. These worms will continue their life cycle and end up in the digestive system from seven to twenty days later. Therefore, it may be necessary for you to worm a horse twice if he has a lot of worms.

Some extremely wormy young horses should not be given a full measure of wormer because it may kill too many ascarid worms. These worms will then swell and block the intestines causing severe colic or even death. For this reason a half measure of wormer should be used, followed with the other half in seven to ten days. Then a full measure could be given again in twenty days. This should clean the horse of internal parasites.

Remember, your horse will reinfect himself with more parasites as soon as you turn him out on the pasture or feed him on the ground. If there are a lot of potential parasite infections under your present management, you will need to worm more often. You may wish to change your management to reduce the opportunity for parasites to infect your horse.

It used to be thought that tubing was the only way to do the job right. Shell came out with a product similar to the Shell pest strips, but the chemical was inserted in a little plastic tube and cut in small pieces. The horse ate these with the grain and he was wormed. Or did he eat them? Those horses that would eat all of the wormer were effectively wormed, but too many ate the grain and left the wormer. Mixing the wormer in a horse conditioner that has many different grains can help disguise the wormer. AID animal products have bought Shell's animal health products so you can still find this wormer under the AID name.

Another group of well liked wormers are the paste wormers. Merk Animal Health Division has Camvet and Combot, Farnam has Equivet T+z and Equivet T+c, Cutter has Horse Paste Wormer and Negabot Paste. The first one from each company is for worming all but bots. The second wormer in each case is for bots plus some of the other worms, but not all. Internal parasites become immune to a given drug if it is used over and over. Therefore, the wormer should be changed periodically to prevent creating immune worms.

Cutter Animal Health Laboratories has brought out two new products called Negabot-Plus paste and Combotel paste. These also are advertised to be effective against bots, large and small strongyles, ascarids and pinworms. They can be used for pregnant mares and foals also.

These are not the only paste wormers available. Many other companies have products on the market. Before using them make sure you are getting a wormer with a broad spectrum.

You should realize that the bot wormer, if used in excess, can harm the horse's liver. Therefore, you want to use it effectively. Possibly two applications could be used to clean all the bots out. The rest of the year, use either Camvet, Equivet T+z, Cutter Horse Paste or other products that do the same job. Before using them, make sure they have a broad spectrum kill and are highly effective.

Recently, a new type of wormer was approved by the FDA for worming horses not meant for slaughter. The active ingredient, ivermectin, is the first in a series of anti-parasitic agents derived from the avermectin family of compounds. The avermectins are highly active, broad-spectrum anti-parasitic agents isolated from fermentations of the soil organism, Streptomyces avermitilis. It is effective against adult large strongyles, adult and fourth stage larvae, small strongyles, adult and fourth-stage pinworms, adult ascarids, adult hairworms, adult large-mouthed stomach worms, neck threadworms and stomach bots.

This drug acts on parasites by inhibiting signal transmission from the ventral cord interneurons to the excitatory motor neurons. It stimulates release of inhibitory neurotransmitter gamma-aminobutyric acid from nerve terminals. Or in simple terms, the susceptible parasites become paralyzed and are thereby killed.

Ivermectin is effective against the large bloodworm larvae as well as fifteen other types of worms plus bots. The kill rate is advertised in the high 90 to 100 percent range. The product is advertised to have a longer residual killing effect than any other paste wormer.

Many small strongyles, as well as other worms, have built up resistance to popular worming drugs, greatly decreasing their effectiveness. This is where ivermectin has another advantage because the worms have no resistance to it at this stage of use. The ivermectin paste is sold under the trade name Zimecterin and Eqvalan.

It has recently been noticed that horses wormed with the ivermectin products can still show signs of tail rubbing days after the worming. The mature male pinworm has been found attached to the horses inner areas of the rectum which causes the horse to rub his tail. To completely kill the pinworm it may be necessary to worm once a year with one of the Zole products.

Because horses can be reinfected with parasites soon after being wormed, they should be kept on a routine worming program. We all put off worming until the horse looks like he needs it. By then the horse has severe internal damage to tissue and organs that cannot be repaired.

Preventive maintenance is so much cheaper and easier on your valuable horse. You will find your hay goes further and your horse looks like he is healthy if you keep the parasites killed.

Foals, weanlings and yearlings require more care and caution when being wormed. Some worming medicines are too strong for foals or weanlings. Be sure of the product and the dose before administering it. To kill the ascarids that most colts have, it may be necessary to worm three times at twenty day intervals and then to repeat the treatment every two or three months. Many colts are held back in growth due to inadequate worming.

Read the advertisements of worming products on the market. Confer with your vet and select a wormer that is effective but safe for your horse.

The cost of worming a horse will vary with the method used. The self administered pastes or pellets will run from $6 to $12. If a vet tubes the horse, it will cost about $15. If he comes to your place, there is generally a $20 house call charge. If you worm just twice a year, you will have a cost of from $12 to $70 depending on the procedure.

You should also look into the 5-in-1 shot for tetanus, Eastern and Western Myoencephalitis and two strains of flu. This is a two-shot series to begin with, then once a year after that will maintain the immunity. You never know when a horse might step on a nail and you will not find it.

Other veterinary costs will include those for shots, health certificates if you travel with your horse, plus the unforeseen problems associated with injuries. You should figure on allowing $100 a year (plus any worming costs) for vet bills. Hopefully, you will get by for less. Many horse owners find they pay more out in vet bills than MD bills.

Shoeing

The horse's foot is made up of bones, elastic fiber, sensitive material and insensitive material. For a horseman to know how to take care of the horse's feet he must first know the parts of the foot and how to examine it.

Before you can examine a horse's foot, you must first pick it up. This can be done by approaching the horse calmly and quietly. Talk to the horse and pet him to reassure him.

To pick up the right front foot, put your right hand on the horse's shoulder. Run the left hand down the horse's leg. Grasp the pastern. This can be done at the front or back of the pastern. If the horse refuses to pick up his foot, pinch the back cord right above the ankle.

Sometimes the horse will lean into your push. If so, remove your hand when the horse's weight is on it, and then, as the horse starts to catch himself, push him off that foot. With his weight off the foot, you can pick it right up. Don't stand directly in front of the knee or the horse may hit you if he tries to pull his foot away.

Shift the foot from the left hand to the right. Next, step over the foot so the pastern is between your lower thighs. Close your knees around the horse's pastern. This frees both your hands. Steady the foot with the left hand and clean the manure and rocks out of the sole and around the frog. Always dig away from your body.

Now that you have the foot cleaned out, observe the outer wall, which is the insensitive material. The white line separates sensitive from insensitive tissue. The sole is hard on the outside but becomes softer as you file off layers.

The frog is the rubbery substance forming a 'V' in the back of the foot. Behind the frog are the bulbs. The hoof itself is divided into the toe, quarter and heel, with a bar extending from the heel along the sides of the frog.

Once the mud and manure are cleaned out of the base of the hoof, you should look for nails, glass or rocks that may be lodged in the sole or frog. These can make the horse lame and can sometimes cause tetanus.

If the horse has shoes on, the wear of the shoe and the placement of the shoe should be observed. The shoes should be changed every six to eight weeks. The hoof grows like a fingernail and when it gets long it will break off too close to the white line, causing the foot to be sore.

If the horse is not to wear shoes, the excess growth must be cut off his feet every eight weeks. If a

Grasp the pastern . . .

Pick it right up . . .

Step over the foot . . .

Close your knees

horse's hooves are allowed to go for four or five months without attention, uneven wear of the hooves may cause a young horse to go crooked-legged and an old horse to experience pain or lameness because of uneven pressure on the foot and leg as he walks.

When you are through with the front foot, just let it down as you move your inside leg and step away. Most of the strain in hoof trimming comes from your nervous system. You sweat from nerves, as well as exertion. If you don't feel competent or safe, let the horse shoer do the job.

To pick up the hind foot, approach the horse at the shoulder and work back to the hip. To pick up the right hind foot, put your right hand on the horse's hip. Your left hand should be worked gradually down to the lower position of the cannon or pastern. Grasp the leg and pull forward. If the horse starts to push back, hold on and pull the foot up while holding it forward. Then step under the leg and to the rear, letting your right arm come down around the hock.

From this position, rest the cannon bone on your thigh. Hold the hoof with your left hand while cleaning with the right. Notice that the back foot is a long oval, whereas the front is more rounded. To set the foot down, just step out from under as you release it.

Look at the outer wall of each hoof. It should be smooth with no lines or wrinkles. You can sometimes tell the type of care a horse has had in the past by observing these lines. High temperatures will cause a line to form on the hoof at the coronet. It then grows out as the hoof grows out. These are generally not damaging to the hoof. If, however, the lines are wrinkled and one wrinkle follows another, the horse has been foundered. Founder is an inflammation of the sensitive tissue of the foot. It is usually restricted to the front feet, but all four feet may be affected. The problem involves pressure or swelling within the hoof that cannot be expressed because of the solid wall and the sole. The resultant pinching of nerves produces severe pain. After founder the hoof is soft and grows remarkably fast. It is hard to keep a shoe on a horse that has been foundered. Do not buy a horse that has been foundered.

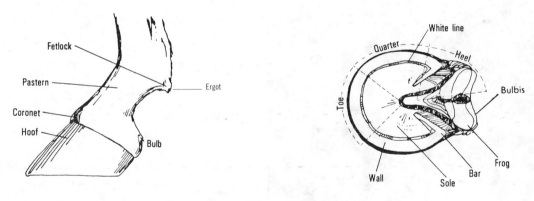

Lower Front Leg

After examining your horse's feet and determining if shoeing is needed, the next step is to pick shoes and a horseshoer. Many people, both men and women, claim to be horseshoers or farriers. Ask around and find out who the better horsemen in your area are using. This is generally a good indication that the farrier is doing a satisfactory job.

Have the horse caught before the farrier comes. If there is a flat, smooth area, use that to stand the horse on. Some farriers like cement to shoe on and others prefer dirt. If the ground is level, the set of the foot is more easily observed.

Be sure to walk the horse so that the farrier can watch the way the horse moves. A good farrier can make minor adjustments that may help your horse travel better.

Grasp the pastern . . .

Pull the leg forward . . .

Step under the leg

 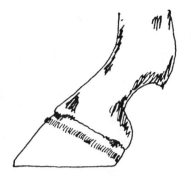 

Smooth hoof wall   Heat lined hoof wall   Foundered hoof wall

A good farrier will work calmly and quietly around a horse. Some horses need a little discipline, but most farriers will not start out with discipline. Be sure you remain calm while helping the farrier. Let him handle the horse his way, as long as he doesn't overdo it. You may have a horse that needs some lessons about holding his feet up.

Most farriers furnish the shoes and nails. There are many styles of horseshoes available, if you are uncertain as to what shoe to use, ask your farrier to help you select a style best suited for your horse and the use you make of him. If, however, you want a particular type of shoe the farrier does not carry, you must buy your own. Shoe sizes start as small as 000; this is generally used on large ponies and young horses. Next come 00, 0, 1, 2 and so on. Few saddle horses take over a size 1 shoe. Work horses need much bigger and heavier shoes.

The shoe is described by the same nomenclature as the hoof, that is, it has a toe, quarter and heel. The nail has a large head with a beveled tip. The beveled side of the tip always goes to the inside of the shoe so that the nail will veer out and exit from the hoof.

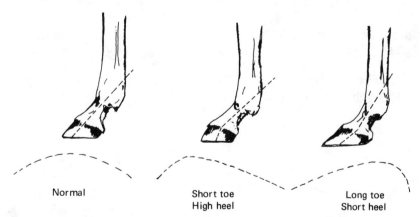

Normal   Short toe High heel   Long toe Short heel

Settings of the Hoof and Pastern

When the farrier has the hoof shaped and ready for the shoe, look to see if the angle of the shoulder, hoof and pastern are the same. If the toe is long and the heel short, the horse will break over too slowly. If the toe is short and the heel is high, the horse will break over too fast. Both of these conditions are undesirable because either can cause the horse to travel incorrectly.

The shoe should cover the entire wall, but should not hang over the heel. Some sloppy farriers will not curve the heels in on the front shoe and the wall of the heel will not be supported.

Nails should come out about a quarter of the way up the wall. This can range from one-half inch

 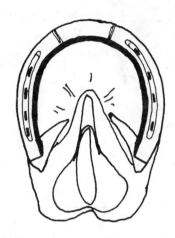

Good shoe set   Incorrect shoe set

on a small foot to a full inch or more on large horses. The nails should be in a uniform line horizontal to the hoof. The nails are cut off and clinched (turned over). This clinch is what actually holds the shoe on. If the nail is cut too short there is not enough to clinch and if it is cut too long it may stick out and cause the horse to cut another of his feet with it.

After the horse is shod, walk him around to see if he interferes, or one foot hits or even ticks another foot. If you hear metal clicking, there is a problem with the set. The farrier should check this and make sure the problem is correct.

The cost of shoeing varies greatly from one area to another, starting at about $10 per horse for shoeing and shoes and going up to $30. Because race horses need more critical attention, their shoeings may cost $30 to $75 per horse.

Your horse may require three to four shoeings a year. At $20 each, this would amount to $60 to $80 a year. Another $30 to $40 will be required for trimming unless you do it yourself.

Remember, a horse is no better than his feet. If you don't take care of them, you are asking for a lame horse at best and an accident at worst.

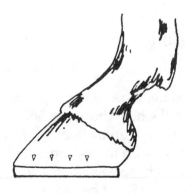 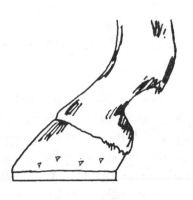

Good nail set   Incorrect nail set

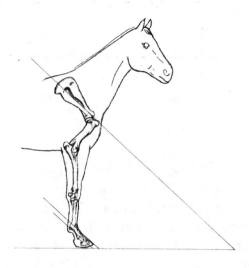

Shoulder pastern and hoof exhibit a common slope.

Teeth

One year in the life of a horse is equivalent to three years in a human's life. A ten year old horse is equivalent to a thirty year old man. Horses, on the average, live to be about twenty years old, but some live more than thirty years.

One way to tell the age of a horse is by looking at his teeth. The teeth develop and wear in a relatively uniform manner that can be predicted. When buying a horse, you will surely want to know how old he is, and you can't always take the word of the seller. Registration papers may be transferred to another horse illegally, and the age may not match with the papers. But if you are able to tell age by the teeth, you can do your own checking before the horse is purchased.

A horse has two sets of teeth. One set is known as the milk, or temporary teeth. This set includes twelve front teeth or incisors and twelve molars. The molars are just back of the incisors past the interdental space or bit area. The first three sets of molars are replaced by permanent teeth in an orderly sequence. The other twelve molars come in as permanent teeth.

The temporary teeth can be distinguished by their small size, pearly color, distinct narrow neck and small fang. The permanent teeth are much larger and stronger and are darker in color.

Some horses develop small round teeth in front of the pre-molars called wolf teeth. These teeth may appear on the upper jaw at about six months of age. Males or females may develop these teeth. The wolf teeth have no function and may disappear on their own. Some need to be pulled if they are present when you start putting a bit in the horse's mouth. If this is not done the bit may bump into these teeth, causing the horse to gap his mouth and throw his head.

The tooth is made up of cement, enamel, ivory and pulp. At the top of the tooth is an indentation called a cup. As the horse ages, his teeth wear down until, by the time he is nine, the pulp can be seen to the edge of the remains of the cup. By fifteen, the tooth is round and shows a portion of the pulp on the top or table surface. By twenty, the table surface of the tooth is triangular. At the same time the tooth is wearing down, the gum is receding. The tooth has different shapes from one end to the other. It is long oval on top, round oval farther down and triangular lower. These shapes can be seen as the tooth wears down.

The foal may be born with four front milk teeth, two up and two down, or he will get them soon after birth. At six months he will have his full set of temporary incisors or front teeth. At two to two and one-half years of age, the colt will lose his four central incisors or nippers (A). These will be replaced by permanent teeth. At about three to three and one-half (B), and by four to four and one-half he will lose his corner incisors (C). You can see the change from the milk teeth of a two-year-old to the mature mouth of a five-year-old. At four and one-half to five years of age the male horse develops four bit teeth also known as canine, or tush teeth. In some cases, the female also develops these teeth.

At five years of age the horse is said to have a full mouth. Up to this point the horse's teeth will generally not vary more than six months from the described rate of development.

Beyond five the method of aging is much less accurate. The normal mouth will wear at a predictable rate assuming a horse is on pasture six months and in the corral six months of the year, with no excessive abrasives, such as sand or grit, being taken into the mouth with the feed. The cups will disappear with wear. This means the indentations in the center of the table surface of the lower incisors will disappear from wearing of the surrounding table surface at the following rate: (1) cups in the central incisors (A) of the lower jaw will be worn out at six to six and one-half years; (2) cups in the lateral incisors (B) of the lower jaw will be worn out at seven to seven and one-half years; (3) cups in the corner incisor (C) of the lower jaw will be worn out at eight to eight and one-half years. At nine the horse is said to have a smooth mouth, or all lower cups are worn smooth.

Using the cups alone to tell the age of the horse can be quite misleading. Horses raised in desert range country tend to be pastured out nine or even twelve months of the year. They are often forced to pick quite close for their feed. Sand and small pebbles are taken in with the grass. This gritty material acts as an abrasive on the table surface of the teeth, wearing the surface down at an accelerated rate. The teeth will be shorter and whiter than normal. A six-year-old may read seven or eight and a seven-year-old will often be smooth.

Barn-raised horses have the opposite situation. Not being required to bite grass off with the front teeth retards wear. They use their teeth in coordination with the tongue to transport feed to the grinders. Thus, the teeth will be longer and feed stained. An eight or nine year old horse may read seven and a ten or eleven-year-old might read eight.

The length of the tooth and the color can help you tell if the cups are reading true. A seven-year-old, pastured out twelve months, will have a short white tooth. While a twelve year old horse fed on hay year around will have long hay stained teeth.

At about seven years of age a hook develops on the upper corner incisors. This is called the

Permanent tooth

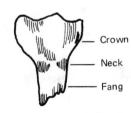

Crown

Neck

Fang

Temporary tooth

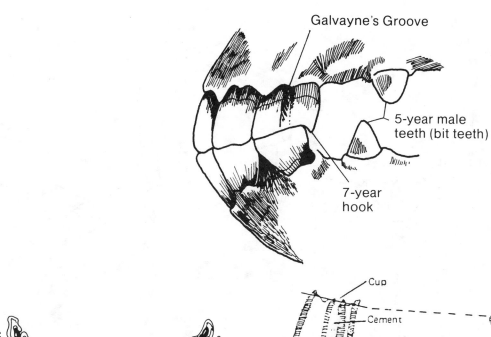

Galvayne's Groove

5-year male teeth (bit teeth)

7-year hook

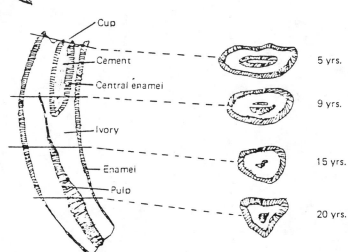

Cup

Cement

Central enamel

Ivory

Enamel

Pulp

5 yrs.

9 yrs.

15 yrs.

20 yrs.

Sectional View

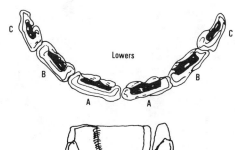

C   C

Lowers

B   B

A   A

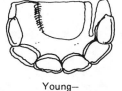

Young—
long oval

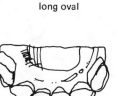

Middle age—
rounding

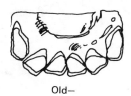

Old—
triangular

Top View
Lower Incisors

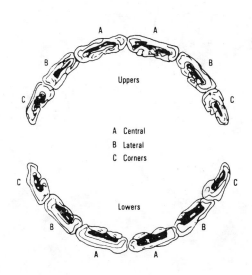

A   A

B   B

Uppers

C   C

A Central
B Lateral
C Corners

C   C

Lowers

B   B

A   A

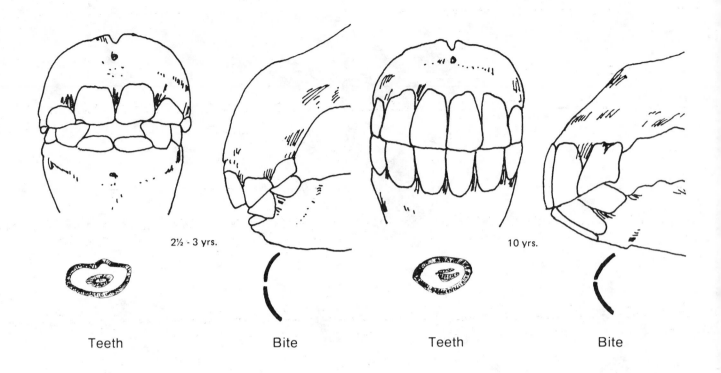

2½ - 3 yrs.

Teeth   Bite   Teeth   Bite

10 yrs.

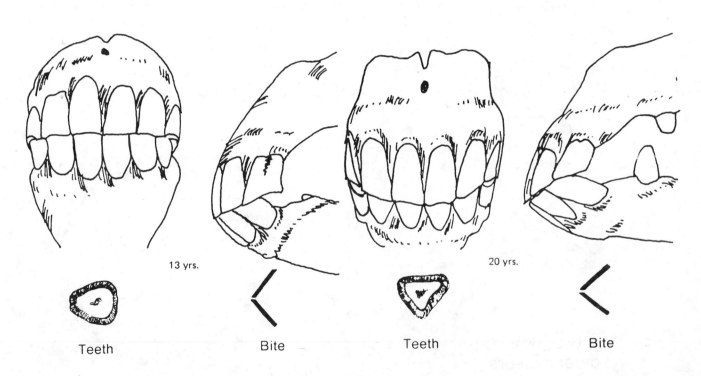

13 yrs.

Teeth   Bite   Teeth   Bite

20 yrs.

Teeth and Age Determination

seven-year hook. Not all horses have this due to the angle at which the teeth meet. It is formed from lack of wear on the back corner of that tooth.

Accuracy beyond nine years of age is quite poor unless the person reading the mouth is a real artist. The methods used are the shape of the table surface, the angle of incidence or bite, the length and color of teeth, and distinctive marks, such as Galvayne's groove. The shape of the table surface changes from long oval to round then to triangular. The angle of bite is almost straight up and down at two years of age. This angle increases until at old age the teeth point out. As the horse gets older, the gum recedes faster than the teeth wear down resulting in old horses having long teeth. The color of the teeth tells whether the horse has been grazing or has been fed in a manger. Galvayne's groove is an indentation with a dark color in the center of the upper corner incisor that starts at the top and with age extends down the tooth. At ten years, the dark color appears, by fifteen, it is halfway down the tooth, and by twenty it reaches to the tip of the tooth. These factors are only guides, but can help place an approximate age on an older horse.

There are some dental variations and abnormalities that you should be aware of.

Parrot mouth : The lower jaw of the horse recedes, so that the upper incisors are prominent or buck-toothed. Most horse associations require gelding parrot mouth horses before registering, because the trait is inheritable.

Undershot jaw : The lower jaw protrudes.

Cribbers or windsuckers : The outer edge of both upper and lower incisors are beveled from biting hard surfaces to suck air.

Sandmouth : Badly worn incisors due to eating in sandy or gritty areas.

Bishoped teeth : Alteration of a tooth by drilling a cup, generally in the corner incisor, to show a younger age for sale purposes.

When buying a horse you should watch for all of these abnormalities. There are enough good horses to pick from that you don't need to consider unsound or deformed horses.

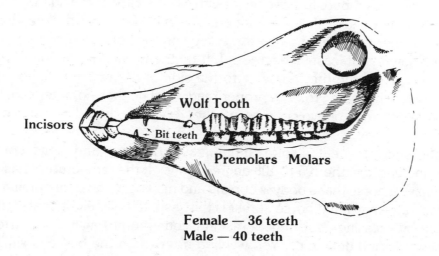

Female — 36 teeth
Male — 40 teeth

Many young horses between two and four have a hard time losing the temporary incisors. They may be loose and even hanging, but will not come off. This makes it uncomfortable for the horse to eat. If this does occur, it is best to pull these teeth so the horse will be more comfortable.

The pre-molars are also shed from two to four years of age. These are harder to observe, but can cause discomfort and loss of weight to a young horse. Many times these teeth wear in such a way that they have sharp edges that cut into the cheek and tongue. These may need to be filed or even pulled. Generally, if a young horse is slobbering his grain excessively, this is a good indication he needs his teeth filed down or "floated". An older horse can have the same problem with his permanent molars. Many older horses need their teeth floated to be able to pick up weight and look healthy again.

It is generally necessary to call a veterinarian to perform these tasks. It is, however, mostly labor or hard work that is involved and the process can be easily learned by any horseman. The cost of the tools is equal to the cost of one floating.

There are many ways to save money and still provide your horse with adequate care. First, become educated as to the needs of your horse. Next, find out how much of this you can physically do, then get training by a capable person.

A general rule of thumb is that a person will annually pay out in feed and care costs an amount equal to the value paid for the horse. This is a very loose assumption, but people that buy the cheapest horse they can find will generally provide the cheapest care for him.

General Horse Care

Check His Vital Signs

There are many times a horse owner could use some horse health knowledge in order to ascertain if his horse is sick or just faking it. Some horses will act sluggish and even limp yet still be in perfect health.

You should know how to take the horse's vital signs, know what normal is and know when to be concerned. One vital sign being irregular is not an adequate indicator. Take all the vital signs and correlate their readings for a proper indication of the degree of your horse's sickness.

It is always easier to wait until you have a sick horse before you worry about being able to read these vital signs. The better approach would be to check your horse's vital signs a number of times while he is healthy. This will give you some practice and it will also give you the specific numbers for your horse to compare future checks with when sickness is evident or suspected.

The healthy adult horse should have a temperature of 99.5 to 101 degrees Fahrenheit. To check this get a rectal thermometer and tie a long string on the holding end so you won't lose it in the horse. Shake it down to at least 95 degrees. Lift up the tail and insert the thermometer with the string protruding. Hold the thermometer to the side of the rectum. If you insert it into a chunk of manure you are not going to get a proper reading. The thermometer should be left for at least four minutes. A deviation of two degrees in either direction should be a sign needing further checks.

Many problems, such as heat stroke, influenza, strangles, and colic could cause the temperature to be increased in the 105 to 108 degree range. If the temperature has dropped to 98 or 97 degrees you have a horse that's body is cooling and may be a sign of oncoming death.

The normal heart rate in an adult horse at rest is thirty-six to forty-eight beats per minute. The pulse can be taken by pressing your fingers (except your thumb) against an artery. Take the count for thirty seconds and double it. You will find arteries on the horse in similar places you would find them on yourself. The inner surface of the lower jaw or the back edge of that jaw will have one. Another is about four inches below the eye. At the inside of the knee or under the tail head are other points to use.

Some illnesses will elevate the pulse to sixty or even one hundred beats per minute at rest. If you question your reading of the pulse, you can place your hand just behind the horse's elbow and feel the heart beat.

The normal rate of respiration for an adult horse at rest is twelve to twenty-four breaths per minute. You can watch the movement of the nostrils or flank to count the breaths.

Generally when a horse is sick, all of his vital signs will be abnormal. If you have checked normal for your horse you have a better gauge than using the wide average ranges. If the temperature is two degrees off or the breath or pulse is more than ten percent above normal, you should consider your horse ill and needs attention. If the temperature is five or more degrees elevated accompanied by quick breaths and elevated pulse, the horse needs immediate attention.

If we were to check the temperature of a horse wintering out we may find a temperature one degree below normal, which may be accompanied by pulse and breath rate at the lower range of normal. This indicates his body functions have slightly slowed down. Any activity would cause these to shoot up markedly.

A normal horse in medium work may have a heart rate of sixty to ninety beats per minute and the respiration rate may double. The body temperature may also be elevated a degree because the body might not be able to sweat quick enough to maintain the normal.

It would be well to work your healthy horse and check his vital signs while hot. You can start off in the spring taking his vital signs then check them periodically as you get him in shape.

By checking him when you stop exercising, then in about five and again ten minutes after rest you will be able to evaluate his recovery time as his conditioning training progresses. This will help you know how well conditioned he is.

Respiratory Problems Can Kill

Many of the respiratory problems in horses are very minor, but about ten percent of the cases are very severe and some horses die as a result of these respiratory problems.

A horse can cough for a couple days and you finally decide you need to treat it. After another couple days the horse has a serious case of pneumonia.

The dry, intermittent cough is a result of a mild inflammation of the airway. As the disease increases in intensity, the cough becomes more persistent and violent. Any increased exercise or stress can bring on violent spasms of coughing. Affected animals breathe faster and tire very easily.

As a rule, the horse has a very effective filtering system for dust and disease. As the air is taken into the lungs, the air is humidified. Almost all dust and foreign matter is weighted down with moisture and deposited in the throat to be coughed back out. What does get by the humidifier has to pass through a number of airways that change directions of air movement, which takes out more foreign matter.

If bacteria or viruses get past these defenses they are eaten up by macrophages, which are little bug-like organisms that originate from the blood. These bugs have large appetites and move about the lung to devour any bacteria and virus which could hamper the lung's exchange of oxygen for carbon dioxide.

Under cold, wet conditions, over exertion, long trailering or changes of temperature and humidity, the horse's respiratory defense system may be inadequate. As a horse owner, you should use good management and sensible use of your horse to minimize stress on the horse.

Symptoms of the onset of bronchopneumonia are noticeable depression, high fever, partial or total loss of appetite, marked elevation in respiration rate, difficulty in breathing where the stomach muscles along the abdomen are used to help force air out of the lungs. There will be an accompanying long drawn out cough that is wet instead of dry. Weight loss will occur after a couple days. The horse will be in pain from the distress of this system.

It is interesting that most all viruses, nine out of ten, infect the horse's respiratory tract. Most of these are of a minor problem causing only mild inflammations of the mucous membranes of the nose, throat and airways. Usually the horse can fight these off by himself, if not under stress.

Once in a while these viruses may act on the respiratory defense system in such a way as to make it ineffective against bacteria. Once this occurs the bacteria grow and generate life-threatening infections such as pneumonia.

It is interesting that most horses will have a strong enough defense system to combat the disease, yet about one out of ten will be hit with a life-threatening infection. These horses may be in the same pen and under the same environmental conditions.

It's hard to know when you need to call the veterinarian and when to treat the symptoms with long acting penicillin. One day you think it is just a mild virus and the next day the horse is in a life-threatening situation.

Watch for reduced appetite and check for an elevated temperature. If you notice either deviating from normal you should call the veterinarian to have him listen to the lungs.

It seems once you see the common symptoms of pneumonia you are late in your diagnosis and you may have a $100 vet bill to save the horse. Be an observant horse owner, provide cover for your horse and think about his nutritional needs all year around.

Giving Shots

If you have horses, they are going to get sick and need shots. Horses also need yearly vaccinations as well as occasional shots of penicillin or other injectable medications. If you can give these shots yourself, you can save a lot of expense and the veterinarian's time.

Giving shots is not difficult, but it does take a little practice. First, you need a needle of the right gauge or size for the job. An 18 gauge by 1½ inch long needle is usually used for deep muscle shots. Penicillin is a thick liquid that is hard to push through a needle any smaller than this.

Most of the vaccinations come with a needle in the individual packages. These needles may be as small as 22 or 24 gauge because the liquid is thin and will flow easier. Remember, the smaller the gauge the larger the hole and the more the horse will feel it, so use as large a gauge as the liquid will allow.

You can buy disposable needles very cheap so there is no reason to use a bent or dull needle. A bent needle may break off in the horse's flesh and cause a major problem. Dull needles cause more pain and are harder to insert than sharp ones.

Needles can be reused, but be sure to disinfect them and check for sharpness and bends. The use of a dirty needle will cause more damage than the shot can help.

Most shots are given intramuscularly — deep into the muscle tissue. These are the easiest kind to give. Shots to be given subcutaneously (just beneath the skin) or intradermally (between the layers of the skin) are much harder to administer. There are few shots that require this kind of administration.

There are only two places to give deep muscle shots. That is the neck and the rump. You can give one on either side so that gives you four options.

For shots of 10 cubic centimeters or less use the neck. This will handle all the vaccines. If you have over 10 cc, then use the rump. There is more muscle to absorb a larger volume of medicine and good blood circulation to distribute the drug.

Do not give horses shots in the chest. Many people do and you even see veterinarians giving them there. You run a much greater chance of swelling and pockets of fluid forming if you give the shot in the chest because of poor circulation in this area.

It is safer for you and easier to give in the chest than the rump. That is why many people use that area. After a few problems with the chest shots, you will stop using this area.

You can still have a problem of an abscess on the neck or rump so you must take precautions this does not happen by using a proper dosage placed properly and using sterile tools.

On the neck there is a muscular area that will be easy to put the needle in and it is a safe area for you to work. Drop down at least four inches from the top of the neck to make sure you don't damage the nerves in the back of the neck. You can feel the muscle in the neck running from front to back. Take a midpoint and use that for your shot area.

You can also give the shot high on the hip, on the rump, or down below the buttock. If you give the shot high on the hip and get an abscess, it will be much harder to drain and heal. Most veterinarians like the area where the hip is rounding, so if there is an abscess it can be drained. If you use the upper thigh below the buttock, it is best to use the inside of the leg. It seems to be less sensitive than the outside.

Before you can give the shot, you need to fill the syringe. First, pick a syringe that is large enough to hold the total dose to be given. Next, wipe the rubber stopper of the bottle with alcohol. Place a sterile needle on the syringe and draw in air to the amount of fluid needed. Shake the bottle of medicine to combine the ingredients equally. Insert the needle in the rubber cap of the medicine bottle and press the plunger on the syringe towards the bottle, filling the bottle with air.

Tipping the bottle upside down, draw out the correct amount of fluid. If there are bubbles in the syringe, you can tap it with your finger and they will rise toward the needle. Push the plunger until the bubbles are removed. It may be necessary to fill the syringe a little fuller so you can clean the bubbles and still have enough medicine.

Extract the needle from the bottle. Holding the syringe upright, press slightly on the plunger to make sure the air has been removed and there is a constant flow of medicine.

Now you are ready to give the shot. Have someone hold the horse in an open area rather than working in a stall. Once in a while you will have to blindfold or twitch the horse to give him the shot, but if you do a good job with the needle, the horse won't even wince without restraints.

If you were to take the needle on the syringe and jab it in like they do in the hospital to humans, a horse would kick your head off. Instead, you should take the needle off the syringe. Place the needle between the thumb and first finger, pointing down toward the little finger.

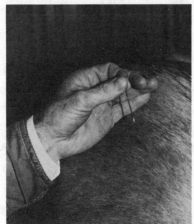 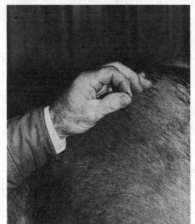

Desensitise the area with a couple taps   Flaten the hand and drive the needle in

Using the little finger and side of the hand, tap the horse in the area the shot is to be given. Tap two or three times quickly to desensitize the area. On the fourth tap flatten the hand out and drive the needle down firmly into the horse. You must maintain a good hold on the needle. Be sure the needle goes straight and all the way in.

Place the syringe on the needle and draw on the plunger slightly. If you get blood, you have hit a vein and need to reset your needle. If there is no blood, go ahead and push the plunger in and extract the needle and syringe together.

Rub the area the shot was given in to press the fluid into the surrounding muscle. If you have followed these instructions, you should have no problem. Once in a while, however, you will have a reaction from antibiotic shots or even vaccines.

All vaccine bottles have a printed warning concerning the possibility of anaphylactic shock. The best way to avoid this reaction is to be sure to read the instructions for the vaccine and be sure to give the shot properly in the location described and in the proper dosage. It is wise to discuss the vaccination program you need to be using with your veterinarian beforehand. He can advise you on safe and necessary vaccines to use and how to use them.

If shock ever happens, call the vet IMMEDIATELY. Try to keep the horse up and walking until he gets there. Anaphylactic shock is not too common, but it sure scares you if it does happen.

If you have to give a shot intravenously, you should get the help of a veterinarian the first time. It is not difficult but there are tricks that help you to find the vein and get the needle in.

Generally, you will use the large vein in the neck which is the easiest to find. Wetting the area will help you see the vein easier. Usually alcohol is used, but clean water may be as satisfactory. There is debate about the use of alcohol on the skin before the needle is inserted.

Place your finger on the neck below where you are going to insert the needle. Find the vein and press slightly. This will restrict the vein and the blood will back up above your finger.

If the horse's head is turned slightly away, it will take away the wrinkles on the neck and make the vein more visible. If you are doing this in the winter, it will be helpful to clip the hair in a small area so you can see the vein easier.

Using an 18 or 20 gauge sharp needle detached from the syringe, insert it in the raised vein in an upward motion. It only needs to go through the hide and into the vein so don't try pushing it too far. The needle should be started almost parallel to the vein or you will go through it. Be sure the point on the needle is next to the vein. That will aid in penetration.

If you hit the vein, drops of blood will be seen at the open end of the needle. Hold the syringe upright and press all the air out of the syringe. Attach the syringe to the needle and draw a little blood into your syringe. If you don't get blood, that means you pulled the needle out or pushed it through the vein while attaching the syringe. You will then have to fish to find it again. As soon as you get the blood in the syringe, start feeding the medicine to the bloodstream. Don't get in a hurry and push too hard. Let the medication mix into the bloodstream rather than stopping the flow of blood as you fill the vein with medicine. Remove the needle and wipe the area with your thumb. Put pressure on the entry hole for a moment so the blood will stop oozing.

Giving shots is not difficult if you follow these simple instructions. It will save you money and your veterinarian's time if you do it right.

Strangles

If we are going to use our horses, they are going to come in contact with many of the disease organisms some time or another. One of the greatest protections is a healthy horse. If he does contract a disease he is much more able to fight off the organisms in a much shorter period of time.

Some diseases can, and should, be vaccinated against. The five-in-one shot for two strains of flu, tetanus, and Eastern and Western Equine Encephalomyelitis is very helpful. Some other vaccines are questionable, such as that available for strangles. This vaccine is known as Strepvax, manufactured by Wellcome Animal Health, Inc.

Strangles is caused by Streptococcus equi, a bacteria. This bacteria is thought to be present in most, if not all, horses. Some have immunity from previous large dose exposures, others have no immunity and the disease attacks once the horse is in a weakened state or is exposed to a form of the bacteria to which they are not immune.

Young horses and those under stress, such as in shipping, may be susceptible to the bacteria. Once the horse becomes susceptible and exposed, the disease takes five to six days to incubate. The initial symptoms are a rapidly rising temperature, reaching a peak of 102° to 106° F, increased respiration rate, depression and anorexia. The nasal passage becomes inflamed and a nasal discharge appears in two to three days. This drainage becomes more voluminous as the disease attacks the lymph nodes. At first they are sore then they become enlarged and very hard. These lymph nodes may rupture, liberating large quantities of thick, creamy pus. Laryngitis usually develops, accompanied by a cough, which can persist for several weeks. Some say the disease will run its course in twenty-one days. If you treat it, it will last only three weeks.

Penicillin is the drug generally used to combat this bacteria. The problem is, however, that the penicillin may turn the horse's natural immune system off. The lymph nodes swelling may be reduced but the bacteria attacks the joints. This may cause swelling in the joints that will break and drain, also. This prolongs the disease.

The bacteria may, if deterred, attack the lungs, liver and kidneys. In these places the pus pockets break and drain into the body cavity, generally causing death. About two out of each one hundred horses contracting strangles will die from the disease or secondary infections.

For this reason, healthy horses can have this disease and come through it with an immunity to further exposure with only three weeks of lost use time. You must isolate the horse and give him complete rest, good feed, and keep him warm and dry if he is going to get through the disease with no side affects.

This disease is quite contagious but possibly not as contagious as has been previously thought. This disease must be passed with contact of the nasal discharge or the pus from the ruptured swelling.

Whenever you have a horse with a nasal discharge you should isolate him to protect the other horses, unless you want to do like some mothers do for chicken pox. It may be that a light case of the disease in the warm summer months may make the likelihood of future problems less likely.

Young horses should build up an immunity to the disease before you start hauling them all over the country. Most of these immunities break down when the horse is put under heavy stress or are in poor condition when attacked. Therefore, you are never completely safe.

One way to limit the problem once you have an outbreak is to clean the stalls where the sick horses are and remove the litter from the premises or burn it so no other horse will come in contact with it. Provide a separate water trough for the sick horse, then disinfect the area, including water container and feeders, once the horse is well.

Why not vaccinate for strangles and remove all the chance of the disease? This vaccine can be as dangerous as the disease because of allergic reactions and infections at the site of the vaccination. Some times the vaccine is not readily taken into the horse's system. The horse gets a swelling at the site of the vaccination which enlarges and must be drained to heal. This may take much longer than three weeks to run its course.

It has been reported by some that half their vaccinated horses had a reaction to the vaccine, while others made out with little problem.

The best policy would be to use the vaccine if you had weak, sick or very young horses that may have a hard time fighting off the disease. Otherwise, keep your sick horses isolated and keep a clean facility, then you shouldn't have too much trouble.

Don't get upset when the horse starts to swell under the jaw and load him up with penicillin. It will just prolong the illness. Let the swelling occur and even encourage it with hot packs so it will come to a head, break and drain, then healing can continue.

You can do more harm than good if you try to override nature's healing process. Remember to give him rest, keep him warm and on good feed. In three weeks he will be ready to work back into his routine slowly but surely.

Colic the Killer

Colic is the number one killer of horses. The most prevalent cause is internal parasites. Improper feeding, such as winter pasture or dry feed with inadequate water, or abrupt changes in the feed can also cause colic. Bringing a horse out of the pasture where there is little feed and inadequate water, then giving him all the alfalfa hay he can eat is a good way to cause a blockage and colic.

Blocks in the intestine prevents the movement of food stuffs through the tract. Twists may occur in the long digestive tract causing the tract to swell with gas and food stuff pressure. Bacteria and virus infections can then cause colic and possibly death.

A horse with colic, regardless of cause, will have an increased heart rate and body temperature. The colic causes pain and as the pain increases the horse will show signs of sweating in relation to the pain.

Restlessness is evident with the horse pawing the ground, biting or kicking the stomach or trying to roll. Once down the horse will get up and lay down again, not being able to find a comfortable position.

Most horses with colic won't eat or drink much, if at all. Many will not be able to pass any feces.

If the horse has a mild case of colic, walking him may be adequate to relieve the bowel and pass feces. You may wish to give him about 60 cc of Pepto Bismal for gas. This would be about two ounces. By using a 30 cc hypodermic syringe without a needle, you could fill it and put it in the side of the mouth and as far back as you could. Raise the head up and plunge the antacid into the back of his throat. Hold his head up until he has swallowed it, then give him another 30 cc.

When you diagnose colic in a moderate to severe degree, the veterinarian should be immediately called. While you are waiting for him to come, keep the horse on his feet and walking. Letting the horse lay down and roll may permit the intestine to kink, then it is in a life threatening condition. If you're lucky, however, the horse will be able to pass the blockage and gas before the vet gets there.

It will generally require administering an analgesic, such as mineral oil, and an antacid into the stomach. A sedative is then given to reduce the pain.

You should walk the horse until he shows signs of reduced pain. Once he starts to relax and loses the desire to roll, he can be turned in a corral.

The horse should be watched carefully for the next twenty-four hours for signs of change. If the horse gets worse, it may require surgery to relieve the blockage or kink. **Even then the horse may die.**

A proper internal parasite control, accompanied by good feed management can reduce most of the colic. This includes providing adequate water to horses in winter pasture as well as bringing the horse up on feed slowly once you bring him in from pasture.

The stress that horses experience when left for long periods of time with inadequate food and water can be life threatening. Vitamin A and calcium will definitely be lacking under these conditions. This can cause night blindness, reproduction failure and poor hoof development. Nerves can be damaged and respiratory diseases can run rampant.

Foals sometimes develop rickets due to the imbalance of calcium and phosphorus. They will not develop properly and will often have permanent structural damage.

It costs to own horses. It requires a lot of careful, thoughtful planning and execution of those plans to keep your horse in proper health. If you want to check your horse to see if you have been doing a good job, just look at his feet. If the hoof wall is smooth with no horizontal ripples, the horse has had no disease or nutritional problems great enough to cause a fever.

When a fever occurs generally there will be a break down of the normal development of the laminae tissue just inside the hoof wall at the coronary band (hair line above the hoof). When this happens there will be a ring formed on the outer wall as well as a weak attachment of the laminae at that point. As the hoof grows out, the heat ring will move down the hoof. When it is directly above the white line, (the tissue separating the wall from the sole of the hoof) that hoof extending beyond the white line may break off easily.

Horses that have had drastic changes in feed, colic or diseases usually exhibit this heat line. If the heat in the body is excessive, such as in founder, the heat rings will be large and repetitive.

Use some good management and have a horse with a nice smooth hoof as proof of your good care.

Bale Twine Colic

You can probably think of a hundred uses for hay baling wire. Many farms were held together with this wire. Most wire was picked up because it had uses and besides the farmer didn't want the cows picking pieces up and getting hardware disease.

Today we find most hay bales tied with orange or black poly-propylene twine. The twine has much fewer uses and doesn't cause hardware disease. Therefore, it is left on the ground, hung on posts or piled up in any spot that is close.

Some feeders just throw out a bale of hay with the strings on it and let the horses feed off the tied-up bale. They feel this will cause less waste of hay.

It may cause less waste, but it may also cause the death of their horse. A horse can't readily distinguish the twine from the hay, especially if he is real hungry. The twine may be chewed up and swallowed.

Many cases of obstructive colic have been traced to these ingested strings. This problem has cost many owners large veterinarian bills and, in some cases, the loss of their horse.

Many times the ball of twine ends up in the cecum. As it travels through the digestive system, the string cuts like a piano wire, which irritates the bowel. Mineral oil will seldom remove these obstructions so they must be surgically removed.

The twine can also freeze in the ground, leaving a loop for a horse to catch a foot in. This could cause a strained muscle, pulled tendon or rope burn at the least, and may cause a broken leg.

It only takes a little effort to pick these strings up and properly dispose of them. This will make your facility look much cleaner. It is easy to spot the feeder that has pride in his work or his facility.

Many times you get the bale of hay out to the corral and remember your knife is in your other pants. It makes a mess of a bale to pull the strings off if you only need half the bale to feed at that feeding.

Go back to your string pile and get a single string. Run this string under the string on the hay bale. Take hold of the loose string with one hand on each side. Now see-saw the bale string with your

Don't leave string on bale

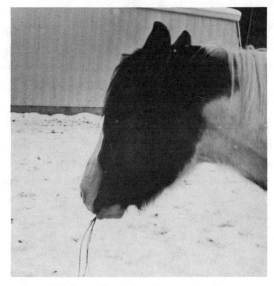

String Can be Ingested

See-Saw string in two

Tie each end then
lace single string between

loose string. It will cut through the bale string quickly. Then do the same to the other bale string.

Feed what you need, then you can save the rest by tying a square knot in the two strings on one end, then the two on the other. Use an extra string to loop through the loop on each end of the bale strings. Go through a couple of times. When you pull the single string by both ends it will bind on itself and hold tight while you tie a knot to hold it.

Cleanliness is next to Godliness so keep those strings picked up.

Scratches

Wet muddy corrals and dirty stalls are typical areas for horses to contract a skin condition known as scratches. Scratches is a fungus infection of the pastern, fetlock and sometimes cannon area. It usually appears as a swelling and redness of the skin in these areas. Generally there is itching in the area and a foul smelling secretion from the oil glands of the skin. The area is very sensitive to the touch and sometimes hard to doctor. Cracking of the skin and formation of small blisters are additional symptoms.

Thread-like fungi invades the hair and skin wherever there have been scratches or abrasions on the skin. These fungi develop in spores within and surrounding the hair. The spores multiply and spread to adjacent tissue.

If this infection is not treated it may develop into grease-heel or grape. Once this occurs the outlook for complete recovery is poor.

If the hair on the leg is long, clip it closely around the infected areas. Wash the skin with a mild soap and water solution. Remove any scabs or drainage before treating.

It won't do much good to doctor the animal if he is left in the muddy, manury corral where he contracted the infection. Move him to a dry, clean area where the infected skin will stay clean and dry.

There are more treatments for scratches than almost any other disease; everything from wrapping the area with sauerkraut poultice to a strong iodine coating. Some prefer salve to keep it soft while others use drying agents. Most treatments for fungus infections will have a positive effect on the disease. The real secret is to keep the doctoring up daily until it is cleared up. This may mean two or even three weeks.

Most people get tired of doctoring the infection after two or three days and think they have started it to healing so they figure it will continue. Scratches are very hard to heal because the spores are hard to kill. They will not be killed if there is a scab or drainage they can get under. Once the skin cracks, the spores invade the sore and the job is more difficult.

If you are seeing a lot of dried drainage around the area you may need to wash it daily before you try to treat it. Keeping it clean and dry will be one of the greatest factors in prompt healings.

Once the area is clean use a twenty percent solution of Clorox as a wash once or twice a day for a week. Then evaluate the progress of the healing. You should see a decreased redness and sensitivity. The drainage should have stopped and the area look more normal.

Depending on how far advanced the infection was, you may need to continue the treatment for another week or more once you see it is working.

Once the drainage has stopped, after the first week, you may want to use 50-50 DMSO and furicin liquid or a sulfide pink eye spray and alternate days with the Clorox to promote more rapid healing.

If after a week you don't see any improvement you should have your veterinarian look at the infection. You may have misdiagnosed it and be treating for the wrong disease. Or you have greased heels to deal with which may need cortisone or other medicines only available through your veterinarian.

It is best to prevent this disease from occurring in the first place. Clean your corrals and bed an area where the horses can stand to dry their legs. Use a rubber curry and clean the legs periodically to prevent mud caking on the legs and to check for early signs of scratches. Look for the hair standing up like the hair on a dogs back. Check for sensitivity. If it is sensitive to the touch, there is a good posibility you have a case of scratches to doctor.

No Hoof—No Horse

It is difficult, at best, to ascertain which leg the horse is limping on, let alone to know what is causing the lameness. How many times have you been riding along and noticed a faint limp? Could you immediately figure out which leg the horse was hurting on?

There are some tell-tale signs that help to figure this out. Since the horse is forced to carry most of his weight on the sound leg, there is generally a sinking or "nodding" of the hip or head as the sound leg strikes the ground.

When the lameness is in the left fore leg, for example, the head will "nod" as the right foot is planted on the ground, but will jerk up as the left or lame leg touches the ground.

Lameness in the rear legs may be detected in the hips. The hip opposite the lame leg drops as the sound foot hits the ground.

Lameness in both front legs is indicated by stiff, stilted action and short stride, which often gives the impression of stiffness in the shoulders. The head is carried higher than usual without nodding. The hind feet are lifted higher than usual while the front feet scarcely leave the ground as the horse moves. When at rest the weight of the body is constantly shifted from one foot to the other and the hind feet may be cramped up under the body in an attempt to relieve the pain in the front feet. Such symptoms of lameness are characteristic of acute navicular disease and founder.

Symptoms of lameness in both hind legs are short stride, awkward gait and lowered head. The front feet are raised higher than usual as the horse walks. It is difficult or impossible to back a horse up that is lame in both hind legs. At rest the horse is uneasy and constantly shifts his weight from one back leg to another.

If the horse is swinging his leg as he advances it, the lameness may be an inflammation in the muscle or joints above the knees or hocks. When the horse does not want to put weight on the leg, the injury is usually below the knees or hocks.

When there is a shoulder injury the horse will show pain as the leg is carried forward. The stride will be short and the toe will be dragged. These lamenesses are less common and should be the last to be considered.

If the lameness is severe enough he will refuse to place any weight on the affected leg. Placing the leg out in front of its normal position may be an indication of this.

Once you have isolated the leg or legs the horse is limping on, you must next try to isolate the problem. Between seventy and eighty percent of hind leg problems occur in the hock or stifle, so this is the main place to check.

Your hands can tell you a lot about the condition of the leg. Place your hands on the sound leg and feel the temperature in the leg. Also feel the bony and fleshy tissue. Now go to the sore leg. Run your hands over this leg feeling for elevated heat, puffiness or hard enlargements on the bone.

Sometimes there will not be a noticeable difference in the two legs. If so, go to testing the joints. Observe the horse walking, then start with the ankle joint, bend it and hold it bent back for a couple minutes. Walk the horse again. If you can tell an increase in the lameness, it is likely that he is sore in that joint.

If you find no difference, bend the hock joint bringing the foot up towards the stomach and hold it. Walk the horse off briskly and see if he limps worse. If so, the injury could be in the hock or stifle.

Go back to the hand test and check for heat or swelling. By pressing your fingers on suspected areas, you may be able to find painful areas.

The hoof itself is a major area for lameness. The hoof should be cleaned out and tested by applying pressure to the soles, bulbs, and coronary band or hairline. If the horse flinches you have found a problem.

The horse carries sixty to sixty-five percent of his weight on his front legs, therefore, they are more likely to go lame or unsound than are the back ones. Many times the unsoundness or lameness is a direct result of the horse's conformation. If the legs are out of alignment they will place an abnormal shock to the joints, thus causing soreness and eventually unsoundness.

Once a lameness is observed the leg alignment should be checked to see if it is possibly the weak link in the structure. Even better, do not buy horses that have poor leg alignment. If you don't know what proper alignment is, you should check the "Conformation" section of this book. It is easy to understand and it makes you a better horseman.

There are many ailments of the legs that could be talked about with their accompanying treatment but this would require much more space. The best way to handle the problem is to treat minor problems and call the veterinarian for anything you are not acquainted with.

A much used remedy is DMSO and furacin liquids mixed fifty-fifty. This can be used on kicks, swellings and joint soreness. If you do not see some improvements after three or four days, you should call the veterinarian.

Remember, do not make the lameness worse than it is by using the horse lame. Be an observant rider and recognize when a horse is hurting. You can minimize your problems by following this simple rule.

Founder

Once the pastures are starting to green up in the spring the first thought is, "Now I can turn old Dobbin out and stop feeding that expensive hay." If you turn out on the early grass you are asking for grass founder.

It is best to wait until the grass is a little more mature and the moisture level is reduced. Even then it is best to turn the horse out for a couple hours the first couple days, then a half day the next day. Possibly he will adjust to the new feed without any founder problems.

Some horses raised in high mountain valleys show grass founder. Most of it is not severe but is evident once the sole is cut into. The blood is close to the surface and the sole is sensitive.

In some cases the horses walk on the outside of the hoof to take the pressure off the sole. This causes excessive wear on the outside wall. Feeding fresh-cut grass clippings to a horse on dry feed can also cause founder. It will taste so good the horse will over eat. At the least the horse will get colic. This will be manifest in the horse wanting to roll or bite and kick at his stomach.

If you want to feed grass clippings, always leave the cut grass on the lawn until it drys. This may take one-half day to all day in the sun. This cured grass will still be tasty and very nutritious so don't feed a horse too much even after being cured.

Grass sprayed for weeds can cause sickness or possibly death when eaten by a horse. Be sure you throw away the first clipping of grass after it has been sprayed.

If you are not going to take precautions when feeding grass it would be best not to feed it at all. Horses require good supervision because you have penned them up and they must rely on you to provide them a proper diet.

Founder can be caused by a number of other problems. The most common is grain founder. Over eating any type of grain or high protein feed, such as dog food, chicken feed, Calf Manna, or the like, can cause founder. Be sure your high protein feeds are safely stored away from the horse's reach.

Watering a hot horse may also cause founder. Hot horses should be given a small drink and then cool them off by walking, before letting them have all the water they want.

Pregnant mares that stand on hard surfaces while heavy in foal and mares that retain the afterbirth may also contract founder.

Prolonged stress, prolonged concussion of the hoof on hard surfaces and nervous stress can cause founder. Founder causes a disturbance of the blood circulation to the feet which results in an inflammation in the hoof. Because the hoof and sole are hard and do not allow much expansion, any inflammation means pressure and pain in the feet.

Founder, or laminitis, is a serious ailment of the fleshy laminae in the hoof. There is a breakdown of the interlocking laminae tissue that holds the intersensitive tissue to the wall of the hoof. The sensitive laminae also supports the coffin bone in the hoof. This is the main bone at the end of the bone structure of the leg. Once this sensitive laminae releases the coffin bone due to deterioration, the coffin bone drops or rotates down on the sole or bottom pad of the hoof.

There are many degrees of founder, ranging from mild or even unnoticed, to severe, where the horse will not move unless forced. In the severe cases the horse will try to avoid weight on the sole. He will stand with his feet outstretched in front so his weight is on his heels, or he will walk on the outside of his hoof so the weight will be on the outer wall. Over a period of time the horse will actually become pigeon-toed. If you are considering buying a horse that is pigeon-toed always check for founder before buying.

With severe founder the horse will have an elevated body temperature and sweating. You will be able to feel heat in the legs and hooves of the front feet. It usually will just affect the front feet, but in some cases will affect all four feet.

The foundered horse will have founder rings on the hoof. These are horizontal rings on the front of the hoof sloping down at the heel. The front rings will be close together while those at the heel will be farther apart.

The rings associated with founder should not be confused with slight ridges on the wall of the hooves, parallel with the hair line, which may result from stomach and intestinal disorders or any illness causing an elevated temperature for a short period of time. These ridges or heat rings occur because of the break-down of the laminae but it is very minor, due to the short duration and extent of the temperature. You will generally see a single ring on each hoof, being more prominent on the front hooves.

Now, what can you do if you find your horse has foundered from one cause or the other? Call a competent horse veterinarian immediately. Early treatment is important since the course of the disease during the first three days determines whether it will develop into a chronic condition. The affected feet should be soaked in the coldest water obtainable. Use ice water if available. Standing in cold running water is also good. Antihistamines and cortisone may reduce the severity of the disease. Butazolidin can reduce the pain for the horse. Making him more comfortable will lessen the stress.

In chronic founder the horse will walk on the heels continually, permitting the toe to grow excessively with no wear. The excess hoof should be removed from the toe. A shoe must be designed to protect the sole which is flat or convex. A very wide-webbed shoe can be used to protect the sole. There should be no pressure of the sole against the protective web. This horse may need shoeing every month to keep the foot in shape and the shoe on.

The easy kept horse is more prone to founder. Horses that convert feed to body weight easily will usually over eat when they have free access to feed. A nervous, thin horse will usually eat a little grain then walk off to do something else.

Shetlands are very prone to founder. They grass founder more quickly than most, so keep them on a lean diet even if it means tying them up half the day so they can't over eat. You don't want to kill them out of the goodness of your heart.

Incidence of founder occurs more in some breeds than in others. Possibly it was more an individual type within the breed, but here is the data available:

Breed	% Founder
Appaloosa	0.5
Thoroughbred	2.7
Quarter Horse	2.8
Arabs	3.3
Standardbred	3.3
Shetland pony	5.2
Morgan	6.0

To reduce the chances of founder remember:
1. Keep feed stored so the horse cannot gain free access to it.
2. Put your horse on pasture in steps rather than all at once.
3. Don't feed or water a horse that has just done a lot of work and is hot.
4. Don't over-do any horse but especially a young horse or one that is out of shape.
5. Give the horse a soft place to stand and don't work him excessively on hard surfaces.
6. Check mares for afterbirth and make sure you can account for the whole bag with both horns.
7. Worm often to eliminate digestive upset or colic.

Splints

As the horse evolved from a prehistoric mammal, he passed through a stage having five then three toes. Through the following centuries the outside two toes, along with their associated bones, receded and the horse became a one toed animal.

What were once five metacarpal or metatarsal bones evolved, with the center one growing thick and strong, forming the cannon bone between the knee and ankle and the hock and ankle. The first and fifth metacarpal and metatarsal disappeared while the second and fourth shortened, thinned and reposed, one on each side of the cannon bone. Today they are known as the splint bones.

In young horses, the splint bones are rather loosely attached to the cannon bone. By five or six years of age, this attachment has usually calcified and the bones are firmly fused to the cannon bone.

The attachment of the splint bone can, however, become inflamed easily during the first few years of life. The inflammation may be caused by a concussion to the splint bone, disease associated with vitamin or mineral deficiency, or strain from excessive training. Faulty conformation, or improper shoeing which puts stress on the leg may also contribute to the development of "splints".

A splint is a calcification or bony growth around the injured or stressed area of the splint bone. This may occur on any of the eight splint bones, two on each leg, but is most prevalent on the inside splint bone of the front legs.

At the onset of a splint no swelling may be visible. The horse may or may not limp, but usually the area injured will be tender if pressed. Lameness is more evident after a workout.

To heal the injury, nature lays down fresh bony growth around the inflamed area. This bony growth will be larger at first. This is known as a green splint.

As soon as you discover a splint, give the horse complete rest so there will be no additional irritation of the injured area. An irritant may be used to reduce the size of the calcification. This may or may not help. Naturally the calcification will shrink, tighten and harden into its final stage. This is known as a cold splint.

Little if anything can be done short of surgery to reduce a cold splint. Once this bony callus is formed and set around the splint bone the splint rarely causes trouble. If, however, the flexor tendon, suspensory ligament, or corpal joint is tied up, the horse may have chronic lameness.

If lameness does persist, it may even be a result of a broken splint bone rather than a bruised one. If broken, the area will remain inflamed and painful. For this reason many veterinarians prefer to x-ray the leg at first signs of a suspected splint to be sure it isn't a fracture. Using irritants on a fracture would hamper its healing, where it may help a splint to shrink.

If the splint bone is fractured then surgery is necessary to remove the broken end of the bone and smooth the remaining broken end. This will eliminate the irritation and the horse should soon be sound again.

Some very young horses develop splints due to nutritional bone disease. Young horses fed inadequate diets, vitamin deficient or an imbalance of calcium and phosphorus, may develop splints. It can also occur by feeding excessive vitamin and mineral supplements.

Be sure you give your young horses a balanced diet according to their growth and energy requirements. In this way you can eliminate the chance of bone problems.

Many people feel if a little vitamin and mineral supplement is good then more is better. Try to let the horse balance his own mineral needs - don't force feed him. By using high quality feeds, the vitamin requirements will generally be adequate.

The largest number of splints in young horses, however, are caused from strain or injury. Colts playing in the pasture may develop splints even before they are ridden. Crooked legs and feet due to poor conformation contribute to these strains and injuries.

It is important to keep the feet of these young horses trimmed properly or even correctively trimmed to facilitate a more proper way of traveling. Long broken hooves may be the reason for one foot hitting the other leg.

It is easy to understand why the big heavy muscled colts have a much greater incidence of splints. These colts create much more strain in play than would a light weight colt.

Once you put weight on the young horse's back the chance for splints is increased. Fast turns, sudden stops and hard concussion to the hoof can all cause the splint bone attachment to be stressed and inflamed. As the young horse gets more tired, he becomes sloppy in his way of traveling and may interfere.

Take care not to over do or ask too much out of your young horses. Give them time to develop their bones. Start with easy training and build their strength and stamina as you increase your demands on the young horse's body.

Lastly, remember that a splint is only a blemish and does not, in itself, devalue the horse's usefulness. It may, however, be an indication of other conformation problems that should be evaluated.

Wounds on the Body and Legs

Every horse owner should know some basic horse first aid. You can make a great difference in the outcome of an injury or illness if you can keep cool and apply the proper first aid treatment.

When you come home and find your horse tangled up in a barbed wire fence, what is your first reaction? Do you get emotional and run to the horse, hollering "Whoa"? Or, do you stay calm, get the halter and wire cutters while calling someone for help to hold him?

Walk up to the horse slowly and talk quietly to him. Take a moment to pet him and reassure him that he is going to be okay. Do not get in a position to get hurt with the horse or wire. Your health is of primary importance and should not be jeopardized. The major damage has already been done to the horse so do not get in a hurry.

Cut the wire and remove it before trying to get the horse to move. In his condition you cannot be sure which way he will jump.

Once you have him out of the wire, take him to a dry quiet area where you can work on him. He may be suffering from shock with possible loss of blood. Nature has good control over loss of blood, so you will only be in a life threatening situation if he has cut a main artery in his neck or one of the major arteries in his legs. In any case, the bleeding should be stopped with a pressure bandage. A feminine napkin works well for a large wound. Seldom is a tourniquet used. If the area cannot be bandaged, use the pad and direct hand pressure until the bleeding stops or medical help arrives.

Once the bleeding has stopped, the wound can be washed out with water and a mild soap. If the wound needs stitching, do not apply any medication before the veterinarian arrives.

Cuts on the body will heal fast and will seldom form proud flesh if taken care of properly. If the wound is shallow it may be easily sewn up to prevent scarring. If it is deep and the muscle has been cut, you can either have the veterinarian stitch it together or leave it open and let it heal from the inside out. Many times the results are about equal.

Cuts on the legs can be much harder to heal cleanly. Wounds on the leg are much more prone to form proud flesh because of the difficulty of the skin to grow together when there is little muscle under it. Nature must lay down granular tissue to fill in the opening. When more granular tissue is formed than desired, it is then called proud flesh. If left uncontrolled this proud flesh will form large unsightly growths that can restrict the movement of joints under it.

If you see an excess of this granular tissue above the hair level, a caustic substance such as copper sulfate or calcium hydroxide can be applied. To prevent it from occurring in the first place, use Granulex and Derma Grow 2. Spray the Granulex on the wound, let it set a couple minutes then rinse it off with water and a mild soap. Do this two or three times. Once the wound is clean and dried, spray Derma Grow 2 on the wound. This can be done once or twice a day.

Small wounds on the knees, hocks and lower legs can be cleaned and Blue Lotion applied. This is drying and will promote rapid healing. Minor wounds above the knees and hocks heal well with the use of either Red Oil or Blue Lotion.

A horse has a strong healing mechanism within the body. Many times he will get better in spite of what we do. The tissue will regenerate with little problem if it is kept dry. Prolonged bandaging has been shown to retard healing and increase proud flesh formation.

Unattended wounds may get infection or may form unsightly proud flesh, so it is much better to keep the horse in and doctor him. Just do not get in the way of the horse's own healing powers once it starts.

From talking to a number of veterinarians one finds there is a lot of controversy concerning when to stitch and when to leave open. If the wound is real fresh and little internal tissue damaged, stitching will generally promote the most rapid healing If the wound is over twelve hours old, the blood feeding the edges of the skin around the wound will generally not be adequate to promote healing. If the edge of the skin can be cut back to tissue with a good blood supply then the skin will heal properly. If the wound is swollen, stitching may also be the wrong choice.

If the horse has a cut with a flap that points up, you will have poor success stitching it because the blood will not feed the flap properly. Flaps that point down can be sewn much more successfully.

Many times it is more feasible to clip the flap off and allow the wound to heal smooth. Loose flaps left unsown generally form a wattle of skin that heals in a lump separate from the wound. This is unsightly and not necessary, if proper care is taken.

Casting low ankle, pastern and coronet injuries have been fairly effective, but even these can have a negative result. Sometimes the wound heals on the outside only. This requires removal or changing of the cast so the wound can heal from the inside out.

A half and half solution of DMSO and furacin can be rubbed on swollen legs to reduce the swelling adjacent to the wound. Do not use this in the open wound for it may retard healing.

If the horse is in pain, you can make him more comfortable by administering butazolidin or "bute". This will reduce the pain and retard inflammation. Buy bute in one gram tablet form. The average dose for a mature 1000 pound horse would be two tablets twice a day. The tablets can be mashed into powder and sprinkled over the grain. It can also be mixed into a paste and given orally with an empty dewormer syringe.

Summer Dry Hoof Problems

The dry weather creates a problem for your horse. He may not get enough moisture in his hooves. You will notice the dry, cracked appearance of his hooves when this occurs. This is how quarter and toe cracks start.

When the hoof grows longer than the sole, it may crack or break off. If it cracks, the pressure of the weight of the horse will cause the crack to separate. If this is not taken care of, it may crack right up to the hair line. Once the crack reaches the hair line and affects the coronary band (growth band), it is too late for any corrective work.

If you see cracks in the hoof, get the horse shod so the pressure will be constant over the hoof, instead of all on the crack. Some horsemen rasp above the crack, thinking this will stop it, but the crack may move up easier because you have weakened the hoof at that point. Use a hot iron and burn the hoof just above the crack. This will change the alignment of the hoof wall cells. It will work like a scar. The scar is always stronger than the surrounding tissue.

It is important not to leave the horse barefooted if he is cracking, or you will have more trouble. Many times it is the front feet that crack the worst because the horse carries sixty-two to sixty-five percent of his weight on his front feet. Therefore, you may get by with just putting shoes on the front feet if you are not using the horse.

It is much better to prevent those cracks before there is a problem. The use of Hoof Flex or a similar hoof dressing will add moisture to the hoof if applied two or three times each week. Use an old paint brush and work the dressing into the hairline, back on the bulbs, and over the hoof, sole and frog. The horse takes most of the moisture into the hoof at the hairline (coronary band). That is why you should try to cover this area well with hoof dressing.

To prevent the loss of moisture in the first place, be sure your horseshoer does not rasp up the hoof wall to make the shoeing job look better. This removes the outer layer of the hoof wall (periople), seen as the shiny covering of the hoof.

Hoof dressing will penetrate the hoof structure readily, allowing the hoof to "breathe", regulating the absorption and evaporation of moisture and accentuating the natural luster of the hoof. Hoof Black and Hoof Clear, used for shows, seal the hoof wall and prevent moisture absorption. These products add to the drying problem.

Wild horses could travel to the creeks and rivers to drink and add moisture to their hooves each day. They wore their hooves smooth on the hard ground. They did not have a shoer rasping up the hoof wall.

Once we put a horse in a dry corral, we are responsible for taking care of his hooves' moisture needs. If we do not do it, the horse is sure to have a cracking problem. Get some hoof dressing and show your horse you care, by putting it on him. It will not do him any good while its in the can.

Winter Care of Horses

We have all been aware and concerned about the nutritional problem that exists with the deer in the winter. These animals are, however, free roaming and can move into the river bottoms to get as much feed and water as they can reach. They are free to find shelter under trees and up draws. We even had one come right in the garage and lie down on a rug next to the steps of the house. What a shock my wife had when she walked out and the deer jumped up right in front of her.

Now, compare the horses in the fields to the deer. With the deep snow they have less feed accessible than the deer because they are fenced in and cannot migrate to where there are better pickings. Most of the fields have no shelter, not even a tree.

Studies with horses have shown as food is deprived, still allowing adequate water, horses progressively lose the natural defenses against bacterial, fungal, and viral infections. Persistent anorexia will limit the horse's ability to cast off these infections.

Many horses do not have access to adequate water and must eat snow for moisture. Have you ever tried to melt snow to get water? If so, you know how much snow is needed to get a bucket of water. Horses will eat enough to wet their throats but they do not get enough to supply their needs for body functions. This may cause colic and may be more of a problem for horses in the fields than the feed is.

Horses pawing down to the grass will still find moisture in the grass at the bottom of the snow unless it is frozen. When the horse walks on an area and packs it down, it soon freezes solid and is very difficult to paw through.

If you are feeding hay without adequate water, you are asking for problems because the horse will gorge himself on the bale set out every few days. Without adequate water, the digestive juices and other body functions are reduced. The hay balls up and causes compacted bowels and colic.

A mild case of colic can be treated usually with good results. If the horse is not treated, he may roll trying to relieve the pain in his stomach. He may roll over and kink an intestine or roll into a ditch or depression where he cannot get up. This can be fatal even if the veterinarian does all he can.

Try to supplement the water supply by watering before you feed so the horse will not leave the water to freeze before he tries to drink it. If it is frozen, it won't do him much good.

Nutritional problems are not restricted to the horses in the pastures. Many people are trying to feed their horses on poor quality, meager rations. This also causes loss of weight and colic. We must be responsible for these horses or else get rid of them. Starvation should not be forced on any animal.

Internal parasites still thrive when horses are undernourished. They are the first to partake of any nourishment coming into the horse's system. After all the worms get their fill, the horse doesn't have much left to survive on. Many cases of colic are caused by worms. In some cases, the worms commit suicide by killing their host.

If your horse is losing weight it would be good management to worm him and have his teeth checked. If he needs his teeth floated or filed, he will not do well even on good feed.

A mature, idle one thousand pound horse in warm weather needs about seventeen and one-half pounds of good quality hay for maintenance. If the horse is pawing for feed he will exert more energy, which means he needs more feed for the energy exerted.

Beyond this, the horse will require added feed for cold temperatures. He needs this extra feed to maintain his body temperature. This means the horse may need twenty-five pounds of feed, or more, depending on the temperature. Can you imagine how much pawing a horse would have to do in two feet of snow to obtain twenty-five pounds of dry weight grass? Few, if any, can meet these kinds of needs. Without meeting the needs, the horse starts to lose weight. Once their weight is down, they lose body warmth and need even more feed just to keep warm.

When the weather turns off wet and stormy, there will tend to be an increase of respiratory infections. It will even be more of a problem where there are so many weak horses with low resistance to infection.

We will most likely see a large increase in pneumonia as spring approaches. The spring rains will wet the hair and reduce the insulation the horse has from the cold. With minimal amounts of body fat the horse will be easy prey.

Wet Weather Contributes to Trush and Ringworm

Wet weather may be a prime condition fostering the development of thrush, ringworm or fungus rash on your horse.

Thrush is a disease of the sole and frog of the hoof. It may be found in any or all of the feet, but is more common in the hind feet. A characteristic foul order always is present. The affected tissue is moist and contains a black thick discharge. When probed, the black area goes deeper than normal tissue and is sensitive in its depths. The animal is not normally lame unless the condition is advanced.

Thrush is usually started by a bacteria, Sphaerophorus necrophorus, but fungus generally is also involved. When the thrush is in an advanced stage, the frog may be partially or completely eroded or dead.

Urine, manure and mud all contribute to the development of the bacteria and fungus that causes thrush. In these conditions it is next to impossible to keep the feet dry and clean.

It is a good practice to dry and clean your horse's feet every few days and examine them for thrush. You will notice it in the "V" around the edges of the frog. Take a sharp hoof knife and cut away any dead or hanging frog. Make sure the frog does not flap over to one side or the other. Under these flaps the manure will be packed down and will generally harbor the bacteria and fungus in a prime environment for growth.

If you find a black stinky area take the hoof knife and clean the black away as best you can. Do not use a knife with a sharp point or you may stab the horse, or yourself, if the horse jerks his foot.

After you have cleaned it out the best you can, wash it with warm soapy water then rinse it off. You can now apply an anti-bacterial and fungicide. Coppertox is made just for this purpose. Clorox and Purex can also be used quite effectively. If you do not find the thrush it is still a good idea to pour a little Clorox around the frog as a preventative measure.

The fungus caused skin rashes are also harbored in the wet manure the horses lie on. These fungi infections spread on the horse's body and are quite contagious for horses they come in

112

contact with. You can discover these lesions by running your hands over the horse's body. Uninfected areas will feel smooth and soft. The affected areas will be rough and hard.

If not treated this can be quite a mess on the horse's skin. In the cool wet sunless days, this infection thrives. The sun alone can affect some measure of cure but the best remedy is a twenty percent mixture of Clorox and water. The books all say to use a strong iodine cover. This seems to burn the good skin as well as the infected and the hair usually has to come off before a cure is effected.

With Clorox the disease can be killed without killing the undiseased tissue. The fungus will be killed without requiring the loss of hair. You should wash the horse daily for a week with the diluted Clorox wash. This should be enough to clean up the problem.

Ringworm is another fungus that can infect the horse. This is usually obtained by coming into contact with another animal that has ringworm. It also can come from brushes or blankets that have been used on a horse with ringworm. This is one of the few diseases that man can catch from the horse. It is easily caught when your skin touches the ringworm lesion.

You can distinguish ringworm by the characteristic round lesion with the hair raised and finally dropping off on the lesion area. These lesions spread and form chains of round lesions.

It is a good idea to wear a rubber glove when examining and treating the disease. The treatment may require the use of a strong iodine solution but a fifty percent solution of Clorox will also do a good job.

Be sure to isolate the infected horse before the disease is spread to the whole herd. Keep cats and dogs away from the stall used by the infected horse or they may contract it and bring it to you without your knowing it.

It may be wise to contact your veterinarian for assistance in treatment of ringworm. Be sure to see your physician if you contract the disease. It is difficult to get rid of if you don't diagnose and treat it early.

Cribbing and Chewing Horses

So many people equate cribbing and wood chewing, but these are two completely different vices. They are both acquired habits that may result from boredom.

A cribber will take hold of an object, be it metal or wood, with his incisors or front teeth. Then he will pull and stretch the neck in a rigid arch. With his wind pipe opened, he will then swallow air. The swallowed air can create gastric upset or colic. The pressure of the bite also causes the front teeth to protrude and show excessive wear. The teeth would be similar to a thumb sucker's teeth in humans.

If you have a cribber, isolate him away from other horses. The habit is frequently copied by other horses. You might say it's catching.

Once a horse has formed the habit, it is very hard, if not impossible to break. You can, however, put a cribbing collar on him, which will not permit him to stretch and arch his neck so the wind pipe is open. This will only help as long as he has it on.

Wood chewers actually chew the wood up. A horse can chew through a 2 x 6 inch board in one evening. The horse does not actually eat the wood, but he can get slivers in his mouth and some slivers do find their way down the stomach. The vice can cause buccal infections, colic and does cause excessive wear on the teeth.

This vice is also catching. If you bring a horse in that has the habit, the rest of the herd will pick it up and devour your fence or building.

This is not evidence of a lack of any given nutrient or just hunger showing. You can balance a ration perfectly and still have a wood chewing horse. Some old timers used to say the horse heard there was "grain" in the wood.

One way to stop this is to use pipe, cable or wire fences. Some like pole fences, so they need a way to stop them from chewing.

A product called Carbolineum Stain, produced by Carbolineum Wood Preserving Co., P.O. Box 23028, Milwaukee, WI 53223, does a good job preventing chewing if used adequately. This has been used at the Utah State University Horse Arena complex for the past 10 years. This is a dark brown oil base stain that contains a creasote base. It preserves the wood and repels insects that deteriorate the wood. Because it is a pesticide it now requires a pesticide number for purchase. See your country agent or an approved pesticide applicator about a number when ordering.

This product is always in a usable state. It doesn't evaporate, separate or settle while standing. One coat will last about six months. After six months it will weather enough so the horses will start to chew again. Carbolineum Stain is only sold in 10 gallon lots, so you may want to get your neighbors to go in with you. Possibly your western store or feed store could carry it in one gallon cans.

Don't be fooled by products from this, or any other company that are sold to stop cribbing. If it doesn't contain the creasote base it will seldom do any good for chewing and nothing painted on the fence will stop cribbing.

There are a number of products sold that are said to stop the horse from chewing wood or cribbing. After putting some products on, some people have had the horse come right behind and chew the fence. No product put on the wood will stop cribbing.

EVR Induced Abortion

It only takes one abortion to put a small breeder in the red when raising foals for sale. How can he know when a mare might abort or what can be done to prevent it?

The disease known as Equine Viral Rhinopneumonitis (EVR) is a highly contagious viral disease of horses. It produces abortions in mares and Rhinopneumonitis in young animals. The source of the virus which initiates outbreaks is a herpes virus. The respiratory disease apparently is transmitted by droplet infection. It tends to occur in the fall in groups of foals that have just been weaned or in young stock under stress. The disease is spread from these young horses to the pregnant mares.

Among mares, abortions have spread from one group to another on the same farm when there was no direct contact between the two groups, indicating the air borne characteristics of the disease.

Apparently the stallion plays no role in transmission of this infection. Pregnant mares transferred from a group in which the virus was present have carried it to new areas.

Dogs dragging parts of aborted fetus or membranes may spread the disease, also. It is imperative to dispose of these materials at once to prevent more contamination.

In foals, lesions are limited to inflammation of the upper air passages and the mucus membranes of the nasal cavity. The disease in weanlings is recognized as a mild fever which usually appears in the fall months. Ordinarily the disease is so mild as to cause little concern. Severe coughing and respiratory difficulty may develop and prolong the period of recovery in the weanling. This is more likely to occur when the disease is complicated by strangles.

Infected mares generally show few, if any, symptoms. They generally abort during the seventh to eleventh months of pregnancy. Those that carry their offspring to full term may produce living foals that die shortly after birth. The mare generally appears normal before and after the abortion and has no ill effects from it. Subsequent breeding of the mare, if not reinfected, results in pregnancy and terminates in the birth of a normal foal.

When one of a group of mares that are six to nine months pregnant aborts because of EVR, all the other mares may eventually abort. The incubation period is approximately three to four weeks and susceptible mares readily become infected upon exposure to the abortion. Because the disease is highly contagious, aborting mares should be isolated, cleaned and washed down with an antiseptic.

It is a good practice to take the aborted fetus immediately to a Veterinary Diagnostic Laboratory for confirmation of the disease. This service is available to all horse owners. You can go through your veterinarian or go directly to the laboratory. The cost runs from $2.50 to $10.00, but $5.50 is about an average price you can figure on.

It seems many horse owners feel the damage is already done so they chuck the fetus across the fence and hope for next year. It is to your advantage to know what caused you to lose a breed bill and a year's feed cost. It may be that you will have the same luck next year if you don't change your management program.

Mares that are more or less isolated from other horses and have had the two shot series of EVR killed virus about one month prior to breeding may get by with a couple shots one in November and another in February. If, however, you have other horses around your mares, or horses coming in and out of your ranch, you may want to go on a program of maximum protection. This would mean giving a shot of killed virus at five, seven, and nine months of pregnancy after the initial series. Do not add any outside horse after November.

You may wonder why you need to vaccinate them so much. The vaccine does not create a total immunity. It is working on a herpes virus that is hard to control. Any stress on the mare may cause her to be susceptible to the virus. If you are going to ship the pregnant mare you want to administer another dose two weeks before traveling. If you know she had been under a strain on the place, you may want to give her an added booster.

The storms and wet from the winter are definitely a stress situation for the horses that do not have protection and adequate feed. These are much more susceptible to the virus when they do come in contact with it.

Foals may be vaccinated with the modified live virus at two to three months of age and then again in four weeks. After that you can go about every three to four months. Yearlings can be vaccinated every six months.

Because the infection is quite mild without complications, many horse owners would rather let the young stock become infected and get over it naturally. There is some resistance that does develop from this but stress can reduce the resistance and cause the horse to become infected again. Think of it similar to cold sores. They both are caused by different strains of the herpes virus and are usually short lived with no after affects. You can't prevent cold sores but you may grow out of them.

A secondary bacterial infection is sometimes a complicating factor. Watch the suspected horses and keep them warm, dry and well fed and they will have little affect from the virus.

Performance horses that are always going to shows or races may need much more concern. You don't want your horse to have 106° temperature for two to five days just when you need them to perform. It may, therefore, be necessary to vaccinate these horses as often as every ninety days, or two weeks before each event. This protection is needed due to the exposure to other horses and the stress that is induced in performance horses.

For the best program for your specific situation, contact your veterinarian.

What is Your Responsibility at Foaling Time

So you have a foal coming this spring. What are you doing to get ready for this blessed event?

You should have recorded the dates the mare was bred. This will give you a good indication of the approximate date of foaling. The average gestation period for a mare is 336 days. A rule of thumb is, subtract one month and add three days to the date the mare was bred. The actual date may vary in some mares from 300 to 365 days.

Many things can affect the length of gestation. The condition of the mare makes a great difference in how long she carries the foal. Mares in poor shape take longer to develop a complete fetus. Her age and the stallion used can have an effect on duration. In warm weather, mares will foal sooner, while in cold weather they seem to wait, possibly hoping for good weather. A colt will usually go two to seven days longer than a filly.

A premature foal born under 300 days has a very poor chance of survival. Many twin births occur prior to the 300th day and do not live, or they are aborted prior to this time. Twins are not to be sought after in horses as they are usually born early and underdeveloped.

During the first heat in the early spring, a mare may produce two follicles at the same time and may, if bred on this heat, become pregnant with twins. It is better to let that first heat go by and try for the second or even the third, if you're trying for an early foal.

By the end of the eighth month the fetus is about the size of a small dog and has all its characteristics. During the next three months the fetus will grow to full size. The mare can get by on a normal ration up until the ninth month. During the ninth and tenth month the mare should be put on a little higher quality ration, making sure adequate protein, calcium and vitamin A are present. This ration should be increased more during the last month because of the large amount of nutrients required by the fast growing fetus. Make sure, however, the mare is not getting fat. A fat mare will have more problems during foaling.

Exercise is also important for the expectant mare. With muscle tone, the mare will have a much easier time foaling. An exercise program can be continued right up until the day of foaling. The exercise should be reduced to a walk during the last couple weeks of gestation.

It is best if the mare can be kept in a green, dry pasture for foaling. If the mare is going to foal while it is cold or wet, be sure to start putting her in a warm barn with good bedding at night so she can get used to it. This area should be at least twelve feet square. Larger would be more desirable.

We know there is a considerable variation between mares' gestation lengths, but a given mare may be quite consistent. If the mare has had previous foals you can estimate closer when she will foal by her previous record.

Some books say a mare will foal within twelve hours of wax appearing on the teats. This is not accurate. Some mares have waxed and dripped milk for two days or more before foaling. Other mares have shown little bag and dropped a foal without waxing (fifty percent don't wax at all).

The man who says he can tell you when your mare is going to foal is really putting his reputation on the line. The way some mares carry their foal, it is hard to be sure they're even in foal in the tenth month without pregnancy testing.

One mare was bred all spring and summer and then assumed open. She was put on the cutter and ran all winter. The owner just couldn't get her drawn up in the gut for racing so he took her to the vet. The vet told him she was over nine months pregnant and to stop trying to pull the gut off her. She horsed (came in heat) right up until she foaled.

When you are in the last couple weeks of gestation you need to be thinking of how you can help that mare have her foal. The best way you can help her is to leave her alone. More problems are caused than cured by helpful hands. Most mares have their foals at night and have no problem, assuming you have fed and exercised them properly and provided an adequate area for them to foal.

It is best to monitor the expectant mare every four hours during the last few days of pregnancy. Once she shows signs of labor, such as restlessness, stall-walking, switching the tail and kicking the abdomen, she should be checked every hour. Sweating over the shoulders, flanks and chest is also quite a reliable sign of the impending birth.

Other physical signs of approaching parturition (foaling) include the relaxing of muscles in the tail head and at the tops of the hips. The vagina will dilate and the bag may drip milk. A mare may, however, foal without expressing any of these signs.

The first stage of labor described above may last for a very short time to the extreme of twenty-four hours and still not interfere with the production of a live foal. No danger exists for the fetus during this period since the placenta (after birth) is intact and providing oxygen and nutrients.

Stage two begins with the placenta membrane's rupture. This will release a large volume of fetal fluid. From the moment the water breaks until the foal is completely delivered and respiration has started, time is precious.

In a short time the mare will start to have sharper contractions and then you will see the front feet of the foal. Don't grab hold and start to pull. Next the mare will bear down and the head and neck will appear between the legs. She will then rest a moment before her next bearing down. This time the shoulders, hips and legs will be expelled.

The normal time required from the start of the second stage to completion of delivery can vary from twenty to sixty minutes. When the front feet and legs are out, the membranes can be opened up.

If the mare has an abnormal, or breech, birth or in any other way is having problems, a veterinarian should be called. You can usually get the mare up and walk her until the veterinarian arrives. This will slow the birth process down and prevent the mare from damaging herself or the foal.

Don't get in a hurry and cut the cord. Let nature take its course and the cord will be ripped in two. There will be much less bleeding and it will allow extra blood to enter and remain in the foal.

Make sure the foal is breathing. If the foal fails to breathe immediately, artificial respiration should be applied. This may be done by blowing into one nostril of the foal while holding the mouth and the other nostril closed. At the same time the chest can be pressed and released. Be careful not to break a rib. You can rub the body vigorously to stimulate the foal. Now he is breathing.

The mare may retain the placenta for one to six hours. Do not try to pull it or you will rip the mare. If the mare doesn't expel this sack within about six hours you should call a veterinarian to remove it.

The mare may retain a section of this sack which could become infected and cause foal founder, it may also cause problems when later breeding the mare.

It is, therefore, necessary to check the expelled afterbirth to be sure it is all there. There should be a base sack with two smaller arm-like sacks extending away from the large sack. These are known as the horns of the placenta.

The placenta should be disposed of after inspection. This does not mean thrown over the fence. Use a solution of iodine to spray or dip the umbilical cord in. This should be done two or three times or until the cord appears dry. It is also good to give the foal a tetanus antitoxin shot for protection if the mare hasn't had the tetanus toxoid vaccination.

Stay with the foal until it is up and nursing. It may need a little help but if it is strong leave the mare and foal alone.

If the foal is straining and seems to be bound up in the bowel you can give it an enema of half baking powder and half powdered sugar mixed with a little warm water. Use a rectal syringe for application. Sometimes mineral oil is used for the enema.

This can be administered the first day to unblock the sticky pack of matter acquired during the fetal growth. Usually one cleaning will do the job but it can be repeated until the foal is having normal bowel movements.

Make sure your foal gets the colostrum milk from the mare. Don't milk it out to relieve the bag. This milk provides the new foal with his mother's natural immunities to disease and is high in growth nutrients.

Milk production requires high quality feeds of adequate quantity. For the first couple weeks hold the hot feed or grain down. This can cause digestive upset in the mare and scours in the foal.

You could feed the mare a bran mash once a day to keep the bowel moving. Once the foal is adjusted to the milk you can increase the mare's feed. This is one time when you need to feed well. If you don't, the mare will take off her own body nutrients needed for the growing foal. This can lower the calcium level of the mare to a dangerous point.

Your foal is strong and healthy now, but is your responsibility over?

Care of the Foal

Your responsibility is greater after the birth of the foal than it is before and during birth. Your foal is going to grow very rapidly the first twenty-four months. About forty-five percent of the mature body weight is obtained by six months of age; sixty percent by twelve months; eighty percent by eighteen months; and eighty-seven percent by twenty-four months of age. The first twelve months of a horse's life is obviously its most critical stage.

Foals have been observed to gain two and one-half to three pounds daily between three to nine months. From nine to eighteen months average daily gain is 1.1 pounds; and from eighteen to twenty-four months of age the average daily gain is decreased to 0.33 pounds.

The above is natural growth, not excessive body weight or fat. By over feeding, you can develop too much body weight for the size of bone. These horses usually break down, or go crooked legged because the legs cannot carry the excessive body weight under stress of the youth's activity.

The foals are very efficient in converting feed to body weight. Up to weaning they will produce a pound of body weight from about four pounds of feed. It takes weanlings about six to seven pounds of feed to produce a pound of weight. Yearlings require twelve to sixteen pounds of feed per pound of gain.

In order to have your foal grow at the optimum rate, you should worm it at two months and each two months thereafter until it is a yearling. Worms can keep a foal from developing normally.

Try to keep the foal's feet trimmed so they are level. Watch for excessive wear on the under side. He may be wearing excessively on the inside. If so, take off the outside to level the base of the foot. If the foal is crooked, obtain the advice of a competent farrier for corrective trimming. Most of the corrective trimming must be done in the first six to twelve months of age. By nine to twelve months, the ankles are set and by twelve to eighteen the knees are set.

The foal must have a high level of nutrition without any set backs. The mare's milk production will increase until the second or third month, then decrease until the foal is weaned. Try to get the foal eating a sufficient quantity of quality feed prior to the decrease in the mare's milk. If not, the foal will drain the mare and stand around wanting more but not eating enough to much more than maintain body weight until weaned.

If the foal is eating well at a creep feeder along with the milk he gets from the mare, he can maintain his growth rate. If not, the foal may be better off weaned at three and one-half to four months and put on a hay and grain ration due to the mare's reduction in milk production.

Daily Milk Production, 1100 Pound Mare

Month of Lactation	Daily Milk Production (37 pounds/day - 100 percent) (percent)
0-1	84
1-2	86
2-3	100
3-4	89
4-5	65
5-6	46

The ration in the creep feeder should be free choice alfalfa plus a formula of seventy percent crimped oats or half whole and half rolled oats, twenty percent soybean oil meal and ten percent wheat bran. Brown sugar sprinkled over the grain at first will entice the foal to eat readily. Start the foal on about one-half pound of grain mix a day as soon as he will eat it. Increase this gradually until the foal is consuming two to three pounds of grain daily.

Calf Manna is also a good feed for the foal. Using a cup or one-half pound a day, plus a mixture of whole oats and rolled barley with a little bran will also produce a well developed weanling.

Over feeding can cause founder in varying stages. The foal may start walking on the outside of his hooves because the sole of the hoof is sensitive. Cocked ankles can also be brought on by too hot a ration, especially if the foal goes from milk and grass to a full feed of grain and hay. By using one-half grass hay and reducing the pounds of grain, you will slow down the rate of gain and usually the ankles will go back into position.

The protein fed to young horses should be of high quality. This means the essential amino acids which make up protein should be in the correct amounts. Some studies have shown the rations with milk by-products as a protein source results in yearlings growing twice as fast as those fed linseed oil meal. When the yearlings fed linseed meal were supplemented with lysine at 0.45 percent of the total ration and weanlings at 0.55 percent, they grew as fast as those on milk by-products. Soybean oil meal is a higher quality protein than linseed oil meal, therefore, it is recommended over linseed oil meal. Lysine is cheaper to supplement than buying milk by-products in most areas.

Once you have produced a superior yearling, don't turn him out on a pasture without supplement and expect him to keep on growing. That second year is also very important in the horse's total development. If turned out he may be able to hold his weight during the summer. If fed properly, he may have close to ninety percent of his mature size by twenty-four months.

Halter break the foal during the first couple of months. This will reduce the external fears and internal trauma when you are feeding and working with him. If he is nervous and over excited he will not gain well and may have undesirable disposition traits in later life.

It takes good management and high quality feeds to produce superior individuals even when the parents are both superior.

Gelding That Good Colt

Are you trying to decide whether or not to geld that fine colt you have? You're not sure when to geld him or what method should be used?

On the ranch, colts were always gelded, hopefully before they become sexually active. They ran with the herd of mares and geldings and many times a long yearling would breed a mare or two.

Bob Miller of Big Piney, Wyoming, always docked the last bone of the tail on each colt he cut. In this way a gelding could be spotted a hundred yards away. Any horse colt that wasn't docked by the spring of his second year was easily spotted and taken care of.

On a ranch the colt was usually front footed and thrown down, then all four legs were tied. It was a fight for both horse and man. By the time the job was done the horse had pulled all the muscles he had and possibly injured some.

On the cowboy's side, one cowboy, holding a horse's head got his finger in the horse's mouth by mistake and come up missing a finger. The horse was just getting even.

When these horses got up, they were so sore from the strain they didn't want to move around. The next day their muscles were stiff, so they didn't feel like exercising. Without exercise they started to swell in the bag and sheath. This made it even more uncomfortable to move around.

Because the colt wasn't halter broke, he just had to endure and hopefully get better. Some didn't make it. Those that did survive remembered the pain man had inflicted on them.

Some people still use this method. If it was good enough for Grandpa, it's good enough for them. Their horses still have to go through the strain and pain.

A veterinarian can give your horse a tranquilizer to put him at ease. He then will give him a shot to put him out. The shot will last for about fifteen minutes. In this time the vet will have one hind leg pulled forward while he performs the operation The horse is relaxed so adequate cord can be pulled down and clamped. Then the gelding will act like a gelding. With a tetanus shot and some disinfectant on the incision, the operation is completed. In a few minutes he will wake up not knowing anything happened.

Let colts relax for twenty-four hours, then start exercising them. It is not enough to put the horse on a walker. The horse must trot vigorously to open the incision, so drainage can occur. The incision will scab over and the fluids that build up have no way to escape, if the horse isn't moved around briskly.

If your colt is broke, you can start riding him the next day. His muscles won't be sore from straining, but he may be a little hesitant about moving out on a trot. Don't overdo him, but exercise him until you can see a marked reduction in the swelling.

It is best to exercise him twice a day, rather than one long session. It will keep the swelling down better and make him more comfortable so he will walk around on his own.

Cut your colts late in the fall or during the winter or early in the spring. They heal quicker with fewer side effects. When it is wet and cold they may stand around more, so you must exercise them. The cold seems to reduce swelling and make for a shorter recuperation period. This can be as short as one week of swelling. In the summer, many times it takes three weeks in the swelling stage before the horse can be turned out on his own to exercise.

It is easier on the horse if you geld him when he is very young. This, however, prevents adequate development. Some horsemen will wait until they are at least yearlings. Most wait until they are long yearlings or two years old.

You can cut stallions as old as five or six and have good luck making saddle horses out of them. If a horse has a good disposition as a stallion, he will surely have a good disposition as a gelding.

Some mean, older stallions will never quiet down and make a gentle saddle horse. They are going to throw that bad disposition so it's best if they are gelded anyway.

So many people feel they have a stallion prospect every time they get a male foal. There are so few that will make a top stallion. Just remember, a mediocre stallion may make a top gelding. A top gelding will always out sell a mediocre stallion. Everyone can use a good gelding, but few people want a stallion around or have facilities to stand one.

Cleaning the Sheath

Most horse owners take good care of their horses. They see that they are wormed, vaccinated and even get their teeth floated when necessary. They groom them regularly and clean their feet.

Most owners of geldings forget one important cleaning. That is the cleaning of the sheath and penis. This is a subject that you seldom hear discussed but it is still an important subject to know about.

A dirty sheath can lead to infection, ulcers and urinary problems. It doesn't matter if the horse is kept in a stall or out on pasture, the sheath is still able to collect dirt and urine.

The horse is one of the only animals that excretes a tremendous amount of fat cells in the urine. As these fat cells are expelled through the urethra, they can cause several problems. At the end of the urethra there is a pocket called the diverticulum. It is in this small pocket where fat cells collect. Mineral deposits will surround these cells, and as they grow in size they become a hard mass. The horse will end up with what is referred to as a "bean".

If these beans do not fall out on their own, they may cause irritation and pain. When this happens, a gelding will start to urinate, but will quit very suddenly. This is due to the discomfort and back pressure on the urinary system. Since the gelding's bladder is full, he will continue trying to urinate then stop in pain.

Often the pain from the bean will become so intense that the horse will not drop the penis to urinate. Therefore, the urine will run out into the sheath and contaminate the entire area. The accumulation of urine in the sheath will cause a greasy-type of material to build up and become dry and flaky. Sometimes the material becomes so caked on the penis and sheath that it causes ulcers to form on the end of the penis or in the diverticulum.

Look at your gelding when he is urinating. If the penis is caked with scaly matter, you should be concerned about getting him cleaned up.

If he is really touchy, you may need to take him to the veterinarian and have him tranquilized and cleaned. If he is a quiet horse you can do the job yourself. Prepare some warm water with a mild soap mixed in. Also have a bucket of clear warm water for a rinse.

You may want to wear a pair of rubber gloves for the job. Take a rag full of soapy water and wash the inside of the sheath as much as possible. Use a 30 cc syringe without a needle or a bulb syringe and fill it with soapy water. Apply a little vaseline around the end of the syringe, insert the syringe into the sheath and squirt the water. Repeat this several times. This will wash the loose material out of the sheath.

Add a little vaseline to the back of the rubber gloves and reach way up into the sheath and take hold of the penis. Put a little pressure on it and the horse will generally let it be pulled out. If he holds it up in, there is nothing you can do, without a tranquilizer, to get him to relax.

You may want to leave your cleaning supplies at the corral until you see your horse urinate. Just as he is finishing, take hold of the penis and go to work cleaning it up. This way you will be able to get all that fatty build-up cleaned off. Be sure to rinse the soapy water off.

When cleaning the sheath always face the rear, working from the left side of the horse. Stay as far forward as you can so he can't kick you.

The older the horse, the more probability he will have fatty globs in the sheath. Two-year olds are usually still problem free.

If you find your gelding has a problem, clean it up, then routinely clean the area twice a year to eliminate the possibility of a problem. Cleaning the sheath and penis may not be the most pleasant job, but it goes along with the responsibilities one has when owning a gelding.

Stress Can Kill

You hear quite a bit about endurance rides these days. There are fifty mile and one hundred mile rides. There are also ride and tie races where one rider rides on ahead and ties the horse up then begins to run. His partner runs until he comes to the horse then rides on past the first rider and ties up and starts running. This continues to the end of the race.

In most all endurance races there are vet checks to ensure the horses are not over stressed. This is good because some people don't know how much is enough for a horse.

Back in 1958, an endurance race from Malad, Idaho to Garland, Utah was held. The distance was only thirty-two miles. There were no vet checks and anything went. It was a hot Fourth of July so everyone participating was promised a case of beer. The winner was to get $1,000. The horses were staggered at the start so they ran against the clock.

The contestants thinned out quite fast after the first twenty miles. Some people, however, just wouldn't listen to their horses. They rode on and on. One little sorrel horse stopped about a half mile from the finish line. The horse was totally exhausted. That wasn't good enough for the rider, for he dragged that horse the last half mile and finished. Within fifteen minutes the horse was dead.

Another rider rode across the finish line then loaded his horse in the trailer. The horse was dead when he went to get him out of the trailer.

There were a lot of sick horses that finished that race and some never recuperated from the foolishness of man for the sight of a buck.

At the Duschesne County Fair in Utah, they run an endurance race of sorts. This is only about two miles long but it is over a cliff and down a mountain side with a river crossing at the bottom. A lot of horses come in all skinned up from this race. Last year one horse and rider fell. The rider was leading at the time so the horse rolled right over him. They were both down for a time but finally got up and finished the race. The next day that horse died from a kinked intestine.

It's surprising in both of these races the horse that won was no worse for wear, and the riders were in fine shape too. The Malad race was won by a Mexican on a big buckskin he had been riding from Blackfoot to Pocatello, Idaho every day or two for beer. The horse took a deep breath and walked off without any side effects. He could have turned around and rode back. That horse never walked in the race. It was a big swinging trot or slow lope for thirty-two miles.

The horse that won in Duschesne that year had only a few skinned fetlocks. He really didn't show signs of stress.

What was the difference between the winners and the losers? It was conditioning. A horse must be in shape for what you're going to ask of him. Many horses will try hard to please you even if they aren't in shape. These are the real losers, because you really weren't worth trying for. A horse can endure much stress, but you better make sure he is in shape. Be sure you know the stress signs in your horse and take appropriate action. Would you want someone to demand that you worked until you dropped dead?

The old timers told of riding from Pinedale to Jackson, Wyoming, do their business and ride home in one day. It is seventy-six miles one way on the road. They went through the hills to cut off some of that distance, but it still had to be one long day. They claimed they could turn the horse loose for a day and go back again if they needed to.

Riding eighteen hours in the saddle in a day, moving cows and calves to the upper ranch then riding home was a common occurrence. Horses got more riding in a day then, than they ever do now. Cattle are trucked to the range or horses are trucked home after a few miles. Most riders couldn't fathom eighteen hours in a saddle or racing thirty-two miles in one hour and forty-five minutes. The horses and cowboys that were in shape weren't any worse for wear. It's dudes that don't ride enough to get in shape or get their horses in shape that need to watch for signs of stress when they go camping or hunting. Use some horse sense once in a while, it may improve your logic.

Azoturia or Tie Up

The old time teamsters told of a disease known as Azoturia. This disease was also known as "Monday Morning Sickness". Horses that worked hard all week would be given a rest on the weekends without reducing the grain being fed. On Monday the horse would become sick within an hour of hooking him up, usually within fifteen minutes.

The timing of the horse becoming ill was the most reliable diagnostic sign. This disease was primarily limited to the winter months and occurred most often in young fat horses.

The symptoms of Azoturia are rapid pulse (sixty to ninety), sweating, stiff gait, trembling muscles and a desire to go down. They will have difficulty controlling the hind quarters and may sit down like a dog.

Horsemen often confuse Azoturia with colic, founder, sleeping sickness or kidney disease. Many times myositis (tying up or cording up) is also confused with Azoturia. Extreme stress or exhaustion is often improperly called Azoturia.

Due to the breakdown of muscle tissue in Azoturia, certain muscle pigments are released into the bloodstream. These pigments eventually find their way into the urine, resulting in dark colored urine. This may be coffee black in severe cases. Thus, the name "Black Water Disease" was coined.

Azoturia occurs when there is a metabolic disorder or an imbalance of chemistry of the body. With excessive carbohydrates and fats fed on the weekend and not burned, the horse finds his system overloaded with energy. The heat from the energy as work begins produces a chemical reaction that causes a derangement in glycolysis with the accumulation of lactic acid in the muscle tissue and blood.

In Azoturia the most important immediate thing is rest. Avoid moving the horse as much as possible. Feed no grain. Drugs useful in these cases include thiamine to stimulate muscle metabolism, tranquilizers to relieve muscle spasm, cortisones to correct the severe inflammation and stress that occur. Pain relievers usually help as well as alkalizers to neutralize the acid accumulations in muscle tissue.

Vitamin E and selenium are being used by most veterinarians when muscle disorders are evident. This disease requires the immediate attention of the veterinarian.

To help prevent Azoturia, condition horses slowly, balancing grain intake against daily activity. Provide free access to exercise areas on rest days. When the horse is rested his grain ration should be cut in half.

Warm horses up before putting them to hard work and cool them off after work. When the season's work is over, reduce the high protein feed gradually to limit the stress on him. Remember, a horse that has had one attack is predisposed to have another.

Myositis (tying up or cording up) may have many of the same symptoms as Azoturia but it may strike the animal on Thursday or Friday instead of Monday. This disease is more common in saddle or light horses where Azoturia is more prevalent in draft horses. Tying up has no seasonal preference.

Where Azoturia has a higher death rate, myositis has practically no death loss. Tying up is more like muscle cramps or spasms. It is believed, however, that similar chemical imbalances are at fault in this disease, also.

Aside from the mild exercises, most of the medical treatment in severe cases would be about the same as for Azoturia.

Horses with chronic tie up conditions are often put on a low level of vitamin E and selenium to reduce the occurrence of the condition. Some people find their horses showing these signs when they reach the top of the mountain. Their unconditioned horse is tying up and exhibiting many of the symptoms discussed above. This may be exhaustion from sheer stress.

Stress and Exhaustion

Exhaustion, heatstroke, dehydration and anhidrosis are terms you should become familiar with. They all relate to over exertion in relation to the condition of the horse and/or climatic conditions.

A horse can sweat over thirty pounds of body fluids out of his body. Under normal conditions an animal loses and replaces body fluids at approximately the same rate. In the body fluids are important chemical compounds called amino acids, carbohydrates and electrolytes. When the horse is over worked his system goes out of balance. By losing too much body fluid they lose the chemicals that permit proper absorption of these sources of energy and protein.

The electrolytes are non-metallic chemical muscle impulse conductors such as sodium, potassium, selenium, chlorine and calcium. Each muscle produces heat as it utilizes energy, releasing electrolytes into the blood. This causes veins and arteries to expand in size to their maximum carrying capacity.

The added circulation carries more heat away from the muscles to cool them down. As water is drawn out of the muscle cells to produce sweat, cells operate with decreased efficiency. Heat builds up in the muscle and the horse becomes weak and exhausted.

Heat is both advantageous and detrimental. A five degree rise in temperature within a muscle increases the rate of chemical reactions by fifty percent or more, thus making the horse more efficient. If, however, the body core temperature rises above 107 degrees, heat stroke, exhaustion and possible death results.

Dehydration can result from lowered volume of body fluids. Horses can normally tolerate a certain amount of dehydration as long as they continue to sweat. It's when the temperature climbs and they can't get rid of the body heat that the problem of anhidrosis arises. This is when the horse can't sweat and heat continues to build up in the body. To check for dehydration grasp a tuck of skin and pull it out. This pinched fold of skin will normally snap back immediately, but if the fold remains for three or more seconds this indicates water loss is serious. If it remains for six to ten seconds the dehydration is life threatening.

Check his breathing. At rest he will breath about sixteen times a minute. He requires twice as much air volume at a walk, four times as much at a trot and eleven times the rest rate at a gallop. Because the volume is not equal to breaths he will possibly increase his breathing to one hundred twenty breaths a minute at a gallop.

Once you stop and rest him he should recover back to sixteen or twenty breaths a minute in a short time. If he doesn't you will know the horse is out of shape for the work you are doing; you are asking too much of the horse.

When the horse is breathing in shallow quick breaths or panting, he is having trouble cooling his body. Staggering may occur and the muscles may stiffen and tremble.

Get the horse in a shady area and put cool water on his head and neck. It will also help to put some down his spine. You need to help him reduce his body heat and replenish his body fluids.

It will help to keep your horse at a reasonable weight. Excess fat on a horse traps heat under the skin. If he has a lot of hair it may be advisable to clip him if you expect the trip to be hot. This will make him much cooler. Cold blood horses have fewer sweat glands than hot blood horses so they will have a harder time keeping cool when it's hot. Hot blood Arabians have a thin skin and many more sweat glands, as nature has prepared them to live in Arabia in the heat. Cold bloods were developed in the colder climate where nature provided them with a thicker skin and more hair to keep warm in winter. They did not need as many sweat glands.

A horse will maintain his body fluids best if you can water him up before you leave, then try to water at least every fifteen miles. This should be more often if you are in steep slow terrain. When you water a hot horse you can give him all he wants as long as you keep traveling after he has drank. If you are going to stop for a while don't let him drink much. He should be given a small drink then walked for a few minutes then give him a little more and walk him some more.

Permitting a hot horse to drink, then stand can cause colic, founder and/or muscle cramping. The blood is busy carrying heat away from the muscles then the circulation is reduced by standing. The cooling system is shut down by the cold water. The muscle and hooves still have excess heat they can't expend.

By walking the horse at the end of a ride you are keeping the blood pumping to help cool the muscles. Take a little salt with you and let the horse have access to it. He will lose two grams of salt for every pound of sweat he loses.

Potomac Horse Fever

The disease, Potomac Horse Fever (PHT), is not only a problem in the Potomac River Basin but in the Rocky Mountain states. PHF has been diagnosed in most of the western states. The spread of the disease is inevitable.

Potomac Horse Fever attacks suddenly with devastating results. It presents itself as an acute syndrome with depression, fever, lack of appetite and watery diarrhea. The diarrhea can be life-threatening due to the loss of electrolytes and severe dehydration. Death can be very rapid —even before treatment can be started.

The cause of this desease is a rickettsial organism known as Ehrlechia risticii. This organism is know to infect ticks, and chiggers, which are thought to be the primary hosts which infect the horse. Flies, mosquitos, lice and other insects are also suspect as carriers.

Horse to horse transmission of PHF has not been observed, thus the disease is not considered contagious among horses.

The disease seems to be seasonal, with most cases seen between May and September, with most cases occurring in the latter portion of this period. The initial clinical signs are usually depression and a mild fever, which may go unnoticed. Seven to ten days later severe diarrhea, depression and lack of appetite are seen. The clinical signs mimic those of Salmonellosis, which is also a common equine intestinal disease, but is treated somewhat differently.

A test is now available for PHF. This is a plate latex agglutination test (PLAT). The Proto Tek development test is being manufactured and distributed by Schering. The PLAT gives results in just over thirty minutes after the blood sample has been separated by centrifuging.

Reliability of the PLAT as a screening tool during active infections is significant to horse owners and caretakers since early treatment of PHF with a Tetracycline drug helps suppress rickettsial replication and staves off full blown illness. Tetracylcine, however, may worsen Salmonellosis, a diarrheal disease, which shares many clinical signs with PHF. It is, therefore, important to test before treating to identify the specific organism present.

Even if there have been no cases in your state, you should take precautions to reduce the chance of its spreading. Be careful to minimize exposure to ticks and chiggers and check horses thoroughly for these insects when in the mountains. Remove any ticks immediately. If the head is imbedded, use a match or hot needle to encourage the insect to release its grip and back out. Watch your horse carefully for the next two weeks for any signs of the above symptoms.

Prompt medical treatment can save sixty to seventy percent of the horses. Horses not treated may have a seventy percent mortality rate.

There is a new vaccine available to help prevent PHF. The vaccine is given in two doses of vaccine thirty days apart. Your veterinarian should have the vaccine now.

It may be a good idea to vaccinated your horse for this disease so you won't have to worry about him contracting it. For about ten dollars you can be safe, rather than sorry. If you have a question, check with your veterenarian.

For your own protection you may want to get vaccinated for Rocky Mountain Spotted Fever which is also carried by the tick. This could save you a lot of sickness if you ride in the tick infested areas.

Fly Season

There are many types of flies that bother the horse. Some are biting and some are just nuisance-type flies.

For those biting flies, such as horse flies and deer flies, there is relatively no insecticide you can put on your horse to rid him of their torment. You can provide him with a dark area to stand. The flies tend to like the light and will not bother the horse as badly in a dark stall or shed.

The biting flies were so bad in Wyoming that the work horses would have a sheet over the harness to help protect them from the hoards of flies.

The face fly is a more recent nuisance that can cause horses much distress. As the flies swarm around the eyes and nose the horse moves his head from side to side or rubs it on his legs. Some horses just keep moving, some even trot around, trying to keep away from the flies. This takes energy and creates a nervous horse. Some horses are much more affected by flies than others. The hot blood horses are more nervous and irritated by the insects than the cold bloods or draft horses.

Face flies and other non-biting flies can be controlled quite effectively by the use of sprays, wipes or powders. There are also new products on the market that can be tied to a horse's halter or around his neck that will repel flies.

Fly spray is not very effective for bot flies either. These flies are primarily an external nuisance and can cause horses to perform erratically while being ridden.

If you really want to reduce the problem for your horse, you can look at stable management programs to reduce the fly population. To combat the fly problem, it is necessary to have a manure disposal system as well as a fly control program. A wide variety of compounds are available for the latter purpose. They include insecticides to use in and around the stable as well as baits and traps that also work well. One word of caution: never use any of these products without first reading the label very carefully.

Cut down the smells and sights that draw flies. Clean your stall daily of droppings, then clean all bedding material at least twice a week. Place the manure pile a little ways away from the barn and have it removed and spread in the fields as often as possible.

In the summer use little bedding in open front corrals, then clean manure often. This will provide a much more fly-free area for the horses to rest in.

Cattle corrals and corn silage pits are strong drawers for flies. If possible, place your horse facility a good distance from these facilities.

Water can also be a drawing card for flies if it sits in the corral. Be sure you have good drainage and keep drinking water tanks cleaned and clear.

Use good sanitation practices around the horse facilities. Feed areas can be swept or raked, and allow no feed to sit and spoil. All afterbirths or dead animals should be immediately disposed of.

It takes work to reduce the fly problem. It is nice to go onto someone's facility and see a clean, well-kept unit that has been freed of many of the undesirable sights, smells and accompanying insects. Most owners could make some improvements.

Health Inspection

When you plan to travel out of state you should check the requirements of the destination state for inspection and test requirements. Most states require health and brand inspections to enter their boundaries. A health inspection can be obtained from an accredited veterinarian at a cost of $7 to $25. This inspection certificate is good for thirty days. This should be a minor physical if performed correctly. The horse's temperature, respiration and heart rate should be checked. His nose should be checked for discharge and his lymph nodes under the jaw should be checked for swelling. This inspection is not to verify soundness but rather to check for communicable diseases that might be transmitted. Strangles, pneumonia, influenza, equine viral rhenopneumonitis, viral arteritis, equine encephalomyelitis, and equine infectious anemia can all be diagnosed if in the early stages when high fevers occur. If no vital signs are taken, the visual appearance of the horse is all that can be used. This will not be adequate if the horse is not showing other symptoms, many of which develop later.

Some veterinarians say the inspection is not absolute anyway, because a horse could have been exposed to a disease and be a few days short of the high temperature stage when he is given a health inspection. Under these conditions the horse will have no signs of illness and receive a clean bill of health. Within three days the horse is in a high fever stage of the disease and the infection could be spread. Yet the horse will have a thirty day health certificate to travel on.

There have been horses inspected and given a clean bill of health, and in a few days came down with strangles. This is not the veterinarian's fault or mistake, this is just a weakness in the health inspection certificate itself. We expect that this health certificate gives the horse a clean bill of health. If done properly it does for one instant in time, but that is not really solving the problem it was intended to do.

Some states have picked out one of these diseases, equine infectious anemia (EIA) or (Swamp Fever) to do a specific test on. This is the Coggins test named after Dr. Leroy Coggins of Cornell University who developed it. EIA can either be acute or subacute. The mortality of the acute form is quite high. The subacute form is the most common form. The signs are similar to the acute form but are not severe and death seldom occurs. Horses tested with the Coggins test may be reactors (or carriers) and show no signs of being ill. Some of these carriers can actually transmit the disease, but others will not.

EIA is transmitted in the blood from infected horses. The most common vectors of transmission are the biting insects, except mosquitos. Hypodermic needles, surgical instruments, dental floats and bridle bits may also transmit the virus.

Symptoms of the disease are unthriftiness and lack of stamina. Anemia may also develp periodically. The infected horse may appear to get better in seven to twenty days, then weeks or months later, during periods of stress, may have another attack. Horses that have the subacute form, or those that survive the acute form, are dangerous to any horse in the vicinity because they are carriers of the disease.

No vaccine is presently available to prevent this disease or no treatment is known once it is contracted. It is interesting that no acute, or even subacute, cases of this disease has been found transmitted in Utah according to Dr. James Schoenfeld, State Veterinarian.

The Coggins test is required by many states on all horses entering the state. This does provide a monitor on horses in transit. The test is accomplished by the veterinarian drawing 10cc of the animal's blood. This blood is sent to an approved laboratory to have the test run. The test takes twenty-four hours to run, but you should allow from three to seven days to get the results so make sure you plan your travel accordingly.

When a reactor is found, they are always retested. The test has not been found to be one hundred percent reliable. Some horses with positive tests on the first test have been found clean on the second test. Horses that have had liver problems will generally test positive. Dr. Cathy Borrett, a DVM in Ogden, Utah, is working with a positive reactor in an attempt to transmit the disease through the blood to a negative reactor. She is trying to show horses with a history of liver problems may test Coggins positive but are not carriers of the disease.

There have been few horses confirmed positive reactors to the Coggins test. You might ask if these animals were required to be destroyed? No, they are required by law to be isolated on that farm for the rest of their natural life or the owner may opt to have the horse destroyed, if he pleases. Usually this means the horse is sold for meat, exposing many horses before being slaughtered.

Remember, only horses being prepared for interstate transit are tested so we don't know how many other reactors we might find if the remaining ninety percent of the population were tested. With this in mind, how valuable is the test program to protect clean horses from the disease? If it has little effect, why put the horse owner through the trouble, worry and cost of the Coggins test. Especially, when we know the Eastern and Western Equine Encephalomyelitis is known to have a seventy to ninety percent mortality rate and we don't even require the protective vaccination that is cheaply available. This disease is a known killer in the Intermountain West.

A number of the veterinarians are not sold on the test program or the results from the test. It appears there is room for discussion as to its use.

Horse owners are so fragmented regarding a unified organization that their voice is seldom heard even as a whisper. It is time that the horse owners form county, multi-county and state horse councils representing all facets of the horse industry and speaking on issues such as the health and brand inspection program in the individual states. Let's see if we can all work with one goal in mind, that of the welfare, betterment and protection of our industry.

Horse Facilities

Horses need shade in the summer and protection from the wind, rain and snow storms the rest of the year. Sometimes trees or gullys may be adequate, but generally a three-sided shed is necessary as a minimum.

Fencing for pastures can vary depending on availability of materials, but stay away from barbed wire and net wire. Both have caused many injuries to horses. Poles are the cheapest form of fencing for pastures, but they do require upkeep. Two by six planks are also good fencing. Some of these can be obtained with a plastic coating that requires little if any maintenance. Even the posts are plastic coated to prevent rotting.

Round training pens are very helpful when working young horses. A forty or fifty foot round corral would be ideal for working colts. The fence should be five and one-half to six feet tall. Horses can be roped or worked loose with a whip in it.

An eighty-five to one hundred foot round corral can be used to lope circles and work cattle individually. The footing should be small gravel, well packed, with a six inch layer of sandy loam soil. This can be worked up when needed, but will pack enough on the bottom for a smooth tight base.

Build your outdoor arenas large enough for what you want to do in them. It takes at least two hundred and fifty feet for a roping arena, by the time you build the chutes and boxes.

For a riding arena make it at least one hundred and fifty feet by one hundred feet. The inside arena may be reduced to seventy-five feet wide if money is tight. Much narrower than that gives problems for some types of training. We have been using an arena fifty feet wide for some time at USU because money was not available to build the quality of facility desired.

Stalls in the arena area are convenient but they cause an arena smell that is hard to dissipate. This can cause horses to cough and be more susceptible to respiratory infections.

Horse stalls built so the open air can circulate through them will reduce these respiratory problems. Make stalls at least ten feet by ten feet. Twelve by twelve is nice for large horses. They take more straw but are more comfortable on the horse.

Using an open front shed with a thirty-five foot depth permits stalls to be built in the back with a four foot walk way and then open corrals. This is a very functional unit.

Be sure you leave a rough surface on any cement that is made for walk ways. A smooth surface will be slick when wet.

Corrals should be built with width between poles. Start your first pole up about sixteen inches from the ground. Do the same with wire fencing if you have to use it. This will reduce the cut pasterns from horses pawing through.

Set your gates up that same height and only use gates that have round pipe. If a horse lies down close to a fence or gate and rolls over he may get a foot or two through the bottom rungs, then he will stand up. If the rungs are close he will not be able to get his foot out. If the gate is open on the bottom of each rung you may get a broken or cut up leg. Its much better to have a round pipe with distance between each rung so the horse can pull his leg out without injury.

It is always nice to have a doctoring chute for floating teeth, clipping ears, doctoring and even saddling if you have a snorty horse. Make this chute very sturdy, with easy opened gates that stay secure.

You can cut a hole in the back of the chute for pulling tails, also. This prevents a lot of injuries as long as you make it high enough they can't kick over it. Make the front high enough they can't get over it, too.

Arena

Arena with tack room and tie posts

Open front shed has
a large door in the
center. The hay
shed is behind open
front shed.

Box stalls
and open
runs.

Automatic waterers
should be grounded
with the
wires encased
in conduit.

Cross tie in the bronc chute for trimming ears, floating teeth or other care.

Front and right side swing open from either side leaves a hole for pulling tails. Board it up so he can't kick you.

Three feet wide makes it large enough to saddle and mount in the chute. A five or five and a half foot long stall is adequate. Board the back of the stall, leaving a hole to pull tails

Make sure the gate locks are horse safe.

Adapting poles to pipe is quite easy.

Poles make safe horse fences.

Tired of muddy poles that the horse has to step over?

133

Pole gate
with two openings.

Slide the poles back
for a four foot walk
through gate.

Slide them all the way
and have a fourteen foot
drive through gate.

134

Literature Cited

1. Fonnesbeck, P.V., R.K. Lydman, G.W. Vander Noot and L.D. Symons. 1967. *Digestibility of the Proximate Nutrients of Forage by Horses.* J. Animal Sci. 26:1039.

2. Balch, C.C. and R.C. Campling. 1962. *Regulating of Voluntary Food Intake in Ruminants.* Nutr. Abstr. and Res. 32:669.

3. Waite, R. and K.N.S. Sastry. 1949. *The Carotene Content of Dried Grass* J. Agr. Sci. 39:174.

4. Nelson, D.D. and W.J. Tyznik. 1971. *Protein and Non-protein Nitrogen Utilization in the Horse.* J. Animal Sci. 32:68.

5. Fonnesbeck, P.V. and L.D. Symons. 1967. *Utilization of the Carotene of Hay by Horses* J. of Animal Sci. 26:1030.

6. Goodman, H.M., G.W. Vander Noot, J.R. Trout and R.L. Squibb. 1973. *Determination of Energy Source Utilized by the Light Horse.* J. Animal Sci. 37:56.

7. Hintz, H.F., S.J. Roberts, S.W. Sabin and H.F. Schryver. 1971. *Energy Requirements of Light Horses for Various Activities.* J. Animal Sci. 32:100.

8. NRC 1978. *Nutrient Requirements of Domestic Animals, Number 6.* Nutrient Requirements of Horses. 4th revised Ed. National Academy of Sciences, National Research Council, Washington, D.C.

9. Fonnesbeck, P.V. 1968. *Consumption and Excretion of Water by Horses Receiving All Hay and Hay-Grain Diets.* J. Animal Sci. 27:1350.

10. Teter, N.C. and J.A. DeShazer. 1976. *Effects of Temperature on Nutrient Requirements of Meat Animals.* First International Symposium, Feed Composition, Animal Nutrient Requirements and Computerization of Diets. (Edited by P.V. Fonnesbeck, L.E. Harris and L.C. Kearl) Utah Agr. Exp. Sta., Utah State University, Logan, Utah.

CHAPTER FIVE

THE NATURE OF THE HORSE

Horse Hierarchy

Do you get trampled every time you walk in the corral to feed? I cannot count the number of times I have had a cranky horse run a submissive horse over me. All you could see was hay flying and me being bumped out of the way.

Some people say they can pick the horse that will win the race, be aggressive at the show or handle the trail best by their dominance in the corral.

The pecking order is a very real social system among horses. It is not established without some bumps, bites, and kicks. Once a horse has a given area to himself he thinks of it as his private domain and he is the ruler. Put another horse in and the first one there will fight for his rule. If the second horse is submissive he will be dominated. If, however, he is aggressive he may win the ruling position.

If the ruler gets sick he may lose his rule by being submissive for a given time. Once he is better, he may again dominate the pen.

Each time a new horse is added to the pen there is a new fight for the rule. The top position is not the only position desired in the social order. Each horse will know who is above him and who is below him in the order. Some horses are very aggressive to the point of being dangerous, in order to show their authority. While others can establish authority with just a bump or by pinning their ears back.

With four pens to work with, I separate the horses so the most aggressive bosses are in the biggest pen together and the most submissive in the smallest pen together.

It is interesting to watch the bosses make their case for their right to be ruler. It may be quite violent but once the order is established, they settle down to living with each other. They know they will get a fight if they push their authority too far.

In the pen of submissive horses you would expect everyone to be so happy to get away from the overly aggressive horses that they would be content to let everyone be. Not so! Every society has to have order, and this corral is no different. They start pushing and biting to establish their position in the order. Soon you have an established order, of which the ruler may be more aggressive that the ruler in the larger pen.

If this ruler is too aggressive, I move him up to a middle pen. In the middle pens there is much less bickering. There is a definite order, but here you can see six horses eat out of the same feeder.

As a young horse matures in the group he may change his position in the corral. As he improves his position it gives him courage to challenge those still higher up. He may move from the bottom of the pecking order to near the top in a few months of maturity.

Some people would have us believe this aggressive attitude is carried over into their training. This does not hold true in most cases. I have horses that have to be penned alone because they are so mean with other horses. Yet, these same horses are pussy cats when around people and are not aggressive to ride.

It depends to a high degree on the type of interaction the horse has had with people. Even if they have learned to be submissive to people early in life, they may still be very aggressive in the corral. They may even want to show this aggression whenever the trainer is present. They don't want other horses getting the trainer's attention.

Trainers in all areas of horse competition tend to agree that you may take a horse that appears to be submissive in his surroundings and he will be aggressive in his competition. This is in part due to the confidence his rider imparts to him. He can feel more confident in his competition as his rider teaches him to handle situations and to work on his own without the rider having total control.

Look at the aggression shown in a cutting horse. This horse may be the most submissive, but put a cow in front of him and watch him take charge.

So what does this all mean to a trainer or someone picking a horse? Should we look for aggression or submimssion?

Depending on which corral I put the horse in I can sell you which ever you want, in the same horse. So don't put too much stock in the researchers that sit and watch every move a horse makes for a couple of weeks, then tell you what kind of personality traits the horse has. By changing the horse to another pen, the same researcher would come up with a totally different personality pattern.

Look for the horse that relates to people in a positive way, and is willing to try to do what you ask, regardless of his position in the herd.

Have you ever had a horse that walked over you, pulled you around, kicked and bit you? What is this horse saying? He is telling you that you are at the bottom of the pecking order. Before you can do anything to train him, you must change this pecking order.

Whenever you work with a horse, you form a pecking order. If you're brushing him and he is pushy and kicky, he is trying to establish his dominance. If you back off, he will know he is dominant.

138

If you straighten him up and let him know you are going to brush him and he is going to stand still, then he will find you are dominant. Use a pair of hobbles if necessary.

A horse will test this pecking order quite often at first. After a while he will accept your dominance. Once he does, training becomes much more productive.

It helps to work your horse in a round pen on a line or if he is well trained work him loose. Put a bridle on and take the reins off at first. The bit will take energy out of the horse as his mind is working on holding the bit. Work the high off the horse. Have him walk, trot and lope on command. Stop him with "whoa" and say "come here". You will be surprised how fast he will start coming right to you. Don't walk to him; always make him come to you. Then rub or pet him on the neck. Let him rest a minute while you talk to him and pet him.

Soon he will learn this is a reward, a good time, so he will want to come to you. Then you can use it in the corral or pasture. Walk out and say "come here" in a commanding voice, and he will at least stand and look at you at first. Then soon he will come to you. Always rub him on the neck and talk to him instead of jumping at him with your halter.

Never take a halter off and hit the horse to spook him away. Always take the halter off and then pet him and talk to him a moment. It will make catching him the next time much easier.

This idea carries through in all your training. Always be dominant, but with kindness. If your horse won't lead it is because he doesn't respect your authority. Get a stock whip and find a fence with some room to travel down it. Get on the left side of the horse with the fence on his right side.

Always make the horse walk so your shoulder is even with the throat latch. This means you can push the horse out in front a little with your right hand. With the whip in your left, out of sight of the horse, tap him on the hocks and make him walk off. Do not walk any faster than the horse but keep up with him. Keep your shoulder right at his throat latch. If he wants to trot, keep up to him. Stop him and face him.

Teach him he must move with you as long as you are turned forward, and must stop when you face him. Never pull on the rope to move him forward, but rather tap him with the whip. Kiss to him every time you want him to move out. Soon the kiss will be adequate without the whip.

You must always remember that you are not going to drag the horse. Always be at his throat latch and always face away from the horse when traveling.

When you are on the horse, the same principle of the pecking order is valid. You must be the dominant one, and he must do what you tell him. Work again in the round corral and work on the different gaits, stop and back. Be firm but fair. Stop and reward him by patting him on the neck and letting him rest. Never run him out of air.

The sooner you establish the pecking order between you and your horse, the sooner you will enjoy the horse. It matters not what the pecking order of this horse is among his stablemates; it is the order between the two of you that you can control. Some horses that are very timid in the herd are quite dominant with their handler, if permitted. Other very dominant horses in the herd may be pussy cats with their handlers. So don't always judge their docility by watching them in the herd.

Controlling That Mean Horse

Some horses just cannot relax and leave the rest of the horses alone. They are always running the others around. These horses need to be taught a few manners.

The first thing to do is try to keep the mares and geldings in separate pens. A gelding may take the mares as his property and no other gelding better get close to them. This can happen even if the gelding has been gelded properly.

Some geldings are cut long so they still produce some male hormones which cause them to act like a stallion. These horses are very difficult to control no matter what you try.

I bought a four-year-old gelding at an Elko, Nevada, sale. He was a show horse that had been penned alone all his life. I put him in a pen with other horses and he'd liked to ate them up.

It's difficult to keep a horse penned alone all the time. They become much less useful in anyone's program. I decided to see if I could set this horse straight right from the start. I put a pair of chain hobbles on him and left him in with the other horses.

He could not move fast so he stopped chasing the other horses. He still could bite, but even that stopped because he couldn't get that close to other horses. Within thirty-six hours with the hobbles on he was a new horse. When the hobbles were removed, he was still cooperative with the other horses.

This may take a little hair off the ankles where the hobbles go, but it is worth a little hide if the horse changes his attitude. Sheep skin covered hobbles will reduce rubbing hair off.

Some mares are bossy and this may help with them, also. It may take a few repetitions to help if they have been in the herd for some time. Do not put a hobble with a chain dragging on the horse. The chain can damage the horse's legs.

Nothing works every time, but it is sure worth a try if you have a cranky horse in the herd.

Behavior Patterns

Protective behavior is seen in mares protecting their foals and in stallions and some geldings protecting mares.

Investigative behavior is highly developed in the horse. This is the reason some come up with porcupine quills in their nose or skunk perfume all over them. Some even get bitten in the nose by rattlesnakes. They investigate with all their senses. This can easily be seen in colts in new surroundings. They will have to see everything, listen to all the new sounds, touch new objects and even taste new things.

Gregarious behavior reflects the desire to be with others. Generally, this is the desire to be with other horses, but it may be satisfied with dogs, ducks, goats or people. This can be a negative or a positive value in training, depending on the cause and to what degree the desire exists. Some horses cannot be taken away from their stable mate, while others could care less. Even after two or three months apart some horses will, in a day, again form that same close bond. A horse that likes being around people is easily trained because it has no basic fears of man. That liking can, however, be overdone if the horse has to be rubbing on you and walking all over you just to be close.

Aggressive behavior can be very aggravating because one horse in a pen of horses is always the boss and then there is a pecking order down through the herd. Feeding and penning in small areas can be a real problem because of this. One would think if you put the bottom horse from each of two pens together that these meek animals would get along. Usually one becomes very aggressive and dominates the other. If one horse is moved to another's pen, the one that has been in the pen will be domineering for a period. If the new horse is very aggressive, he may soon become dominant in the pen.

A pecking order is always established by horses and there is little a manager can do except shuffle the horses into different pens. By putting the more aggressive horses together and the less aggressive horses together, they tend to be able to take care of themselves better. You can always depend on having a few horses get kicked or bitten. The only alternative is to pen each one separately.

Modifying behavior so it tends to make the animal more at ease and teachable is the trainer's goal. Putting a horse on the fight accentuates his aggressive behavior and creates patterns that are hard to handle and even harder to change.

Inheritance

There are many misconceptions when it comes to a horse's instinct, or inherited ability to work cows, commonly called cow sense. This implies that some horses are born with the understanding of how to herd a cow. The justification for this belief is seen when an unbroke colt seems to work a cow on his own. Just try putting a steer into a medium size pen with a horse and watch the horse try to put him over the fence. This will happen if the colt is a healthy athlete with a lot of energy. This is an athlete's desire to be active and playful. Horses have never been crossed with cattle or in any other way been permitted to know what a cow is going to do. Many horses can be made into cutting horses, regardless of whether they, or their ancestors, have ever been around cows. Thoroughbreds and Arabians are good examples of this.

Trainability or brain power has a fairly high likelihood of being inherited. This is another factor that may be associated with cow sense. Some horses are very slow to catch on to heading a cow, while others start to come to it in only one or two sessions. The horse's attention span, or length of concentration, is highly correlated to its teachability in any activity, but especially in working cows.

Aggressive behavior is also an inherited tendency. Disposition can be improved by watching for this in the mare and stallion and breeding a horse with a desirable disposition to another horse of like qualities.

Working With The Horse

A wild horse will run to get away from danger. Nature provided him with exceptional speed and a strong sense of smell and hearing. If cornered, a horse relies on kicking, biting and striking with his front feet to defend himself. Usually he will not be aggressive to a human unless he feels excessive fear or because of previously terrifying experiences. Old broke horses use these same means of aggression when they are spoiled and ornery or downright mean.

How can a person know what to expect from a strange horse? One way is by observing his radar. By watching his ears you can tell where his attention is focused and what his mood is. When you walk up to him in a corral, he may have his ears forward towards you. This means he is watching you and thinking about what you are going to do. If his ears are drooping to the sides, his attention is on nothing particular. He may be daydreaming or even asleep. If you touch him before you get his attention, you may startle him and he may react adversely. Always talk to a horse that has relaxed ears to make sure he knows you are there.

The horse to watch out for is the one with his ears pinned back against his neck. That horse may bite, strike, or kick. If you learn to read the attitude and attention of a horse and act accordingly, you can greatly cut down the chances of getting hurt. This tool of watching a horse's ears is one that older, experienced horsemen use without even realizing it. If they didn't, they wouldn't be old, they would be dead. With time and practice this attentiveness will become second nature to the young or new horsemen, too.

Working with mares creates special problems. When in heat they are unpredictable, but just prior to and after heat they may be even more dangerous to handlers, riders and other horses. They will tend to kick and bite much more readily. Young mares are usually more unpredictably aggressive than old mares that are used to what is happening in their body.

Ears forward

Ears drooping

Ears relaxed

Ears pinned back

142

Stallions should always be assumed unpredictable. Some stallions are very gentle and easy to get along with, but when a mare in heat is close by, the stallion's disposition may change drastically. Others are dangerous all the time. Penning a stallion away from the other horses usually adds to his aggressive attitudes. Some managers run a young stallion with an old cranky gelding that will teach him a few manners. Some pasturebred stallions act like geldings under any circumstances other than when they are loose in a pasture with a mare in heat.

Geldings tend to have the most even disposition, but some are very aggressive in a corral with other horses. Some geldings retain stallion characteristics of fighting for mares.

As a horse becomes comfortable around humans, he may repress some of his natural instincts and rely on the handler or rider for guidance. Sometimes this can cause the horse to go places and get into predicaments he wouldn't otherwise do. This puts more responsibility on the handler or rider to be careful of what is asked of the horse. You may get him and/or yourself hurt because of your thoughtlessness.

You must realize that the horse has good vision and keen senses, but the visual potential can be restricted by the horse's massive body. This makes him rely more heavily on his other senses for safety. Working around horses requires a clear understanding of the horse's vision area and the safety and danger zones that you must deal with.

Understanding the horse's natural instincts and responses is a must for safe handling and training of the horse.

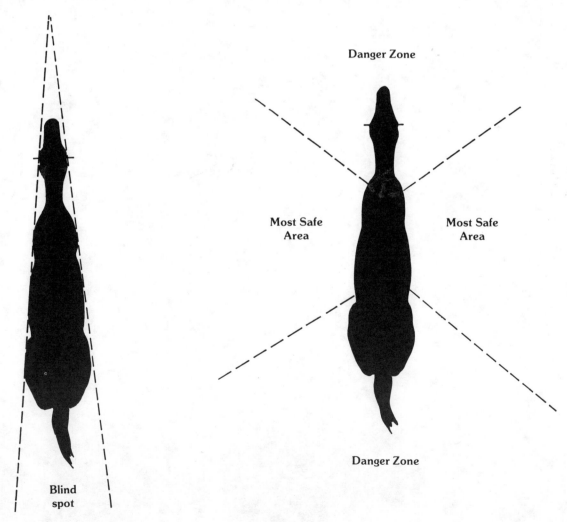

CHAPTER SIX
LET'S RIDE

Catching The Horse

Haltering

Before moving toward the horse, open up the halter at the buckle. Place the buckle in your left hand first, then take up the long tip. Last, hold the halter rope with your fingers on the left hand.

Always try to approach the horse toward his front left (near) shoulder. If you must start on his right (off) side, move to the left side as soon as the halter rope is around his neck.

Starting from the left side, you approach the horse slowly with your hands at your side. Talk to the horse as you walk towards him. Remember to keep your hands down and do not show him the halter.

Once you are within a half arm's length of the horse's shoulder, reach out with your right hand and pat the horse on the shoulder or neck. Move in closer, extending the right arm up the neck and toward the small of the neck.

Now take the end of the halter rope with the fingers of the left hand and transfer it to your right hand by going under the horse's neck with the left hand. Most horses now assume they are caught, and you can halter them. Put your right hand back over the horse's neck. Hand yourself the long belt end of the halter. You now have the halter open under the horse's chin. Move it up and catch his nose in the nose opening. Pull the halter up on the horse and fasten the belt in the buckle snugly.

Problems in Haltering

1. Rushing at the horse with your halter extended. (Slow down and relax.)
2. Horses that turn their rear end to you every time you approach them.

   a. Sometimes two people can corner the horse so he can't escape.

   b. Grain can be used to entice the horse to turn around.

   c. A whip can be used to tan the horse's rear end until he will always face you. Use a long whip so you can stay out of reach of his hind feet.

   d. A rope can be used to rope the horse while his head is in the corner and soon every time you enter the corral the horse will face you because he wants to see what's coming.

   e. A flipper crotch (slingshot) with a pebble can be used to hit the horse's rear end so he will turn around to see what's happening.

   f. A rope can be allowed to drag from a halter left on the horse or a chain can be attached to the leg. This would be a last resort because of the chance of the horse hurting himself.

When removing the halter from a horse, never jerk it off and scare the horse away. Always take it off easy and pet the horse to reassure him you are his friend. Walk away from the horse, don't let him turn and run away from you.

Hold the halter...

Approach the horse...

Put the rope around the neck...

Hand the strap over the neck...

Then catch the nose

Buckle snugly

Leading

Take the halter rope from around the horse's neck and you are ready to lead him. When leading the horse, stay on the left side. Hold the rope about a foot or so from the halter. Turn the direction you are going and start walking. Do not face the horse when leading. If you have a problem leading him, give him more rope.

Some horses do not lead well. This is a problem you must overcome before the horse is of any functional value. There are many ways to encourage a reluctant horse and one may be just right for yours.

1. Slip a loop over his rump and then if the horse doesn't lead by the halter, give a quick jerk on the back rope. Repeat this until he learns that when he comes with the lead rope he will not get jerked on the rump.
2. Put a rope over the withers and around the heart girth of the horse, tying a bowline under his chest just behind his front legs. Run the rope between the front legs and use it in the manner as in 1 above.
3. Move the horse so his right side is next to a fence and with a whip in your left hand and the halter rope in your right, move the horse forward with him between you and the fence. When he doesn't want to move, tap him with the whip on the rump or legs without turning around. Try not to let him know what is hitting him. He will learn that quick response to the halter rope prevents the sting on the rear.

4. Sometimes a dog that will heel livestock on command can be used. When you say "Get 'em", the dog will heel the horse. Soon, even when the dog isn't around, you can say "Get 'em" and the horse will move rapidly forward. Make sure the dog doesn't help you when you don't need his help.

Ready to lead

Don't look back

Teaching to lead

Tying Up the Horse

Once you have put the halter on the horse and are ready to saddle him you need to tie the horse to a sturdy object. **Never tie to anything that he can pull out of the ground, break, or otherwise damage.*** Just think of what could happen if the horse pulled an object loose — what damage that object could do to horse or handler. Always tie to a post at a height of about four and one-half to five feet off the ground. Leave about eighteen inches of rope between the object you are tying to and the halter. If shorter, the horse may get upset and fight being tied too short. If longer, he may get a foot over the rope or his head wrapped around it.

Always use the slipknot when tying a horse that is haltered. For this knot take the long end around the object to which you are tying him, then make a small loop with the slack of the rope hanging down on the outer edge of the loop. Grasp the slack end about a foot below the loop. Take it under both the loop and the main line coming from the halter, then over the top of the line from the halter, through the loop and snug the knot tight, then slide it tight against the post.

There are other knots that can be used, but this knot can generally be released in a hurry; therefore, it is safer for the horse.

Slipknot

Tie to a sturdy object

When no halter is available, a rope looped around the horse's neck can be secured with a bowline knot. This knot will not pull tight so it cannot choke the horse. Many horses every year are choked to death by well-meaning people tying a slipknot about the neck and then tying the other end to something solid. The horse then pulls back and hangs himself.

149

The bowline can be tied by closely following a short saying. You form a loop with the length of rope running to the tie post. The loop you have made is a rabbit's hole. The extension from the hole that passes under the loop is the tree. You can hold the tree up with your fingers holding the loop. Then take the end of the short piece of rope in your other hand and pretend it is a rabbit. Now the rabbit comes up through his hole and goes around the tree, then back down his hole. You hold both ends of the rabbit (or the two pieces of rope lying side by side) and shut the hole by pulling the tree and the loop end. This creates a knot that will not slip and when adjusted snugly against the horse's neck will not come off. The other end can be tied to something solid with a slipknot just as if the horse had a halter on. It is best to try to have a halter available so you won't need this knot, but a good horseman should know the bowline for emergencies.

Bowline

Moving Around the Horse

Once the horse is securely tied with the slipknot, you must never go under the halter rope to get from one side to the other. To most, this seems like the safest place to be. It can be very dangerous and many people have been hurt by horses lunging back. Broken poles have hit the horse handler in the head, or the horse that does not break loose may lunge forward once he hits the end of his rope. Thus, he may land right on top of the handler with his front feet.

Go way out...

Or directly behind

Never under the halter rope

The correct way to move from side to side of a tied horse is to go around its rear end. There are two ways to do this.

1. Go way out around the horse and come up to him on his opposite shoulder. This seems like the safest possible way, but can be less safe than the other alternative if a horse turns his rear end as you approach him.

2. It is best to go directly behind the horse by putting your hand on his back and working along his side until your arm is on his rump, then go right around his rump. Some kicking horses cannot be handled in this manner, but most horses can.

When going around the horse's rear end, stay within a foot or less of the horse's tail and legs. If you are two to two and one-half feet away, you'll feel the maximum force of a kick. At three to four feet you may get the end of the kick, which would not be as great. By staying close to the horse, a kick will be more of a push than a kick because he hasn't got the force of the thrust in motion.

Most horses will not kick if they know where you are. Never touch a horse on the rear end or legs without first speaking to him and making sure he realizes you are there.

Horses sleep in a standing position and sometimes appear to be awake when in reality they are in a sound sleep. If you startle a horse into wakefulness by your touch, he is likely to jump, kick or run away. This won't happen if you speak to the horse before touching him, and make sure he looks at you or in some way shows that he is aware of your presence. Be sure the horse always knows where you are and what you are doing when you are around him.

Grooming

Always groom your horse before riding. This will prevent dirt and manure from caking under the belly where the cinch goes and on the back where the saddle could cause irritation. By grooming just these places it is possible to avoid the problems of soreing the horse from dirty skin, but a good horseman will groom the entire horse.

Many tools can be used when grooming; the metal or rubber curry, and the hard bristle and soft bristle are the most common brushes. For the mane and tail there are the scotch comb, the metal comb and the large hair comb. Items such as sponges, mitts, towels and wool cloths could also be a part of your grooming equipment if you show your horse. Each tool has its time and place and you should become familiar with all of them.

Because sensitive bone is close to the surface on the head and lower legs, never use a metal curry on these places. Usually a hard bristle brush will get them clean. To remove patches of mud, one can carefully use the rubber curry. If there is only a little foreign matter on these areas, a quick brushing with a soft bristle brush is adequate.

When grooming a horse, face the front of the horse when working from the shoulder forward. Face the rear when working from the shoulder towards the tail. Always place your closest hand on the horse. This hand will be an indicator of the horse's movement. You can feel the horse getting ready to move and you have time to move before he steps your way. By extending the hand on the horse you are able to push away from him or let him push you away. Without a hand on the horse while you are grooming, you have no way to anticipate movement and may be bumped, knocked down, and possibly get stepped on. **Always keep the near (or closest) hand on the horse while grooming**.

Through the winter and into the spring the metal curry can be used on the horse's body because of the large volume of hair over the body. Once the horse has shed off in the spring, however, the metal curry should not be used for more than mane and tail cleaning. Some horses even find a stiff rubber curry too rough on their skin in mid-summer. Sometimes a brush is all that is needed over the entire body, depending how dirty the horse is.

Mane and tail combs tend to take out many hairs with each use. Prolonged use can greatly reduce the horse's volume of tail and mane. This is especially a problem with some Appaloosas, which lack heavy mane and tail hair to begin with.

Always untie the horse to brush his head. Do not stand in front of the horse while cleaning it. Always remember to stand by the neck or shoulder and reach up to brush his head. Many horses do not like their heads fooled with. If the head is clean, leave it alone. On the other hand, some horses would have you brush their heads all day. Be considerate of the horse's likes and dislikes, but if his head is dirty get it clean. On the other hand, don't stand and brush his head all day and forget his rump.

When brushing the legs, never squat down next to the horse. Always bend at the waist to reach the lower legs, keeping the near hand on the horse at all times. Some of you readers may need some exercises just to get limber enough to groom the horse, let alone ride him.

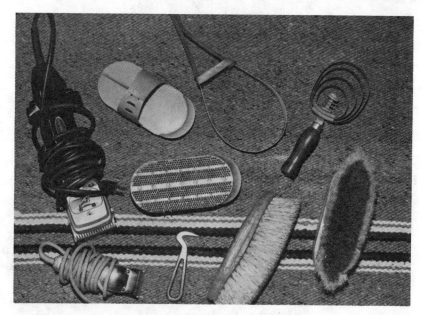

Grooming equipment

For grooming, it is especially important to have the horse tied the proper length (eighteen inches of rope). If he is tied on too long a line he will be able to reach around and bite you on the rear end as you lean over to brush his legs. When brushing his back legs, try to keep yourself as far forward as possible and still be comfortable and functional.

If the horse's body is quite dirty or dusty, a circular motion with the curry will loosen the dirt and bring it to the surface. Then a brush can be used to flick away the dirt. With a brush, short flicking strokes are best, since this will lift the dirt up and sweep it away. One must learn to use either hand with equal dexterity. This is true for many maneuvers with the horse.

When cleaning the tail pull it to one side or the other. Do not stand directly behind the horse. If the horse is touchy about his tail you can sometimes put him against a fence and pull it through to work on it. Tails get long and straggly as they grow. Some people desire a long flowing tail on their horse, while others prefer tails pulled up to the hocks. Pulling the tail is an art in itself. Some use a dull knife and make many passes through the thick tail to thin it. Others take a pair of

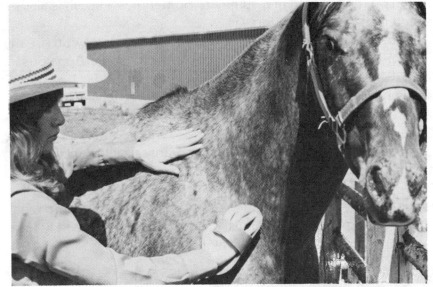

**Face front from
shoulders forward.**

**Face rear from
shoulders back.**

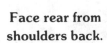

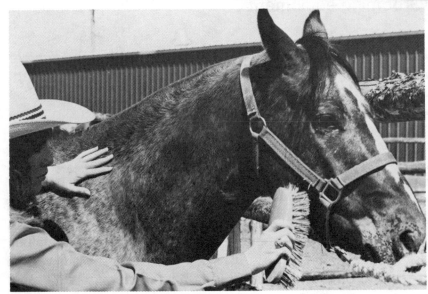

Grooming the head.

scissors and whack at it. Still others pull it out with their fingers and obtain many blisters as a reward.

The metal curry is a good tool to use on tails. By holding the lock of hair to be pulled securely with one hand, the curry can be pulled down and through the lock until the hand holding the lock is reached, then sharply drawn across the lock. This will thin the upper lock and leave it the length to the hand. After thinning and shortening the upper locks, the total length of the tail can be shortened and thinned in the same manner. The fine hairs at the top of the tail head can be pulled by hand, if a show-styled tail is desired.

The mane can be thinned and shortened in the same manner or rated and pulled by hand. Some show styles call for a four- to five-inch mane that has a straight line. Others still like a roached mane. This can be done with electric clippers. The hair should be cut right down to the skin level, leaving a patch at the withers and a patch forward of the ears, called the foretop. Even if a mane is desired, a bridle path should be cut. This should be cut about the length of the ear.

The legs can also be groomed cleaner by clipping the hair from the knees and hock down to the hoof line with electric clippers. This is not necessary with a fine-haired horse. A pair of scissors can be used to trim the fetlock and around the coronet.

Brushing the legs

Cleaning the tail

Saddling the Horse

There are some differences of opinion about using a pad or blanket against the horse's back. Some pads are made of blanket material but have padding, which should satisfy both groups. At any rate, if a pad is used, it is placed against the horse with a blanket on top of it.

First, check the pad to make sure it is clean and free of dirt, burrs and manure. Standing on the near (left) side of the horse, place the pad firmly but gently on the horse's back about six to eight inches ahead of the base of the mane. Then slide the pad back in place. Each horse will need the

Set the pad...

Place the blanket...

pad in a different place, depending on its withers and shoulder positions. Proper placement know-how comes with experience.

Next place the blanket over the pad so that the front of the pad and the blanket are even. If a 30" x 60" blanket is used, always fold in the middle and place the fold to the front. Always remember that pad and blankets should protrude ahead of the saddle one to one and one-half inches.

Pick up the saddle and place the off (right) stirrup on the horn. Then pull the front and back cinch over the seat of the saddle. Set the saddle firmly but gently on the back of the horse. The front of the bars of the saddle should ride against the rear of the shoulder blade. By placing your hand under the pad, the shoulder blade can be felt. Then feel the front of the saddle for the bar. By matching the front of the bar to the back of the shoulder blade a good position can be selected.

Prepare the saddle

By setting the saddle a little forward and rocking it back in place it will be easy to locate the proper position.

With the left hand on the horse, go around behind the horse to the right side. Take down the cinches and the stirrup. Check to make sure the cinches are straight and clean. Also check to see that the front cinch centers in the center of the heart girth between the front legs. If it doesn't, adjust the cinch in the billet so that it does fit properly. This is very important, because if the cinch is set uneven it may cause a sore on the horse's side.

With the right hand on the horse, go back around to the left side of the horse. Put your hand under the front of the blanket and pad and lift up an inch off the withers. This will give a little air to the withers and prevent the saddle tightening from binding the blankets tight against the withers. Put the left stirrup up on the horn. Take the latigo from the keeper, then reach under the horse's stomach and get the cinch by bending at the waist while facing the rear. If you tie the horse too long, he can reach around and bite you on the rear end. You will only do it once. If you were to face the front, a horse could cow kick and get you with a back leg. Run the latigo through the outer portion of the cinch ring; starting next to the horse, run the latigo towards you, and then up to the dee ring on the saddle. Insert it through the dee ring from the outside toward the horse. The latigo then goes back down through the cinch from the horse's side then out through the same place that it went through the first time.

Now pull the latigo firmly, but not until it is tight. You will tighten it again before you ride. Place the pin in the cinch ring through the hole in the latigo, then place your hand between the first and second loop of the latigo and pull down. This will set the pin so it won't come out.

157

Saddle in position...

Check the pad...

Take down the cinches...

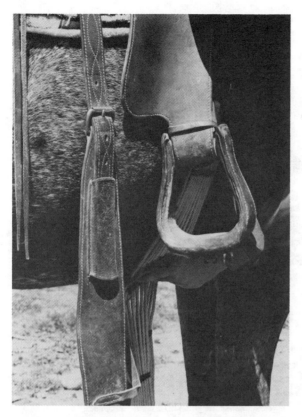

Center the cinch...

Take down the latigo...

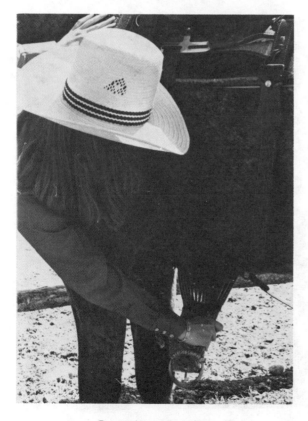

Get the cinch...

Then twice around and buckle

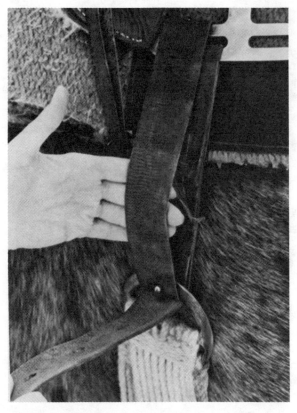

Set the pin...

Leave a little slack

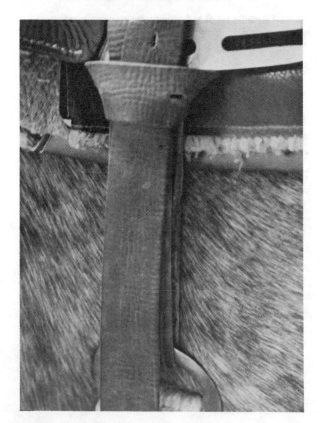

If no buckle, tie a knot

Catch the back cinch...

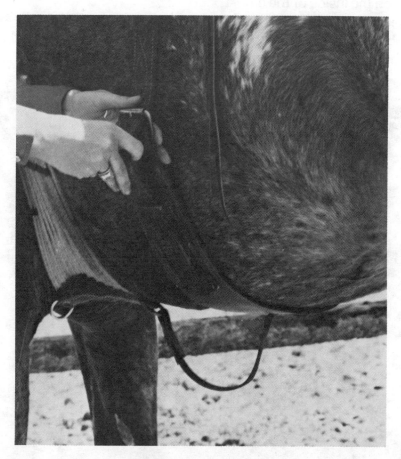

And buckle

If there is no pin in the cinch, the latigo can be tied off by bringing it up to the dee ring and passing it through the same as the first time. Bring it out on the left side then across the dee ring entering the dee from the rear and continuing up and forward then down through the loop that was made by the pass across the dee. Before final tightening of the cinch, the bridle will be put on and the horse walked a few steps.

Reach back under the horse and catch the back cinch. This cinch is tightened until it is just touching the horse's barrel. Remember to do up the front cinch and then the back cinch, never the reverse. Always make sure the front and back cinch are connected. The connecting strap in the picture has too much slack and should be shortened.

Bridling

Pick up the bridle and make sure it is straight and you know where everything goes. Place the headstall over your arm, then lay the reins over the arm as well.

Untie the horse from the post and unbuckle the halter. Now slip the halter down so the nose of the horse is no longer in it. Do it back up around his neck.

Put the headstall of the bridle in your left hand with the reins still over your arm. Holding the crown piece or top, catch the horse's nose between the cheek pieces or sides of the headstall. Now place the right hand between the horse's ears, taking the crown piece in the right hand. The left hand now holds the bit with the first two fingers. The little finger supports the chin strap while the thumb is held on the inside of the bit.

Without bumping the teeth, move the bit towards the teeth. Before the bit touches the teeth, insert your thumb in the side of the horse's mouth. Press down with the thumb on the gum. As the horse opens his mouth pull the bit into his mouth with the right hand.

Unbuckle the halter...

Catch the nose...

Hold the bit...

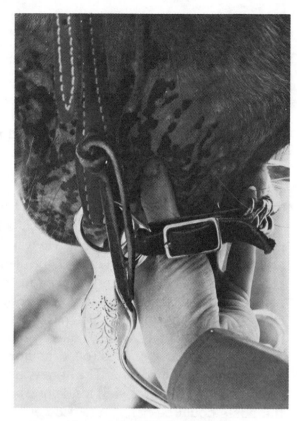

Insert your thumb...

Pull the bit in

Tip the ear forward...

Move the left hand to the crown piece and, using the right hand, tip one ear forward and place it through the crown piece. Then the other ear is placed in the same manner. Remember not to fold or bend the ears, as this will make the horse hard to bridle. Next, do up the throat latch.

If you are riding out in the cold, you should warm the bit in your hands before putting it in the horse's mouth. A cold bit can freeze the tongue to the bit and cause a sore mouth. In the summer time, cool hot bits to hand temperature before using.

The bridle should be adjusted so that the bit just wrinkles the corner of the horse's mouth. The chin strap should have about one finger space between it and the horse's chin. The throat latch should have about two finger spaces between it and the horse's throat. Now that the horse is bridled, remove the halter and hang it on the post.

Some people leave the horse tied while bridling but this can cause problems if you bump the horse's teeth and he pulls back. He will fight the tie rope. If he is not tied he may take a step backward but will have nothing to fight. This will lessen the chance of getting hurt when bridling.

Different bits have different chin strap connections. Where the chin strap connects will make a difference on how tight it should be. Some bits will not need to be pulled up into the horse's mouth as much as others. If you have questions, always check with a competent horseman.

A fellow brought a horse to the University to train that was real hard to bridle. The only way he could get the bridle on was to let the horse start to eat grain and then grab his ear and ear him down while he bridled him. The horse was terrified of being bridled of course.

By bridling the horse with a side pull bridle that could be undone over the poll or crown piece, the horse could be handled (A side pull is similar to a hackamore in that it doesn't have a bit). Each time the horse was bridled he was rubbed over the eye and down the nose. There had to be a bond of trust formed. Soon the horse could be bridled with a bit and regular headstall by anyone in the class.

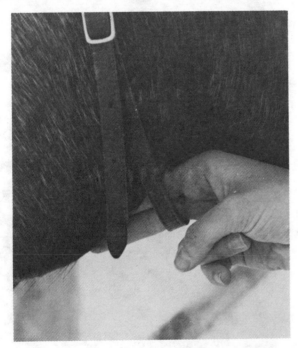

Throat latch - two fingers clearance

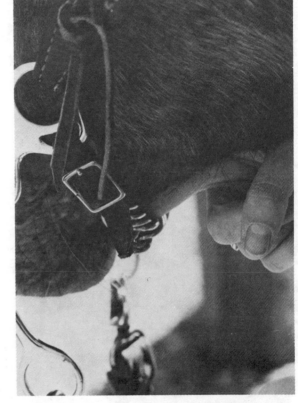

Chin strap - one finger clearance

164

At the end of the quarter, the owner came to pick him up. At that time he was shown how easy the horse was to bridle and told just how to do it. He stepped up to try, the horse went to pieces. The horse didn't trust that man because of past experiences that he still vividly remembered.

It is so important that you choose the right headstall and bit for your horse and then bridle him in a way that is comfortable to him. Most horses will act bad if they think they are going to be hurt or if they are being hurt by a bit that is too narrow or a chin strap that pinches on the bit.

The single ear headstall has been in style a long time, mainly for looks and for the fact that you can't lose the throat latches. Some are made with a small ear hole that irritates the ear. Lately some students have been hurting the ear putting it through the small hole. Then there is always the dummy that wants to put both ears through the small hole. A brow band headstall, where both ears go in the opening, is easier to adjust for most people so we are going to the brow band bridle. These don't irritate the ear quite as much.

Remove the halter

Mounting

After leading the horse a few steps, tighten the cinch by pulling on the latigo, then reset the cinch pin in a tighter hole. The cinch should be neither too tight nor too loose. It is hard to set a standard, but one way to tell it is too tight is to slide your hand between the horse and the inside of the latigo. If you can't get your finger in, it is too tight.

A horse with a high wither will hold a saddle from moving from side to side while a low-withered horse will permit a lot of side motion with equally tight cinches. On some high-withered horses, the saddle slides to the rear. These need a breast collar (strap that is attached to both sides of the saddle in front and around the horse's chest) rather than a tighter cinch.

Before mounting always check the stirrup for proper length. One way to get an approximate length is to place the stirrup under your armpit, then set the extended fingers on the seat jockey at the base of the pommel and cantle. If you can't reach the seat jockey you need to shorten the stirrup. If your hand extends past the seat jockey up onto the seat, then you need to lengthen the stirrup. These adjustments are made on the leather strap behind the fender.

Standing at the horse's left shoulder, take the reins in your left hand and place them on the horse's neck about eight inches forward of the saddle. Take the slack out of the right rein and

**Lead the horse before
tightening the cinch
and again before mounting.**

Check the stirrup . . .

then shorten the left slightly tighter. This is to make the horse turn towards you if he starts to walk off. By turning your wrist you can turn him even more without moving your hand from his neck.

Face the rear of the horse. With the right hand, reach around the stirrup to grip the inside of the stirrup. Now turn it around to face you. Lift your leg up and place your foot into the stirrup. The right hand is now placed on the horn. Wiggle the saddle - this is a cue to let the horse know that you are going to mount so he will stand still. Bounce around until you are facing forward with your right side next to the horse. Keeping your head up, give a bounce on your right leg moving your weight onto the left leg. Once you have raised your body up on your left leg, swing the right leg over and sit down easy. Do not flop into the saddle. If you let your head and shoulders lean over the horse and he moves toward the left side, there is a good chance you will lose your balance and go over on your head. Once you have obtained your seat and caught the right stirrup with the right foot, adjust the reins in your hand so they are even.

If you are long-legged, you will have no problem getting your left foot into the stirrup; therefore, it may be easier just to place the right hand on the horn facing the front and place your foot into the stirrup. Now the move upward is the same as previously discussed.

Another way to mount is the jump mount. This is easily undertaken once you learn the above method. The only difference is how you place your left foot into the stirrup. With the left hand on the reins and the right hand on the horn, face the front so that you are turned directly facing the open stirrup. Lift the left leg toward the stirrup at the same time you jump with the right leg. Stand close to the stirrup and jump straight up. Don't stand back and try to jump towards the horse. There is much more chance of kicking the horse with your toe and startling the horse.

Turn the stirrup . . .

Place foot in . . .

Grip the horn . . .

167

Face forward...

Bounce up...

Sit down easy

Jump Mount Sequence

169

Once the left foot is in the stirrup, let the right leg go back down and touch the ground. Then mount as above.

Many people like to mount with the left hand on the horn holding the reins, and the right hand on the cantle or back of the seat. They say they feel more secure. The only problem is that they have the rein hand in a position where they cannot adjust if the horse moves off. They also have to let go of the back of the saddle to get their leg over the seat. In this position the left hand is all they have for balance. If the horse moves, they will generally lose their balance. In any case, this type of mount generally results in your rear end hitting the seat hard, which will startle the horse.

Dismounting

Bring the horse to a dead stop. Take the reins in the right hand, then place the left hand around both reins on the neck at the same place as when mounting. With the right hand on the horn, wiggle the saddle from side to side under you. This is a cue to the horse that you are going to get off and he is to stand still.

Position your left foot in its stirrup so you have good footing but will not hang up. Free the right foot from the stirrup. Step into the left stirrup, raising your body out of the seat. Swing the right leg over the horse's rump. The right leg should be bent at the knee and raised at the hip. Do not wipe your foot on the horse's rump. Now step down to the same place you mounted from. Do not turn around facing the rear when dismounting, because you have less control and knowledge of what the horse is doing. Once your right foot is on the ground, take the left foot out of the stirrup. Do not jump out of the left stirrup on the way down. You may startle the horse and cause a problem.

Once you are on the ground, let go of the right rein and hold the horse with the left. Reach under the neck with your left hand and pull the right rein down. With both reins in the right hand about eighteen inches or more from the bit and the slack in the left hand, you are ready to lead the horse.

Stop...

170

Swing leg over...

Step down

Putting Away the Horse

The first step in unsaddling is to place the halter around the horse's neck and do it up. Do not tie the horse up. Next, undo the throat latch on the bridle and with the left hand on the crown, push the headstall off the horse's ears. Do not continue down with the headstall until the horse has released the bit from his mouth. If he holds onto the bit, you can insert your right thumb into his mouth and he will let go of it. Had the headstall been pulled down before the bit was released, the chin strap would have created a bind on the horse's chin and the bit could not come out. The horse would throw his head in the air from the pressure. If this happens, let go of the headstall and the bit can fall out. You may need to take hold of the bit to get it out. It is always best to do it

171

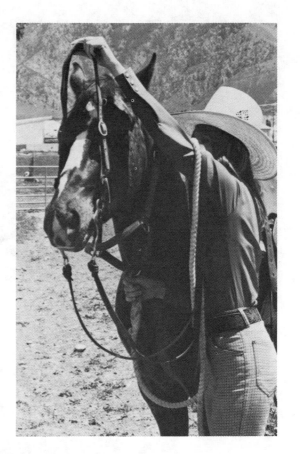

Do up the halter...   Slip bridle over ears

right and this won't happen. From this situation it is easy to see why it is best not to have the horse tied while unbridling. Once you have the bridle off, you can put it over your arm while haltering the horse.

Now that the bridle is off, unbuckle the halter and catch the horse's nose in the nose hole of the halter, then do it back up. The horse should then be tied up again as previously discussed.

After the horse is tied up, put the bridle on the saddle horn or take it back to the tack room and hang it up. Do not lay it down in the dirt or tangle it up.

Put the near stirrup on the horn and unsaddle. Always remember to undo the back cinch first, then loosen the pin in the latigo and undo the latigo. Be sure to thread the latigo back through the keeper. No one wants to handle a latigo that has been dragged through the mud and manure before being put up.

With the left hand on the horse, go around to the off side and put the stirrup over the horn and the cinches over the seat. Returning to the near side, lift, do not drag, the saddle, blanket and pad off all at the same time. Take them directly to the tack room and place them in their proper place. Do not set them down in the sand or dirt.

If you are tall you can omit pulling the cinches and stirrup up because you can hold them up out of the dirt as you return to the tack room. Doing so, however, will prevent walking on or tripping over them as you carry the saddle.

Tie up the horse...

Thread latigo through keeper . . .

Undo the back cinch...

Lift up...

Slide off...

Keep cinches
out of dirt

174

It isn't always necessary to brush the horse down after the ride, but if he is hot and wet it is a good habit to get into so you don't put a hot horse up before he has cooled out. Drinking too much water at this time could cause colic or even founder.

After he is thoroughly brushed, untie your horse and lead him to his corral. Enter the corral with the horse, then turn the horse around facing the gate. Now take the halter off. In this position the horse cannot beat you to the gate and escape.

Reining the Horse

Types of Reins

(1) Split reins are two separate reins. They can be made of leather, nylon, cotton or other strong material that can be held easily. They can be flat or round, depending on the likes and dislikes of the rider.

This type of rein is held in the left hand. The reins run from the bit through the thumb and forefinger and out the bottom of the hand. The forefinger can be placed between the reins for best control. Place the right rein on top and the left on bottom. This is in keeping with the flow of the reins. The slack of the reins run down the left side.

Split reins can also be held with the rein coming from the bit passing up through the bottom of the hand and out the top. This hold gives more forceful control, and in young riders may cause hard or forceful hands.

A left-handed person can reverse his hands on the reins. This will leave his main hand free for roping or playing games if so desired.

(2) A roping rein is a single rein that runs from one bit shank around the neck and back to the other bit shank. This type of rein is used by ropers and goat tiers so that they can dismount and leave the horse without the rein falling on the ground. Barrel racers also use them because they are easy to handle and impossible to drop on the ground while racing.

This rein is held with the hand over the rein. The hands can easily be changed in barrel racing.

(3) The romal and popper is a combination of the split rein and the roping rein. There is a roping type rein with a whip-like extension in the middle where it is held. This type of rein is used mainly in the show ring. It is held by passing the doubled rope rein up through the left hand, with the right hand holding the popper.

Methods of Reining

(1) The indirect or neck reining is a cue type of reining. It is used on horses that are trained to the cue of the rein on the neck. To neck rein a horse, move the right rein against the right side of the neck to go left and the left rein against the left side to go right.

Using this method the rein is pushed lightly against the neck when the inside front leg starts to leave the ground. A horse being neck reined cannot be forced by more pressure. The added pull on a neck rein will only pull on the bit on the opposite side that you wish to go. It will pull the horse's head out of position and cause the horse to misbehave. A green broke horse will not respond to this type of reining.

(2) The direct rein or plow rein is the type used for draft horses. The left rein is pulled to go left and the right to go right. This is used on colts or problem horses. More pressure can be applied to the reins and the horse can be guided by controlling the direction his head is pulled. This should be done with a pull-release-pull method instead of a hard, constant pull. The pull is punishment and when the horse moves his head the release is a reward. As the horse stalls, the

Split reins - out the bottom

Roping rein

Romal and popper

Left turn   Right turn

pull again is the punishment. Soon the horse learns that a small pull means to turn and he actually turns on the release. The pull is just the cue to start his head.

When using this type of reining one should use a snaffle bit, side pull or hackamore (not to be confused with a hackamore bit). These head gear permit a direct pressure to the place you want it.

(3) Squaw reining is the use of both neck reining and direct reining. Here again the snaffle bit, side pull or hackamore should be used. This type of reining is used to teach a horse that has learned direct reining how to neck rein. The left rein is pulled to go left, but the right rein is pressed against the neck. Soon the left pull is eliminated and the horse is working off the neck rein.

When direct reining, take hold of both reins in the left hand with your thumb up and ring and little finger between the reins. Reach down the right rein with your right hand and take hold of the rein with your thumb up. Take the slack up and take hold of the horses mouth. Pull until you get a step. As soon as you feel the horse move his foot, release the pressure an inch. Then pull again until you get a step. Use the pull-release (punishment-reward) method to teach him what you want. A constant pull will teach him little.

To turn left, slide your right hand up the right rein to where it comes in contact with the left rein. Open your two top fingers and take hold of the left rein, too. Now reach down the left rein with the left hand, remember, thumb up.

Do not lean over to the side you are turning to. This puts weight on the shoulder you are trying to get the horse to lift. Your weight should be on the inside back pocket.

There are two methods used for squaw reining. The first and most widely used is to take the slack of the left rein and run it over the neck to the right side. The slack from the right rein is run to the left

177

side. The right hand holds the right rein and the slack of the left rein. The two hands each holding a right and left rein. This works well for most riders but it tends to cause the rider to lose his grip on the reins and the reins soon are too long. A skilled rider will be able to gather up this slack but the beginning trainer will get himself in trouble with the loose rein.

Another alternative for two handing a horse is to take the rein in your right hand with thumb up and lower two fingers between the reins. This is just the same as the direct-rein method. With your right hand take hold of the two reins about 10 inches down from your right hand. Be sure the thumb is up on this hand, too. Take hold of the left rein and pull a couple inches of slack in the left rein out of your right hand.

The left hand is now holding both ends and the left rein. Release the left rein from the right hand and you have the reins set for this method of two-hand riding.

If you find your reins getting long, take hold of both reins with the right hand and take a new position with the left. This is easy and quick. This method also allows you to slide one hand farther down the rein if a direct pull is needed.

Generally, the inside rein should be raised and pulled inward toward your stomach when squaw reining, because this tips the nose to the inside and raises the head, neck and inside shoulder.

Direct Rein

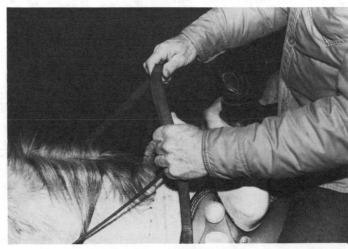

Squaw Reining

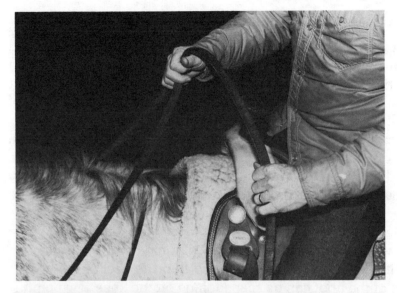

Step 1

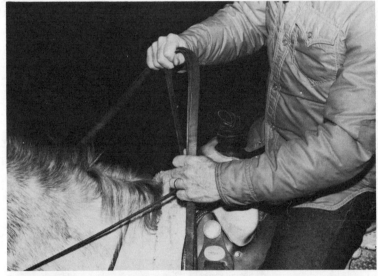

Step 2

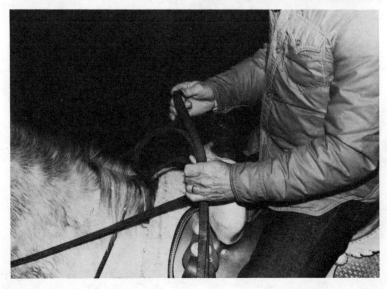

Step 3

Posture and Cues

Basic Body Position

First stand up in the stirrups, then let yourself back down into the saddle by bending knees and pushing heels down, with your crotch maintaining most of the contact with the saddle. The chin should be up, the shoulders back, and the chest out. The small of the back is held in. This is what is referred to as sitting tall in the saddle. The opposite of this is a slump position with the small of the back out. This sets a person on his back pockets in the back of the saddle.

A horse normally carries sixty-five percent of his weight on the front feet. If the rider is to be a part of the horse when riding, he must distribute his weight in the right places at all times. On a walk the rider can sit up tall without riding the back of the saddle. This puts the weight slightly forward so that approximately sixty-five percent of the rider's weight is being carried by the horse's front feet.

There should be leg contact from the crotch to the calf. A short-legged person will be able to maintain contact over his entire calf, while a long-legged person will only be able to maintain contact at the upper portion of the calf. The leg should be bent so that the heel of the boot is directly below the shoulder and the toe of the boot can be seen looking off the knee. By pointing the index finger of the right hand straight down while sitting up straight, you can see if it points at your heel. If not, make the proper adjustments. The foot should be placed so that the ball of the foot is on the tread of the stirrup with the heel lower than the toe. The foot should point straight ahead or not more than thirty degrees out. Female riders tend to point their toes out more than males because of their basic skeletal and muscular structure. Because of the masculinity in some females and the femininity in some males, however, there can be all variations of toe positions in each.

The more the toe points out, the more the knee will be rotated out and away from the fender, thus, the less leg contact a rider will have. Losing leg contact causes the rider to be looser on the horse and more apt to come off in a quick turn or under a situation that requires quick leg responses.

Good Posture

A good leg exercise on the ground is to get your legs in an upside-down "U" shape with your toes up and your heels right below your shoulders, spreading your legs apart so a horse can fit in. To get in this shape you must bend your legs and lower your hips. If you try to stand straight up you are going to be in an upside down "V" rather than a "U". This will cause you to have no calf contact on the horse.

Upside down U

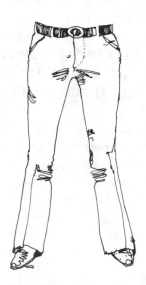

Upside down V

An exercise for the foot that helps is to stand on the bottom step of a staircase and look upstairs. With the ball of the foot on the step and the heel hanging over, bounce on the foot, letting the weight go down into the heel. This will pull the muscles in the back of the leg. As you ride, you should have the same type of pressure in the back of your leg and in the instep of your foot.

Now that your legs and feet are in the proper position, let's move to the arm and hand. The arm should bend at the elbow to about a ninety degree angle. Tall riders will have a greater than ninety degree angle and short riders may have less than a ninety degree just to clear the horn.

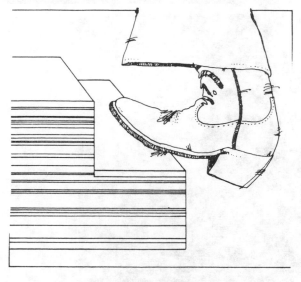

Bounce a little!

When using split reins, with the index finger separating the two reins, the hand is held so that the rider sees the thumb and forefinger as well as the top and part of the back of the hand. The hand should be positioned just above and in front of the horn.

With the elbow tucked into the body, the forearm and hand can swing left or right in a horizontal plane to turn the horse. The hand should never drop below the saddle horn when turning with the rein in this position. Remember, you are not turning the horse with force, but rather with the rein as a cue.

For a rider to have good contact with the horse, the hand and arm must be supple and relaxed. The reins should be held so that contact is maintained with the horse's mouth but without putting pressure on the bit. The difference between a tight and a loose rein is only one inch, or even less for finished riders. The horse must be able to trust the rider's hands in order to feel relaxed while working.

Some riders like to ride with a slack rein or a rein that hangs in a loop below the neck. If the horse has been trained to respond to very light cues, the rider can get away with this in slow, easy work, but most riders gather up the reins for fast reining, with the exception of cutting horses that are trained to work with slack rein.

Reins too tight

Reins too loose

Having contact with the mouth does not mean you need to apply force to turn. Force will cause more problems than it solves. A horse will soon become afraid of the reins and throw his head in the air to try to get away from the pull. This fear of the rider's hands can prevent the horse from learning any other type of cues because the horse is so worried about being jerked and hurt that he cannot concentrate on anything you are trying to teach him.

Turning The Horse

A horse should learn to turn in response to three cues: (1) hand or reins, (2) body weight shifts, and (3) leg pressure. Before starting a turn, always collect the horse (get his attention) by a slight pull on the reins followed instantly by a release, then go right into the turn. This action is known as the dwell. The dwell tells the horse to get ready to do something different. Some horses tend to daydream or lose contact with the rider when walking. The dwell brings the horse back to the alert position.

To turn left, the right rein is pressed against the neck. Always turn your shoulders so that you are facing into the turn. The body weight is shifted slightly into the left or inside back pocket. The horse can feel the slightest movement of weight so teach him to work in response to small shifts instead of throwing your weight around to get the horse to turn. The left foot moves away from

Leg and foot cueing

the left side of the horse so he feels he has some free space. The outside or right leg and foot are pressed against the horse at the cinch or heart girth area.

The horse's basic desire is to move away from pressure so he will move away from the right leg and into the free space you provide by shifting your left (inside) leg away from him. He also moves away from the right rein. By putting your weight in the inside back pocket, you put your weight over the pivot foot thus helping to stabilize the inside rear foot.

There is a great deal of controversy among horsemen as to where the weight should be placed when turning a horse. Some riders like their weight on the outside of the turn because they feel a need to release the weight off the inside leg of the horse so he has freedom to move. Others do not change the weight, but rather hold it directly over the horse's center of balance and move with the horse while others prefer the pattern mentioned above. Each method can produce horses that turn well. The horse learns from repetition. With consistent reining and leg cuing, all three approaches can develop a good turning horse. A finely trained horse will turn when given any one of three cues (hand, leg or body).

Another cue that can be used on a turn is a voice command. A kissing or clucking sound used whenever you want more action will cause the horse to wake up and move at a faster pace. This is true especially if this cue has been used in conjunction with discipline so that the horse knows if he doesn't move he will be disciplined.

Use three cues when turning

At A Walk

While at a stand, collect the horse. Then squeeze with your legs while making a kissing sound. This will move the horse forward. Once on the move, sit tall in the saddle. Do not lean forward or backward but stay right over the horse's movement. Do not rock your body with the horse's swinging motion. The hand should be allowed to move with the swing of the horse's head. This may be accomplished just with the fingers, depending on the horse's action. If the horse is not moving into the bit put more leg, and if necessary, foot pressure to him.

Maintain constant leg contact with the horse. Watch his ears to see what he is looking at and where his attention is focused. After a while you will be able to feel changes in muscle movement

At a walk

through the saddle that will also indicate what the horse is going to do. With experience, you often can anticipate a quick lateral movement and be able to compensate so as to stay with the horse.

Stopping

The horse needs a pre-cue to let him get ready for a stop. This pre-cue is followed immediately by the stop cue so the horse cannot "scotch" or start to slow down before the stop. The pre-cue used is a voice command "Whoa", followed by a pull on the reins, then a release, then another pull. This first pull is firm and its release does not totally remove pressure from the mouth. The second pull is to set the horse in his tracks. He is not to move off from where he stopped until you cue him to do so. At a walk, leg and body cues are not quite so important to the horse, but the rider should practice so they come naturally in all gaits. As you pull the reins, let the small of your back out, drop your hips

Cue on third leg position. Stop on fourth position.

Make him come to a full stop.

185

(take a deep seat). At the same time, lower your heels and squeeze your legs. Do not stand up in the stirrups or move yourself away from the saddle at any time.

The rider's hand should be kept low, just above the saddle horn. In order to do this during a pull, the reins may need to be shortened in the rider's hands. Learn to walk up the reins with your fingers. Hold the reins tight with the little finger, then reach the thumb and forefinger forward on the reins and grip with them, moving the rest of the hand up to that position. The process is similar to a snail crawling. (For a more advanced method see Chapter Nineteen.)

Backing

The same cues are used to back the horse as to stop him. First, give him a verbal pre-cue of "Back". Then move your weight slightly forward and squeeze your legs. At the same time, use the pull-release, pull-release technique.

Your weight is shifted toward the horse's front so that his rear legs will have less weight to lift. Backing does not come naturally to a horse. If given the alternative, a horse will very seldom back, but rather will turn and go, or try to go forward.

Backing

By squeezing his body with your legs you encourage the horse to draw his rear legs up under him. This makes it easier for him to carry the weight that is put on his back legs when backing. If he does not get his back legs under him, which shifts a larger than average portion of his weight onto them, he will have a hard time backing properly. Many horses with straight back legs have a problem getting them up under them. Horses that are camped out in the back (legs sitting too far to the rear) have even more problems.

The pull-release on the rein is a punishment and reward system. The pull makes the horse start the backward movement. The slight release while he is moving back tells him he is doing what you want. If he stalls, pull until he starts to move again, then release. Soon the horse learns to back after the first pull, during the release. Some get so good you have to cue them to stop backing.

Riding The Trot

The trot is the easiest gait on the horse for covering ground. It is like jogging for a human. It takes less total exertion than faster gaits and can be maintained for long periods of time. Because it is easy on the horse, a rider should learn to be comfortable with this gait. There are three different methods of riding the trot: (1) stand, (2) sit, and (3) post.

The stand trot is ridden with all your weight on the balls of your feet with the heels down. The reins are shortened because you have moved closer to the head. Your body slopes forward with the shoulders and chest directly above the horn and your rear slightly poked out. The contact with the seat is on the crotch, not the back pockets. The horn is always held for balance with the right hand. This is one time when you can hold the horn and not be criticized. When riding the stand trot, the shock of the vertical movement of the horse is absorbed in the rider's knees and ankles. When a stand trot is done properly the rider's head moves in almost a horizontal plane. Your legs, however, soon tire of this position, so an alternative is needed.

A sit trot requires lots of practice. The object is to try to keep your pants against the saddle from one calf around to the other while the horse moves up and down. It is best to practice this method at a slow, collected trot or jog.

The reins are held slightly tighter than a walk (but without giving more than contact pressure). This permits instant control of the horse's speed. Some horses can be trotted on a loose rein if they are trained to maintain a slow speed, but many need a rider-control system. The rider's elbows should be close to the body. If the elbows bounce, the shoulders will bounce, and then the whole body bounces. Therefore, arm, shoulder and chest muscles must be under control. The hips and waist must absorb the shock of the horse's vertical movement. As the horse moves down from the rider, the rider's pelvis and small of the back rock forward stretching in an upward tall seat. Then the pelvis and the small of the back collapse backward as the upper torso is compressed downward as the horse moves up. In other words, as the horse comes up, you press down into the seat, but you remain in total contact with the seat throughout the gait. If done properly, the rider's body moves with the horse.

When the rider does excessive bouncing, the horse will be upset from the pain in his back. Gentle horses will usually try to trot faster, causing more bouncing. Green horses may bolt and run or start bucking. That is why it is best to learn to ride on gentle horses that have had a lot of use and are settled and dependable.

The post trot is a combination of the stand and sit trot. The reins are held about the same as for the stand trot to start with. The right hand can hold the horn. From a standing trot position, move yourself towards the rear of the saddle until your thighs contact the cantle where it enters the tree. Do not sit on your pockets to make contact with the saddle. Use the crotch and base of the pockets to make contact with the saddle. Next pull your waist forward as if you wanted to touch the horn with your belt buckle. Let your hips break forward, then backward. The forward and backward movement is timed to a one-two rhythmic beat with the rhythm of the horse. You should come up with the horse's outside front foot. This can be timed by watching the shoulder movement.

From the knees down, the legs do not move. From the knees to the shoulders the body moves forward and backward. This movement absorbs all the vertical movement of the horse. The rider should never lose contact with the saddle from one calf around the seat to the other calf. The seam of the pants under the thigh stays in one place on the saddle, while the outer thigh rolls forward and backward. The crotch slides back and forth on the seat, but maintains contact with the seat. If done properly, the rider's shoulders and head will not move much from a horizontal line as the horse trots along. This method of riding the trot is by far the easiest on the horse and rider for extended periods of trotting.

Once the rhythm is mastered, you can let go of the saddle horn and just enjoy the ride. This method of posting was used by the old-time cowboys on the big ranches. When long distances had to be covered in desert country before any cattle were sighted, the easiest gait for the horse was a trot. These cowboys knew if they wanted to have enough horse left to do the day's work and then to take them home, they had to conserve their horse's energy.

Stand trot

Sit trot

Today some dudes look at a western rider posting and see it as bouncing. The method is sometimes laughed at by these same people. After a few miles on a brisk trot, most of these dudes will drop their horse to a walk, because their legs are tired from the stand trot and their stomach can't take any more of the sit trot. Then, as the rider posting the trot keeps on going, they stop their laughing.

The sit trot, however, is the only method permitted in a Western Pleasure class at a horse show. It is questionable why the post is not permitted when an extended trot is asked for, because a sit trot can only be maintained for a short time at an extended trot. Many riders cannot ride an extended trot and still stay sitting in the saddle even for short periods of time.

Stopping at the trot can be accomplished just as discussed in the section "Stopping". Correct timing of leg and body cues become much more important at the trot, however.

Lope and Gallop

To ride the lope you must first know something about the lope. This gait is generally considered a fast three-beat rhythm. First the hind foot hits, then the other hind foot and the opposite front foot strike at about the same time. Next, the remaining front foot strikes the ground. The last front foot that strikes the ground is said to be the lead. A horse that lopes with the left front foot striking the ground after the right foot is in the left lead. If the right front foot strikes the ground last, then the horse is in the right lead. In a right lead, the right back foot lands slightly ahead of the left back foot and vice versa for the left lead. Some horses do, however, travel in one lead in front and another in back. This causes an uneven, rough gait. It is known as being disunited.

If you watch a loose horse that hasn't been broke, he will take either lead with no hesitation.

The horse should always be on the lead to the inside of a circle or turn. A barrel horse must be on a right lead for a right turn around a barrel and a left for a left turn. In pole bending a horse will change leads on each pole. In cow cutting, the horse changes leads with each direction the cow takes. From this you can see it is important that your horse knows both leads and knows how to change leads.

Some people will say their horse is just right footed and will only take the right lead. More likely the horse could take either lead before he was broke. It is the rider that is just right handed. On the ranch a horse is usually loped on a straight away. A cowboy will always lean the same way and kick the same way each time he lopes. Soon the horse will learn to lope only on one lead. Horses broke in this manner are very hard to train to use both leads, but they can learn and will work well with proper training.

Right lead initiated by left hind leg.

189

Right lead foot last to leave ground.

Some people make their horse afraid of the lope and want to run away every time they let them out. A good cure for this is starts and stops. By loping short distances such as twenty or thirty steps then stop and start again, soon the horse will learn he is not going to run, so he will relax and slow down. Your bouncing is one reason the horse gets excited and tries to run away or go faster than you want. You must keep from bouncing, by learning to ride the rhythm and balance of the horse without shifting your weight or fighting the saddle.

Once you can tell the lead by watching the horse, try to tell the lead when you are on his back. If you relax, your lead foot will go slightly ahead while the off lead foot will be straight down. If you need to kick the horse, it is always done with the outside foot, not the lead foot. Your lead foot should stay in the slightly forward position with no pressure against the horse. A well trained horse will change his lead if you change your feet position.

To properly ride a lope, you must know that the back outside foot of the horse initiates the lead. Many people think it's the front inside foot, so they just worry about the front end. They end up missing back leads on every other change.

If you want to position the rear end properly for the lope, you must teach him to two-track or half side pass. This is moving the horse's body at forty-five degree angle to the fence. This will make a double set of tracks. To get the horse to do this, hold the head towards the rail but allow him to go down the rail. Now push his rear end away from the fence with your heel closest to the fence, pushing in at the back cinch. Put your weight in your back pocket closest to the fence. If he doesn't respond, have someone come along the side of him and poke him just in front of the flank as he moves down the fence so he will move his rear end over and make the two sets of tracks.

Once you have him two-tracking in both directions freely, you are ready for the lope. On the two-track you were holding the horse to a walk with the reins. For the lope, just put the horse in the same position and give him a release on the rein pressure. Your leg next to the fence should be pressing him at the back cinch and the other leg should be away from the horse so he has a place to move into. Your weight should be on the outside back pocket. He will be free to lope and in that position he will not take the wrong lead. Lope a short distance, stop then start again.

Remember, for a left lead, rein the horse's head lightly into the fence, moving your lead foot away from the horse and slightly forward. With the outside foot, press or kick the horse at the back cinch. This will move the horse to the left, causing the horse to lead with his left feet. Your outside leg should remain straight down while loping. Do not let this foot go forward or you will end up sitting on both back pockets in the back of the saddle. Instead, you want to keep up over the front of the horse because that is where the forward momentum is going to place the majority of the horse's weight. You will also find that the front end does not have as much bounce in it as the back end.

Another problem many riders have is that they bounce hard as the horse trots for a time prior to loping. It is much better to have the horse trained to go from a walk to a slow lope. If there is excessive bouncing at the trot, the horse, if gentle, will not go into a lope. If he is a young, unsettled horse, he may try to run away or even buck. A rider's bouncing hurts the horse and can cause so much frustration that the horse will actually try to unload the rider. A rider that is having this problem should stand trot until the horse is into the lope. It is, however, more difficult to properly cue the horse into a lope if you are stand trotting. It is recommended that you try all these maneuvers on a trained horse to get the feeling before trying to teach a green horse the maneuvers.

As soon as the horse starts to lope, let his head come back to a straight line in the direction of travel. After a horse learns his leads and the cues, the head need not be reined to the outside.

The gallop is a four-beat gait just a little faster than the lope. Some horses go from a trot to a gallop without having a collected lope. The rider rides the gallop the same way as the lope discussed above.

The flying change of leads, or change of lead while the horse is in a lope, is a more advanced manuever that will not be discussed here. At this stage, if a change of lead is desired, let the horse drop down to a trot for a couple steps, then change directions, picking up the proper lead and loping slowly in that circle.

Some trainers prefer to let the horse turn his head toward the inside of the circle. If the horse has been taught his leads by loping in tight circles, his head must be to the inside to get him to lope in this tight circle.

Cruise Control On Your Horse

When you get a horse finished, he should have a speed or cruise control on him. You should be able to set the speed you want, then drop the reins and he will remain at that speed until you step on the brake or touch the accelerator.

Riders have a hard time staying off the brake or the gas once they get the desired speed. If they bounce their rear end on the saddle or their hands on the reins they keep upsetting the cruise control.

To train a horse to have a cruise control, you need to work on cues for each gait. Say "walk" and start out on a walk. Give the horse a loose rein. That means an inch or two of slack. If he starts to go faster than a walk, stop him and back him a step or two and start again. Keep this up until he understands he must stay on a walk.

For a trot, say the word "trot", and let him move out on a loose rein. Use the word "easy" and check up the reins if he moves out too fast. If he is aggressive at the trot, just stop him and back him, then start again.

You have to make the horse realize you control the gas feed. If you want more speed, such as an extended trot, you should ask for it. Make him stay on the extended trot. If he breaks to a lope, stop him and start again.

Once your horse realizes you have the gas and the brake you have a big advantage in riding. It is so much more fun to ride at your desired speed, rather than being taken for a ride at your horse's speed.

For a lope, use a kiss to obtain the gas needed. A kiss means to speed it up. Use it in a turn, a side pass or a lope. Don't use it at a walk or a trot, however.

If your horse is standing still and you cue him for a lope with your outside leg back at the back cinch and kiss, expect him to give a little hop and step right into a slow lope. Don't ask for the lope on a tight rein. He knows he should slow lope unless you give him more gas.

If your horse won't slow lope, work on the stop, back and start again. Show him there is no use getting in a hurry because there is no place he is going to go. It takes many stops and starts to get the point across.

Remember to use a loose rein. You have to learn to trust your horse, just as he has to learn to trust your hands. If you bounce your hands in his mouth he will get all kinds of signals. He won't know what to do. Learn to let your hands float away from your body so the rein pressure, or lack of it, doesn't change.

You can always get a horse to run, so why not work on controlling his speed to a slow lope. Check him and say "easy" to slow him a little. If he is really aggressive, stop and start over just as soon as you feel him moving out on you. If he is close to being slow, use a light see-saw action on the bit and say "easy". As soon as he backs off on the speed, stop the see-saw.

You can see all the stopping that is involved. That means you'd better have a good stop first. Make him stop square, then back.

When stopping say "Whoa", wipe the reins upward on his neck and take a deep seat. Relax your knees so you don't rise out of the saddle. If you fly forward, your horse will have to stop on his front feet to catch you.

As soon as you feel him stopping, say "back". Make him realize that is the next movement. That will make him come to a complete stop so he can back. Try it, it works.

Punishment and Reward

Punishment is thought of as spurring, whipping or jerking. Any of these can be used to extremes, but spurs, bats and pulling can all be effective forms of punishment. Some people like to take punishment to the extremes with hitting and kicking the horse, while others like to starve them as punishment. These are uncalled for and not a true horseman's way of punishing.

Training horses can be a good place to learn a lot about yourself. It is easy to punish a horse harshly when you lose your temper. The mature approach is to control your emotions and analyze the situation to see if you have asked more of the horse than he was capable of performing with his level of training. Would more repetitions of the desired act do more good than a whipping? Ask yourself this before punishing your horse.

Many times the horseman hurts himself more than the horse when he loses his temper. If you can't control yourself, you will never be able to control the horse you want to use or train.

Starving or abusing a horse has no place in training. If you can't handle a healthy horse, you better find another job or activity because you will never become a horseman.

To be effective, the punishment must be administered at the time of the wrong behavior. The horse must be able to relate the punishment directly to the behavior. But in all cases, the horseman should be very certain that the horse is at fault, rather than himself.

Remember, there is a difference between punishment and cruelty. Creating fear in the horse is the poorest way to train. It is better to have the horse relaxed and willing, rather than tense and ready to explode all the time.

Rewards should accompany desired behavior. These rewards should be given consistently for the desired behavior. The horse must relate the reward to the right action, just as he relates punishment to a wrong action. Consistency is the best policy, for horses learn by repetition.

A reward can be a pat on the neck or a quiet, reassuring voice. Always provide the same reward for a given activity. Soon the horse is desiring to please because he wants the reward. It is much better to have him work to earn a reward rather than to avoid a punishment.

Both punishment and reward must be used in training horses; each has its place. A horse must never be allowed to run over or abuse you. In any relationship, mutual respect precedes love or affection. You must gain the respect of the horse and most of the time this requires some punishment to convince the horse you mean business. Soon you can gain his confidence and affection with reinforcing proper behavior with rewards. Many trainers try to put on an act of being hard or having little affection for the horses they train. Most trainers, if they accomplish anything, do form a bond of mutual respect and even affection for their horses.

Remember, horses learn through repetition, so keep reinforcing his memory and habitual action with repeated lessons, always accompanied by punishment and reward as needed. As the training proceeds, the need for punishment will decrease or be absent, while the reward is continued after each maneuver.

Think About Your Riding

Have you ever danced with a partner and found their feet in the same place as yours were? Their body was always blocking your moves or forcing you to pull them around the floor? Without coordination, rhythm and balance it is hard for two people to function well when doing anything. It is the same way when trying to ride a horse. If you are not turning with the horse then he has to drag you around the turn. When he stops, if you fly forward he will start stopping on the front end because he has to catch your weight as you go forward.

You have a large responsibility to become a partner who is sharing half the responsibility of being in the right place at the right time. You must cue your horse to tell him what you want him to do, but don't force him. Think of it as making something like backing easy for the horse to do, and going ahead difficult when you are asking him to back. You don't force him to back, just create a barrier so he can't go forward. Maintain pressure on the reins and squeeze your legs until he gives a step back, then release the pressure as he moves back. Set the pressure again until he gives a step. Let him find the hole or open area and move into it. Don't pull and pull until he backs from force. This principle applies to all training. Always make what you want him to do easy and the opposite action difficult. Provide a hole for him to go to by moving a leg away from one side while you block his move to the opposite side with your other leg.

How many times have you been told to go do something without good instructions. You usually end up going back to get better instructions. The horse has to understand what it is that you want him to do, so you must make sure your instructions are clear and put in a way he can understand. Make sure you don't ask more than his level of training will permit him to understand.

If your horse is having a problem with a maneuver it is usually you that is creating the problem. It is funny that a horse can take both leads so easily running loose in the pasture, but put a rider on his back and he can't do anything right.

Remember, when you are training a horse you have to over exaggerate cues so the horse will easily relate to them. The horse learns fast to voice cues so always use them in training. Once the horse learns the companion cues, such as legs, hands and body for a maneuver, you can omit the voice cues for shows.

You must ride with an awareness of what the horse is focusing his attention on. If his attention is not on you, you can't direct it. By watching his ears you can tell where his attention is focused. You want his attention but you also want a relaxed horse. If you are not relaxed your horse will not be relaxed.

Just try getting on an unfamiliar horse and see how tense you are. You find the horse is tense too. There is no way for one of you to relax if the other one is tense. No positive learning can occur as long as you or your horse are tense. There will be negative learning occurring though. The horse will block against you, out of fear, and you will turn around and block against him out of your fear of what he might do.

When you are afraid, you always give confusing cues such as squeezing your legs to hold on when you want to him to slow down. You tell him one thing with your legs (go) and another with your hands (stop).

Give your horse something to do when you are riding him. He is always learning, so make sure he is learning good behavior. If you are asleep, he is going to have idle time and in that non-positive time he will be learning negative activities.

Your frame of mind has a lot to do with how well you communicate with your horse. Don't go out to do some training because you and your spouse or parents have just had a fight. That is no time to train. You can't take your frustrations out on a horse one day then expect he will be calm and quiet the next day. It takes a lot of riding to repair the damage you do out of frustration.

At a time like that just go for a ride and show him some country without asking too much of him. Remember the horse is not your slave, he is your partner and that is the only relationship in which you will ever be able to accomplish any training.

Train when you have peace of mind and are in a happy mood. Pick times when you are not pressed for time. Sometimes you have to try hard to create such an atmosphere to work in. Without it you just won't do the horse any good. Remember you can't teach experience; it only comes with time. So put the time in and the experience will come.

Will Rogers said, "The outside of a horse is good for the inside of a man." Just make sure it is good for the inside of the horse too.

CHAPTER SEVEN
SAFETY

Most accidents with horses can generally be traced back to carelessness. It may not be the carelessness of the person that is injured. Many times an innocent bystander or rider can be hurt because of someone else's careless handling of his horse or someone's thoughtless actions around a horse. Therefore, it is important to work around your horse and to ride in a defensive manner. This means taking extra precautions that might not be necessary if you knew you were all alone with your horse and could be sure no one or thing would appear by surprise. But you never know this so it is best to take extra precautions whenever you work with a horse. You need not be afraid of a horse, but you should respect his ability to hurt you and take precautions so that he doesn't.

Catching, Leading and Tying

Try to approach a horse from his left front side. If the horse has his rear to you, do not walk up and touch him. Always make him turn around. Touch him on the shoulder or neck first, don't dab at his face.

When leading a horse, use a long lead rope, but hold it about a foot from the halter and never wrap the rope around your hand. Walk at the side of the horse. Do not let the horse pull you. Do not try to out-pull the horse, for he is stronger and you will lose.

Tie the horse with the proper length of rope using a slipknot that can be easily released. Make sure he is tied far enough away from other horses to avoid fights. Never go under the halter rope or step over it while the horse is tied up. Once he is tied, go around behind him with your hand nearest to him on his rump and walk close, rather than at arm's length.

Saddling and Bridling

Set the saddle on the horse's back, do not throw it. Don't let the cinch or stirrup hit the horse on his right side. It may startle him or the cinch ring may even injure his knee if it hits hard enough. At any rate, it will cause him to be jittery about being saddled next time. Always do up the front cinch first, then the back cinch. Remember to undo the back cinch first when unsaddling. Tighten the cinch a little, then walk the horse a few steps and cinch the saddle tight enough so it won't slip, but not so tight as to make the horse uncomfortable. Walk the horse a few more steps before mounting. Check all your equipment to make sure that there is no excessive wear, especially on the latigo or right billet.

Mounting

Adjust the stirrup so it will be close to the proper length if you don't know exactly where to set it. If you do know where to set it, make sure it is adjusted correctly, so you don't have to get off and do it again.

Always have the reins adjusted so you have control of the horse. Do not let your foot get caught in the stirrup by putting your foot in up to the heel of your boot. Sit down easy. Do not bounce in the saddle. Make the horse stand until you are ready to move him. Never mount inside a low building or near an obstacle, such as a tree or fence that the horse might run you into.

When dismounting, always collect the reins in your left hand and make the horse stand still while you get off. Take some of your foot out of the stirrup. Step down soft and easy. Don't scare the horse as you come off. Let go of the right rein as soon as you are on the ground.

Hold the rein about twelve to eighteen inches from the bit while leading a bridled horse. If he pulls back, do not jerk on him, but rather give him rein and move with him easily while talking calmly to him. Pulling hard on a bridle may cause the bit to hit the teeth or pinch the tongue.

Riding

Never drop a rein or you may lose control of your horse. If a horse starts to run away, always circle him even if it requires pulling one rein sharply around. Always keep your heels down so your weight is applied to the stirrup on a slight incline at the ball of your foot. This is very important, for a horse may be frightened and jump to a side without notice. If your heels are down, you have much more balance and stability. If your toes are down, you have little chance of staying on and more chance of catching a foot in the stirrup.

If your horse is afraid of obstacles, try to quiet him while facing the obstacle. Then move him past the obstacle as easily and quietly, but firmly, as possible. Do not punish him or he will have a bad experience and may be worse next time. If he attempts to run, stop him and make him face what he is afraid of.

When going up or down hill, always walk your horse. If the terrain is rough, be sure to slow down, take it at a walk and, if necessary, get off and lead your horse. Never ride or stand closer than one length's distance from the horse in front of you. If you get closer, the front horse may kick your horse or even you. This can happen when you are on a horse in a group that is standing still. Always make your horse stay parallel to a horse by his side. Don't let him turn so that you and he are facing the other horse's hind feet.

Walk your horse to the stable. Never let him run the last mile home or you may be knocked off at the barn door.

Stirrup Hobble

Does your saddle hurt your feet and ankles when you ride? Possibly it is because you need to have your stirrups turned. Short legged people especially have a hard time keeping their stirrups turned enough because they have to shorten the fenders so much.

Unless you buy a handmade saddle, which will generally have preturned stirrups, you are going to need to turn the fenders. First take the stirrups off and wet the fenders three-quarters of the way up to the seat. Use a deep bucket and put the fender right into the bucket. Wet the adjustment strap as well. Don't worry about getting them too wet.

Now the fender is wet, put the stirrups back on and turn the fenders and stirrups around about thirty-five degrees past perpendicular (the position you would ride in). Mold the fenders to arc around where your leg will be.

Many people use a broom handle to stick through the stirrups to hold them. This will permit the stirrups to go back to perpendicular which is not enough turn.

I have designed a stirrup hobble that you place on the stirrups to keep them set at thirty-five degrees past perpendicular until they dry. You can purchase one by writing to: J'Wayne McArthur, ADVS Department, Utah State University, Logan, Utah 84322-4815 and send a check for $5.00. The stirrup hobble will be sent postage paid.

Once you have the stirrups turned it is most desirable to place the stirrup hobble on your saddle while it is not in use. This will maintain the turn in the fenders so you don't have the pigeon toe feel every time you mount up.

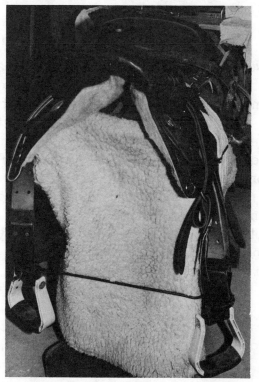

Use a Stirrup Hobble

Some saddles have fenders which are too long for a short legged person. You may need to cut three or four inches off the top of the fender, then reattach the fender to the stirrup strap at the top. Do not move the stirrup up to the wide part of the fenders to shorten it, because this causes the fender to be much harder to turn. There should be two and a half to three inches of narrow leather below the wide part of the fender for the stirrup to fit in and turn.

More kids have a poor ride because of the length of their stirrup or the inadequate turn of the stirrup. These kids might place high in a show if only their saddle properly fit them. They are not knocked down because the saddle doesn't fit, but because they polish the saddle (moving backwards and forwards) or bounce bad. Both of which could be corrected, or at least helped, by proper stirrup length and seat size.

It is not adequate to use Dad's roping saddle and pull the fenders up high so there is no movement in them. Johnny will slop and bounce around in the big seat. He will have to reach with his toes to find stirrups that are lying parallel to the horse's side. Johnny needs a saddle that fits if he is going to do his best.

Don't look for the big heavy saddle that must be made good because it is so heavy. Find a light weight barrel racing or cutting saddle for them. They can feel the horse much easier through these thinner leathers and they can even lift the saddle.

Most cutting saddles are made on sixteen or seventeen inch trees, a youth generally needs no more than a fourteen inch tree. The Buster Welch tree in a fourteen inch seat gives a great feel of the horse.

You do not have to have a silver plated saddle to win. You just have to have one that fits you and your horse.

Also, when riding in the hills your knees tend to get tired. You can raise or lower your stirrups a hole and it will relax your knees. Change them every once in a while and you will enjoy the ride more.

Common Sense Horsemanship

Control your temper. Never punish a horse for something that was your fault or due to the horse's inexperience. If you are going to discipline your horse, do it at the time the horse needs discipline. Make sure it is timed so the horse knows what the discipline is for.

Do not tease your horse. He could become mean and unpredictable. Be kind, gentle, and firm with him and you'll develop a responsive horse.

Each horse is an individual. You should know your horse's personal temperament and peculiarities. If you let anyone else ride him, be sure to tell them about his characteristics.

Never yell or make loud noises when you are riding or working around your horse. This can upset him and lead to jumping, bucking or kicking.

Do not race or try any cute tricks while riding, especially when you are riding with others. You can cause someone else to get hurt.

If your horse hasn't been prepared for riding by proper feeding, shoeing and conditioning, you may be unsafe on his back. He may also be in danger of injury because of your lack of attention to his needs.

Remember you must get a horse's attention and have his respect before he will freely do what you want. And only after you have his respect can you gain his affection. Without respect, there can be no affection.

CHAPTER EIGHT
So You Want to Train

There are few accomplishments that can equal the satisfaction of training and showing your own horse. Once you have felt the satisfaction of riding a horse you've trained yourself, you will never want to ride anything else.

Halter Breaking

Barn-raised horses are used to having humans around. Because of their inquisitive nature they learn not to fear man. This is brought about by seeing the person who feeds them bringing hay and grain walking among them. Many times the young horses will come up to smell or touch, and sometimes even try to taste this person.

The range-raised horse, on the other hand, has not had this contact with man. Just the sight of man or any movement by him will put a range horse in a fright. These horses, therefore, take special care and different handling before they can be brought to a point where they can be halter broke and ready to saddle.

Barn-Raised Horses

Foals can easily be handled from birth to two months of age. After that, they start getting stronger than you are.

You can press them in a corner next to their mothers and slip a halter on them. It helps to have someone lift their tail up over their back once you have them cornered. This seems to make them stand still.

Use a long rope on the halter so you can control the foal without being too close. Lead the mare and let the foal follow. Turn the mare and pull a little on the foal to turn it.

After the foal is coming to the pull and not fighting the rope, you can tie the foal's lead rope around the mare's neck, using a bowline knot. Lead the mare around and the foal will follow. Turn the mare many times so the foal will be pulled around.

You can repeat this for a few days then start leading the foal yourself. Pull him from one side, then pull from the other, getting a few steps each way. Do not try to pull straight ahead at first. Always reward the foal with a pat on the neck and a kind word when he comes to the pull.

As soon as he starts to give to the pull, you can tie him to a strong post at about his eye height. A good precaution to use in tying a foal up for the first time, is to use a rubber innertube to go around the post twice, then nail it in place. Tie the foal's lead rope (about two feet long) through the two wraps of innertube, but not around the post. Tie the mare close by to make the foal more at ease. When the foal pulls back he will not hit a solid point but will find more resistance as he increases his pull. Soon he will stand on a loose lead. This is the time to groom the foal, pick up his feet and in general, gentle him. The foal will learn to respect the rope from this procedure, because he is taught through punishment (pressure on the halter) and reward (slack rope with no pressure) that it is easier to stand on a loose rope than to hang back.

What you've done so far has not taught the foal to lead, but only to respect pressure on the lead shank. Now start working with him each day. Face the way you want him to travel. Don't face him while you're pulling. When he comes, stop and pet him and tell him that was good. If he doesn't want to come, give him a firm pull to the side and then a quick release. Do not try to out-pull him. As soon as he starts moving from side to side you can start moving him more forward. This may be the second or third day. Don't get in a hurry to have him leading forward. Just because you did it the first day doesn't mean the foal is halter broke. It takes a lot of repetition to reinforce the concept in the foal's mind. Soon he will lead forward easily. Now move to his shoulder and make him walk up with you rather than behind you. Once you accomplish this you have taught him to lead.

Older, barn-raised horses, such as yearlings, take more work, more strength, and more repetitions to accomplish the same results. Some breeders would rather wait until they are ready to work with a colt before they halter break him. They feel they can go right on with his training rather than turn him out until he is a yearling or nearly two-year-old and find he has forgotten most of what was taught at two months.

Range-Raised Horses

The first thing you have to worry about with a range horse is how to catch and get a halter on him. Some like to run the horse in a chute and halter him there. Some range horses would try to tear the chute down and in the process injure themselves. If you can get a halter on without getting hurt or hurting him, this can be a good way to start.

Another way, that is not recommended, is front footing him. Once the front feet are roped, the horse is thrown to the ground and held down while a halter is put on. This can put the horse on the fight, causing the halter-breaking period to go much slower than necessary, and involving considerable fighting of the rope.

Many old timers would rope a horse around the neck and choke him until he was about to pass out. Then they put a halter on and gave him some air. This took some of the fight out of him.

Some Indians used this method, and as the horse started to gasp for air the Indian would breathe into the horse's nostrils and talk to him, while putting on a war bridle. As the horse regained his senses, he would think the Indian had given him back his air. This method works well, and a horse given this treatment will have a desire for your smell or breath. He will walk up to you when you walk into the corral and put his nose up to your face and smell. It makes it easy to catch him. Some people would say that this method sounds quite hard on the horse. It doesn't damage the horse or put him on the fight any more than he would be if you just rope him, and it may prevent him from damaging you. You must let him know you are in control from the start, or you will have much more trouble trying to train him. Once he is caught, put a halter or a hackamore on him, then you can go ahead and work easy with him, trying to get his trust. Always stay in command and don't let him turn away from you. Pull him from side to side a step at a time. The hackamore with a rawhide nose band or rope nose band will make him pay attention to you. If he acts reluctant, just give it a jerk and he will change his mind.

Another way is to rope the horse in a small corral with a six-foot fence. Once he is caught he will start running and wanting to fight the rope. Don't pull on the rope, just let him run on his own while you stand in the middle with your end of the rope. Once he stops, start walking up to him slowly while talking quietly. If he wants to run some more, let him. He will soon turn and face you again. Start to walk up to him again while putting a slight amount of pressure on the rope so he holds his head toward you. If he tries to run, move with him holding his head in and he will soon stop and face you again. Work your way up the rope again and touch the horse's neck. Stay away from his head for a while. Loosen the rope on his neck a couple of inches and talk to him. If he moves away, start talking your way up the rope again.

Once you can walk up to the horse easily you can either put a halter on him or make a come-along halter with the rope, by pulling a foot or so of slack from the loop around his neck,

200

Say "Come here"

Blow into his nose

putting a turn in it, and raise it over his nose. Now you can more easily control his head, but you do not want to put him on the fight by jerking him around. You are going to have to take the time to teach him to trust you, not fear you. Pull him sideways with short tugs and releases. Once he takes a step, walk up and loosen the pressure on his nose and pat him on the neck. Move to the other side and tug on that side until you get a step. Never ask for more than one step to start with and never pull straight ahead.

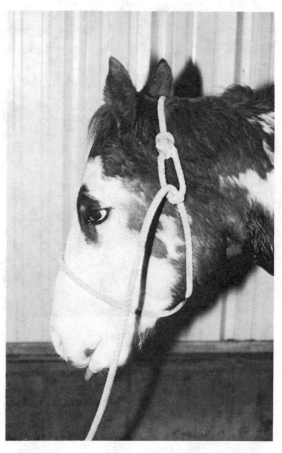

A quick come-along or war bridle.

You are now pulling him off balance and he is moving toward you only to catch his balance, but if you reward him for this action he will feel he wants to come to the pull. This takes time and patience. If you have neither, then get someone else to train your horse because that's the name of the game.

An older horse, such as a yearling or two-year-old, can take longer periods of handling with positive results. Spend an hour or two the first day with such a horse. Follow this up each and every day for a week or more if needed. Pull and reward and pull and reward until he is following you around. When you're leading him, always face the direction you want him to go. Never face him and pull him towards you. When you face him, he should learn to stop and stand still.

Don't tie this kind of horse up solid during his early training. If he hits the rope hard he may start fighting it and you don't want that. Once you feel he has learned to respect the rope, snub him to another horse and pony him around in a bigger corral or pasture. This will further reinforce his respect for the rope. Now he is ready to be tied up. Most likely he will not fight the rope. Be sure to tie him high and on a relatively long line (about two and one-half feet to play on) since a shorter one will most likely make him nervous and try to hang back. The truck innertube around the post is a good precaution here, also.

If you are having a problem with the horse not moving forward after you have pulled him from side to side, you might want to try one of the aids discussed in the "Leading" section.

Horse Loop

Catching wild or spooky colts can be a big problem for the novice trainer. Roping skills are not practiced by many horsemen. It is becoming a lost art, especially some of the specialized loops such as the horse loop previously used to rope horses in a corral.

The horse loop is so easy and smooth to use that it looks like there is no skill to it. This loop can be thrown with any type of lariat, either left or right handed, from the ground or from horseback.

To rope horses, start the throw by building a loop half again as large as a calf loop. Set the loop face up on the left side of you. The hand should be palm up.

Start the swing as if you had a bucket of water you wanted to swing around you. You will have to start out at arm's length with a little speed to create centrifugal force. Swing the rope out to the left as you start up. The arm is outstretched and comes up diagonally across the body. By the time it reaches the right side it is up head high.

The palm is up all the way around. Start bending your elbow and lowering your hand as it goes around your right side, then around your back. The loop should flow out from the ground and remain straight out and away from your body all the way around.

Don't try to throw this loop. The momentum developed going around your body is the force used to reach the horse. It is similar to the hammer throw in track and field events.

As the loop comes around your back and around your left side, your hand turns so the palm is still up and open. Keep the palm in this position as you extend your arm for the throw. Let go of the loop when your arm is completely outstretched in front of you.

The total action of this loop is smooth with no jerks or quick up and down motions. The loop should be round and open from the time you start with it on the left until it approaches and settles over the animal. The aim of the loop should be slightly higher than the object being roped. The loop is to settle down over the horse and not hit him in the head. He will not be afraid of being roped if you throw a clean loop.

As the rope settles over his head, pull the slack quickly. If the slack is not pulled, there is a good chance of roping him low on the shoulders. This will give him even more of an advantage in a tug of war.

Ranch horses learn to face the roper once they are caught, then walk right up to the roper. Sometimes, just throwing the rope on them, even if you don't catch them, will cause them to come right to you, if they are rope broke.

Roping the horse is also a good way to teach the horse to face you in the corral. After a few times of being roped when he gets his head in the corner, he will face you and watch you when you walk into the corral. If he faces you, walk up and catch him. If he turns away, rope him again.

Practice this loop on a six or seven foot fence post. More accuracy and distance can possibly be obtained with this loop in less practice than with any other loop.

If you want to practice for roping calves off a horse, begin by roping a bucket on the ground. Start with the loop hanging down from your left shoulder. Bring it up over the imaginary horse's head and around, just as above. This time you can use a smaller loop and hold your slack line with the right hand as the loop goes out to the calf. Pull your slack and dally for the drag to the branding fire.

This loop was used on cattle associations where there were mixed herds of cows with different brands. The calves were let mother up, then a brand could be read on the cow as the cowboy roped her calf. As he pulled it to the fire, he would call out the brand. The brander would get the proper iron out of the fire and stick it on.

If the roper had swung his loop around his head a few times, he would have had everything stirred up and calves would not have stayed mothered up.

If you can't rope well, or even if you can and don't have good corrals, you need to figure another way to catch the horse. Some leave a halter and long lead rope on him once he is caught. This can teach the horse to carry his head to the side or to jerk his head up every time he steps on the rope. If you must use this, try not to use it very long.

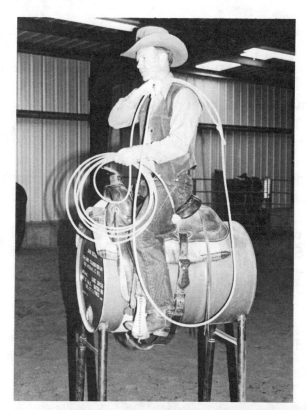

Practice the horse loop off the barrel horse.

The barrel horses will make for practical dry roping. Dallies can be taken without worrying about losing a finger.

Another way is to leave the halter on and use a grain bucket. When the horse sticks his head in the bucket, snap the lead strap on without disturbing his eating. When he takes his head out, he is caught. If he is halter broke but just won't come up to you even with grain, sometimes a stiff wire with a hook in the end can be used to hook his halter, if you can get that close. If the horse doesn't jerk away, you are all set.

Cornering a horse with the help of another person can work if the horse isn't too spooky. Some horses will run right over the top of a man, or will just keep turning their rumps to you and kicking if you touch their rumps. These kind need the rope. Teaching them to face you when you walk into the corral is imperative. The rope will do it. Some like to use a whip on the rump or flipper crotch or even an old B-B gun to hit him on the rump. These will all make him face you, but they don't catch him for you.

The old timers would put a soft hackamore on an unbroke range horse and tie him with a long, soft cotton rope to a log small enough for him to move, but too big to pull any distance. They would then put him in the middle of a pasture and leave him for a few days, coming back to water him once in a while. This made the horse respect the pull of the rope, and he would be quite easy to handle on the end of the rope from then on. Some did get hurt and all of them got a few rope burns even with the soft cotton ropes. The process made him respect the rope, but did not teach him to lead.

If you start by tying a range horse solid to a post, there is a good chance he will hurt himself while fighting the rope. Some have even pulled their neck out of joint and gone around for six months with a crooked neck.

Once you feel the horse is halter broke, don't just turn him out and think he will remember all that you have taught him. Catch him at least once a week and lead him, tie him up and groom him. The more often you work with him the better he will be. Then when you start to break him, he will be halter broke and gentle.

CHAPTER NINE
RESTRAINTS

When you are working with spooky, nervous horses, when shoeing, grooming or doctoring, it is sometimes necessary to use restraints to provide safety for yourself as well as the horse. Up to now, in what has been discussed, most horses would not have needed restraints other than the rope or halter. As the training effort increases, there are many times when a simple restraint will be needed to make the horse immobile. This may be needed to speed up his learning. Sometimes you need to let the horse fight himself rather than you. He has so much strength that you cannot possibly physically restrain him. If he wins a tug-of-war or a foot-picking-up lesson, then the training problems are increased. Remember, the horse must respect your ability to control him. You can teach bad habits much more easily than good ones, so be sure you are in control of the situation even if it means using a restraint.

Tying Up A Hind Foot

In the following sections such as grooming, sacking out, saddling and mounting, the practice of tying up a hind foot is very common. This is known as scotch hobbling. First, take a twenty-five foot cotton rope of 3/4-inch diameter. With one end, make a loop around the neck just in front of the shoulder. Tie a bowline so it will not slip. Now, if the horse will allow you to pick up his foot, put a heavy strap with a metal ring in it around the off side back ankle. You can use an old cinch and go around the ankle twice. Run the loose end of the rope through the ring or cinch rings. Run the end of the rope through the loop that is around the neck. Now pull the hind leg off the ground about five inches. The horse will generally fight this, so have the horse untied and have someone holding the lead rope on the same side you are working on. Do not fight the horse's head; he needs his head for balance. Do keep him turning toward both of you but let him fight himself rather than you. Once he has stopped fighting, tie a slipknot around the two ropes going down to his foot.

To get the best of the situation without a fight, you can have the slipknot pre-tied to the proper length so when you put the strap around the ankle the rope is already tied off properly. If you tie it so that the leather hobble hangs just below the horse's knee, it should be about the right length.

Lift the horse's off back foot up and take the hobble under the belly and fasten it to the pastern. Let it down easy and step out of the way. You can have someone hold the halter rope up but don't pull on it. Let the horse fight himself until he settles down.

The safest way to tie up a back foot is to tie the right foot to the left side, or the left foot to the right side. This brings the foot up under the belly and in this position the horse cannot kick you as you walk by the back foot. If you tie up the left hind to the left side, the horse can lift his leg up to his belly and kick out the length of the rope. If you are working close, you could get kicked.

If he won't let you pick up his hind leg to put the strap on, make a loop on the ground and let him step in it, then pull the foot up. Or you can let him step over it so the rope is between his hind legs, then bring it around and through the loop on the neck. Sometimes this is too slow and you get in trouble. Both of these methods can result in rope burning the horse's hind leg. The 3/4-inch cotton rope will help reduce the burning, but once you pull the foot up, don't let the horse pull slack away from you. This can be done by putting a bind on the rope by going up through the loop on the neck from the horse's side, then out and up, over and around the two ropes going down to the hind leg.

 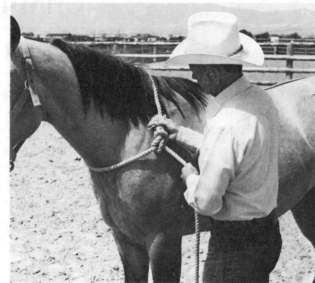

Tie a bowline

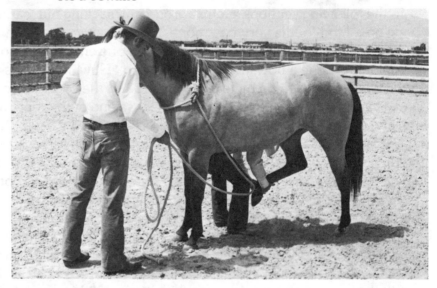

Fasten strap around pastern

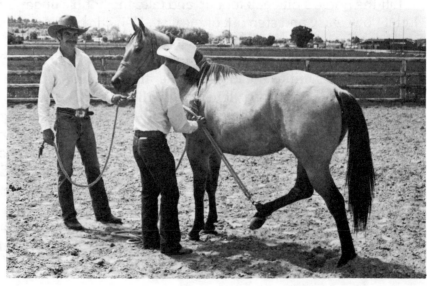

Tie leg off the ground

210

Pre-tie rope

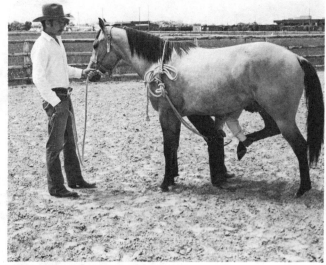

Fasten strap around pastern

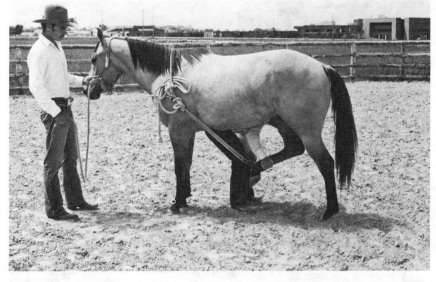

Make sure foot can't reach ground

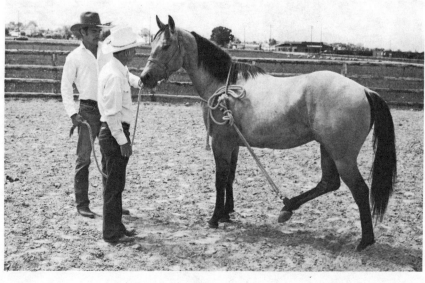

You're ready to go to work

211

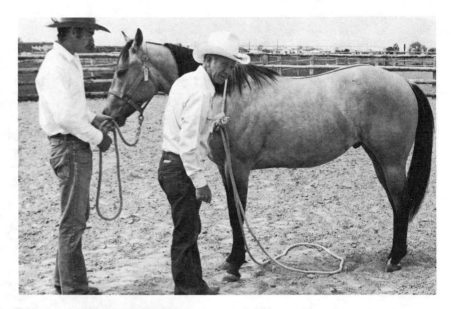

Set rope and trap foot

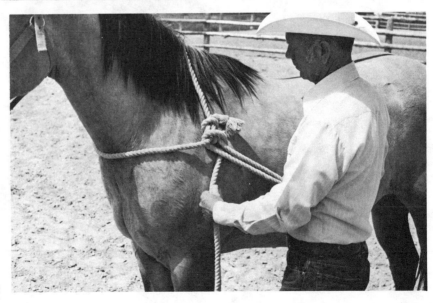

Take a bind wrap—take up slack

212

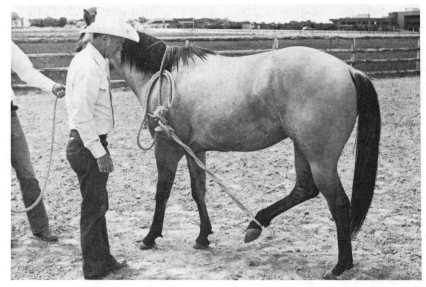

Twists keep foot
from coming free

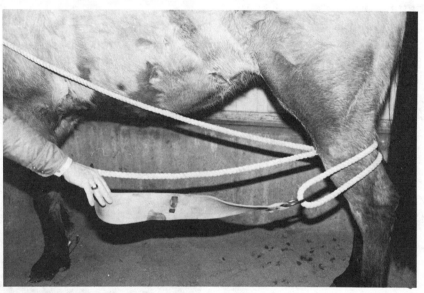

Run rope through
near cinch ring

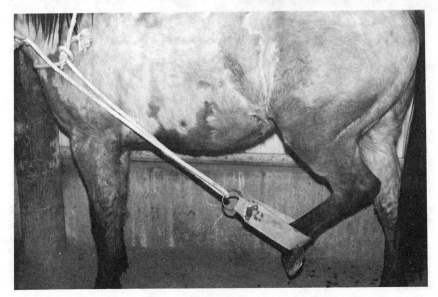

A pony cinch would
work well

213

Once you have the foot raised so the toe is off the ground, tie a slipknot around the two ropes. Pull on the rope around the foot until you have raised the foot up. Now use the slack and put a hitch around the pastern. This will prevent him from kicking out of the rope.

If he wants to fight the restraint, just turn his head loose and let him fight it until he stands still. If he falls down, just start grooming or sacking him out while he is down. He can get up when he is tired of this situation. If he doesn't want to get up, pull his head towards the side his legs are on and give him some encouragement to get up. Once he is up you can walk all around him, brush down all his legs, pull his tail, and climb all over him and the only thing he can do with his leg tied up is fall on you if you are careless.

Tying Up A Front Foot and Hobbling

When you pick up a front foot of a horse and he continually pulls it away from you or straightens it out, you can tie it up and let the horse stand for twenty minutes on three feet. A few sessions like this and he will realize you can take it away from him any time you please, so he'd better cooperate.

A leather figure 8 hobble can be used for this tie. Undo it and put the pastern of the horse in where the first foot would go. Run the tip through the center ring, then bring the hoof up and quickly strap the buckle around the forearm. Another way to tie this front foot up is to put a rope around the horse's heart girth then tie the foot to this rope.

Do not stand in front of the horse at any time while putting it on or working with him while it is on. Generally, a horse will try to pull its leg forward, and this can get to the point of striking and rearing on some rank horses.

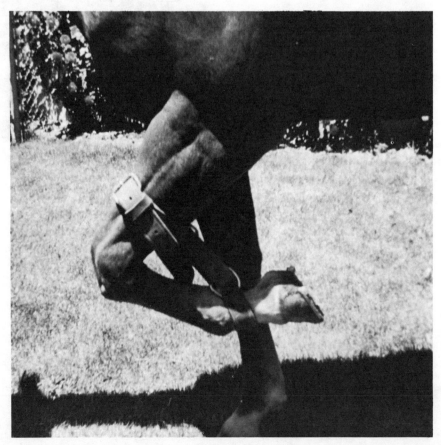

Tying up front foot

Tying a front foot up does not take much locomotion away from the horse so it is not a good restraint when sacking, saddling or mounting.

After you have tied a horse's back leg up once or twice and he has quieted down, it may be adequate to hobble both his front feet while sacking and saddling, just to keep him from walking around. Some trainers hobble the front feet for mounting and dismounting training also.

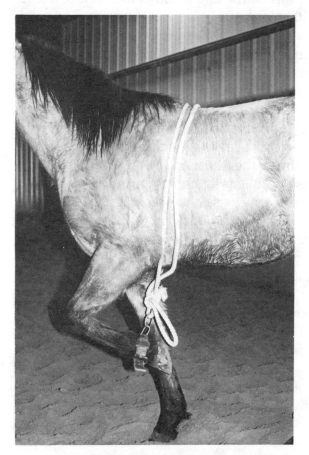

Hobbling one foot

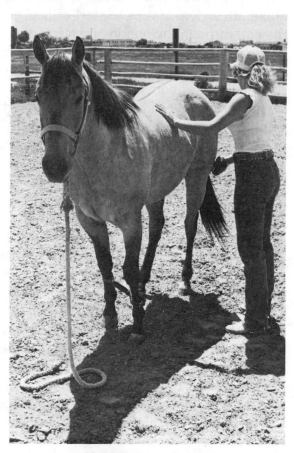

Hobble around cannon

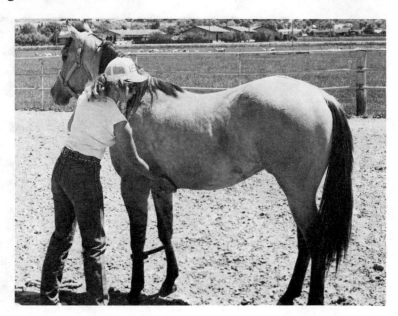

Start grooming

215

War Bridles

The war bridle comes in many shapes and sizes, but possibly the simplest and most effective is the 3/8-inch rope made into a loop. With the hondo hanging down the left side of the horse's head, run the rope up over the poll and down to the right side of the mouth. Put the rope under the upper lip so it is at the top of the upper gum. Now thread the end through the hondo. Have about fifteen feet of rope to start with so you are left with a long pull rope. It is easier if you thread the end through the hondo and place the loop on the head, but you need to be sure the hondo is hanging down from the left ear so you can form a bind that will pull up on the upper gum.

To use this bridle you first must get the horse's attention, so give it a couple of sharp pulls and release. Now if you are going to pick up a back foot just start down from the hip. If the horse starts to kick, give him a couple of good jerks on the rope. Try again on the foot. If he still doesn't want to let you, jerk him a little more and a little harder. This method is punishment with the only reward being that you aren't jerking the rope. It is quite effective, even though it sounds cruel.

Excessive use of the war bridle can cause horses to throw their head in the air every time you pull on the halter rope. This is undesirable and can cause problems later for showing at halter.

Never overdo any restraint and hurt the horse. Some people use a chain snapped into one side of the halter running through the mouth or under the upper lip and back up to the halter on the other side. Chains generally damage tissue and can injure a horse's mouth permanently.

Another type of war bridle is also called a come-along. Trainers find if they say they are using a war bridle on an owner's horse, he may get upset, but if he is told that a come-along is being used he doesn't seem to mind.

This bridle is formed by placing the loop of a rope around the horse's neck with the hondo on the right side. Leave about six inches, then make a half hitch and place it around the horse's head with the hitch on the right side. Now take the end of the rope over the bridge of the nose and under the rope on the left side of the face.

This bridle puts pressure on three pressure points on the head: the poll, the brow of the nose, and the chin. It can be used to teach horses to lead, or will work on horses that lead but won't trot beside you. It can also be used to load horses. When loading, however, it is better to force his rear than his head.

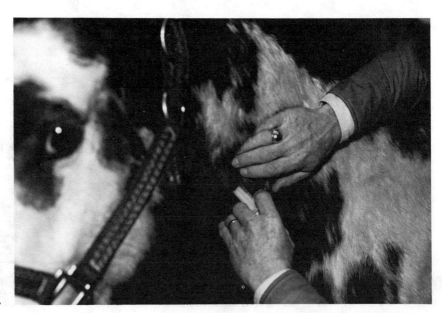

If the treatment is going to be severe, a tranquilizer may be needed.

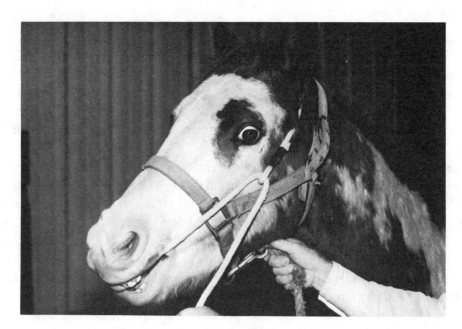

Lip rope

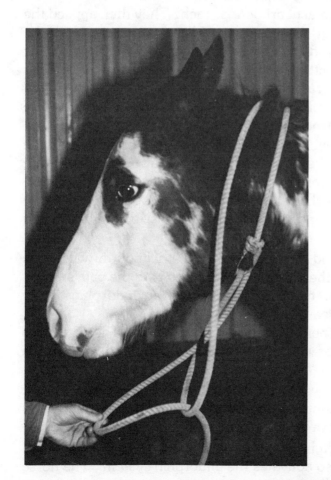

War bridle—Come-a-long

217

Twitch

A twitch is a device that is placed around the upper lip and then tightened to apply pressure. Many trainers will put a twitch on almost every horse when they are going to clip the ears or roach. This saves time and fighting. Many vets use a twitch and then follow with a local or general anesthetic when working on horses. Horseshoers also find this a helpful tool. If you use this tool, be sure not to stand in front of a horse while putting it on. Many horses will rear or strike and you can get a foot or knee in the stomach.

There are many types of manufactured twitches. The old timers used a stick and piece of twine or small rope, or even a small chain. Just put a small circle of rope around the upper lip and then put the stick through the rope and start to twist. When it starts to tighten firmly, start doing what you were going to. If the horse is uncooperative, tighten the twitch tighter. Every horseman should keep one of these gadgets handy. They can save a lot of fighting and will reduce the chance of the horse or you getting hurt.

There have been several explanations for why the horse stands subdued while being twitched. Some think the horse's attention is distracted from what is being done, focusing his attention on his lip. Others feel the pain induced by the pressure on the upper lip leads to a decreased perception and awareness of pain produced by treatment performed on another part of the body. Yet some feel the horse just becomes insensitive to painful stimuli.

Lagerweij and Nelis of the University of Utrecht in Utrecht, the Netherlands, wondered about this phenomena enough to perform a study to check their hypothesis.

Using thirty-seven horses, they recorded the normal heart beat of each. They then applied the twitch and again checked the heart beat. The heart beat decreased by eight percent with the twitch on. The horses were more calm and their eyelids drooped as if sedated.

With the twitch on they applied a painful stimuli with a needle along the back of the horse. The heart rate increased back up to the basal or normal rate after the pain stimuli.

This pain inflection was then repeated later without a twitch and the heart rate checked. The rate had increased by twenty-two percent above normal without the twitch.

What caused the heart rate to decrease with a twitch on? We know that the body can produce adrenalin when alarmed. The adrenalin speeds up the heart rate. The body also has a heart rate reducing drug. This substance decreases the sensation of pain. The twitch may, like acupuncture needles, result in activating this pain decreasing mechanism. The effect of acupuncture is partly explained by the release of endorphins. The Netherland researchers hypothesized that the twitch caused a similar release of endorphins.

By injecting endorphins into the blood stream and running the pain test without a twitch, the researchers found no difference in heart rate from the data using the twitch with the pain stimuli. This result indicates that the effect of the twitch on heart rate is mediated by endorphins in the body and that these endorphins can influence the heart rate of horses.

Blood samples were extracted in the first experiment with the twitch and pain. These samples showed an increase in endorphins. Thirty minutes later blood was extracted and showed the blood back to normal.

The horse appears sedated and the heart rate lowers with the twitch, whereas painful stimuli activates the horses heart rate to increase significantly. Thus, the twitch must not create pain unless it is placed on excessively tight. The twitch can be thought of as Western acupuncture.

When we relate the sedating qualities of the twitch to that of twisting or biting the ear of the horse, one could wonder if this type of restraint also activates the endorphin system. The horse with an ear bit will stand in a similar stupor as if twitched.

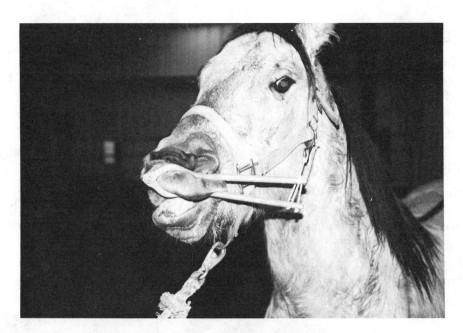

One man twitch

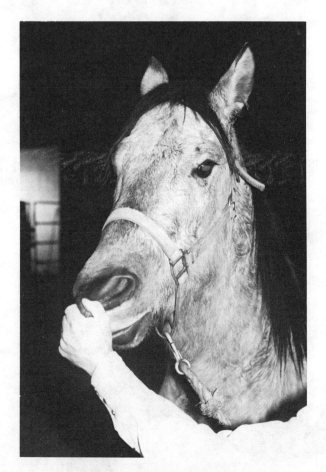

The hand may be enough

Earing Down

When earing a horse down, grab the ear with your thumb up and twist the ear. If you grab with your thumb down, it is hard to hold on when a horse puts his head up. If you twist good they usually will hold the head medium low and out. If he was really a mean one, the old timers would bite the end of the ear. This really made them stand still. Watch out that you don't get hit in the head if you try it. Some old timers ended up toothless for one reason or another.

There are pros and cons to this method. It generally makes a horse ear shy if you use it repeatedly. If you are out where you haven't any restraining equipment and need to perform simple first aid, it is very effective and should be used. If the horse is fighting being bridled, you can get a grip on the ear with the right hand, even with the upper portion of the headstall in your hand. Some horses a trainer gets are already spoiled about being bridled. This can be corrected by bridling properly (see "Bridling") so the bit doesn't bump the teeth. Make the horse stand while he is being bridled, holding the ear as a last resort. Always rub the ear and head afterwards and quiet the horse. After a time or two the older, spoiled horse will realize he is going to get bridled one way or the other and he will quit fighting.

Earing down

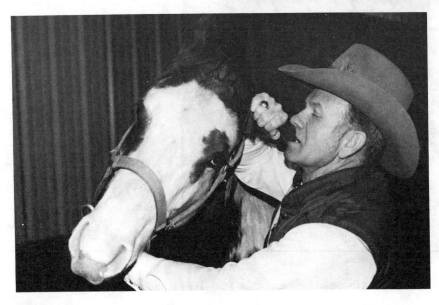

Get a bite but watch his head

220

Running W

The running W is another restraint used by some trainers for saddled horses. It is made with two ends of a pair of hobbles with no chains, but rather a ring on each to run a rope through. Tie the end of a fifteen foot rope to the right stirrup, then run down through the right ankle hobble and back up to the cinch. Have a ring tied securely on the cinch, go through that ring, and back down to the hobble on the left ankle. From there run up to the left stirrup. Take hold of the end of the rope and when the horse acts up you can pull his feet out from under him and say "Whoa". Some people use this if they are afraid of a horse bucking them off. They jerk the horse down a few times then they get on. The horse is afraid of having his feet jerked out from under him, so when he goes to jumping around the rider pulls a little on the rope and says "Whoa" and the horse stops and stands still so he won't get his feet pulled out from under him.

This should be a last resort method. There is too much chance of injuring a horse's knees when he goes down. It would be much better to tie up a hind leg for a while, then snub the horse up. Some older, spoiled horses might respond to the running W, but whatever you do, be careful. Knee pads should be used on the horse if you choose to use this method.

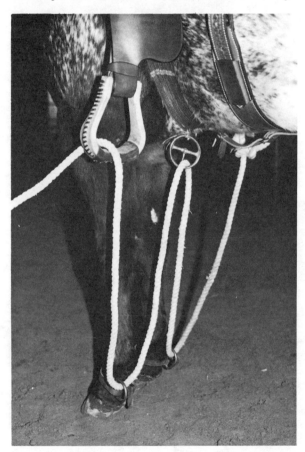 

Running W

CHAPTER TEN
Sacking Out

You've all ridden horses that you can't move your hand on or flop your leg without them jumping sideways. This is the result of a bronc buster getting in a hurry to ride and not doing an adequate job of sacking out the horse. Sacking out takes a lot of the spook out and helps him realize movements aren't going to hurt him.

Let's start with a halter-broke, barn-raised horse. The range horse will be discussed later because he can be handled a little differently, if needed. Always have the horse untied or he will hang back and damage the nerves over the back of his head (poll). Hold the lead about two feet from the halter. Don't try to strong-arm the horse into staying close, but always keep his head toward you.

Use a saddle blanket, feed sack or rain slicker to start with. Let him smell the blanket. Next, rub it on his neck and shoulder. If he has been handled a little he will not mind this. Now move the blanket to his back and down his rump. There is no need to start out slapping him with the blanket and putting him on the fight. If he is behaving himself, start laying the blanket over his back and neck, then pulling it off. Now start throwing it on and making a lot of movements. Keep it up until he does not get upset about any motions.

His legs are next; swing the blanket so it wraps around a leg, then pull it away. If he wants to kick, keep doing it until he stops. Rub his head with it and throw it over his head and let it sit, then pull it off. This should be done while working from both the horse's left and right shoulders. Don't stand directly in front of him. Hold the rope with one hand and swing the blanket at him with the other. More repetitions will do more good than hitting him hard and getting him tired from fighting.

Let him get acquainted with it

Some horses won't stand still to be sacked out the first time or two. That is where tying the hind foot up comes in handy. Never fight the horse, let him fight himself. He will give in quicker with less wear and tear on both of you.

Don't be afraid to use restraints on the horse. Generally the horse that has been restrained and made to submit to sacking and saddling will, in the end, be the most quiet and dependable horse. It's the horse that learns that he can occasionally win the fight that is hard to handle in later training.

A stick with a feed sack wrapped around one end can also be used to work down the legs. This will be a more continuous feeling, similar to your hand as you move it down the horse's leg. Let the horse kick at it but just keep going up and down the leg until he gets tired of kicking at it.

After three or four sacking-out sessions, the colt will stand still and act like you want him to. Now you have accustomed him to overcoming the fear of movement. Next, you can use a feed sack with some tin cans in it. Start over and accustom him to noises that he will naturally be afraid of. You may need to go back to tying up a hind foot to make him stand still.

Remember, never leave a horse tied up at the halter to sack him out because he will always hang back and most likely will damage the nerves over the poll. Once you damage these nerves the horse will hang back every time you tie him up. The pull of the rope irritates these nerves and he fights to get away from the pain. If you do damage these nerves, stop tying the horse solid for two or three months, while the nerves heal. Then be very careful not to damage them again. The innertube around the post is a good preventive measure, as well as a good prescription after the damage.

Back to the range horse. Some trainers like to rope-sack a rough horse out when they first go to roping him. To do this you need a good round corral with high, secure fences. First walk into the corral with the horse and start swinging the rope. This will scare the horse and he will start running. Don't rope him, but just keep swinging it and make the horse run until he starts to slow down. Now throw the rope at him. He will take off running again, but he is getting tired now. Keep throwing the rope on his back and at his legs. When he is tired enough he will stand while you rope him. Then walk up and take it off and throw again. Rope him until he just stands there. Rope his front feet and let him step out of it. Then rope his back legs and let him step out. After a horse has gone through this a couple of times he will never be afraid of a rope swinging or touching him.

Even the barn-raised horse needs to be sacked out with a rope. The above method will work with him too, but it won't take as long or be as hard on the horse. Some trainers do it with a long halter rope. They swing it over his neck, over his back and around his legs. You never know when a lead rope or catch rope might get under a horse. If he goes to pieces there is a good chance he will hurt you or himself or possibly both. Get him used to as many things as you can while you are starting him, then he will not be distracted or spooked by these or similar sounds, sights or movements when being handled or ridden.

Don't think you have the job done, for you are going to have to do it all over again from the saddle when you start to ride him. If you are not thorough in this training, you are just asking for problems later in your training.

224

Sack him out

Don't forget his legs

Slap it on

Put your weight on his back

Sit up and pat him

Slide off the back

226

CHAPTER ELEVEN
First Saddling

Some horses will stand quietly while you saddle because of all the sacking you have done. If the horse is not quiet, get someone to work with you. Put your helper at the halter and tell him to always stay on the same side you are on. If one of you get on each side, the header will always pull the horse's head to his side and that puts the horse's rump towards you.

Let him smell the saddle after you have set the blankets in place. Now move back and ease the saddle on his back. Jiggle it a little. Take it off and set it on again with a little less ease. If he stands, fine; go around to the right side and take the cinch and stirrup down. Make sure your helper moves with you to that side and controls the horse.

If the horse throws the saddle and blankets, it will scare him and make it harder to saddle him for a while. That is why it is best to restrain the colt by tying up a hind leg again. With the leg tied up you don't have to be so easy. Set it on and off and back on. Repeat it until he is very much at ease. Now take your cinch and stirrup down and cinch it up, but not tight. Now let the leg down. He has learned not to fight that leg tied up or what you are doing when it is tied up. Next time you won't need to tie it up, but for the first experience you didn't have to take a chance that the horse might get the best of the saddling.

Some trainers will put the horse in a round corral and tighten the cinch and let him play a little with the saddle. He most likely will run and jump. The first time, it may be advisable to tie the stirrups together under his belly so they won't hit him. There is no sense in making him buck, even if he can't throw the saddle. It may give him some ideas for later on. Some trainers don't even like to turn them loose with the saddle on. They would rather pony them off another horse which can serve the same purpose of getting the horse used to the feel of the saddle, its sounds and movements.

An alternative for tying up a hind foot is the bronc stall. This is a stall that is no more than thirty inches wide and just long enough to accommodate the horse. It must have a butt strap or bar so the horse can't hang back. It works about like a bucking chute. The horse cannot do anything because he has nowhere to go. If he likes to rear, just attach a rope to one side of the chute, then

Blanket him

227

Set it on a few times

Don't let him throw it

Cinch him up

228

cross it over to the other side just above and in front of the withers. Now attach it solidly to the other side of the chute. This will keep him down. Go ahead and put the saddle on and off as much as you want. Don't use the bronc stall more than a couple of times. Get him out and make him stand in the corral while you saddle.

You will be repeating the saddling over the next two or three days as you get the horse ready to drive. Don't get in a hurry to prove you are a bronc buster. Anyone can get on and get thrown, but it takes patience and planning to do the job right.

CHAPTER TWELVE
Bridling

The snaffle bit can be used easily and effectively by novice trainers. If you follow the ground work described in the following pages you will be able to produce a horse with a light mouth and a fine rein.

The goal is to keep the mouth soft, so you will want to pick a snaffle with a 1/3" x 1/2" diameter bar at the sides of the mouthpieces. Some even use rubber-covered bits, but these don't get a hold of the horse enough. You must have his attention and respect without hurting his mouth.

The width of the bit is also important. If you have a three year old Quarter Horse that is well matured, you will need a wider bit than if you are starting a two year old Arabian that is quite small. The Quarter Horse could use a five-inch mouthpiece while the Arabian should have no more than a 4 1/2-inch mouthpiece. A 4 1/4-inch may be even more desirable.

Most snaffles are made in five-inch mouthpieces. If you are going to be training small horses, you should invest in the narrower bits. If you only get a small horse to train once in a great while, you may make do with a five-inch bit with some leather inserts on each side of the bit.

The headstall should be made of sturdy material. Generally leather is desired, but some of the double-stitched nylon headstalls are quite adequate and much cheaper. Don't worry about how nice or fancy your training equipment looks. You are going to use it at home, so just make sure it is functional.

The single ear headstall is the most common in the West, but the brow band is easier to get on a young horse and it causes less ear irritation when bridling.

Cutting horse trainers use a nose band bridle called a side pull. The nose band can be made of metal or rope. Some have a double rope nose piece. The reins are fastened to a ring on each side of the cheek. A running martingale is always used with the side pull. The side pull works directly off the pressure point over the nose. It cannot cause pressure under the jaw like hackamores do. This head gear will put a stop and back on a horse. It will also make a horse give his head side to side without the chance of hurting a horse's mouth. Most people feel they won't have enough control, so they don't try them. The side pull is only as severe as the rider makes it but it can handle runaway race horses or broncy colts.

The hackamore can also be used if you understand its function and have the hands to use it. Don't think this is the softest on the horse. It can be as severe as you want to make it. Novice riders usually misuse it and cause sores on the jaw bones of the horse. Then every time you touch the reins the horse's head goes straight in the air.

How To Bridle

To most horsemen this seems quite basic and even unnecessary, but many horses are hard to bridle because of poor bridling procedures by the previous rider. Young horses are especially hard to bridle because it is new to them and many of them have sensitive teeth. Between two and five years a horse is always losing or gaining teeth. Those of you that have been around babies that are teething know how irritable they can be and how tender and sore their mouth can get. If you notice a tooth is loose, get the pliers and pull it. The horse will be irritated for the moment, but will feel much better the next day.

231

Realizing the possibility of problems with the teeth of a young horse, the trainer should use the procedure discussed in the "Bridling" section to minimize problems of head throwing.

The snaffle bit should fit up against the corners of the mouth, but need not wrinkle it. As you start working the horse in a snaffle he may have a tendency to gap his mouth open. By lowering the bit in his mouth one hole in the headstall he will have to take hold of the bit, which will make him keep his mouth closed. A low cavesson (nose strap) or figure 8 nose band will help to keep his mouth from gaping, also.

Even though you have a snaffle bit and it requires no chin strap for leverage, it is a good practice to place one on loosely so the bit cannot pull through the horse's mouth when pulling on one rein.

Catch his nose

Open his mouth

Lay the ear forward

Be gentle with the ears

Let him get used to the bit

CHAPTER THIRTEEN
Bit Training

The bit training can start at this point or could have started before saddling. The first step is to put a snaffle bit and headstall on the horse. Take the reins right off. Tighten the bit until it just touches the corners of the mouth. Let him go for a half day with it on. He will learn to eat and drink with it on. Do this for two or three days. These can be the same days you are sacking him out if you are in a hurry.

Make sure there is nothing the horse can catch his headstall on and hurt himself. Some horses have cut their tongues and damaged their teeth by catching the bridle on the fence and jerking back. If you don't have a good, safe corral to turn him in, you will have to stay close so you can watch him.

With the saddle and bridle in place, take a rein and attach it to the bit. Now tie the other end to the stirrup. The head should be pulled around until the horse has to circle. If the rein is too long, the horse will be able to walk straight ahead. The purpose for this is to teach the horse to give to the pressure of the rein on the bit. If he fights it he will find he is fighting himself and will give in sooner than if a rider is on his back trying to jerk him around. He only has the bit and rein to concentrate on instead of a rider.

Tie him around to one side for fifteen minutes then the other side for fifteen minutes. This should be done in the morning and afternoon for a couple of days. If he doesn't want to move, get in the corral and move him around so he gets the pressure of the rein. As soon as he is giving easy to the pressure, it is time to drive him.

Take the stirrups up short then tie the stirrups under the horse's belly with a short cord to hold them in place. Now use two fifteen-foot reins. Connect one to each side of the bit, then run each through a stirrup, or you can use a ring tied to the dee ring in the saddle instead of the stirrup. This will keep the reins from pulling low, making the horse put his head low. If you go through the stirrups it is best to tie the reins around the saddle horn so the horse can't get his head too low. Have someone hold the horse until you are in place behind him with both reins.

The most functional area to drive a horse is at the end of corral that is rectangular with about twenty to thirty feet width at each end.

The horse now knows what to do when there is pressure on the bit. Put a little pressure on the side closest to the end fence to start him to turn. As he starts to turn left, for example, move around quickly to the right. Do not let any pressure develop on the right side. Let the horse move almost to the other end of the thirty feet, then pull on the right rein. This will again turn him into the fence. Move quickly to the left and drive him to the other end. If he gets excited and tries to run, just pull his head into the fence more often and make him turn quicker. This will soon take the edge off him and he will quiet down.

After he starts to settle down, stop him and talk to him. You don't need to walk up to him, just put him at ease with your voice and hands on the reins. Move him off again and drive him for about an hour with short breaks for both of you to rest and assess his progress. You can try some figure 8's and circles if he is quiet and not trying to run away with you.

After he is stopping with a small amount of pressure, start him backing. Say "Whoa" and stop the horse. Say "Back" as you pull, until you get a step back, then release. You may want someone in front of the horse to tap on his chest as you pull and release. As the horse takes a step back, release the pressure. Pull again and release on the step. He will soon learn that as long

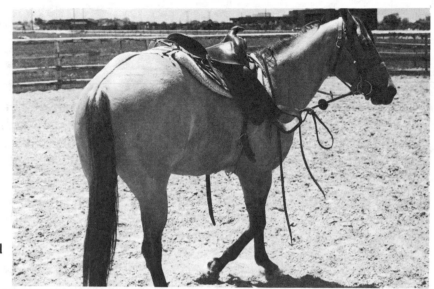

Tie him around

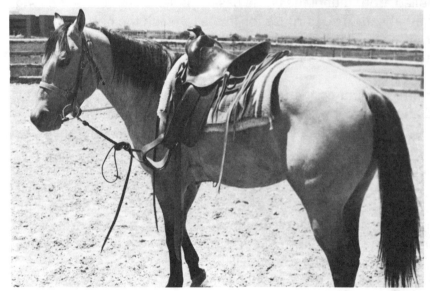

Do it both ways

A bitting rig works well

236

Get horse ready to drive

Rings can be used
instead of stirrups

Work into fence

Stay behind

Work slow and easy

Pull one side, give the other

Drive him around

Stop and back up

as he backs there is no pressure on his mouth. Be sure to use voice commands and reward him with your voice when he does well.

While you're driving the horse, teach him to stop. Drive him into the corner and say "Whoa" and pull on both reins, then release. If he doesn't stop, say "Whoa" again and take hold of his head and position it right into the corner. He will stop now. Let him rest a minute, then move him into the fence for the next turn. If the horse is nervous about the reins on his legs you should drive him longer and get him over his spookiness. Some horses need to be driven four or five times, while others can be ready to ride after only a couple of drivings.

These and all other skills are learned only by repetition and in small individual segments. Trying to teach too many maneuvers at a time is fruitless. It will confuse the horse and frustrate the trainer.

To persuade the horse to give in easily to pressure on the bit and to hold his head in a collected position, you can tie each rein to the dee rings on the side of the saddle. If you have a bitting rig or harness to bit him up in, tie them to the side rings. Observe the natural way the horse carries his head with the bit in his mouth. Now tie the reins in the dee ring so the forehead is back about one-half inch more than normal. A collected head position cannot be described for all horses because they all differ slightly, but generally the horse should look normal. If you want to move his headset back, just shorten the reins a little each day but don't try to do it all at once and don't leave him tied too long the first few days (probably twenty or thirty minutes). This type of training can also be done each day before you ride.

Sometimes it seems like you will never get to riding the horse. But if you want a good horse don't get in too big of a hurry. The better ground training the easier the riding training.

Tie both reins back.

CHAPTER FOURTEEN
Mounting

There are a number of ways to get on a young horse for the first time. Some will cause an unexpected exit. It is best to do it right and take some of the risk out of this step of training. This is possibly one of the most important steps, for you can cause a continuing problem if you don't handle it right.

Tying Up A Hind Foot

By tying up a hind foot you are in control of the horse. By now he has learned to accept a hind foot being tied up and will not fight it. Whenever you mount take the reins in the left hand and lay that hand on the mane about eight inches ahead of the saddle. Shorten the left rein so you can feel his mouth. Don't pull, but have it so that if the horse starts to move you can turn your wrist and make the horse turn towards you. While getting on, without a foot tied up, it is dangerous to let the horse turn away from you for he could kick or step on you. With the foot tied up he can't do any more than turn his front feet. With the right hand take hold of the horn and wiggle it a couple times and say "Stand". This is the cue to the horse that you are getting on. He should learn that when you wiggle the horn he is to stand still.

Turn the stirrup with your right hand, then place your left foot in the stirrup. Take hold of the horn and wiggle it again. Bounce around so you are facing forward. Give a bounce, lift yourself up and sit down slowly. If the colt starts jumping, just stay with him. He will either stop or fall down. If he goes to fall down, just step off as he goes down. Don't get upset and jump off, for this will cause him to do the same thing next time because he knows it will get you off.

Now that he has quieted down, get on and off twenty times. Slide your foot over his rump. Sit down a little harder and slap the saddle and your leg. You need to sack him out now while you are on. Wave your hands and legs so he gets used to movements. This is the big advantage of doing it this way. You don't have to be quiet and slow so you don't scare him. You want to get the scare out of him.

Get on and off both sides. You can even slide off his rump. Do whatever you have a hankering to do. Just don't hurt him or make him overly frightened.

You might say, that is not the way you mount. You put the left hand on the horn with the reins in that hand and then put your right hand on the back of the saddle. You've probably gotten by fine so far, but you are open to some basic problems. In the first place you cannot change the pressure on the reins without removing your hand from the horn. To be able to seat yourself you must also remove your right hand from the cantle before you can get your leg to the other side. With only the left hand to balance, you do not have a chance if the horse moves quick. Generally, a person that mounts this way will hit the saddle a lot harder than someone with two-handed balance.

If you want a young horse to buck, just plop your rear in the saddle hard when he doesn't have a foot tied up. Do it right and you can save the horse's back and your rear end.

Snubbing

If you have a helper that is a real good hand, you can have him snub and lead your horse. Have him dally the halter rope around the horn and teach the colt to lead for a few minutes. Use a gentle horse to snub on. Have the snubber give the colt about eight to ten inches slack. Walk

It's time to mount

Get off and on easy

Sack him out

Don't get stepped on

Get right up

Settle down

Sack him out again

243

behind the snubbing horse and come up between the two horses. Make sure the young horse has his body at a ninety degree angle to the snubbing horse. Now mount as describe above. Always remember to jiggle the horn every time you get on or off so the horse can learn the cue.

Now you are on, you can move your arms and legs to get the horse used to movement. If he starts fighting, he will be climbing on the snubbing horse and jerking back. If the snubber gets scared and lets go, you will learn to ride bucking broncs.

Once your horse settles down, get off and on a few times and make him stand. Be very careful you don't get pinned between the two horses. If they knock you down you are bound to get stepped on.

Hobbling

The basic problem with hobbling is that a horse can learn to run with hobbles on. He can also buck with them on. If you are going to use them to mount with, be sure to hobble the horse a few times before you are ready to work on mounting. Let him get used to the hobbles and teach him to stand with the hobbles on.

Mount as discussed above. Then when he settles down, get him used to movements of your arms and legs.

Hobble him—teach him to stand

Mount until he stands well

Tying To A Snubbing Post

Some novice riders tie the horse up close to a post, then mount and dismount. The problem is that the horse could hurt himself and you very easy. This may be fine for a horse that has no desire to move away or one you have tied a leg up on first and got him used to your mounting. If the horse is the least bit skittish you are better off in the middle of the corral or arena.

Some trainers use this method on broke or green horses that want to walk off when they are mounted. If you mount properly and sit down easy you won't need to restrain your horse to make

The snubbing post is the poorest choice.

him stand still. Even under these circumstances it would be better to hobble the front feet to teach a horse to stand rather than using a post.

Cheeking

The old-time cowboys had a lot of good methods to handle horses, but most of them believed in riding the buck out of a horse. The saying was "If he's gonna buck, get it out of him when you're ready for it, not when you're not expecting it." That is why most ranch horses would try you every morning. The only problem with this idea is that they learn to buck and then they try you every time you ask them to do something.

Cheeking is the practice of taking a grip on the cheek strap on a headstall and pulling the horse's head toward the left side. The rider mounts by rolling up from the front of the saddle. In this way a horse has to turn into the rider and the rider can strong-arm him long enough to get a seat. Many of the ranch broncs cow kicked with their back feet. This method kept the rider from getting kicked while mounting.

If you have done everything right up until now, you may be able to turn the horse enough to keep him from bucking, but chances are that he will try you. If he throws you, you really have a big job ahead. Once they get the idea that they can get you off their back by bucking, they will become quite proficient buckers.

If you can ride a bucking horse and want to do things the hard way, you can start him by teaching him he can't buck you off, so he better straighten up and line out. One day you may be surprised and create a bucker.

The very poorest is the practice of having someone on the ground snub the horse on a longe line. The horse is too strong for a man on the ground and if the ground holder pulls when a horse goes up, he could cause the horse to lose his balance and fall on the rider.

245

CHAPTER FIFTEEN
First Ride

The first ride leaves a lasting impression on the horse. If it is not an unpleasant experience he will not be on the fight the next time. If, however, he gets the best of the deal, or he is abused because the rider loses his temper, he will be ready to fight next time.

If the horse is snubbed up to a quiet but stout horse, he will learn quick. Let the snubber lead the horse for a few laps around the arena or corral just so the horse will get used to the snubbing horse and his rider.

Mount as discussed in the mounting by "Snubbing" section. Get a good seat and take a loose rein. Let the snubber lead you around a couple of times or more until the horse seems to be at ease. If he doesn't want to quiet down, put him on a hard trot for fifteen minutes or so until he wants to slow down. Don't start fighting him as soon as you get on. Let him settle down, then he will be more teachable.

Have the snubber give you a couple of feet of lead rope and then start turning your horse with slight pulls as you walk in a figure 8. As soon as the horse gives to the pull, learns to stop and stops well, give him a little more rope. Soon the snubber can just hold the rope in his hand and keep up with your horse. If you get out of control he can pull the horse's head and dally up again.

If you have followed the previous instructions diligently, it will only take a half hour or less of snubbing and you can go right to riding. It is good to snub him for a few minutes for the next two or three days in a row just to keep the young horse quiet. Don't put him on the fight or you will not be able to teach him what you want.

Some trainers use a round corral to take the edge off a young horse. They will turn them loose or use a longe line and make them run in a circle until they can see the horse is starting to quiet down. The round corral is a very good tool and can be used to advantage if you don't have a snubbing horse, rather than creating a fight that you may not win.

In many articles you see the author using a longe line and advocating its use. The longe line is a poor substitute for a round corral. The problem with a longe line is that it causes the horse to get

Snub close and walk

Now trot

Give him some rope if he is being good

in the wrong body position. A horse will normally go into a lead with his rear end slightly to the inside of the lead he is going to take. The longe line pulls his head to the inside, which causes his rear end to move out. You will find that many horses have a hard time taking an inside lead when their rear end is to the outside. It also causes a horse to flip his feet to the outside of the circle. A hot walker tends to do the same thing. A bare-footed horse will wear the inside off the outside front foot from pushing off of that foot each time he takes another step with his inside foot.

If you don't have a round corral to work him in, pony him off another horse if he is too high, but stay away from the longe line and the hot walker. Either can be used in moderation, but some riders think they can train horses on them.

CHAPTER SIXTEEN
Reining the Young Horse

For the first few days the horse will need to be pulled around with the reins. If leg and body cues are used, the horse will soon start reacting to these cues. Soon he will be working more off the leg cues than the rein cues.

Handling the Reins

For the basic methods of handling the reins see Methods of Reining in Chapter Six. If you really want to learn to handle your reins proficiently use the last method where the left rein has a loop in it. This method permits quicker adjustments in the rein length and position of the hands.

Put a bridle on a chair or post and work with the reins until you can use this method. Once you use it you will never go back to the reins crossing from one side to the other.

No matter how you hold the reins you should be able to let go with one hand and grab the horn with the other if the horse is about to buck you off. With the hand on the rein, pull his head around as much as you can.

You may say a good rider won't have to grab the horn, but if it is a choice of grabbing the horn or being bucked off, it is much better for the horse's training if you grab and stay on. If you can ride with balance, that is much better. Don't grab the horn, but do use your reins to put the horse in a turn into the fence. If you can turn the horse into the fence, he will have to get his head up to see what he is doing. Turn him into the fence a couple of times and he will start thinking about the turn rather than bucking.

Some trainers feel that if you pull hard on a horse he will put his head down to try to counteract the pressure and then go to bucking. They feel if you don't put hard pressure on the mouth when a horse gets upset there is less chance of him bucking. You can turn your horse with one rein and spook him with your hands or legs and get him moving off, rather than just pulling straight back on his mouth. Turning to the side will generally take his mind off bucking. As soon as you get on, start with the turns. Never try to make the horse start off straight away for the first few rides. These are some safety thoughts you should try to remember.

Now, back to training. Lead the horse around by pulling out low on the rein you want him turning toward. Let him walk thirty feet and turn him into the fence again. Always have a fence that is high enough that he can't get his head over or else use a barn wall. Just don't take him out in the big pasture and try to start the schooling.

In the beginning of a horse's schooling, never let him get out of control far enough that you need to take hold of him hard. You want to keep your horse at a slow enough pace that you can control him with a light to medium touch. If you get reckless and let him start running off, you are going to have to get hold of him hard to shut him down. Then you have done something you wanted to avoid. It's better to try to let him run into a corner and stop him easy.

Always keep your horse under control. Ask him for only as much as he is capable of doing responsively with light pulls until you finally have him coming along well. As he gains confidence, you can ask him for a little more. Still, do it with the calmness and quietness of a light hand.

When you start with a two year old colt and expect him to give you his undivided attention for three or four hours at a time, you are fooling yourself. A two-year-old has about as much interest in what you are doing as a three year old child would have. Ten minutes of attention is asking a lot.

Direct rein

Squaw rein

Weight on inside back pocket

Ride with no mouth pressure

Let him stretch out

Stop and back up

By the time he is three, he will have a little more control of his mind but will still not want to work for more than fifteen minutes on training techniques. You have to work him for a few minutes on one thing then let him relax by trotting some circles or slow loping. Then go back to some more training.

As he matures and gets more interested in what you are having him do, his attention span will increase. He will still have a short attention span for each specific maneuver you want him to learn, so mix up the training and the exercise.

Some people are more sensitive to the ways of a horse, or any animal for that matter, and what makes him tick. It is easier for these people to get along with horses. Some people are gifted with sensitive feeling hands, but even such hands need development. Good hands come with a lot of experience and have a delicate feel for the horse's mouth. Some people grab a paintbrush hard; they paint houses. Others have a delicate touch on the brush; they paint beautiful pictures. Are your hands those of a house painter or an artist?

It all goes back to take and give (punishment and reward). If you know how to take up on the bit and then release to get your way quietly, training will be a lot easier for you and your horse. If you are too hard on him, you will scare him and make training hard for both of you.

The worst enemy a man can have in developing hands is a temper. You have to learn to control that before you can hope to develop good hands. Anybody who has ridden horses very long will say he has been mad at one time or another. Almost every time he has lost his temper he has messed up more training in five minutes than he can correct in a week.

So, before you can develop a good set of hands, you have to develop a way to control your temper. Once you can do that, you may become a horse trainer.

The horse must learn to respect your hands but not be scared of them. Whenever you start jerking a horse's mouth, you create fear in him and he will try to get away from the pressure. You must form a bond of trust between you. If the horse can trust your hands, he will be willing to respond to your requests. Some horses are more willing to please than others, but it is by building a bond of trust that you will be able to get a horse to want to please you.

Once in a while you see a horse working well out of fear of not doing it right and getting punished. If such a horse gets into a bind or new situation, however, many times he will do the wrong thing and blow up because he is scared of the trainer. This isn't the type of relationship you want to create. Your hands are your tools for creating either of these conditions, so learn to talk to your horse through them.

That doesn't mean you have to have your hands in his mouth all the time. Sometimes it is just nice to give him a little slack and let him relax. Try not to have your hand in his mouth unless you need to tell him something. If he is trotting out easy, give him a little more release and let him relax. You can always gather him up when you are ready to do something different.

In order to stay light on the bit, a horse has to have a live, moist mouth. If his mouth gets dry, pretty soon he gets hard-mouthed and has no feeling. Some horses are born with a soft mouth and some aren't so fortunate. You can take a horse and develop a nice mouth on him if you have good hands.

The main part of any kind of a handle you get on a horse starts with your hands. When you start spinning that horse, you want to turn him with your hands, but you adjust the speed of the turn around with your legs. By pressing with your leg, the horse speeds up and by releasing he slows down. The leg cue starts at the knee and moves to the heel. Some riders always start kicking with the heel first.

By using two hands on the reins, you can keep him in position and keep him going the same way as his nose. You can't do that with one hand. If you ride with only one hand on the reins, a horse is going to lose some of his form. The horse's head will come out of position and the first thing you know, he's following his ears instead of his nose for his nose is pointed the other way.

In neck reining you want a lot of touch on your horse's neck. A horse should respond to the weight of the reins against his neck. If you put more pressure on the neck rein, it will pull on the bit on the side you are going away from. This will turn the nose away from the turn, so it is important that you have a light touch on the neck, or else use two hands on a snaffle bit. With two hands you can develop a light touch on the neck and still position the head.

Cues and Aids in Turning

Let's refine the turning process and analyze what we want the horse to do. First of all, the horse can turn better when the inside foot (of a turn) leaves the ground. With this foot up he can step out and then follow that lead. If you turn while the inside foot is down, the outside foot must cross over the inside foot and sometimes hits the inside foot.

Now you know when to turn, let's look at how to turn. Naturally, the horse will move away from pressure. This is a key to all training. When you pull out on the right rein connected to a snaffle bit, the bit puts pressure on the left side of the mouth. This makes the horse move right. As the horse takes a step, he is rewarded by a release on pressure. Soon the horse turns on one small pull. The reward is no further pressure. Another reward that can be used is the pat on the neck or a kind word in a quiet, reassuring voice. The horse will learn from this that a quick, positive response to pressure receives a reward, while a negative response receives more pressure with no reward until positive action occurs.

To help tell the horse what to do, you should learn to use your legs and body correctly. If you press him on the left side with your leg, he will move away from the pressure. At first, pressure isn't enough. You can slap your foot against his shoulder. He will naturally move away from the movement of your leg and the pressure it creates.

Think of your legs as gates. If you want the horse to go left, open the left gate. You can also crowd him with the right gate. If you're going right, open the right gate.

What happens when you crowd the horse with both gates? He knows he must get out of the pressure so he will go faster. If you put a barrier in front of him by holding pressure on the bit, he will start to back out of the pressure.

To open the gate just move your calf and foot out away from the horse. To crowd with the gate you start the pressure in your knee, down your calf and if that isn't enough you can use your heel. Don't start with a kick. That just upsets the horse.

You can move the front or the back of a horse with your leg, depending on how you cue. Press at the front cinch to move the front end and the back cinch to move the back end. Many riders cue too far back when asking for a front end turn. This confuses the horse.

For the first couple of weeks don't confuse the horse with cues to the back cinch. That comes later when you have fair control over the front end. A trainer must be consistent with his cues. He must constantly remember that the horse not only learns maneuvers with his cues, he learns maneuvers in segments. You can't expect a horse to do a roll back before he learns to stop, pivot and bust out. You may have to walk a horse through a simple maneuver a number of times over a week or more before you speed it up to where you want it. If you get in a hurry, you will accomplish less than if you show patience and reason.

Look the direction you're going

Cue the front to turn the front

Cue the rear to turn the rear

Reward the horse

CHAPTER SEVENTEEN
Riding the Young Horse

Once the young horse is giving to pressure, turning, and will stop a little, it is time to start putting the miles on him. Ride him in the pasture or the hills whenever possible. The arena is a nice place to work on maneuvers, but the open country will make him think of the things around him and not worry about the man on his back. As you ride through the sagebrush, rein and leg cue him around each turn in the trail. He will probably make the turn anyway, but when you reinforce his natural tendency with a rein and a leg cue, he will learn to respond to them when there is no trail.

Another good maneuver for teaching the young colt to neck rein is by trotting through the poles. Use the direct pull and leg pressure. At first, it will take direct pulls, but soon he will start to respond to the indirect neck rein and leg pressure. Soon he will be moving just on the neck rein. Sagebrush and trees work even better as obstacles to turn around.

When you're out riding and you feel he is getting a little tired, take down your rope and swing it a little. Drag it and throw it. He will soon get used to the rope and this will carry over to many other things that you want to do. A little slow roping in the corral will also help settle him. If he is coming well, go ahead and heel a few steers.

If he really gets aggressive when you're roping, tie on to a log and drag it for ten or fifteen minutes. This will slow him down and also get him used to pulling from the saddle horn. You never know when you might need him to pull a steer or even firewood.

Get yourself invited out to help move cows. Working cattle will help settle him down and also take his mind off of being silly. You've got to keep your horse busy and keep him guessing. If you don't, he is going to out-smart you. Constant work in the arena will usually make a cheater out of him.

If you don't have access to the open country or cattle, you can build yourself a set of trail obstacles and work on them periodically to give the horse a change. See the section on "Trail Class" for help in teaching him to be cooperative and relaxed.

Always get the right lead

255

Balance up over
the horse.

Horse in free
flight.

Stop and let him
rest often.

Try to get your horse to relax and trust your hands. When you are out on a ride, don't over-rein him as far as pressure goes. For this reason, always keep him at a speed you have control over. If you feel that he is getting out of control, say "Whoa" and stop him then start over.

You have a lot of time to get him collected. Creating a supple mouth is what you want to work on now. You have to be able to handle the front end with your hands before you start bringing him together with your legs or collecting him.

Use your hands to teach him that you expect him to give his head to the slightest pressure. When he wants to forge ahead, pull and release a little, then pull again. As soon as he gives to the pull-release, let him relax. A solid pull will have a tendency for him to put his nose in the air and push into the pressure. You must use the pull and release method. This isn't to say that you can't pull on him. When he won't respond, set him down and back him up. Make sure he knows you are in command. You don't want to scare him, but don't let him scare you either.

Whenever you are going to be asking the young horse to turn and you are using two hands, remember to use a ring snaffle, side pull or hackamore. If you use a bit with a shank and direct rein, or pull the direction you want to go, you will cause the portion above the mouthpiece to push the cheek in against the molar teeth and cause pain. This will take the horse's mind off what you are trying to teach him.

If, however, you are riding circles or just moving out and want to gather your horse up, two hands can be used on the shank bit. It is best not to get in a hurry to get into the shank bit and when you do, go into a short shank snaffle. Get one that has a curve back on the shanks. A Tom Thumb is not desirable because the shanks are too straight down and create too quick of a communication and have poor leverage because of their shape.

After the horse is started, don't be afraid to change from the ring snaffle to the side pull or hackamore and then back. If you are going out for a ride, use the short shank snaffle. Learn to use each of these and the variation will relax your horse and keep him light mouthed and interested and that's what you want.

No bridle can be a cure all. You can overdo any type of equipment and that is also true with the side pull, but it has its place in your training.

The side pull is just a headstall with a nose band on it. The reins attach to the side of the nose band, thus the name, side pull.

Young horses are often afraid of the bit in their mouth. They put all their attention on that bit and forget what you are trying to teach them. The side pull is just like riding them with a halter until you take hold of it. Then you have more control than with any bit you can use.

Race horses that have learned to run into the bit will be hard to renovate for a saddle horse because they like to lean on the bit. By using a side pull they have nothing in their mouth to push on. They soon relax and start to work for you.

Always use a running martingale adjusted so it does not pull the reins down when your hands are in a normal riding position. The martingale will only take hold when the horse gets his head too high or you get your hands too high. The martingale should be used with both the side pull and ring snaffle.

Work the horse in a side pull for a week or so, then go back to the ring snaffle for a week. This will keep the horse's mouth soft because it doesn't have time to callous up from the bit.

If the horse is lugging or pushing on the bit put him into the side pull. If his nose gets a little sore put him back in the bit.

You can ride a horse for many days or weeks in a side pull and not hurt him. He will only feel the pressure when you take hold of him. The rest of the time he will feel very free and relaxed. He knows you have the control, from past experiences, and will control his actions. You will be surprised how much respect the horse gains for the side pull.

When a horse puts his head down to buck all you have to do is hit him on the nose with the pull of the reins. His head will come up and he will not be hurt in the mouth like he would by jerking a bit.

The real trick in using the side pull is learning to trust your horse and the side pull. Give him some rein and leave him alone until you need to tell him something. You will have the feeling you need to have a hold of him all the time. You must trust him and he will relax and trust you.

You hold and handle the reins just the same as you would with a ring snaffle. You won't notice any difference in the turns, but the stops and backs will be much easier to teach with the side pull.

If the horse won't turn one way put the metal nose band on a couple times and take hold of his head firmly and give a strong pull then release immediately once he moves. It only takes a few sessions and he will give to the pull.

Ask him to stop, if he doesn't make him pay with a strong back. Soon he will be stopping and putting it in reverse on cue.

This is possibly the most important training device you can have in your tack room if you use it properly.

When you are riding you must have his respect, as well as on the ground. If he is being obnoxious, put him in an extended trot and let him go until he wants to slow down, then trot him some more. A trot is the horse's best gait. Trotting also helps put a stride on him. While he is trotting, you can start teaching him to lighten up on the bit. Once he is a little tired he will learn faster and cooperate better. Don't run him out of air, however, for he won't be able to concentrate on anything when he is out of air.

You must have his respect when you are mounted, as well as on the ground. If he is being obnoxious, put him in an extended trot and let him go until he wants to slow down, then trot him some more. A trot is the horse's best gait. Trotting also helps put a stride on him. While he is trotting, you can start teaching him to lighten up on the bit. Once he is a little tired he will learn faster and cooperate better. Don't run him out of air, however, for he won't be able to concentrate on anything when he is out of air.

Don't be afraid to lope him out in the country, but be sure he is a little tired from trotting first. When he wants to slow down, push him a little farther then say "Whoa" and bring him to a stop. Don't try to stop him fast, but rather a nice even come-down stop. Even if he has to take a few steps before he stops, just use a pull-release, pull-release rein pressure. Don't worry about any leg cues at a stop to start with because this will drive him into the bit and may scare him.

A horse can move free and easy out in the pasture, but you can put a man on his back and he's uncoordinated. During the first ridings, a horse will trot rough and lope all wobbly behind. After you trot him and lope him a little, he will learn coordination and balance with a rider on. This is what a trainer has to teach him - how to move with a man on his back.

For the first month just ride him and try to take the spook out of him. Teach him to relax and trust you. Teach him the cues you are going to use for the different gaits, such as verbal commands. To start with, tell him "Walk" and make him stay on a walk. If he breaks into a trot, pull him down to a stop, start over, and say "Walk". If you can feel him going to break into a trot, tell him "Easy". When you want to trot, click to him and lift up on the reins, say "Trot" and squeeze both legs if he doesn't want to move out. If he tries to break into a lope while he is trotting, pull and release slightly and say "Easy".

Lift your rein a little, squeeze your knees and kiss. You will be on a lope. Slow him down and make him learn to lope slow. Tell him "Easy" and make him come down with your hands.

You can talk to him as you ride. Use a calm, quiet tone. If something happens, don't stop the calm tone and holler, or you will scare him. Sing or whistle as you ride to help relax him. If he starts acting up and shying, don't miss a note at the soothing tone and don't clinch your legs.

The communication works in reverse too. As a rider, you should listen to the horse and feel his movements so you know what he is thinking. Country riding is as much to make the rider relax

Four reins on a snaffle
Turn with snaffle bit rein
Stop with curb bit rein

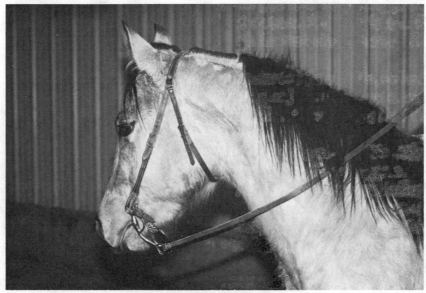

Move to the short shank snaffle

Metal side pull

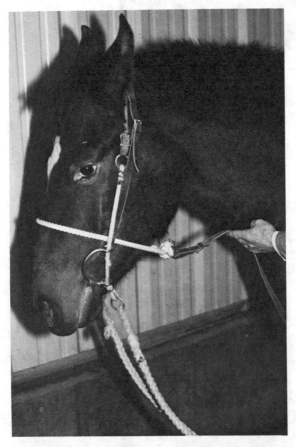

Gag bit with tie down. Tie down strap should be able to touch neck.

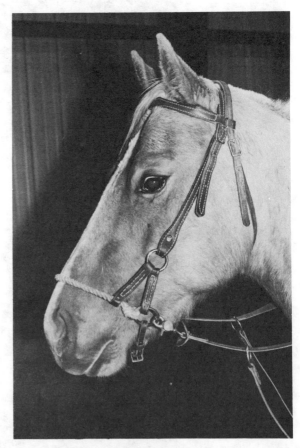

Rope side pull

and trust the horse as vice versa. If you are not used to riding colts, you need to cover more miles to help build your own confidence and develop a bond of trust between you and your horse.

Unless you are breaking horses for other people on a monthly fee, there is no reason to hurry the training. If, however, you are working for other people, they will expect quick results for their money. These visual results can be obtained by pushing the training ahead before the horse is settled. A horse trained in this manner will not be as safe to ride, neither will he have his maneuvers firmly instilled in his mind. If an unexperienced rider tries to use a quick-broke horse, the horse is likely to react adversely to poor hands and off-balance riding.

It takes time to break a horse. It isn't a one month shot, but rather six months to a year before the horse is really settled much. After the horse has three years of good riding, he may be dependable, but even then a horse is never completely dependable for youngsters or unexperienced riders.

After a month of easy riding over a lot of miles, you are ready to start moving the young horse up into the bit. This is called collecting him. With your legs, you drive the horse's rear end up under him a little and push him into the bit. If you have done a good job of teaching him to give to the bit, you will be able to tuck his nose and have a collected horse that is gathered up and ready to learn new maneuvers.

There's been a lot of controversy over which type of headset a horse should have. Some trainers and judges want to see a horse with his head behind the vertical, while others want the head held in a natural position. This is with the nose out a little past the vertical.

They each had reason to support their position. Some trainers felt a horse had to be collected and up into the bit to perform to his best. If a horse is strung out he will not be able to get his weight on the hind end like they want. These riders always had more hand and leg contact, which kept the horse ready all the time. It also kept him in a nervous state.

The natural headset theory was built around the thought that a cow horse was able to stop and spin with a natural headset. The cutting horse had his head forward of the vertical and the rider used little hand and leg pressure when the horse was working.

This horse learned to work on a loose rein and respond to a very slight neck rein and leg pressure. The horse could slow trot and lope or move out briskly with no false gait as seen in many artificial headset horses. This horse could flat spin 180 degrees to head a cow. He could slide on his own without a rider's hand holding his head up.

The natural horse can spin with normal balance. He is just running in a tight circle with his hind feet moving slightly forward as he turns.

The big headset on the Western Pleasure horse is out and the natural look is in. This is long overdue. Both riders and judges should realize that the unnatural headset and the false gait is no longer what is in fashion.

You no longer need to fight the horse's nose in all your training. You can teach him to relax and work on a loose rein because he is comfortable and not afraid of your hands and legs. This doesn't mean you want him all strung out. You still want his hind legs up under him, but teach him to be collected on a loose rein.

If you permit him a little freedom with his head, he will be more relaxed and easier to work with. If he relaxes too much and lowers his neck below the horizontal, lift your hands up and forward on the neck. Work the bit in a light see-saw motion. Don't make it uncomfortable, just noticeable. This will usually elevate the head and tuck the nose at the same time.

As soon as he does what you want, stop the action and give him a little slack. Use this when necessary in training, and when you are in a show you will only need to lift and wiggle your hand. He will get the message and respond with a more alert appearance.

Remember, the natural look is in, so work on making the horse look natural, not artificial in his gaits and maneuvers.

When you ride him, you may want to use a running martingale adjusted so the reins can run from the bit to your hands without bending down to go through the martingale. With this length martingale, you are not always pulling on his mouth. When the martingale is too short you can't feel his mouth and you pull harder. A martingale should only come into play when the horse lifts his nose out of position, or when you get your hands too high.

Make sure martingale is long enough.

As you ride around the arena you can bit the horse up by holding your hands in a fixed position down by the swells. If you feel the horse leaning on your hands, squeeze your legs to move his hind legs up under him. This will shift his weight a little and lighten his front end. It will also cause him to hit the bit harder at that moment and then he will have more incentive to back off the bit. A natural headset and collection can be achieved simultaneously. If you work the young horse on a loose rein consistently at all gaits, he will learn to keep his headset and he will learn to keep himself collected, or he will get stopped, backed and started again.

A horse can be flexed at the poll and still be strung out in back. To be collected, a horse must keep his hocks under him. You accomplish this with leg pressure, not just by using your hands.

If you have not taken enough time to get your horse to relax and trust you, you may find that he gets nervous when you start collecting him. If you continue the training while he is nervous, he may start switching his tail. This is a hard habit to break, so it is best to prevent it even if it takes more easy riding.

A maneuver to relax the horse can be done while you let him stand. Take one rein and pull-release ever so lightly to get him to turn his head. Once he starts to give his head, ask him for a little more until he will touch your outstretched foot with his nose. Work on both sides and make it a relaxing experience, not a fight, or you haven't taught him anything.

If you are going to make a kid's horse or a beginner's horse out of him, don't get him too polished because he will fall apart under novice hands and possibly get someone hurt. If a kid's pony is what you want out of your horse, just keep riding him relaxed.

Have you ever considered where your horse's feet are when you lope, stop or turn? They are beneath the horse, but just where? When you turn on a walk you should turn to the right just as

Suppling exercises

**Turn as the horse starts to pick
up the inside foot.**

263

Stay in balance with the horse

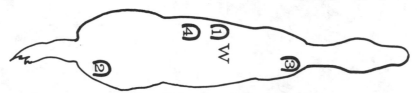

A walk is a four beat gait.

Get a collected trot

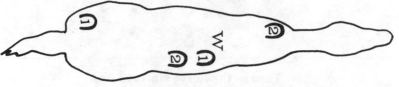

A trot is a two beat gait.

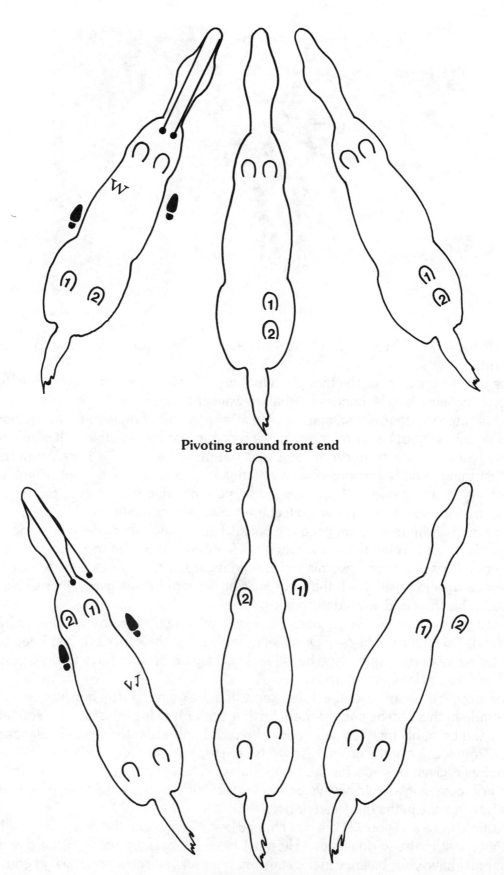

Pivoting around front end

Pivoting around rear end

the horse starts to lift the right foot. If you turn as he lifts his left foot he will have to cross his legs to make the turn.

Most riders just turn whenever the thought hits them. They stop when they decide to and the horse lopes on whichever lead he chooses, usually always the same one.

If you want to improve your riding, start paying attention to the movement of the horse. The professionals do this without a second thought, for it comes naturally to them. It didn't when they started. They had to concentrate on the legs and the movement of the horse until they had it down. The first thing to do is get someone to watch you as you ride. Tell them "Right" each time the right front leg hits the ground. If you don't look, you may find it difficult to feel it. Shut your eyes and concentrate. Now you can start to feel the movement of the horse.

Once you have the front feet down, go to the back. This is much more difficult. Once you have this down you can start turning the horse when his front foot is just ready to leave the ground. When you pivot a horse he must have his inside hind leg up under him as a pivot foot to make a 90- or 180-degree turn in position. If that foot isn't under him he will generally run his rear end around instead of his front end around the back.

Remember to put your weight in the back pocket to which you are going. This stabilizes that hind foot which is up under the horse. Don't lean one way or the other but just keep your body evenly over the horse in the same plane he is in. This way he doesn't have to drag you or try to catch up with you as you lean to and fro.

Now for the stop. You want to let the horse know you are going to stop him just as his back feet leave the ground. In this way he can set them further under him for the stop. By squeezing your legs the horse will bring his hind legs up under him more and allow for a good balanced stop. If you pull as his front feet leave the ground, he will try to stop with them.

A lead requires a given position for the horse's legs. The front and back on the inside of the direction the horse is going should always be leading out. If you can't feel the leg movement, you will never know if you are in the right lead or not.

Watch a cutting horse and you will see him change leads every time the cow changes directions. He cannot move fast in the wrong lead.   He must have his balance going in the direction he is moving. You must have your balance in the same manner. If you relax you will find your lead foot ahead slightly and the off foot straight down from your shoulder.

266

If you fight the saddle by putting both feet out in front, pushing your rear end into the back of the saddle, you will bounce or polish the seat. To ride a lope you must sit up straight and ride over the front end of the horse not dragging behind him. Always ride the horse with balance and rhythm rather than pressure and pull.

On cold days ride bareback a lot and feel the movement of the horse's legs and back. Start to find the rhythm of the horse not just the security of your saddle.

If your horse is supple and you have good hands and sensitive cues, you are ready to move into some new maneuvers, speed up some old ones and polish everything up. You might say, "Oh boy, here is where I put the spurs on and really go to kicking and jerking." The spurs can give you more trouble than help. They also can cause your horse to start bad habits, such as switching his tail and kicking out when you spur. Possibly later on, when you have taught the horse the maneuvers and you are ready for the final touches, you can use the spur a little to speed up the action. Don't get in a hurry, now you have him relaxed to where you can teach him something.

After you have ridden a young horse for sixty days it doesn't hurt a thing to turn him out for two weeks and let him rest and think about what he has learned. Some people think they have to keep riding a horse steady for a year or two or he will forget what he has been taught. More trainers will tell you that the horse will come back, after a rest, with more interest in what he is doing. He will not have forgotten what you have taught him before the rest.

In the first sixty days you will want to accomplish a lot of basic maneuvers. But you don't want to plan on polishing them in this early training. There is plenty of time to put a finish on your horse over the next year or two. Don't be in a hurry to use one hand and neck reining. Most of the maneuvers to be taught can be more easily taught by using two hands to position his head. Two-handed handling isn't a sign of a poorly-trained horse, it is a sign of a trainer that knows how to use his hands properly.

CHAPTER EIGHTEEN
The Kid's Horse

What is it that you are looking for in a kid's horse? If the child hasn't ridden much before, you'd better be looking for a well-broke, gentle horse if you love your child.

Some novice horse owners think they should buy a young horse so the child and horse can grow up and learn together. They will, all right. The horse will be full-grown in a couple of years and will have learned how to buffalo the child. The child learns, if he doesn't get hurt first, that he really doesn't like to ride because he does not have control of the situation. Soon the horse is sold and the parents take a deep breath of relief and put their checkbook away.

The first thing to realize is that you will pay for the horse once when you buy him and then you will pay almost that much again each year to keep him fed and healthy. You might as well get a good one because it won't cost any more to feed and take care of him than it does for a pungo.

When you are looking for a kid's horse, you want to go to a reputable dealer or have one with you when you go to look at the neighbor's horse. It is easier to get taken on a horse than almost any other item you may purchase. Some people feel "buyer beware". They don't have any different principles when it comes to children.

A good trainer can take a horse that has been broke a few years and work with him slow and relaxed and be able to tell if he will make a kid's pony. First, he must be sacked out from the ground and mounted with everything from sack lunches to boards or anything else a kid might want to carry on him. The horse should be ridden double. He should be mounted from both sides and mauled all over. When a horse that is to be ridden by a kid needs to be corrected, he should be corrected quietly but firmly. You don't want the horse to learn to be afraid and jumpy with the thought of getting a whipping.

Once the trainer feels the horse is ready, the child should be schooled in a small arena or corral. If you just turn the two loose and say "Learn to ride", you will let him develop bad habits that will be hard to break later and you take the risk of him getting hurt by doing something that is just not safe.

If you want to get hurt skiing, just go up on the lift and start down the hill with no instruction or previous experience. Once you are out of control, you are asking for a bad accident.

It works the same way in riding. Teach the child the proper method and make him stay in control and you can relax and watch him enjoy his horse and progress in his skills of riding.

It may be necessary to have a good rider get on the horse and ride him every once in a while to keep him minding the rein. Most children are too small to give many leg cues, so a horse must be trained to respond totally to the rein cues. Old broke ranch horses sometimes make good kid's ponies. They are settled in their ways and have had about everything done on them. Don't be afraid of a little age on a kid's pony, as long as the horse is sound and does not stumble. It is better to start with one the child will have to get after than one that is ahead of his rider. This builds confidence in the rider.

A trainer can make good wages retraining old horses and selling them for kid's ponies. This takes time and a lot of mauling before you can feel good about selling them for kids to ride, but there are both financial and emotional rewards.

Once a youth has learned balance and gains some confidence, you can sell his first kid's pony and buy him a trained show horse to start working with. If you start him on a trained show horse you will worry about the horse being ruined and you will keep getting after the child until he doesn't want to ride. Take it easy and let him learn on a horse that he can't hurt and that most likely won't hurt him.

CHAPTER NINETEEN
Teaching Maneuvers

This section contains basic maneuvers a horse should know to be useful. Before you start working on the young horse you are breaking, it might be wise to practice these maneuvers on broke horses that know the maneuvers. This will give you a better chance to learn balance, rhythm and cues. You can't teach a young horse until you have learned yourself.

Not every horse will be able to make a fine handling horse. Some horses find one maneuver easy and another difficult. Some horses will put their mind to learning and others won't.

If you are trying to pick a horse that will be able to do the job, look for a horse with a well proportioned head, wide between the eyes and large expressive eyes. The neck should be slender and of proper length for the body. The back should be short and the hip long and sloping.

If the horse's hind legs are slightly set under him he will be able to slide stop, back and spin easier. If you go too far with this theory, you get a horse that will break down from curbs behind and below the hocks from the strain on the ligament.

Another feature to look for is a long, flexing pastern. A horse with short, steep pasterns will be a rough riding, straight legged stopper.

The cross of the Thoroughbred and Quarter Horse generally makes good handling horses. Lightning Bar and Three Bars horses crossed onto King, Poco Bueno, Skipper W or Leo lines make some of the best. The longer, more slender neck of the Thoroughbred brings added balance to the front end. It is more important to have a well V-ed up chest set on correct legs than to worry so much about that heavily muscled rear end. The horse will go unsound in the front sooner than the rear because of the weight stress placed on it.

The heavy set deep muscled horses are not the ones to pick if you want an athlete. You want that leaner horse with the long muscling.

Whatever horse you pick, you need to teach him how to handle himself with you on him. This section should help you to train your horse to handle the way you want him to.

Slide Stops

Training horses is a very dynamic activity. Sometimes you no more than find a way to do something than you figure out an even better way to do it.

There is a lot of meditation and thought that goes into figuring better ways to teach a horse to do what you want him to do. Once he learns, you have the reward for all your thought and effort.

At Salmon and Idaho Falls, Idaho, I had my sale horses slide stopping without a bridle and they topped both sales. I had seen a picture of a horse doing just that in the Western Horseman magazine. There was no explanation, so I had to figure out how he might have accomplished such a feat before I could train my horses to do it.

The old-timers told the story of blindfolding a horse, running him towards the barn wall, and just before he hit it they would say "whoa" and step off. After the horse got up, they would do it again and again until when they said "whoa" that old horse just stopped in his tracks.

There are some similarities in what we are going to do, but with much more tact and less trauma. The horse has to learn to stop on cue, so you don't have to get in his mouth and hurt or scare him.

Ropers cue their calf roping horses by dropping the reins on the neck or touching the neck in front of the saddle horn. The horse knows if he doesn't get set down he will get a big jerk on his withers. If he sets his back properly, the back cinch will hold the saddle and the jerk will be distributed over the back.

The first thing you must do to teach a horse to stop is get your horse to trust you. He must be able to walk, trot, and lope on a loose rein and be able to give you a little more speed, then stop without being afraid you will hurt him.

Once you have this trust built up you can start on the slide stop. All maneuvers start out simple and so does the slide stop. Much of the training can be done at a walk and trot.

When you want to stop, there are three things that must happen simultaneously. When you are ready to stop, say "whoa", let the small of your back out and drop your hips in the saddle (take a deep seat) and wipe your reins on his neck in an upward motion without touching his mouth (start with your hands low). Remember, these movements must all be done at the same time. Next make contact with his mouth and make him stop, then back.

Use a ring snaffle or a side pull with a running martingale for the first few lessons. This will not scare the horse when you back him up. Remember, never jerk the horse, or you scare him and hurt his mouth.

Once he is stopping on the cues, it doesn't matter what bit you put on him because you won't have to put any pressure on it for the stop. He will also be able to back off your legs and voice cues with little, if any, pressure on the bit.

If you have a problem getting him to back, use your feet on his shoulders to drive him back. Once he respects your feet, then all you need to do is move your feet forward and he will put it in reverse.

There is a count of "one" from the time you say "whoa", let your back out and wipe your reins, until you touch his mouth. There is another count of "one" until you say "back" and move your feet forward.

At first, give the horse a chance to stop on his own even if he takes a couple steps and a count of two or three. He will learn to stop on cue and not be afraid of the stop. If you try to rip his head off, he will always be afraid of your hands and the stop.

Once he is stopping at a walk and a trot on his own, you are ready for the slide stop. Be sure to put skid boots on and let him get used to them.

Any time you start jerking or pulling hard on a horse to make him stop, you cut down on the prettiness and length of the stop.

**Robert Chown, Western Horseman, March, 1987.
Courtesy Western Horseman**

Courtesy Western Horseman

Lope around a few times until you can feel he wants to stop. Ask him for a slight speed up for three to five strides then say "whoa" and use your other cues. That horse will bury his tail in the ground without you touching his mouth.

At a slow lope it is a little harder to get a slide because of the momentum and the leg movement. As you increase your speed you get both hind legs reaching up under the horse at about the same time.

When stopping at a lope you must pick the right moment to ask for a stop. That is when the lead foot is the only foot on the ground. The next step all four feet are in the air so he can move both hind feet up under him for the stop. Most riders can't feel this segment of the stride so they have a hard time getting the proper timing to stop their horse. You will see some riders looking down over the horse's shoulder to see when the lead foot is reaching out, or looking at the hips. Either way the rider is out of position. A rider must learn to feel the leg movements of the horse under him through the seat of his pants. When the rider feels himself being lifted and moved forward, he should know that the back feet are coming up and reaching for another footing. As soon as the horse starts lifting you up say "whoa", take a deep seat and wipe the reins upward on the neck.

A horse's head is normally going to come up when he stops. He uses his head and neck to balance the lowered rear end. If you don't have to get in his mouth he can use his head as he needs to balance himself for the stop. If you take hold of his mouth first, it may scare him and he will be worrying about the hurt instead of trying to stop. Let him have time to think about the stop, then take hold of him if he doesn't try to stop.

If you aren't getting him to think about the stop, ride him towards a fence or barn. Ask him to stop just before he is to it. Give him the cues then don't let him turn out. He will have to stop.

Not every horse will be able to make sliding stops, but all horses can learn to stop on cue. You must realize that it takes many repetitions of a lesson before the horse will learn and retain the lessons. Don't give up if he doesn't get it right at first. Make sure you are doing things right. Don't ask too much too fast.

If he stops well, let him stand and rest. This is his reward for stopping well. If he runs through the stop, stop him and back him hard. Soon he will be looking for the rest reward. After the backing, pat him on the neck and let him stand and relax for a couple moments before you start out again.

You can work on this stop at a walk and trot as much as you want. He will get better each day and before you know it you will have a beautiful slide stop. You can even demonstrate it with no bridle with only a leather strap around his neck. Use the strap around the neck like the reins and let him stop on cue because he knows how and he enjoys it.

Once you realize the horse is stopping because you taught him how, your reward will be great.

We don't want to be that hard on the horse. We want him to learn to like to stop, so always reward him by letting him stand and relax a minute.

It is important to consider the ground surface when stopping. The best footing to work on is a hard pack with a couple of inches of sand on it. If the ground is too boggy or heavy, you may pull a muscle or tendon. Do not try to work on a stop on grass or slick surfaces. You may scare your horse, and on slick or hard surfaces you may burn the fetlocks or the back legs if the horse is really trying to put the brakes on.

Once your horse is starting to sit down, you better put skid boots on him to keep him from burning himself. If he gets a burn he may not want to really sit down again. It will take a lot of work to get him to stopping again once you burn him.

Once the horse is stopping well, leave him alone. You don't have to show everyone how far you can make him slide. Try not to stop in the same place very often or he will start scotching (anticipating the stop). If he starts this, take him out and lope him in a field for a while. Then stop him a few times and leave it alone.

For a long sliding stop you need the right surface and shoes on the back feet that are about 3/4-inch wide and smooth. Some have trailers or extensions on the heels. It requires more speed, such as a run, to drive the horse's hind end up under him, while holding the front end up. The sliding stop always looks impressive, but unless you have a use for it, it is better to get your horse to stop without a lot of sliding. In both roping and cutting you don't want your horse sliding around. It all depends on what you are looking for.

Once the colt is stopping satisfactorily, you may want to try him in a short shank snaffle. This will tend to make your horse bring his head down a little more than the ring snaffle. You may have to move your hand forward and lift the reins to bring the front end up. The ring snaffle tends to bring the head up, but many times the horse sticks his nose out. It may be necessary to use a tie down or a long training martingale once in a while to hold his head in position. Don't let the horse start relying on these for balance by using them all the time.

Don't overdo the stopping or you will sour your horse on it. Keep him interested and learning.

Backing

Horses do not like to back because it is an unnatural movement for them to make. You will seldom see a loose horse back. He will move forward or turn to get out of a tight spot. A horse naturally carries about two-thirds of his weight on his front legs. In order to back, he must shift some of this weight to the hind legs. The hind legs then, must support more weight and also pull the body backwards. Many trainers prefer a horse with slightly under-set legs so he can get his hind legs under his body.

Backing will be a new experience, so it is best not to get in a hurry about teaching this movement. During the driving training a young horse should have started moving back with the verbal command of "Back" and the pull and release pressure in his mouth. If you are having trouble getting him to back, have someone get in front of him and tap him on the legs with a strap or stock whip. Don't scare him so he gets afraid to back.

While in a halter you can raise his head slightly to lighten the front end and get him to move back. Always use the verbal command "Back" when backing. After he has taken a couple of steps, stop and let him relax. Pat him on the neck and tell him he was a good boy. Step him forward a few steps, then back him again. If a horse starts to freeze on you, don't just pull harder. Move him a step or two forward, then try backing again. It takes his mind off of the backing for a moment.

One of the real problems a horse has with backing is with his head straight ahead of his body he can't see where he is going. He is moving into the blind spot in his sight spectrum. His hips block out his view in this area. Until he has learned to trust the rider's judgement, he will be reluctant to move back into unseen areas.

Backing from the back of a horse isn't difficult if he has learned the word "Back" and how to get his front end lightened up.

The pre-cue is the verbal command "Back". Next take hold of the horse with the reins. Move to the center of your saddle and squeeze your legs. This will make the horse move up into the bit, driving his hind legs under him. He will find he can't move forward, so he will have to back to get away from the pressure. As soon as he takes a step, slightly release pressure on the bit. Pull again and as he takes a step, release. After a few steps, stop and let him rest. Step him forward and try it again.

With this method he will be rewarded for each step. Soon, after the first pull he will move back on a released pressure until he is told to stop. This is the goal, backing on a release after the cue and first pull.

Some trainers like to use a see-saw of the reins, or pulling alternately on one side, then the other, to move one side, then the other. Some have good luck with this method. Every horse responds differently, so you have to find out what works best, but as a rule, the pull-release-pull will move him back with less side motion.

Once he is backing easy and you want to increase the speed and distance, you can use more leg pressure or even take your feet and reach up on his shoulders and jab him a little as he is backing. This will generally put him in fast reverse.

Here again, you can't spend long sessions on backing. It is best to work it in with the rest of his training. Be consistent on your cues and reward him when he does it right.

Watch to see that the horse isn't getting his head too low or tucked up too much. If he isn't lightening up the front end, just lift your hand up and move it up his neck as you pull. This will elevate his front end. If his head is too high, lower your hands back to the swells. Concentrate on the horse's body position and adjust it with your cues and body position.

Move forward and squeeze legs to back.

275

If the horse starts to back crooked, you need to work on the cue to the rib cage to move his rear end. It's just as easy to get a horse to respond to rib cage cues as it is to neck cues. It takes repetition and patience but there is no reason why you can't guide a horse in reverse just as well as you do going forward.

Side Pass and Half Pass

The side pass is a lateral movement when the horse faces north or south and steps east or west. The outside foot steps over the inside, both front and back, to move the whole body in one side direction at the same time.

The side pass is used for opening and closing gates, moving sideways along a log in a trail class and for obstacles in open country. It is a movement that requires the horse to work slow and relaxed, moving with each cue from the rider.

Very similar to this movement is a half pass or two-track. This is where there is lateral movement, but there is also forward movement. It is easier to start with a half pass maneuver and get him so he can handle this, then the forward movement can be stopped and you have a side pass.

To start your horse on a half pass walk him down the fence. Turn his head towards the fence using both a direct and a neck rein. If you are going to go to the left, turn his head to the right fence, shift your weight to the right, and squeeze on his right rib cage behind the back cinch with your leg. Your left leg should move out away from the horse's side so he has an open gate to move into. If he stops and tries to turn back, it means you are holding him too tight. Let him walk down the fence then try to get his body on a 45-degree angle moving down the fence.

If your horse is having trouble crossing his front feet, work him on a walk in a large circle. Make the circle smaller and smaller until he has to step over with his outside foot. Change directions and work on that circle until he steps over. The further he will step over with the outside foot the better will be his side pass, half pass, pivots and spins.

It is a good practice to use shin boots on a horse while you are working with him crossing the front feet. Many horses bang one leg against the other if there is no forward motion in their stepovers. This can cause splints and sore legs.

Once he has learned to step over with that front foot, you can start the half pass. In this manuever he will have to step through with the outside back foot as well.

The ideal is to have the horse's spine straight from head to tail. Facing northeasterly he will move north. Facing northwesterly he will also move north.

Let him walk north, then using your outside leg press the horse in the rib cage behind the back cinch. This will put the rear end to the inside of the arena making a separate set of tracks. Be sure to move your weight to the outside, freeing up his inside legs.

If he will not give to the leg pressure, have someone on the ground use their fist in the rib cage and push him over as you cue him and hold his head toward the fence.

If your horse is really stubborn you can use a spur in his ribs to teach him to respect your leg cues. He must trust you, however, and want to work for you so don't overdo the punishment. Be sure to reward him by removing the pressure, or spur, the instant he gives to the cue.

Once he has learned to step over with his front foot and to step through with his back foot you have mastered a half pass.

A full side pass can be accomplished by moving his body to a 90-degree angle to the fence and move him sideways with the same cues. Don't ask him to travel too far at a side pass in either direction.

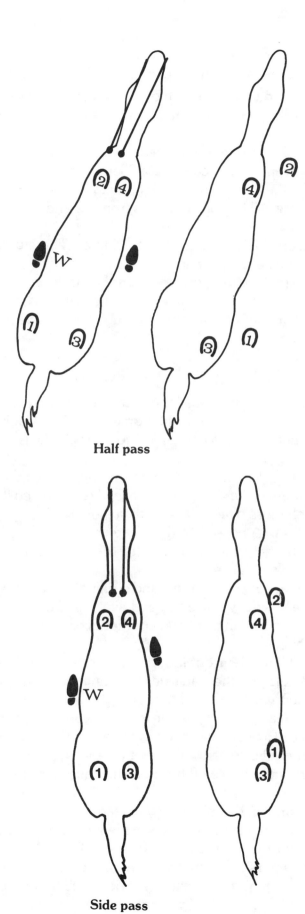

Half pass

Side pass

Half pass—step through

Weight out back on side pass

Horse's body straight

Sometimes a couple of fence posts can be used to practice on. Lay them end to end and make your horse step over one. Now, move him along the log in one direction, then the other.

After the horse has the side pass and half pass down well in both directions you can ask him to trot at a half pass. This will make him more willing to work in the side pass at a walk. Do not overdo the training at any one time.

You wonder what good all this work has done? For one thing, the horse has learned to give to leg pressure and to move laterally. With this movement you can be confident that you will pick up the proper lead when you lope. Just by moving the horse's rear end to the inside of the lead, the horse will always start out with the inside lead. He will be able to do this from a stand still, walk or trot.

Remember, the lope is initiated from the back outside leg, not the front inside leg. Therefore, if the hind outside leg steps under the horse's body as in the half pass, it is in a position to drive off. He will have his inside front leg free and will step out with it, putting the horse on the inside lead.

You must also remember the horse is trying to lift the front inside leg on the side pass, half pass and lope, so you should be on the back outside pocket of your pants to push the outside hind leg down to allow the front inside to be free to reach out.

Understand the Lead

For a horse to make turns in a collected and smooth way at a lope or faster, he must be on the proper lead. When loping in a clockwise circle, or to the right, the horse should be leading out with the right front foot. He is said to be in a right lead. When loping counter-clockwise, to the left, the horse should be in a left lead.

Before a person starts trying to teach a horse his leads, he should be sure he can see the leads from the ground, then get on a horse and feel them while riding. Once a lead is explained it is not too difficult to tell from the ground, but it is much more difficult when riding the horse.

The lope is considered a fast three beat rhythm. A horse in a right lead will have the following sequence: First, the left hind foot hits, then the right hind foot and the left front foot strike at about the same time. Last, the right front foot strikes the ground.

A horse that is loping with the left front foot reaching out farthest and striking the ground last is said to be in a left lead. The back foot on the lead side will also be set down ahead of the outside back foot. Some horses do, however, travel in one lead in front and another in back. This causes a rough, uneven gait. It is known as being disunited.

While observing the lead from the ground, look for the front foot that reaches out farthest and hits the ground last. Also, look to see if the back leg on the lead side is striking the ground ahead of the other back foot. In this manner you can tell what lead any horse is in.

Now, get on a broke horse and try to tell what lead you are in as he lopes. If you can't, don't feel alone. It takes a lot of concentration and practice to become proficient at leads. Some people like to stand up in the stirrups and look over the shoulder to see which foot is reaching out farthest. This is not the way to do it, because it can throw the horse off balance and cause him to change front leads.

The first thing to do on a lope is sit on your crotch in the middle of your saddle. Put your weight in your outside back pocket and sit tall. Don't slouch on your pockets in the back of the saddle.

Let your legs relax and you will find that one leg moves ahead of the other. This is the lead the horse is on. Try to ride with your lead foot at the horse's elbow and open, not touching the horse below your knees. Your outside leg should be straight down against his rib cage. In this position you can ride in rhythm with the horse. If you let both your feet go ahead, you will end up pushing

Leg Positions on a Right Lead

First position: left hind leg initiates the right lead.

Second position: weight on left front and right rear legs.

Third position: weight on right front leg. This is the time to cue for the stop.

Fourth position: horse is in free flight. In this position he can get his hind feet under him for a stop.

into the back of the saddle and polishing the seat by moving forward and back in the saddle as the horse lopes.

Another way to tell leads is to look at which shoulder of the horse is in lead. Generally, you can see a difference. Some horses are so smooth it is hard to feel which lead you are on. Some can even lope slowly in a circle on the wrong lead.

Many riders might ask, "Why worry about leads? The horse should know which foot to have where." A loose horse generally will make the proper lead choice. A rider not acquainted with leads, however, generally will develop a horse with a single lead. When he breaks his horse, he will use the same weight shift and kicks whenever the horse is put into a lope. Thus, the horse moves out with the same lead each time. When loping, the horse is usually started off in a straight lope, rather than in a circle. This also permits the single lead.

If this horse changes leads at all, it will be while he is abruptly changing direction at the lope. Even then he will generally just change his front lead and keep his back legs in the same lead all the time.

When you see a horse lope into a turn, then break down to a trot in the turn and lope out on the same lead, you can bet he was on the wrong lead and didn't know how to change. Some horses are just too lazy to change leads. In order to perform maneuvers properly, a horse must be

Weight on outside back pocket — first leg position.

Changing from second to third position.

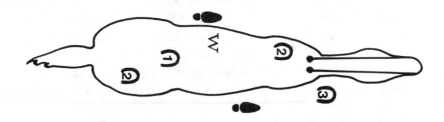

A lope is a three beat gait.

proficient in both leads. You may find he is smoother on, and easier to get into, one lead than the other. Some people feel that a horse is left or right footed, like people. Most likely it is not the horse that is left or right footed, but rather the trainer who broke him. It is your responsibility to make sure your horse learns to do all maneuvers one direction as well as the other. This means practicing one direction as much as you do the other.

Leads and Flying Changes

Now that you know your leads and can feel them in the seat of your pants, you are ready to train your horse to lope properly on command. Find a large pole corral or an arena to work in. A rectangular enclosure is the best.

For a left lead, start along the fence at one end of the arena. Direct rein the horse's head to the fence on your right and lay the left neck rein against his neck. Move your left foot forward and away from the horse. Pull the right leg back, against the horse's rib cage at the back cinch. Shift your weight to the right back pocket and ask for a half pass. Once he is stepping through with his outside hind foot, ask for a lope.

In a lope, sit up straight similar to the posture on a walk. Your inside leg will be slightly forward and open. Your outside leg will be straight down and closed against the horse. If you need more speed, use only the outside leg to squeeze or kick with.

Do not let your outside foot go forward, or you will end up sitting on your back pockets instead of your crotch. This will put you on the cantle with your weight on the horse's loin behind his balance. There, you will take more of the horse's up and down movement. This will cause you to bounce or polish the saddle.

Sit in the middle of your saddle and ride the balance of the horse, not the support of the saddle. In this position he won't have to drag you every step of the way.

Once the horse is loping in the proper lead, it is important to let him have his head in a normal position with a loose rein. It is also important for you to keep in balance with the horse. You should sit still with no weight changes that would confuse the horse. Moving your inside leg back to kick could cause him to shift front leads to accommodate your body position.

If you have to trot the horse before you lope him, you will usually end up bouncing. This may scare him into the lope, or he will buck or just trot harder. Try to get him to step into a lope right out of a walk on the half pass.

Some trainers post the horse into a lope. Coming up with the outside front foot is called posting on the outside diagonal. This will put your weight on the outside hind leg as the horse steps out with the inside front leg. This will help him take the inside lead. Unless you are proficient at posting, you are better off leaving this method alone. It also has a tendency to make the horse think he is supposed to trot every time before he lopes. That is not what you want to teach him.

Most young horses are afraid of the lope when you are on them. It may be because you are bouncing. Their first thought is to run. You must make them feel at ease when they start to lope and as they continue to lope. One way to do this is start out using a one hundred foot straight away or half the arena when you start them to lope. In this way they don't get much speed up before you stop them at the corner.

As soon as they are stopping easy in the corner, you can use the full side of the arena. This time start the lope and stop three times down one side. Walk across the end and do the same down the other side. Turn around and go the other direction in the same way.

After your horse has learned to work off your leg and body cues, it won't be necessary to turn his head to the outside. Put his rear end in position with your legs and body and the horse will take the proper lead.

Some trainers prefer the horse to travel with his nose slightly to the inside of the circle. This helps for tight circles. The natural carriage of the head, however, may be the most desirable for your horse.

Flying lead changes are much easier to teach a horse if he is willing to take each lead on cue. If he isn't, you will really have a hard time with this maneuver. That is not to say you can't get a lead change. You can jump out on the front inside shoulder and the horse will jump on that leg to catch you. You will seldom get a back lead change and will most likely scare the horse as he changes.

Most young horses need help in making the change of lead on cue. You must have your cues down properly and maintain the proper body balance.

Start the training by slow sit trotting a figure eight. Your legs should be as they would be on a lope for that lead. Sit on your outside pocket as you start trotting in the circle of the eight. Make the figure eight more like two D's back to back or use a long narrow figure eight. This will give you a straight line to change the lead.

As you come out of the circle into the start of the straight away, pick up on the reins a little then release - this is called a dwell. It is a cue to tell the horse you are planning a different gait or maneuver. It is to get his attention.

After the dwell, shift your legs for the opposite lead and shift your weight to the other back pocket. As you make these shifts, press the horse with your outside leg at the back cinch. If he is trained to half pass you will feel his rear end move slightly to the inside of the next circle. You will feel like he is now side trotting in that direction. Once you feel this, move your outside leg to the straight down position and sit trot that circle to the right.

After a number of repetitions with the trot, you will feel that the horse knows where you want his body for each circle. Keep him relaxed and enjoying the training.

Ask for a right lead at a lope and lope the right half of the figure eight. As you come to the straight line between the circles break him down to a trot and make your cues to change leads and circles. When you feel him flowing into the next circle, ask for the lope again. This should only take three or four steps at first. Soon, it will only require two steps, then one, and next you have a flying lead change with no break down to the trot.

Remember, if you put the back end into the circle he will be able to push off with the outside hind leg as he reaches out with his inside front leg. This will put both the front and back legs on the inside lead. If, however, you put the front end in the lead, it is not for sure the back lead will be right. For this reason it is important to have a horse that will half pass and has rib cage sensitivity.

When you are working on flying lead changes be sure to keep your horse collected. Unless his hind legs are collected up under him, he won't be able to react properly to the rib cage cue. You can keep him collected and relaxed only if you are relaxed.

It will take a number of days working slowly on each segment of this movement to accomplish flying lead changes, but if you have patience, both you and your horse will enjoy it.

Where are you going to use the flying lead change? The poles require a lead change at each pole. The barrels require one lead change between the first and second barrel. A cutting horse will change dozens of times in a two and one-half minute performance. Reining horses have to change many times during their pattern. The pleasure horse needs to be able to change leads when you are riding out in the country just so he won't trip and fall down. Ranch horses need to change so they don't let a cow get away as they run through the brush and rocks.

The flying lead change is not a difficult maneuver, but the rider must have the feel of leads and ride in balance and timing with the horse in order to execute it properly.

Pivots and Spins

Just as in most other maneuvers a horse is trained to do, the pivot and spin can be taught in many ways. In some areas the trainers lift their horses up and turn 90-degrees before the horse comes down in front, while other trainers teach their horses to keep walking with their front feet and pivot on their back feet.

The walk around pivot and run around spin are by far the best, if you will spend the time to develop them. This maneuver has the advantage of giving the horse more balance because he is always low to the ground and both his front feet never have to leave the ground at the same time.

Start this maneuver by walking your horse in circles. Make the circle smaller and smaller until you feel him step his outside front foot across in front of the inside foot.

If you have done a good job on the half pass you shouldn't have much problem getting him to step over. This maneuver is much easier for a trim legged, slender bodied horse. A broad chested, chunky horse will have a hard time with this type of maneuver.

Without a little forward motion, the horse will have a hard time stepping over in front. He will hit the outside leg against the inside as he tries to turn. If you back him up while stepping around, you will find him stepping behind with his outside leg. This will never make a good spin.

Try this maneuver with your own legs. You will find the only way to make it work is with a little forward motion. Try stepping behind with your outside leg and you'll see how tangled up you get.

Open your inside leg, close the outside leg at the horse's heart girth and put your weight in your inside back pocket. Direct rein with the inside rein in a lifting motion so you will bring his inside shoulder up. Use the outside rein to tap his neck and to make him get around.

Don't ask for pivots or spins at first. Just get him bringing the circle down smaller and smaller until he is stepping over well. As he comes to the center of the circle, step him over and move him out of the circle briskly. Then start on a circle in the other direction.

When the horse is stepping over correctly with ease, you can speed up the turn by kissing and squeezing your outside leg. The tap of the neck rein will also help speed up the motion.

Remember, don't lean forward and pull low on the inside rein. This will put weight on the inside shoulder causing the horse to drop it. Lock your inside elbow into your side and lift your hand up a little to lift the horse's inside shoulder. This also shifts your weight over the rear pivot foot.

As you turn to look in the direction you are going, you put body English into the saddle, which the horse can feel. Once you understand how to balance your weight over the pivot foot you will be able to help your horse do what you ask of him.

If your horse is the chunky, muscle bound type, he will have trouble crossing his front legs far enough to have a good walk around pivot let alone a run around spin. For horses that have trouble with these maneuvers, you can try the hop around pivot.

In order to lift up and pivot in 90-degree hops, a horse has to move back on his hind legs to get the weight off the front end. This requires elevating the horse's head and front end. Some horses find this maneuver quite easy, but some start rearing and lunging around.

A horse that stays low in front and walks his front feet around will be able to control his balance much better. Some horses are more natural at a pick-up pivot, however. A trainer should start the young horse turning to see which way the horse likes to work. If he is a natural pick up pivoter then don't change him to the walk around.

To pivot a horse 90-degrees, he needs to be giving well to pressure on the bit and to leg pressure. If he isn't, he isn't ready to start pivoting.

For the pick up pivot, shift his weight to his back feet by stepping him back a step and lifting up on the reins. Once you feel the horse has moved his weight back over his hind legs, start his nose

**Work on the front end step over. This is the
basis for all pivots, roll backs and spins.**

in the direction of the turn with a direct rein while you neck rein him lightly on the opposite side. Your outside leg moves up to the heart girth area. The outside leg will turn the front end. Hold the reins so he can't move forward. If he doesn't want to come around, bump him with your leg. Once his nose has been turned he will follow it. Only ask for a 45-degree move at first. Then walk him out and let him relax.

Whenever you start to turn a horse, his back inside leg should be well up under him for balance and as a pivot point. Therefore, you must learn to feel where his legs are as he moves to a stop. If necessary, back him a step to get the proper hind leg under him for the direction you plan to turn.

The real problem you have to worry about is getting the horse too high. If you can keep him low and pivot him, this is just as functional a pivot as any. Your body position will play a big role in whether he comes up or stays low. As you squeeze with the outside leg and turn his head to the inside, rotate your body in the hips so that you are facing into the turn and your weight is on your inside hip pocket. Never lean into the turn or lean back, for these will both throw your horse off balance. You want to feel as if you are a sky hook that can just pick your horse up a little and turn him around. Your body English will give you this feel. If you face straight ahead or behind the turn, your horse will not feel the incentive to turn because he can't feel you turning with him.

If a horse doesn't want to give his head to the turn and keeps throwing his rear end out, you need more work on reining. It will help to step off and tie your rein to the stirrup so the horse has to turn and arch his body. Trade sides and do the same thing again. Usually one or two sessions with this type of training is all that will be needed. Tying the reins to his tail will also make him bend in the middle and turn his head into the turn. Only leave him tied five or ten minutes each way.

A high fence or wall can help you get started with this maneuver, but don't use it long because the horse will think he only has to pivot when he is next to a fence. By continually pivoting into the fence one way, then the other, a horse will learn what you want and soon he will start cheating on the turns.

Some novices think if they put a pair of spurs on and jab him in the shoulder he will really get around. He may jump around at first, but he will be afraid of the turn and when you get him away from the fence he will be jumpy and lunging when you start jabbing him with your spurs. If you need a little help to get him around, use the tip of your rein or a flat bat to tap him on the outside lower neck or shoulder to speed him up.

Once he has mastered a 90-degree turn, you start putting two 90-degree turns together and then three and four until you have a spin. Most trainers find they can't get many continuous spins out of a horse that pivots in 90-degree turns, but then how often, other than in a reining class, will you need to spin a horse? A cutting horse will never be required to turn more than 180-degrees in any one motion.

It isn't necessary to spin him a dozen times a day to keep him tuned up. Just walk him around each way a couple of times and leave it alone. You can always increase the speed if you need it.

Many reining classes ask for only a 90-degree pivot and then a 180-degree pivot. These can be accomplished with either method of turning. The first thing to remember is to stop your horse and let him settle before you start the pivots. It helps if you have a slight dwell between the 90-degree and the 180-degree turns. It gives the horse a chance to collect himself for the other direction.

If you have the opportunity to work cattle or turn back for a cutter, you will be able to let the horse learn while he is doing something so he can see a use for the maneuver. If you are not trying to make a reining horse, don't worry about teaching a spin. It looks impressive but it is not too functional in every day riding.

Roll Backs

A roll-back is a turn of 180-degrees that is executed from a run down. The horse should go into a stop, but before he gets stopped, roll over his inside hock and bust out again in a run. Many people think they are doing a roll-back, when they lope down, stop, circle around and lope back. This is not a roll-back.

To perform a roll-back you want to trot through the maneuver. First, trot down to where you are going to execute the roll-back. Stop with the horse's inside leg forward and pivot him around facing the other direction and trot back. You are using the stop and pivot previously discussed.

**Just as he comes
to the end of his slide
turn him over his
inside pivot foot.
This requires that front
foot step across.**

Don't let him
stall. Keep him
moving around
with your leg.

Bust out for
the next slide
and rollback.
Don't confuse him
with your body or
he will scotch
on the next stop.

Once you have shown the horse what it is you are going to ask him to do, then speed it up to a lope. If you plan to make a left roll-back, put your horse in a left lead so he will have the left hind leg up under him and the left front leg out in front when you roll him back over his hock. As he comes out of the left roll-back he should be in a left lead.

A right roll-back should start on a right lead and turn to the right, then come out on a right lead. The leads are not as much of a problem as one would think because as the horse stops he should have both legs up under him and when he comes out of roll-back it is natural for him to reach out with the inside leg, which will put him on the proper lead.

As you lope down, pick your spot for the turn. Start your stop just before you reach it and then just before your horse comes to a stop, roll him over his inside hock with a pivot. As soon as he starts to straighten out give him some rein so he can move out.

When you put some speed into it and start to stop him, his hind legs will come up under him. Just before he stops, pivot him around as discussed earlier. This is one of the prettiest maneuvers you can make if it is executed properly. It puts together a number of the things you have been working on up until now. It is a practical maneuver too. In almost any cutting contest you will see many partial roll-backs as a horse tries to recover and beat a critter to head him before he gets to the fence.

Some common problems you should look for are poor stops, slow turns and trot outs. When you stop him, don't get his front feet off the ground or it will take too long to get him down and coming around. Make sure the stop is straight. If he is sideways a little it will be hard to turn properly.

Once you start your turn, use your body English and your legs to get him around. Then don't let him stop and wonder what is next or just trot out. Bust him right out of his turn and he will come out on the proper lead.

Training Time Flow Chart

First Week
Halter break
Sack out
Work on stop and back while leading

Second Week
Let horse wear bit
Tie from side to side
Drive
Mount and dismount
Tie both reins back

Third Week
Snub and ride
Ride not snubbed
Tie both reins back
Go on ride
Work on walk, trot, stop and back

Fourth Week
Go on ride
Work on walk, trot, lope, stop and back
Start trotting circles for front leg cross over

Fifth Week
Work on fourth week maneuvers
Start on pivot and half pass

Sixth Week
Work on fourth and fifth week manuevers
Work with cattle, if possible
Work on trail obstacles and side pass

Seventh Week
Let horse rest

Eighth to Twelfth Weeks
Work on fifth and sixth week maneuvers
Speed up manuevers

Thirteenth Week and over
Start specializing on specific training

CHAPTER TWENTY
Training for Performance

The Western Pleasure Horse

Good Western Pleasure horses are the quiet, smooth-moving horses that look good traveling. Not many horses can qualify as a horse that is a pleasure to ride. Some are so rough you can't set them and some are so chargy you can't handle them quietly.

This is a class you can start working on as soon as your horse has learned to stop, back and pick up his leads on cue. After riding a horse for thirty days a good trainer can tell if a horse will make a pleasure horse. He must have good conformation and eye appeal before the judge will usually look at him, but most of all he must have an easy, smooth way of going.

You must train a pleasure horse to walk out in a medium speed. You can't have him passing everything up and you don't want him dragging, as if he would like to stop all the time. Give him a loose rein and make him hold a steady pace. Work on the loose rein. Take hold of him if he goes too fast, but then give him back the loose rein.

A loose rein is important in this class, but most riders don't realize what a loose rein is. Some give a horse four or five inches more slack than is normal and have the reins hanging way down. A loose rein may be accomplished just by lowering your hand a little more than normal. In this manner you can still lift it up a little and have more contact. When you give a horse four or five inches of rein out of your hand, you are in a poor position to stop or turn. If you pull up with your hand real high, a judge will knock you down.

Learning to walk up and down the rein with your fingers as you ride around will also help. If you keep one eye on the judge, you will see when he asks the announcer to call for a change of speed or a stop. Go up your reins a little if they feel too long for a stop. If they call for a change of gait you are still ready to ask your horse for that. Then let the reins slide a little, but not much. Being able to walk your reins will allow you to ride with a looser rein at the walk and take them up a little as you gain speed, if necessary.

If you have a head set on your horse and have created a supple mouth, he will work on a loose rein, but if you have pushed him too fast and started collecting him for slide stops, spins and roll-backs he is probably up on the bit too much for a winning pleasure horse. A pleasure horse must be relaxed and at ease, if he is going to show well.

At a jog or slow trot he should be smooth and steady. You should sit down and not bounce. If he is jigging, then he will be hard to ride. He will show he is nervous and excited. The judge will spot him right off.

Sometimes a judge will ask for an extended trot. This doesn't mean to see how fast he can trot, but rather just extend out a little. Remember, you still must sit this trot so don't let him throw you all over the place.

The judge will call for a lope, both to the right and to the left. It may be from a standstill, a walk or a trot. Your horse should be able to step into a lope from any of these positions and do it in the proper lead. If he happens to miss a lead, break him down and pick up the proper lead. Don't just let him lope around on the wrong lead and show everyone you don't know leads any better than your horse.

This lope should be slow and collected and very smooth and flowing. Sit in the middle of your saddle and ride the horse, not the saddle. Many riders like to sit back and put their feet forward, trying to brace against the saddle. They will generally polish the seat this way, or just bounce.

You want to sit up tall and ride with good posture all through this class. This will add to the smooth, classy look you are trying to portray. Elbows should be in, toes up and heels down. Look like you are enjoying being there, don't be a sourpuss.

When the judge calls for a stop, pull your horse down to a nice even stop as soon as he is in the right position, but don't overdo it and show the judge a slide. Don't pull your horse's head up or lift him for this stop. For the reverse, don't pivot him around or try a roll-back, but rather walk his front feet around smoothly and quietly to the inside of the arena. Keep everything smooth and flowing without any jerks or quick stops.

When the judge has you line up, give yourself some room. He may ask you to dismount and you know he is going to ask you to back. As the judge comes down the line asking for a back, walk up your reins with your fingers until you have a good hold on the reins. If your horse is sticky to start to back, ask him to take a small step forward, then put him in a smooth, collected back. Make it straight using a light pull. Don't put your hand in his mouth and force him back.

You've got to figure a way, while you are showing, to get in a position to be seen. A lot of good horses don't get seen in a pleasure class, especially when they get into heavy traffic where they are hidden from the judge. In a big class a judge can miss a good horse. That's the breaks if the rider doesn't show him to the judge. Remember to always pass on the inside of another horse.

A rider's dress is another way of getting the judge to look at you. Dress like a dressed-up cowboy, not like a dude. The judge can usually tell the difference, and will not be swayed by flashy and overly expensive dress and equipment.

In training your horse for the Western Pleasure class, you must work on slowing and smoothing his trot and lope. A slow trot is quite easy to ride but a fast trot is much harder.

In training, a lot of people will let their horses fast lope or even run around an arena until the horse is tired. They figure they will slow him down when he gets tired, but all they do is make him an endurance horse. It is hard to ride him until he is tired every time you go to a show. He will be all sweaty and look terrible.

It is much easier to teach a horse to slow down by breaking him back to a walk or even a stop if he charges from a trot to a lope or goes too fast at a trot. It works the same for slowing a lope. This will also reinforce his leads because every time you drop him back to a walk or trot from a lope and then start loping again, he will be required to pick up the proper lead. It takes a lot of consistent work to slow him and smooth him.

You want your pleasure horse to have limited head movement. He shouldn't swing or bob it excessively during the show. Some horses naturally bob or swing their heads a little. It is better to choose a horse that doesn't have exaggerated characteristics.

The ears are another thing you have to watch. A good pleasure horse should have his ears forward and alert. If you have a cranky mare or stud, you want to be sure to stay out of the crowd and stay on the inside so you don't get pinned in. Sometimes you can speak to your horse or just lift up on your reins to get his attention back on you instead of the other horses. Young geldings will usually get over this if you ride them around other horses a lot.

The last thing to work on is the extended trot, because you want to make sure you have settled him down, slowed him down and made him relax. To extend the trot you need to push him a little more into the bit, but try to hold him from loping. If he goes to loping, ease him down to a trot. Don't jerk him down or get after him or he will get to be afraid of the extended trot. This gait has to be smoothed out as much as possible and you have to learn to ride it at a sit. You can't post or it looks like your horse is too rough to sit.

In the class, the rider should always make sure he knows where the judge is and where he is looking. If you miss a lead behind the judge and you pick it up before you get to him, you will not get knocked down. If you have to gather up your reins, do it behind the judge, but when you pass the judge do everything just right. Remember, he might turn around any time so don't just ride for the judge but ride properly during the class. The audience doesn't like to see people winning that they saw making mistakes.

Don't expect to win at first, but season your horse and yourself so you are both relaxed. Then you will start winning.

Bitting the Horse Up

Some horses carry their heads too high, either because of fear of the bit and the rider's hands or because of the horse's physical conformation. A thick throat latch prevents a horse from being able to tuck his nose in. Necks that are set high on the shoulders also cause high heads.

In order to teach the horse a proper and natural looking head carriage, it is sometimes necessary to restrict the horse's head with the reins, so that the horse will learn to stay behind the bit and give to it when it is pulled.

Nothing will help if the horse can't learn to trust your hands. This may be because your hands are rough on the horse's mouth or the horse has had such traumatic experiences that he will never trust a rider's hand if he gets excited.

There are a number of things that will help, assuming you don't have one or both of the problems above. You can start by bitting the horse up in a corral and letting him stand. He will push on the bit but will soon learn the only way to get off the pressure is to break at the pole and tuck his nose.

Next, tie a rein to each stirrup and longe the horse on a walk and trot. This will work his mouth on a side pull from each stirrup as the horse moves each side separately. This will also cause him to move off the bit.

Another good way to train for head set and teach the horse to stay behind the bit is to use a snaffle bit with long reins. Run the reins under the horses front legs and up over his back. Wrap the left rein around the right and the right around the left over his back.

Pull the slack so the head is tucked an inch or two more than the horse likes to carry it. With each lesson you can adjust the length a little until you have the horse tucking and breaking at the pull the way you want him to do. This goes for all three training methods.

With the reins under his arms and over the back, put the horse in a round corral and work him on a walk and trot. The action of the legs moving will give a see-saw action to the bit. It will only take a few rounds before he will find that by tucking his nose he gets away from the see-saw.

When you're riding the horse and his head gets out too far, all you need to do is see-saw lightly and he will tuck his nose. In a show you can wiggle your hand from side to side and he will get the message, once he learns to tuck and to trust your hands.

From this you can see the need for hands that are still when they are not telling the horse something. If you can feel little pulls in your hand as the horse strides along, you know you will be sending signals to the horse that he can't make out. That's because you don't know you're sending them.

The horse moves off the bit because he doesn't enjoy that pressure in his mouth. Make sure you aren't creating more pressure once he has moved off the initial pressure.

Don't be afraid to use this on a colt you're breaking or an old horse that is aggressive. You can use a snaffle, or on the older horses use the bit you ride him with. Remember, start out with only a little change in head set and work up to where you want the horse's head.

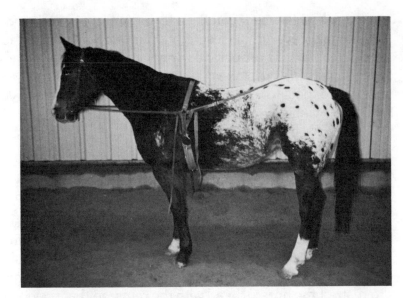

Bitting Rig

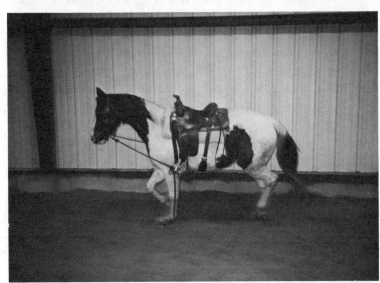

Stirrup Action on Mouth

Leg Action on Mouth

Head Sets

There's been a lot of controversy over which type of head set a Pleasure horse should have. The Pacific Coast trainers and judges wanted to see a horse with his head behind the vertical. While the Southern horsemen wanted the head held in a natural position. This was with the nose out a little past the vertical.

They each had reason to support their position. The Pacific Coast people felt a horse had to be collected and up into the bit to perform to his best. If a horse is strung out he will not be able to get his weight on the hind end like they want.

These riders always had more hand and leg contact which kept the horse ready all of the time. It also kept him in a more keyed up state.

The Texas theory was built around the thought that a cow horse was anything but collected in the same sense as the Coast riders thought of it. The cutting horse had his head forward of the vertical and the rider used little hand and leg pressure when the horse was working cows.

This horse learned to work on a loose rein and respond to a very slight neck rein and leg pressure. The horse could slow trot or lope or move out briskly with no false gait as seen in many·Coast trained horses. This horse could flat sweep 180 degrees to head a cow. He could slide on his own without a rider's hand holding his head up.

Bob Lomis and other top trainers have used this 180 degree turn to develop a 360 degree spin that is flat with just a little forward movement. That means the horse doesn't have to be backed up on his hind quarters and hop around to make a spin. The Texas horse can spin with the normal balance on his front feet. He is just running in a tight circle with his hind feet moving slightly forward as he turns.

In a past Intermountain Quarter Horse Journal, there was an article by Don Balzer stating that "the big head set on the Western Pleasure horse is out and the natural look is in." This was long overdue. Both riders and judges should realize that the unnatural head set and the false gaits are no longer what is in fashion.

You no longer need to fight the horse's nose in all your training. You can teach him to relax and work on a loose rein because he is comfortable and not afraid of your hands or legs.

This doesn't mean you want him all strung out. You still want his hind legs up under him, but teach him to be collected on a loose rein. You say, "but how can that be done?"

Why don't you start out by letting the horse know that you want a slow trot. Let him move out on a trot on a loose rein but as soon as he gets aggressive and you feel you want to slow him down, just stop him and back a couple steps. Try it again. You may only go twenty or thirty steps then stop and back.

Pretty soon he will start to realize there is nowhere to go so he might as well slow down. As long as he is going slow, let him trot on a loose rein. Soon you'll find that he will slow down if you just pick up on your reins and release.

To make this work, you have to teach him that you trust him on a loose rein. Give him a loose rein each and every time you trot. If he takes advantage of it, stop him and back up a step.

Remember to stop and back correctly. Don't jerk him down. Just pick up your reins, way "whoa", take a deep set and wipe the reins on his neck. If he doesn't stop, put pressure on the bit and shut him down. Soon he will stop on the release rather than the pull. Always say "whoa" and draw out the word. Don't say "whoa" briskly or harshly. Make it a word that won't scare him but is still firm in tone.

A horse should not be afraid of the stop and back. If a horse is afraid of a maneuver, he will be undependable in performing it. In all maneuvers, build a bond of trust that will allow the horse to relax and work because he knows how and wants to please you.

If you permit him a little freedom with his head, he will be more relaxed and easier to work with. If he relaxes too much and lowers his neck below the horizontal, lift your hands up and forward on the neck. Work the bit in a light see-saw motion. Don't make it uncomfortable, just noticeable. This will usually elevate the head and tuck the nose at the same time.

As soon as he does what you want, stop the action and give him a little slack. Use this when necessry when training, then when you are in a show you will only need to lift and wiggle your hands. He will get the message and respond with a more alert appearance.

Remember, the natural look is in. Work on making the horse look natural, not artificial, in his gaits and maneuvers.

Western Equitation

If you are really serious about the sport of riding, you will always be trying to learn so that you improve your ability to ride. The better you ride, the better your horse will perform. Until you have learned balance and rhythm, you will not be able to get much out of your horse. Most anyone can slouch around on a horse and learn to stay on but that isn't being an equestrian. An equestrian is an artist in the sport of riding, as equitation is the art of riding. You might say you know riders who place high in the show ring and don't have good posture. This may be true, but think how much better they could do if they did practice good posture.

It is best to start out with good posture and proper seat and hands. If the proper position is practiced, it soon becomes a habit and a good one to have throughout your riding lifetime.

When you are training a young horse, you will vary your hands and seat as needed to over-emphasize some aspects of training, but the goal is to go back to the basic position once the horse knows what you want.

Good equitation starts with mounting the horse. Once the horse is saddled and bridled, lead the horse a few steps and tighten the cinch. Before mounting, always make sure the stirrups are the right length for you.

Stand at the horse's shoulder, take the reins in your left hand and place them on the horse's neck about eight inches forward of the saddle. Take the slack out of the reins so you can make sure the horse stands still while mounting. He should be trained to stand very quietly while you mount and dismount. If you have taught him to stand still by wiggling the horn as a cue, it will help when you are in the show.

Face the rear of the horse. Turn the stirrup with your right hand and place your left foot in the stirrup. The right hand is now placed on the horn. Bounce around until you are facing forward with your right side next to the horse. Keeping your head up, give a bounce on your right leg, moving your weight into the left stirrup. Once you have raised your body up on the left leg, swing the right leg over and sit down easy. Once you have obtained your seat and caught the right stirrup with your right foot, adjust the reins in your hand so they are even.

Next, stand up in the stirrups then let yourself down into the saddle by bending your knees and pushing your heels down, with your crotch maintaining most of the contact weight with the saddle. Your chin should be up, shoulders back and chest out. Your back is held straight. This is what is referred to as sitting tall in the saddle.

Your feet are the foundation for a proper position. If your feet are parallel to the horse's body with the heels lower than the toes, the toes straight ahead and the foot straight and flat in the stirrup, the lower legs, knees and thighs will be correct. If these are all correct, it will be easier for your seat and upper body to be correct.

To put your heels down, just let the weight of your legs go in the stirrups from the back of the stirrup and then raise your toes up. The stirrup should hang at a right angle to the horse so your

One hand on neck, the other on horn.

Have good posture

Keep your head up

foot can sit parallel to the horse. If you ride the outside of your foot you can't have a good foot position.

There should be leg contact from the calf up to the crotch. If you are long-legged you will only have contact from the knee to the crotch. The leg should be bent so that your heel is directly below your shoulder and the toe of your boot can be seen looking off the knee. You don't want your legs out away from the horse's barrel.

With your legs in this position and getting into a "tall-in-the-saddle" position, you will find that you are sitting in the middle of your saddle. Don't sit back on the cantle or you will have your feet way out in front of you and you will be behind the motion of your horse. To be able to have proper seat position, you need a saddle that fits you. If you are small you may need a fourteen-inch seat. A sixteen-inch would make it impossible for you to stay up over your feet. Be sure your saddle fits you.

Looking from the back, a rider should have square shoulders with the shoulders pulled back. The spine should be on the same perpendicular line as the tail of the horse. The saying is "chin up and chest out". This does more for some than others.

There should be a vertical line from the shoulder to the elbow. The elbows should be held close to the rider's ribs. Relax your upper arms and let them bend normally to your sides.

The rein hand, usually the left, should extend a little in front of the horn and slightly higher so it will clear the horn as you turn. Short-armed people will have their hand over the horn, while long-armed riders may have theirs further ahead of the horn.

The rein arm should be in about a 90-degree angle at the elbow. The non-rein hand can be placed on your belt buckle. From the back, both elbows will look symmetrical. If you wish, you can choose to place this hand on your thigh.

For a rider to have good contact with the horse, the hands and arms must be supple and relaxed. The reins should be held so that contact is maintained with the horse's mouth, but without putting pressure on the bit. The difference between a tight and a loose rein is only one inch, or even less for finished horses and riders. Having contact with the mouth does not mean always having pressure on it. Learn to feel the horse's mouth with your fingers and not your hands and arms. Talk to your horse through your fingers and you will have a horse that will trust you and respond to the slightest request.

Hold your head relaxed but in a position with the chin up and your eyes looking above and between the horse's ears. Don't rock your body or let your head bob as the horse moves.

When dismounting, take the reins in the left hand and the horn in the right. Take the right foot out of the stirrup, lift up and swing your leg over and step down so you are facing the front of the horse. Don't let go of the horn or neck until you have both feet on the ground.

Showing in a class of Western Equitation requires that you have a horse that can win a Western Pleasure class. Then you must ride in the proper position and in balance with your horse. In a pleasure class, the horse is being judged, but in the equitation class, the rider is the main one being judged.

There is also Bareback Equitation that requires all the proper positions without a saddle. This class really requires good balance. Not every Western Equitation rider can be a bareback equestrian, but you train for it in a similar way, only without the saddle. A lot of bareback equitation practice can help develop better balance and self-confidence when showing in a saddle.

Whenever you ride, concentrate on improving your posture. Make it a habit to do it properly. You will be a better rider and can teach your horse much more.

The Trail Class Horse

Some trainers don't like to work on trail obstacles because it takes so much time and patience. Most riders don't think it is a very exciting event. But if you really want to feel satisfaction from creating a bond of trust between you and your horse, try this activity.

We have all seen the cowboy who rides up to a ditch and the horse balks at crossing. What does he do? He starts overhauling the horse until he forces him across. What has he taught the horse? He has put a fear of water into the horse. The next time the horse comes to a ditch he will remember the remember the last bad experience with it. If he is forced over enough, he will get used to crossing but will never feel good about it.

A trail horse should be calm, but alert and agile. He should always be able to be controlled by hand, leg and voice cues. During the last year or so, more speed has been added to trail classes. You may be asked to start out in a given lead and lope half way around the arena before stopping abruptly to go over the first obstacle. Points are given for free easy-way-of-going and control. A big old dead-headed horse can't walk off with all the trail class trophies any more. This is a real improvement.

When you pick a horse to work the trail class, you may find that a pleasure-type horse will work well. A slender horse has a slight advantage in backing through obstacles and being able to bend or arc around obstacles.

It is important that you have your horse well cue-trained so you can move his rear end in a 360-degree circle around the front end or the front around the rear. He should be able to side pass and back slow while under your control. Your horse should respond well to voice commands such as "Whoa" and "Easy". You need these when trying to back through difficult obstacles.

A trail horse should be trained so that he knows he is able to do what you ask of him and that nothing you ask him to do will harm him. Even though sometimes he won't like doing it, he will perform well because you ask him and he trusts your judgement. Then you have a trail horse you can win on. You must then remember never to ask him to do something he can't accomplish or that might possibly hurt him. If you lose his confidence, you'll find it hard to regain.

To train a trail horse you should let him look at an obstacle and even smell it, then give him time to think about it before doing it. Don't expect too much to start with. Start with simple obstacles. It will take repetition of an obstacle before he understands what is expected of him. This doesn't mean you should work all day on an obstacle, but rather work a few minutes a day for several days and it will be much more indelibly impressed on his mind.

Pause often during the training. Pause before and after an obstacle to give your horse time to think about that obstacle. Never punish him while he is maneuvering through an obstacle. You can correct him, work with him and try to help him understand what you want. Once he understands the obstacle, never let him refuse that obstacle. Remember to take time, have patience and build a mutual confidence between you and your horse.

Start with simple obstacles such as one pole on the ground next to a fence. First get someone to stand by with a whip. Leading the horse from the ground, walk over the obstacle. Let the horse come up to it and smell it and even paw it the first time. Now ask him to cross with a slight pull on the reins. Do not face the horse while leading him and be sure to stay to the side because he may jump the pole and land on top of you.

If he doesn't want to cross have the helper with the whip just tap him low on the back legs. Do not whip him. If he jumps, take him back over it until he walks over it. Now stop him with it between his legs. Pat him and put him at ease.

Now it is time to mount and ride over the obstacle. Encourage him to go slow and put his head down. This will get more points from a judge than the horse that has his head in the air and walks rapidly over the object.

Add a couple more poles and start over. Now block the poles up six inches. If he is knocking them over, try to slow him down and even stop him in the middle of the poles. Teach him to place his feet, rather than just ambling over the obstacle.

Tires work well to develop foot position. Set up four tires, two by two. Set them up next to a wall or fence but don't put them too close together. Now lead him between the tires a few times.

Stop him in the middle, let him stand a minute or two, lead him on through and mount up. Slide the tires tight against each other. Using your reins to restrain his forward movement and your feet to encourage a longer step, make him step slowly and deliberately in the center of the tires. Don't let him back up or he might hook a tire with his hoof and pull it towards him, thus scaring him. Once he is doing this well, add more tires.

In trail classes you can never be sure what you may be asked to do, so teach your horse as many obstacles as you can. Loading in a trailer and opening a gate should always be stressed because they are so often a part of a trail class.

When loading into a trailer, you want him to get in without being led, then to stay in until he's asked to back out. Using grain in the trailer at home, once he is in, can help teach him to stay in for a few minutes. Always put your stirrups up over the saddle.

Ground Tying the Horse

Have you ever been in a situation where it would have been convenient to drop your reins on the ground and have your horse stand?

Some trainers hobble their horse each time they get off to leave him for a few minutes. Others use a stake (picket) line and hobble.

You will have a hard time teaching your horse to ground tie if he can't stand to be away from the other horses. As soon as the reins hit the ground he will light out for home, or the nearest horse. You must ride your horse alone, so he gets used to being by himself.

Use a ring spike about eight inches long as a stake. Punch a hole in the end of your rein so the spike will go in, but not through the hole.

The arena will be the best place to start your training. Work your horse until he is a little tired. Stop and dismount, now take your reins down. Get the ringed spike and stick it through the hole in the rein.

Let your horse see you drop the reins on the ground as you say "whoa", then "stand". Push the spike in the ground and step on it hard. Step away from your horse and see what he does. He will most likely try to follow you. If he does, he will hit a tug on the rein when he reaches the end of the slack.

Walk over and back him up. Take the loose rein and drop it again. Say "whoa", then "stand". Walk away again. This time let the spike hold him for a moment. If he pulls hard on the spike go back and give him the tug, drop the rein, and say "whoa", then "stand" again.

This may take many lessons before he really understands what you want. Horses learn through repetition, so keep on working on this lesson at the end of your riding each day.

Once he has the idea, stop using the spike and just use your other cues. Be sure to use the cues the same each time.

If you have him trained in the arena, take him out and try him in the open country. The first few times use the spike. Don't carry it in your pocket. Tie it on the saddle or put it in your saddle bags. If you were to get thrown or rolled on with the nail in your pocket it could be your demise.

There are some horses that just won't stay once they find out they can move off the spot they were left. It is best to use a figure-eight hobble around the cannon bones above the ankles. This will usually ground the horse, if it is put on high and snug.

After you walk home a couple of times you will be more interested in this training. To be successful, you must have patience and time. It takes many rides with a lot of stops to see any results.

298

Trailering

While we are talking about loading, we should also consider some factors in hauling horses. Your horse trailer should be checked for safety. There should be proper air in the tires, the hitch should have safety chains and the ball should be replaced every few years to prevent crystalizing and breaking off. It will help to oil your ball hitch to reduce the heat when traveling. This is the major cause of crystalizing.

The trailer should be level. It should not be nosing down or tailing down. The horse has a hard time riding in an unlevel trailer. Having a ball hitch mounted at two levels will permit the lower hitch to be used when empty or when you are hauling only one horse. When you are loaded heavy, you can use the upper hitch. By using the two hitches you will be able to level your trailer.

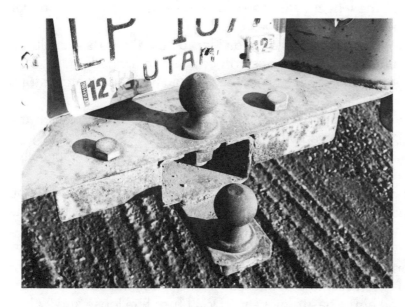

Two levels of hitches permits leveling your trailer

Horses hauled in a trailer with a high hitch, as you see on many four wheel drive units, will sit on the tail gate and rub out the tail hair and cut into the tail.

Dividers should be less than half way to the floor to allow for more spread of the feet and better balance. A foot wide divider is usually adequate.

Floor boards should run from front to back in the trailer. Boards running sideways have more of the horse's weight on one individual board. If it breaks, both legs go down through the floor to the pavement. If they run from front to back, only one leg would go down and the horse would have the other leg to balance on so he could pull the other leg back up. The use of floor mats will help prevent the horse from sliding around and going through the floor if it breaks. Be sure to take them out often and clean the floor boards. Check for broken or deteriorated boards.

The trailer should be six feet six inches tall to prevent bumping the horse's head when loading and to give plenty of head room while hauling. Underseal on the roof will reduce sound and sweating of the metal.

Set the butt chains ahead far enough that the horse cannot lean on the tail gate. Cover the butt chains with a soft rubber hose to prevent soring the horse. A 1 1/2-inch round metal pipe makes a good butt bar also.

Some people don't tie their horse while others do. If you have a proper head divider and your horses haul well, you may not need to tie them. If there is a chance of them fighting or turning their heads around, it is best to tie them. Put quick release snaps on the tie chains. These can be released even if the horse is pulling back.

Always remember to tie them after the butt chains are done up when loading and untie before the butt chains are undone when unloading.

Check the inside and outside of your trailer for sharp objects that may injure a horse. Have them filed or rounded so they are not going to be a problem. The license plate is a danger if exposed beyond the trailer. It is best to bolt them to the back door with the nuts on the outside.

Windows on each side are much easier to use when tying or feeding. The center window requires you to get up on the hitch to see what you are doing.

There should be ventilation in the trailer. Most trailers have air vents in the roof at the front. Horses need air and they need to get rid of body heat so an air escape should also be available.

Trailer brakes should be working and the wheel bearings repacked each year. Check trailer springs for broken leaves and check shackle bolts for tightness.

If you are using a pickup with a rack on it, be sure there is a divider to hold the horses in place. You can blow a tire or break a rim if both horses shift to one corner in a non-divided rack. Dual tires are much safer if you are hauling horses in a rack. Again, tires should have adequate air for a maximum load.

Pickup beds may not be strong enough to support horses. Many accidents occur when the horse's leg breaks through a wheel well and is chewed off by the tire.

Whatever you haul in, be sure your tail gate is shut and correctly fastened. Some people have arrived home and found the horse fell out somewhere along the way.

Once loaded, the horse must depend on you for sane driving. You cannot corner fast or stop and start quickly. Horses climb the sides of the trailer because of a bad ride. Try not to let the horse have a bad experience and you most likely will have a quiet rider.

A big problem for beginner trailer towers is over correcting a swaying trailer. If the horses move to one side, it may require a major correction. Do it as slowly as possible. Don't jerk it back or you will put an opposite movement in the horses and that may cause you to roll the outfit.

It is always best to restrict the area the horse has to move in. Don't turn him loose and let him move from side to side and back to front. This will cause less sway and less distance to fly forward if you have to turn or stop quickly.

If you are hauling short distances it is best not to feed hay in the trailer. A little grain in the manger once the horse is in leaves him with a good feeling about loading. Hay can ball up and cause choking and colic when a horse is nervous. On long hauls it may be necessary to feed in the trailer. Feed small amounts and more often.

Some horses won't urinate in the trailer so it is best to unload horses every five hours or so and let them have a half hour rest. Horses get tired from riding just like you do, so don't go too far in one day. There are horse motels in some areas, so plan ahead to have adequate facilities for your horse to have a good night's rest too.

Gates can be a problem if you don't know how to approach them. If the gate is hinged from the right and swings toward you as you approach it, you should ride up to it with your horse's right side against it and his head facing the gate opening. In this manner you can use your right hand to unlock the gate and then side pass the gate open toward you. Ride around the end of the gate and side pass the gate closed. Back up and lock the gate. If it swings away from you, you will have to side pass it open first, then ride around it and side pass it shut.

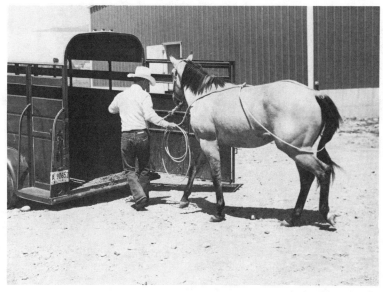

A butt rope may
help the first time
or two

Give him time to
look, smell and feel
the trailer

Give him a little
grain and let him
relax

301

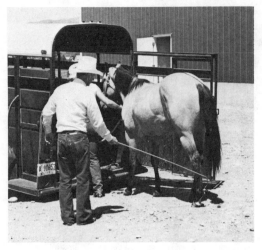

Use whip on back legs

Boost him in

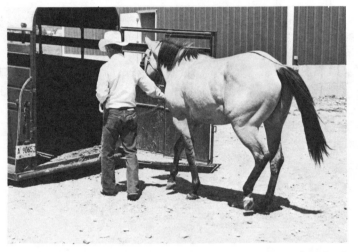

Now he loads

Back him out

302

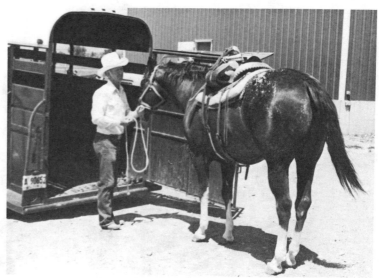

Put your stirrups up

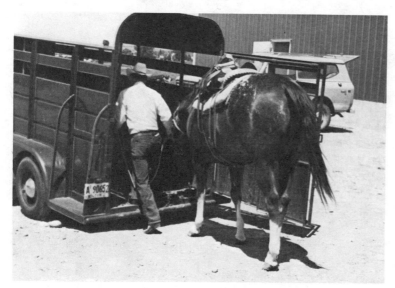

**Let him look
and smell**

If, however, the gate is hinged on the left as you face it, then you should ride up to it with the horse's right side against the gate, with his rear end toward the gate opening. Position him so you can unlock the gate with your right hand. Side pass him to the left until the gate is open well. The smaller the gate the wider it must be opened. Now back him around the end of the gate until his rear end is facing away from the gate opening. Side pass him left until the gate is closed. Then ride forward a couple of steps and lock it.

You are probably wondering, "Why do it different ways? Why not just ride up with the left side of the horse against the gate?" The reason is that you should not change hands on the reins during a class.

Another maneuver to practice is the side pass. Many times the side pass will be used as one of the regular maneuvers in the class. It is also used in other classes as a tie breaker. You want to

**Forward step
through gate**

304

Back through gate

be sure that your horse moves freely in response to leg pressure both front and back and in both directions.

Backing through the "L" is probably used as often as any other maneuver. To start with, use a straight back. Once he has that down, move to a 45 and then to a 90-degree or "L" turn. It is sometimes permissible to walk through forward and then back up, but generally it is not permitted. Therefore, it is important to teach your horse to walk up to the starting point and back through without having seen the layout on a prior walk through. Here again, leg cues are of the utmost importance.

You will lose points for stepping on a pole or moving forward to reposition. The key is to go slow and make every step of your horse go where you want it to. Your cues must be well administered and in balance with your horse's movements. If you cue at the wrong time you may just cause a collision of feet, so remember where each foot is and where you want them to move next. Don't get in a hurry.

You may be asked to make a 180-degree turn in a back up pattern around barrels. This will require your horse to be very supple and bend his body around so he can back out straight.

Many trail classes have sound or movement obstacles that can terrify the inexperienced horse. If you have done a good job of sacking your horse out while you are on top of him you will have a real advantage. Use the rope around the horse. Teaching him to pull by the horn and stand while something is pulled up to him. Always take it one step at a time and make sure the horse knows what you expect of him.

Bridges and teeter-totters can give you problems. Start with a piece of plywood on the ground, get him used to that, then find or build a raised bridge. Make sure the construction is sound on all obstacles. The teeter-totter should be practiced without the center bar first. Let him walk over the boards you are going to use for the top. Next, put the side closest to the horse down and let him walk up it until it teeters to the other side. Try to stop him and let him stand for a moment. Once he has this down, make the end closest to the horse the high side of the teeter-totter. Now teach him to put his foot up on it to push it down, then walk across. This generally is the way it will be in a show.

Trail class training instills in your horse a trust of your judgement. He will do what you ask because you have shown him that obstacles will not hurt him. Be sure you do not hurt him or scare him and he will be very willing to perform the maneuvers asked of him.

This is a good way to work with a young horse that you don't want to ride too hard. It requires a lot of slow work that doesn't stress the horse's physical endurance or bone structure.

A trail class is a way of testing a horse's functional ability on the trail. If you have done a good training job with a good variety of trail obstacles, you should be able to go out on a trail ride and feel quite comfortable with your horse's ability.

Most trail classes don't include up and down hill travel. A horse has a tendency to want to run up and down hills. Always keep him on a walk when the hill has a considerable slope. The horse will over do himself going up hill and will get out of control going down hill if you let him choose the pace.

If the terrain gets too steep, use a traverse and switch back and traverse the other direction. This will take longer to get to the top, but it will be much easier on you and the horse.

If you have sacked him out adequately with slickers, sounds, and movements he will not be spooky when he is out on the trail. If he does become afraid of anything on the trail, stop him and make him face whatever he is afraid of. Don't try to ride him up to it at first. You may need to get off and show him that you are not afraid of it. If you have gained his trust, he will soon relax and come up to it.

The horse will usually pick his way through the brush and trees if you give him his head. It is very aggravating to ride a corral raised horse in the hills because he has never learned to pick his way through the country. A horse raised in the open will learn to follow deer trails and will not attempt going straight up or down hills. He will pick the easiest way through an area.

It takes many rides in the hills for a corral horse to learn these tactics. They can learn, so go out often and help him pick the way through for a while. Let him stumble over some sagebrush and bump into a few trees just to learn there is an easier way.

If you are going to be out riding in the open a lot, you should work on ground tying your horse so he won't run off and leave you every time you drop the reins.

Use a long ring-shank nail and punch a hole in the end of your rein. Every time you get off around home, put the nail through the rein and poke it in the ground. The horse will soon learn to stay where the rein is dropped.

You can also hobble him, then tie one rein around the hobbles so he cannot get his head high to hop around. Work on this at home and when you get in the hills the horse will stay where you leave him.

Do not let him get attached to another horse. Ride him alone a lot and ride with different horses. If he does get attached to another horse start penning him alone. There is nothing worse than a horse you cannot take away from another horse.

The Reining Horse

After you have taught your horse all the maneuvers previously discussed, you are ready to put it all together in a pattern. Most horse shows have some type of reining class for you to work toward entering. There are snaffle bit futurities as well as reining classes for hackamore horses. Older horses will be required to show in a curb bit.

Once the horse has learned the cues for each maneuver, you can move to a short shank snaffle and get the horse used to neck rein rather than the direct rein. This shouldn't take long if you have ridden your horse with a shank bit for pasture rides to relax him. Once he is in the curb bit, you can try a few different ones until you find what he will work best with.

Professional trainers pretty well agree that you must take it easy and not ask for a lot of fast action with slide stops and spins at home. If you know your horse knows how to stop, don't just keep putting him in the ground hard or he will get tired of stopping and even become afraid of the stop. Work on the maneuvers as individual activities, then put a couple together and a couple more. Try the pattern a time or two, then leave it alone. If you teach the horse the pattern, he will start anticipating cues and start scotching on you.

Many different patterns may be used in a show, so if you are going to exhibit at reining, you should memorize each one and try it a time or two or even take an old broke horse and run him through it a few times until you get the timing and distance problems worked out. You should never take your finely-tuned reining horse out and run him a dozen times just so you can get the pattern down.

Let's look at a reining pattern that is in common use in 4-H and open shows. The AQHA has now discarded this pattern for more difficult patterns, but to start with this is difficult enough.

When you start the pattern, move out on a lope and build to a run. The run will be driving the horse's hind legs up under him for the stop. When you get ready for the stop, pull-release and pull with a slightly lifted hand motion. At the same time, move to the front of the saddle and squeeze your legs with your heels locked down for a brace. As the horse plants his hind feet, move back in your saddle and sit deep, with your feet pushed forward. He should come to a complete stop. Make sure the stop is straight. If you need to, cue him over a little to keep him straight. Now back him straight back at a brisk walk. Again, make sure he doesn't go crooked.

Stop and settle him for ten seconds. If you take a deep breath and relax, it will help him to take a deep breath and relax here. Now walk him back to the center of the pattern and move into a collected lope in a right lead to start your smaller figure eight. Make the eight as even as possible, both length and width. The lead change should be made in the center of the eight or just before. The next eight is larger and faster, but still very much in control.

As you come to the center of the second eight, move your horse out straight through the eight toward the marker for the roll-back, or if there is no marker, to the point where you are to make the roll-back. Drive a little past the marker then slide your horse to a near stop and roll him over his hocks to the left, coming out on a left lead. Bust out on a run down to the other marker, pass it and roll back, coming out on a right lead. Come out strong, but then pull him to a slide stop at the center of the arena. Stop and let your horse settle a moment, then do a 90-degree pivot to the left

REINING PATTERN
(Ride the pattern in the order shown).

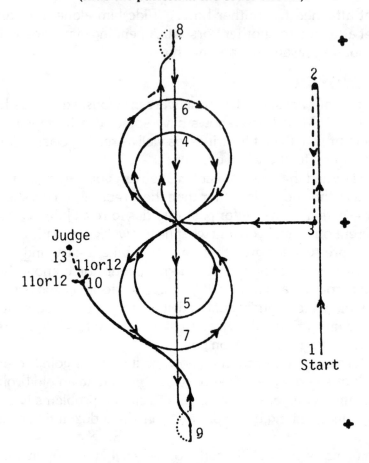

The arena or plot should be approximately 50 x 150 feet in size. The judge will indicate the locations of the markers on the arena fence or wall. Kegs or other markers within the pattern area will not be used.

1 to 2 -- Run with speed past center marker (stay 20 feet from fence or wall).
2   -- Smooth, balanced stop.
2 to 3 -- Back.
3   -- Settle horse for 10 seconds.
4 & 5 -- Ride small figure eight at a collected lope.
6 & 7 -- Ride large figure eight with speed.
8   -- Left roll back over the hocks past the end marker.
9   -- Right roll back over the hocks past the end marker.
10   -- Smooth, balanced stop.
11   -- One-quarter pivot left or right.
12   -- One-half pivot in opposite direction.
13   -- Walk to judge and stop for inspection until dismissed.

or right, then a 180-degree pivot to the opposite direction and pivot back to the beginning position. Stop, then walk him up to the judge for inspection until dismissed.

The judge will be judging you on neatness, dispatch, ease, calmness and speed with which you perform the pattern. Excessive jawing, open mouth or head raising on stop, lack of smooth stop on the haunches, breaking gaits, refusing to change lead, anticipating signals, stumbling or falling, wringing tail, backing sideways, not using markers, changing hands on the reins, losing a stirrup, holding on or two hands on the reins, or any unnecessary aid given to the horse by the rider (such as talking, petting, spurring, quirting, jerking of reins, etc.) to induce the horse to perform will be considered faults and scored accordingly.

With this in mind, go to a few shows and get your horse used to all the noises and other horses. Even show him in some Western Pleasure classes just to get him accustomed to crowds. You are going to have to season him before you can hope to win the big ones. A lot of top trainers spend all their time training and showing, so don't get upset if you don't win at first. It takes time to get it all together, but there isn't any reason why you can't beat them if you have the ability and desire to work for it.

When you get back home, go back to your ring snaffle and tune him up and keep him coming. The thing you don't want to do is burn him out at home. Ride him every other day just to keep him legged up if he is working good. It sure won't hurt to take him out and rope some calves on him or work some cattle to give him a change. Remember, don't work on that pattern too much and don't keep putting hard stops and spins on him and he will last for a long time.

Training The Cutting Horse

To train cutting horses especially, and horses in general, a trainer has to have a natural ability with horses. This is something that can't be taught. It's either there or it isn't. This is much the same as a natural ability to sing, dance or paint. Lessons can help improve the skill, but only a natural ability will have the polish and finesse that it takes to do the best job.

Some trainers have an eye for a horse. They can pick a horse for disposition and ability, get the most out of him and know when the horse has reached his capability. Such trainers are able to tell what the horse can do best and what training each should have.

A cutting horse trainer has to have the ability to read cattle or tell what a cow might do or is going to do. Some people can be around cattle for years and not gain this trait. Others find that they can read what cattle will do without a lot of effort.

It is hard to teach a horse what to do if the rider is always a step or two behind the cow in his thinking. He must be a step or two ahead to be able to position a young horse where he should be.

Some trainers choose geldings while others leave geldings to their last choice. This indicates that stallions, mares and geldings can all be made into cutting horses. There are horses of many conformations that can be seen cutting cattle proficiently. Most trainers agree, however, that they like a middle-of-the-road horse. They like a long, clean neck, short back, long sloping hip, back legs set up under a little, sloping pasterns and shoulders and a deep heart girth. Most prefer medium muscling.

One of the first things to look for is soundness. A horse should have his legs set straight under him and have good feet. A lot of horses aren't built to take the shock and strain of the cutting work. It's very costly and disheartening to work on a horse for six months and then have him break down on you.

Some say a horse is born with cow sense, others call it athletic ability, but whatever it is it must be in a horse if he's going to make a cutting horse. If the horse doesn't have the desire to work, no amount of training can put that desire in him. If he doesn't have that desire, he will never make a good cutting horse.

Once you have selected your horse and have him trained so you can stop, back, roll-back and side-pass, plus cue him into his leads, you are ready to start cutting training. You could have been working around cattle all the time you were training your horse to do the above maneuvers, but it is best to have a good handle on him before you start cutting.

The first thing you need to do to learn to work cattle is to get a stick and go into the arena on foot with ten head of older cows. Start walking through them, move one to the outside and try to keep her away from the rest. At first you will try running fast all over the place. You will keep pushing the cow and causing her to move.

Once you have gotten your run out, pick another cow and move her out quietly and slowly. Try to let her stand and look at you as much as you can. Try to make as few moves as you can while keeping the cow out of the herd. At first your horse will be like you, chargy too, and you will have to slow him down and back him off the cattle a little.

The next thing to do is learn how to handle the cattle. You will see if you walk briskly through the herd they will scatter, but if you step slowly and quietly they will just part a little. This is what you want your horse to do - just part them.

Get another cow out and watch her a moment. Move her until she is sideways. Move parallel to her up to her head. You will see as soon as she can see room to turn she will try to duck out and beat you back to the herd. Try it again, only this time stay on her hip and you will find that you end up driving the cow from side to side. As you move up even with her she stops.

These principles are all important in cutting cattle. If you want an animal to turn, you have to show the cow a place where she can turn, by moving parallel toward her head. As you move about a foot or so past her head, she will make her turn, hoping to beat you around. It is your responsibility to get around and head her until you have her turning the other direction. If you are too close to her, she will beat you every time, so you must stay back.

Some riders are afraid of losing a cow and they will not get up to their head. They end up working from one wall to the other, just driving the cow. If you are training a ranch horse, this might be acceptable because you want to drive the cow out to the "cut". You have no reason to allow the cow to try and turn back on you. In competitive cutting, you have a different goal and should try to let the cow work back and forth to show your horse's ability to handle the action.

Now that you are tired, get on your horse and have someone that is ready for a little jogging help with the training. People cutting is much slower and less demanding for a young horse. It also gives a novice cutting rider a little more time to position his horse and learn with the horse.

Start by following a person down the fence holding the horse out ten feet from the person. You can make a styrofoam cow for each side of the person to help the horse relate to cattle. Move the horse up even with the person and have the person stop. So the horse doesn't learn voice cues you are giving that person, use a nod for each direction and a shake of the head for a stop. You can also pre-arrange some maneuvers.

Let the horse stand and hold the person for a couple of minutes, then move him toward the person a step or two. The person can turn and start to walk the other way. Put your horse's head even with the cows shoulder and move him along with his head turned in a little, looking at the styrofoam critter. Move him up even with the person and have him stop, then stop your horse. Move your horse a little beyond the head and have the person turn and go down the fence again. Stop and roll your horse around and out distance the person until you turn him back.

Let your horse walk by the stopped person, a couple of lengths if he isn't paying attention, then stop him and roll him back then make him catch the person. Make him realize that the farther he goes by the more effort it is going to take to get around and catch up the other direction.

Now speed it up to a trot. Soon the horse realizes when he moves beyond the head of the cow he is going to have to turn around and hurry to get it stopped again. He will become hesitant about pushing beyond the person. Now he is learning something. Within a couple of fifteen or thirty minute sessions, he should be watching the styrofoam cow to see what he is going to do. Speed it up a little and make him get around and head the person. You are teaching the horse to rate the cow and also to head her in this way. Do this for four or five days until the horse is watching and reacting somewhat on his own.

Move away from the fence and get in the middle of the corral or arena to teach him how to position himself for cutting and teach him how to fade back.

You want to teach the horse to work in an arc across the arena with the sides of the arc back towards the would-be-herd. Some riders go across the arena in a straight line, but this gives the advantage to the cattle. A horse should be taught to fade back on the sides. By doing this it will take the pressure off the cow and allow her to stop and turn rather than try to beat the horse to the wall.

Look at it this way. When you walk up to someone you like to stay a certain distance away when talking. The better the acquaintance, the closer the distance. This may be an eye contact area or a sensitivity area that you like to protect. Cattle have a similar sensitivity for closeness. Gentle cattle may let you work within five feet of them while wilder cattle may work twenty to thirty feet away from you. Once you find this distance with each animal, you can tell how much to fade back to allow them to stop and turn. If you press them, they will beat you and your horse will start losing confidence. Working on people will help him build his confidence up. That is what you have to have to get him to start thinking about what he is doing. If you start on fast cattle, your horse will get discouraged and quit trying.

Visually separate the arena into thirds. Now you want to work in the center third, or just a little into the side thirds. In order to do this, you must teach the horse how to turn the cow. You must create an escape route for the cow by pushing a little ahead of her without missing her. This will cause her to turn back. If you don't she will run from one side of the arena to the other. Once you start using turn back men the horse will be working defensively because the cow will be forced toward him. For now don't put that pressure on the young horse.

Have the person move across the arena. Move parallel to him and as you approach the start of the side third, move ahead a little and have the person reverse. Work in this center third area for a few sessions.

Next, move the person over into the side third towards the fence. Now make the horse fade back, but face the fence. Don't let him turn toward the person. Always teach him he has to stop and roll over his hocks to get back in position as the person turns the other way. Let the person get a head start and make the horse hurry to get around and head him. This will teach him to get around and be there.

Move the person in toward the horse a little on some of the crosses. Now teach the horse to give ground and maintain his distance. To position the horse, you are going to have to use your hands and help him learn. Don't jerk and spur or he won't enjoy the work. It's a lot easier to get his cooperation if he likes the game. Once he becomes afraid of what you are going to do, he can't concentrate on the person or cow and he will sour fast. That doesn't mean you have to baby him, but after you have brought him around and move him across, stop him and let him stand and

311

look at the person for a minute once in a while and let him relax. Then step him ahead a step and be ready for the next turn.

After a week of this type of work, he is ready to look at some cattle. You many wonder, "Why not just go to the cattle so he can get used to them?" You can, if you like, but remember you can't position a cow very easily on a young horse and you sometimes have to react faster than a young horse can handle. Another reason is that cattle are expensive and it is hard to keep fresh cattle. After they are worked a little, the cattle will sour and a sour cow is the worst thing to try to teach a young horse with. Cattle sour faster with a young horse because he will surely miss a few and this will give them the idea they can beat him around at the fence, or they will start crowding him too close and this will upset him and he won't be able to handle it.

Some cutting trainers use a mechanical cow, which takes the place of a person, but these are expensive. A good horse is going to be able to work people and get about as much out of it as with a mechanical cow.

You still have to have access to cattle to train a cutting horse. Once you have taught him position and how to rate a person, you need to start letting him get used to cattle. Start by riding amongst a herd of cattle and let him learn to accept being hemmed in on all sides. Stop him and let him stand and relax a minute as the cattle mill around.

Pick one out and drive her slowly to the outside of the herd. Once she is on the outside, let her go then slowly walk back through the herd and drive out another. Bring out five or six. Do this for five or six days until your horse is feeling relaxed and quiet in the herd. You can also be cutting people a few times each week to keep him interested and in a learning position.

During these days you are training your horse, work him before each cutting lesson. Do some quiet pleasure maneuvers first to limber him up and relax him, then work on backs, stops, pivots, roll-backs and leads.

Pressure to head the cow can scare the horse that isn't used to working them. The round corral can help build confidence without putting pressure on your horse. Put one cow in a round corral eighty-five to one hundred feet in diameter. The cow will stay close to the fence trying to find a hole to get out.

Make your horse move parallel to the cow with his head about at the cow's shoulder. Make him watch the cow. Don't get too close to the cow. Each cow will react differently to the distance the horse is to her. By moving closer to the center of the corral, or moving away from the cow you take the pressure off the cow and she will slow or stop. Once the cow stops, make the horse stop. When she moves make him move with her. Move him up so his head is even or a little ahead of the cow. She will stop and turn back. Stop your horse and bring him around and make him catch her.

After a number of turns, he will learn that when he gets beyond the cow she will turn. He will soon start staying back a little. You will have to encourage him to get ahead of the cow to head her. Now he is thinking defense. You can always create the offense.

When the cow stops and faces the horse, make him face the cow. Step him slowly forward. When the cow doesn't like the pressure, she will move one way or the other. Make your horse move with her. After a few lessons on approaching the cow, your horse will start to creep towards the cow because he knows she is going to turn to run as soon as she feels the pressure. He doesn't really want her to turn and run because he knows he will have to catch her when she does. He is working defensively and you must press him into the offensive advance.

You can spend two or three days a week for a couple weeks in the round corral working on the basic body position of the horse and getting him to accept more pressure from the cow by heading her and controlling her movements. This fence work is really good practice for the horse and helps him learn how to get position on the cow. Now that he is watching cattle, take him into the herd and peel off a slow cow and move with her until you have her fifty or sixty feet away from the herd. Don't drive her, but just move with her. By moving this far, the young horse has room to fade back as the cow comes in.

Have your turn-back helpers head the cow back, but don't let them push her. If she turns toward them, they can turn her around, otherwise they can just sit there.

Make the colt stay about ten feet away from the cow. Be sure you don't let the horse move to the cow. Make him stay back and give ground. Position him so he can work her in the center third of the arc. If the cow just wants to run, stop your horse and get another cow. Running from side to side won't teach him anything. Work two or three cows slow and easy. Make your horse stop, step back and roll around in a sweeping motion.

If the cow runs toward the fence, remember to give ground and stop a little before you get to the fence. This takes pressure off the cow. If she tries to run down the side, then you must go right to the fence to cut her off. If you run right up to the fence ahead of the cow, she will reverse and beat you out of the turn and possibly beat you to the fence on the other side. Down to the herd she will go. If you give ground and stop a few steps before the fence, you can sweep around when she turns and head her by the far side of the center third of the arc and be back in position. Once the cow runs to the fence and you have moved over and dropped back a little, just stop. Make your horse face the fence, assuming the cow is still facing that direction and have him turn his head and look at her. As she breaks, sweep him around and head her. If she stops in the middle facing the herd, turn your horse so he is facing her. In this position he can break and turn either direction to counter her move. If she doesn't want to move, don't push her. Back up a step or two, giving the cow a place to go. Once she moves, swing over and block her. If she will work with your horse right there, he can box her in that center area and just sweep from one side to the other with her. If you can see she's about used up, block her move and she will stop. Then, quit her and get another one.

Whenever the cow turns and faces your horse, turn him to face her. He will have a natural tendency to want to do this anyway, but only let him when the cow is facing him. That way he can move either way to block her.

If a horse is missing a cow or over-shooting her, you should teach him to shorten his stride in order to maneuver better. If he is continually missing her, let him go ahead, but make him stop and hurry him back; that will shorten him up. He learns that it isn't going to do him any good to get too far out in front of the cow. He knows he has to hurry faster to get back if he does.

Remember, on a colt you need to work the slow cattle in the beginning, those that just walk and trot. When the cow walks, walk your horse. When she trots, your horse trots. If you run a young horse unnecessarily, it will give him less chance to shut the cow off and get her turned than if you were on a trot. He can trot fast enough for most any of the beginning work, so when you are training your horse trot him a lot. Try to work on a loose rein and have him stop and turn. Don't let him move ahead or run through his turns. If he does, he will do it when you work cattle.

Another thing to keep uppermost in your mind is that when you start working cows, you can't always be riding your horse's head. You must try to work him off a loose rein. You have to pick him up and position him, but then give him back his head. If you've got a heavy hold on him, he can't think about very much but you. If it is all punishment and no reward he will stop trying to please.

When you have headed the cow and have her under control, you can quit her and get another one. Never quit because you might get beat. Make the horse try to head the cow, then quit her.

If you see you have an old sour cow, it is best to drop her and get another. It will scare the horse to make him work her.

Knowing when to end a session is critical. Don't let your horse get tired and irritable before you quit. Stop while he is still interested.

Once your horse is looking at the cattle and working a little on his own, you can cut back to working cattle only two or three times a week. If you keep pushing him every day, he will get tired of the whole thing. If you find he has lost interest, turn him out for a week and give him a rest. When you catch him up again, he will be ready to go back to work

Many shows are won or lost in the herd. Not because of points lost, but because of position as you come out. Never let your horse move into the herd too fast; teach him to sneak in. Go in from one side or the other and start out at the middle of the arena. Work your horse forward and the cattle will naturally separate in the middle. Usually this will leave one cow sitting right out on the edge in front of you. Make your horse set up and pop that cow out away from the herd. Take a stand and wait for the cow to move. Most likely she will work your horse a few times right there in the middle where the action is supposed to take place.

The next cut doesn't have to be a deep cut. If you can see a cow you can peel off, take her and go to work. Don't pick the big black in the back and go after her. Always take what is in place to work unless you know they are sour.

It won't take long before your horse can stay on the cut, even if two come out together. Let him stay on the cut and the other cow will generally slip off and go back to the herd.

Another thing the judge will really notice is if your horse has basic form. Can he stop and roll back or sweep with his front end low and his head toward the cow? This all goes back to the way you taught him to stop and back as well as pivot and roll-back. If you pull him up in the air, he won't look good cutting cattle, so keep him low from the start.

As your horse's training progresses, pick faster cows and push him a little. You don't want to just work fast cows, but try one every once in a while to give him a challenge and something to work for.

Under normal cutting you will move the cut out from the herd about thirty-five feet and work anywhere from three to five feet away from the cow in a head-to-head position, shifting from ten to fifteen feet when you drop back towards the fence. The closer you are, the faster the horse is going to have to respond, so don't let him crowd. Once you have faded back a few times, you have to hold your ground or you will start the herd to moving. A horse learns as he gets seasoned just how far to give ground and when he has to stand his ground.

When you go to a cutting, you will have herd holders on each side of the herd and two turn-back men. Your horse needs to get used to these horses and their movements. These four riders can be of real help or they can cause you a lot of problems. Herd holders should help you get your cut out of the herd by keeping the herd from running off. If you go in from the left, the man on that side should move out in front of the herd and let the herd sift around the cutter and then when the cutter comes out, he should get back out of the way. If he stays out in the middle, the cut will go to the side and give you a poor position to start off with. If you go in from the right, the right herd holder should come out. If the arena is small, it may be best not to use herd holders.

The turn-back men should try to help you, but not push the cow over you. They don't need to be too active unless the cow turns away from the cutter and moves out. If the cutting is going well, the cow will generally turn into the horse. If you crowd the cow, she will turn toward the turn-back men, so you should stay back and draw the cow towards you.

It is best not to use your cutting horse as a turn-back horse. A turn-back horse has to push the cattle and you don't want him to learn to crowd.

Some people think a cutting horse is working totally on his own. A good cutting horse has learned to handle the cattle pretty well, but he has a silent partner. A cutting horse is generally no better than his rider permits him to be.

Training The Roping Horse

Before you start trying to train a roping horse, make sure you know how to handle a rope proficiently. You should learn on the ground by dry roping. Then know how to ride a horse with balance and confidence. Next, put them together on a trained rope horse until you become proficient. Once you have done all this, you may be able to train a rope horse, if you study hard, analyze a lot and have patience.

It is so easy to make a fool out of a horse when training him for roping. For this reason, you might want to start on an inexpensive horse, because chances are fifty-fifty that you will make him either a roping horse or a crazy horse.

Start by putting away your spurs and hard bits. You are going to have to be willing to allocate time each day for training and be consistent in that training.

Once you are committed to training a rope horse, the first thing you need to know is what type of horse to pick. Some trainers like mares, some like geldings, but few like stallions because they are less predictable, plus they take more care when traveling.

Most trainers agree that a roping horse should have a medium to slightly short neck, but still a slim, refined neck with a natural head set. This makes it easier to rope over. A horse of about 14 1/2 to 15 hands and about 1,000 to 1,200 pounds would be best. This gives the horse enough size to handle the stock.

He should have withers to hold the saddle. A mutton-back horse will have trouble holding the saddle during quick turns or if a rope is pulling from the side angle off the horn. A deep heart girth will help the horse absorb the shock from the stop and jerk of the rope. He also needs a strong loin and short back to help in the stops.

Medium to heavily muscled front and back upper legs, along with a long, sloping hip and sloping shoulders that are also medium to heavily muscled will give him the driving power, as well as the stopping and holding ability. He should have a short cannon that is wide and flat. The pastern should be relatively short and the hooves large enough for that size of horse. He must be totally balanced in his conformation to be good.

Perfect conformation does not matter if he has no desire to follow cattle, no heart to try hard, or is too spooky to trust. There have possibly been as many old cowboys hurt in roping accidents as in bronc rides. The old ranch cowboys had to rope off of their broncs and that made it even worse.

In training the rope horse, you must pick one with a good disposition. That doesn't mean he is asleep all the time, but rather that he doesn't go to pieces every chance he gets.

If you are looking for a rope horse prospect, look for a four or five year old horse that is broke well with a good stop and rein on him. If you start training a young colt, you can burn him out before he gets trained. If you choose an eight or nine-year-old, he may be set in his ways and it will take two or three years before you get him trained just right, so he won't have too many good years left.

It helps if your prospective rope horse has had some ranch work and has been around cattle. This will give him the desire to look for the cattle and find the shortest distance to them.

Start with a gag bit if the horse is chargy or heavymouthed at all. If he has a real good mouth, you can go ahead and use a grazing bit or hackamore bit on him.

With the gag bit you aren't going to hurt his mouth when you have to get hold of him to position him and to stop him. Try to stay off his mouth as much as possible, but you have to show him where to be and how to stop and that takes more hand sometimes. The more you can use leg cues to move him over and cues to stop him, the better off you will be. The more you can stay out of a horse's mouth, the better he will finish and the more he will feel comfortable about roping. If he is always worried about your jerking and kicking, he won't be learning about roping.

Most trainers put a tie-down on the rope horse so he can get used to balancing on it for the stop. This should be adjusted so you can push the strap up and touch the neck when the horse is standing in a relaxed head set.

When training a calf roping horse, a neck rope is also needed. This rope goes around the neck of the horse and the rope you are going to use is run through it. This makes the horse face down the rope once you catch something. Some trainers like a nose rope or wire in place of a neck rope. A wire is placed around the nose about where a hackamore would fit, then a small piece of rope is attached to it in a small loop and the rope run through there. This is hard on a horse if he gets his head out of place on the stop. Some horses fight it, but it is a good way to keep your horse looking at the calf on the end of the rope.

Skid boots are another thing you need on a rope horse to keep from burning his rear fetlocks. Put them on and let him get used to them during early training.

Don't ever longe a horse you are going to make a roping horse out of. The first thing he will try to do is run one way or the other around you when you are down to the other end of the rope. Longeing should always be left for someone else to use on their horse.

Many horses are afraid of ropes. It takes time and patience to get him used to a rope. Put him in a small pen, sit on him and swing the rope until he is at ease with it. Take him out on a ride and throw the rope a little. He will be much more afraid of the rope being down around his legs or over his rump. Be sure not to let it get caught under his tail or you might end up on the ground.

As you ride around on a walk, rope his front legs but don't pull the slack. Have someone ride behind you and heel him and you heel his horse as you go out on a long ride. Remember not to pull slack and trip him. After an all-day ride of being front footed and heeled, he will come back quite a bit less afraid of the rope. Remember, don't start hitting him with the rope or he will always be afraid of it. He must learn it isn't going to hurt him or he won't lose his fear of it.

Put a calf or goat in the arena and just follow it around. Because of the price of calves, it will be cheaper to use goats for part of your training. Some trainers even prefer them to start with because they are slower and move more from side to side so a horse learns to follow better.

Make your horse watch the calf (or goat), but don't let him start cowing it, or working it like a cutting horse. He should be following it not heading it. For a week just follow the calf around on a walk or trot or even a lope when necessary. Make your horse rate the calf by staying about five to ten feet from the hip of the calf. At first, make him follow directly behind the calf, but as he gets better trained you can move him to one side or the other just a little to help your throw. If you're right handed, the horse could follow slightly to the left of the calf so you don't have to rope right over the horse's ears. If you're left handed, teach him to move to the right just a little. When you are through training for the day or are going to give him a rest, take him to the box and tie him in it to let him rest. Don't get him too tired before giving him a rest.

Don't start busting a horse out of a box until you have him running at the calves, stopping and knows pretty well what he's doing with the calf. He will learn how to run out of the box quick enough, but you want to keep him from getting crazy about the box. In the early training, you can sure make him crazy if you bust him out of the box each time.

When you first start roping the calves, just start one down the left fence if you are right handed. Run him slow and rope him, using a break-away hondo. This way you don't have to get off and turn your horse loose. Stay up there and set him for a stop, then back him up as the calf breaks away. You can use the fence to make him back straight. Next, use a pen for the calf to come out where the horse can watch him. The horse will soon pay attention to that calf as he is ready to come out of the pen. After a few times of break-away roping, let someone take a hold of the rope and put pressure on it. Have them turn one way, then the other, at the end of the rope as you turn your horse and face their direction.

If he doesn't like the pressure on the horn, you need to log him a little. Tie a railroad tie or log on the end of an old rope and have your horse drag it around for fifteen minutes a day for a week or so. He will soon get used to pressure on the horn.

If the horse isn't working well, you can break-away rope for two or three weeks before you tie on to one solid. Some horses get scared of the rope coming back at them when it breaks away and want to start scotching on you because they are afraid the rope is going to hit them each time you throw. If you have this problem, go ahead and rope the calf and have someone throw the calf while you stay on the horse and make him work the rope. This is the next step after the break-away roping. This will teach the horse to take the jerk and to keep the rope tight.

If you are having trouble making the horse hold the slack once you are off him, you could try putting a rope on the hind foot of a big calf and run the rope through the nose band and up to the horn. The calf will start kicking and the slack will pop the horse a couple of times. He will find out he has to keep the slack out to protect himself. It will also teach him to keep his eyes on the calf.

Some trainers put the horse on one side of a pole corral and a big calf on the other side, with the rope around its neck tied in a knot that won't choke the calf. The rope goes through the poles and up the nose band or neck rope on the horse and to the horn. When the calf pulls, the horse will start to walk up, but after he hits his head on the poles a few times he will start watching the calf and holding the slack tight.

The jerk line can also be used to teach a horse to keep the slack tight. This is a small rope running from the rein through the gullet in the saddle and down long enough to reach the calf. As the trainer runs down the rope to the calf, he lets out slack on the jerk line. If the horse isn't backing, he can pull the jerk line and make him back. Once he reaches the calf to flank him, he can back the horse one more step to take the calf off balance just as he flanks him. It will help in putting him down. Once he is down say "Whoa" and just let the horse hold pressure at that tension.

Rope a couple more and get off and tie them down. Don't expect miracles. It will take a lot more schooling before he is working the rope well. Give him time to learn and have patience.

You want the horse to stop on the cue of pitching your slack. You don't want him stopping as you throw, or he will make you miss a lot of calves. If he starts stopping before you pitch your slack, just rope a calf and make him follow until you pitch slack, then let him stop. He shouldn't be sliding much on the stop because this gives slack in the rope and it is just that much more distance for you to cover once you are off.

To teach the horse to back on the rope, ride up to a log with a hook on one end and rope it. Pitch your slack and step off. Let the horse drag the log up to you. Use a jerk line if necessary. Then put your weight on it. That extra weight will signal the horse to hold the slack at that distance. If he doesn't want to drag the log back to you then you need to put him in an alley or narrow pen to teach him to drag the log while backing up. This teaches him to put some of his weight into the rope and it also teaches him to stay in the right place without moving around.

Now for the box work. Walk or back your horse into the box, turn and face forward. Turn him to the left a quarter turn. This is the position you want him in when you are ready to rope. In this position you can see the calf and so can the horse. His rear end should be back in the corner, but not touching the box. You don't want him sitting on the fence or he might hurt his hocks or ankles when he breaks out of the box.

You should let a few calves out of the chute and make the horse stand there and watch. This is called scoring the calves. Move him more straight around in the box as you score a few calves. He must allow you to position him and not try to take over the box.

Pick a slow calf and come out with it. Let the horse catch it as he wants to and then rope it. Run some more slow ones and come out and just rate them. Your horse will learn very quickly how to bust out of the box so don't worry about teaching him that right off.

Now do up the barrier string. Walk the horse up close and trip it. Do that a few times. Walk him into it so he trips it. It may scare him the first time or two, but keep it up until he is not afraid of it. Then trot and lope him through it until he doesn't even worry about it. You don't want him concentrating on the barrier or trying to jump it if you are close to breaking it. A balk or jump at that moment would be a bad start for any run.

Once the horse is working well and you are satisfied with his training, you can rope a few calves a couple of times a week and he will stay ready. If you try to rope ten or twelve a day you will just burn him out and make him crazy. Take him out in the pasture to exercise him and let him relax. Then each time you are going to rope, ride him a little to take the edge off, and warm him up so he will be attending to business when he goes into the box.

Most of the problems with a roping horse are the results of the training and handling given him. In other words, they are the rider's fault. You can ruin a roping horse prospect faster than about any other type of using horse. You must analyze what you want to accomplish, then determine the training methods. Try the method, but use patience and repetition. Don't get the horse too tired or he will get mad and start fighting you. Don't be afraid to ask for help from a well-known trainer of rope horses if you need it.

To be a roper you must be a little bit of a gambler. When you put down your entry fee, you are gambling on three things: 1) your ability, 2) the ability of your competition, and 3) the luck of the draw. It takes a lot of gambles to season you and your horse until you are winning.

There are calf roping horses and steer roping horses, both heading and heeling. Each horse has to have specialized training for his type of roping, but basically they all must come out of the box, rate the cattle and handle them once they are caught.

If you are going to train a steer-roping horse, you should realize that a heading horse needs to be strong and fast. He must be fast enough to catch the steer - some steers run like they were AAA stock. Once you catch the steer, the heading horse has to slow him down and turn him for the heeler.

A heeling horse can be slower and doesn't have to be as strong, but he must handle well so you can move him around quickly to get in position for the heel loop. Sometimes a calf horse will work well as a heeling horse, but don't use a well trained calf horse to head on. It will give him the idea that he doesn't have to stop when you catch the calf.

Remember, don't overdo the training. Run a few steers and give him a rest. You can break-away rope a lot more cattle than if you are actually catching and letting the horse take the jar and working the rope. Always have patience and good horsemanship and you will develop good horses.

The Barrel Racing Horse

Some horses can make a turn around a barrel and some cannot. Not all of the good ones turn the same. You need to give a horse a little training to see how he or she turns, and see if they have the speed required to win.

There are three major styles of turning the barrels: 1) the run-around; 2) the roll-back; and 3) the front-feet turn. The horse that walks or runs around on the front feet is possibly the poorest choice. The roll-back horse is possibly the next poorest choice. This horse must stop his forward movement before he can roll back and move out for the next barrel. The run-around horse seems to be the most desired by the top barrel racers.

Most trainers agree it is best to start with a three or four year old well-broke horse. This type of horse is settled down and can go right to work learning the pattern and the method of turning around the barrel.

Barrel racing horses come in all shapes and sizes. If you look at the top ten in any given year, you will find short, stocky horses, long, Thoroughbred looking horses and anything in between. The ideal horse desired is much the same as the reining or cutting horse. He is a middle-of-the-road horse with medium muscle, a slender neck and a long hip with hind legs set slightly under him for the stops and turns.

To start training a barrel horse, walk him in small circles and get him to bend in the middle with his head to the inside of the circle. Each time you stop, back him up a couple of steps to teach him to get his legs under him, then bend him around your inside leg and start another circle in another direction. Always use body English and look in the direction you are going. Next, trot him in circles, stop him, back a step and turn and go the other direction.

As you turn him, using a ring snaffle bit, teach him to give to light pulls on the inside of his mouth. If he is heavy, tie him around for a while each way and let him learn to give to the pressure.

Next, walk him around the barrels using the inside pull-release on the bit and use your inside leg and foot pressure between the front and back cinches to cue him to arc or bend around your leg in the turns. At first the horse will have to be positioned for each barrel. Start by moving into the barrel wide so you have room for the turn. This will also prevent him from turning the barrel prematurely. Move him past the barrel before you let him stop, back a step and bend him around the barrel.

Work him up to a trot, then go up to a lope once you feel you both have everything under control. If he feels high, work him down on some long trotting in the field before the lessons. Keep him quiet and stop and let him relax every once in a while. He will learn better if he feels a relaxed atmosphere during the training.

As you lope him you want him in the proper lead. He should start in the lead that you will need for the first turn. If he comes into it on the wrong lead, he is going to lose time in the change.

One way to run the barrels is to lope to a point about five feet to the left of the right barrel, if you are running at the right barrel first. About two lengths from the barrel check him up a little, slow him down, and make him rate the barrel. He must go into a stopping motion and as he slows his speed he can start his run-around turn by turning his head into the barrel and arcing his body around the barrel. This forms a pocket for the rider's leg. As he makes his turn, keep him in close to the barrel as he comes out. He should be taught to bust out of the turn as he comes away from the barrel.

Another way is not to check him at all but let him check himself and take the barrel at his own speed. Some say this makes a smoother run and doesn't upset the horse as much because you

319

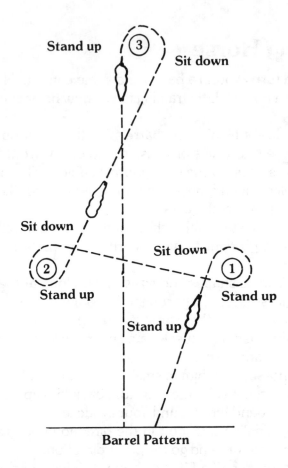

Barrel Pattern

shouldn't be pulling and jerking on him for the slide and turn as some riders do. The method will all depend on the horse. If the horse has a good rein on him and knows how to bend before you start on barrels, he may be able to handle the speed in the turns, but if he is less experienced it would be best to slide and turn so he doesn't get running past the barrel before he makes his turn.

There are many different ideas about how to teach a horse to run the barrels, but start with one and give it a fair try. If your horse just won't work well that way, you may want to change methods or evaluate your training. It may be you, not the horse, that is having trouble with the speed and the turns.

The rein used is generally a roping rein that is short so you have no extra slack to handle. Once the horse is trained, only the hand closest to the barrel is handling the rein each time, so this requires a change of hands between the first and second barrel. A direct pull will be the best for most horses.

Start with a ring snaffle for basic training because you can use two hands and position the horse. Most horses will need a tie down. They will use it to balance on in the stop turns and it will prevent the rider pulling the head up. As the training progresses you may want to use a hackamore bit for the stops, so you don't hurt his mouth. Some trainers like to use a gag bit because you can get a hold of a horse and not hurt his mouth.

Try to get speed between the first and second barrels then check him about two lengths away and let him drift out a little to form the pocket. Slide him into a run-around turn and break him out for the third barrel. Get a lot of speed out of him here and then do the same around the third barrel. As you start out of the third barrel, put your all into bringing him out of the turn with speed when you are in competition.

320

That doesn't sound like it would be too hard, does it? Well, it takes a lot of slow training to get there. First you must walk the horse through the turns and teach him to bend around your leg to form a pocket. If he starts slicing the barrel (cutting the barrel too short by dropping his shoulder into the barrel), you are going to have some hurt legs and knocked over barrels. The horse has to learn to give his head to your pull as he approaches the barrel. If he puts his head to the outside, he can't arc his body and he can't turn. You should remember, if he is getting too close to the barrel, don't turn his head away from the barrel because this will throw his barrel (stomach) towards the barrel you are turning. By holding his head into the turn and cuing him hard on the inside, he should arc and move his middle away enough to get by the barrel.

Don't worry about teaching the horse to run at the barrels. After you have taught him to make the turns slow and easy, you can speed it up to a slow lope, but bring him out from each barrel with snap and drive, then let him slow up a little before the next one. It only takes a few times at the run and he will know what you want, if he has the ability to run. If you run him every time, he will start worrying about the run and forget properly shaping the turns.

Just as with all other events, the rider has to ride in balance to help the horse do the best job. The basic body position for the run is standing up in the stirrups, but still having your crotch on the seat with your weight over the horse's withers. As he goes to stop, take a deep seat, push the horn and use body English, turn and look at the barrel as you start around it. Don't lean in or out but stay on the same angle as your horse with your weight balanced so as not to affect his balance. As he comes away from the barrel, move up over his withers as fast as you can. You will find a lot of force trying to push you back in the back of the saddle. Use the horn and get up over him. Work on these two maneuvers at a walk, trot and lope. The horse will relate them to the maneuver that accompanies them, and will run when you stand up and start to stop when you sit down deep. Keep your feet right under you. Don't let them swing back, or you lose your balance. If necessary, tie them so they can't swing back.

The horse must change leads between the first and second barrels. When you come out of the first barrel, make him switch leads as he comes out of the turn before he starts his run to the next barrel. This may require turning him just past the straight away run and then bust him back to pick up that lead.

Some people think they should teach the horse the pattern so he is so schooled in it he won't forget. It is best to teach him how to turn a barrel and how to get away from it and rate the next one for the slide and turn. You can mix the pattern up a little just so he won't start cheating and trying to run for the barrel and turn too quick and miss it. Don't let him run by the barrel or he will think he can pull out of the turn when he wants.

As far as aids in speed go, some barrel racers use a lot of spurs. Whatever you do, don't wave your legs in and out kicking for all you're worth. This can defeat your purpose. You are just knocking the wind out of your horse and causing more wind resistance, which will slow you down. A horse that is trained well and is trying to do his best won't need to be spurred or batted. In fact, you may distract him from the barrel and cause more problems, which will reduce your time. Voice commands work well on some horses. Voice commands could be used as a cue to speed it up. A cluck just as you come out of the turn may make him get away from the barrel a little faster if you have used a cluck for speeding him up during his training. If you use spurs and/or a bat, use them sparingly and effectively or you will spoil the training you have accomplished.

It takes a lot of runs to get a horse seasoned so you can depend on him, and even then he will have good days and bad, just like people. Consider his feelings and study his problems so you can help him to do his best. Always ask him for a good job, but don't punish him after a run or during a run. Harsh punishment in barrel training will generally result in a spoiled horse. If he needs some help, slow him down and show him how you want it done. You can work barrels longer at a trot than you can at a run. Anything that you need to teach him can be learned better slow than at a run. Have patience and perseverance, and never lose your temper.

Once you are satisfied with his ability, slow down on the barrel training and just keep him legged up. Lope him and run him a little on the straight away to keep his wind strong. He will sour if you keep running the pattern for speed every day. It may be enough just to run the barrels at the rodeos once a horse is "finished" or completely trained. The rest of the riding can be out of the arena. This helps the horse maintain a stable disposition and he will have his mind fresh and ready for the barrels at the next rodeo. If he develops a problem, you must take him back to the arena during the week and work it out. This can usually be done at a trot rather than a speed run.

Pole Bending

Pole bending is just as much an art as barrel racing. It takes the same kind of a horse and similar training to develop a low time in either.

A Quarter Horse will run 300, 400 and sometimes 440 yards in his two year old year. This will be at a straight away with no lead changes. A barrel horse must make at least one lead change and four quick bursts of speed. A pole bending horse has ten lead changes and two bursts of speed.

With this demanding activity in pole bending, many trainers prefer to wait until a horse is three or four years old before pushing his training in the poles. The more mature the horse's body, the less chance there will be of injuring him.

Once you start your training on poles you need to analyze the pattern and your horse. The rules state that you can start from either side of the pattern. With this in mind you need to figure out which lead your horse likes best. If he likes the left lead then start on a left lead on the right side of the pattern because the first pole will require a left lead. Had you started on the right lead on the right side you would need one more lead change in the pattern, which would cut your time.

If he likes the right lead start on the left side. Start by loping in a right circle before you get to the starting line. Come right out of that circle with the speed, rather than starting from a stand still.

If the rider rides straight down to the first pole and makes his turn he is usually too close and goes wide on the first turn, then is in bad shape for the second pole. To correct this, it is best to make the run to the first pole a little bowed to the outside. Like the barrel, this leaves a pocket to turn around.

In a left lead running on the right side, you can arc the horse out all the way down the straight away. Then when you get to your first pole you have a pocket to work with. Coming around the back of the pole, you can hold tight to the side of the pole as you round it. This will put you in position for the second and consecutive poles. If, however, you go wide on the first turn you will likely hit or be in bad shape for the second pole.

A horse has to be able to change leads quick and smooth. He must be looking at the poles and know how to pace the turns. This comes through training and repetition. You don't need to start looking for speed. A lot of the training can be done on a trot.

Your body, legs and hands can help your horse know when to make the turns. Once he has the idea of the pattern down you can work on your technique.

Sit in the middle of your horse. Don't lean to the front or you put too much weight on his front legs. Don't sit in the back of your saddle or he will have to drag you around every turn. As you come to the pole, turn your shoulders toward it and look at it. When at top speed you should be able to slip each pole by your shoulder as you turn into it.

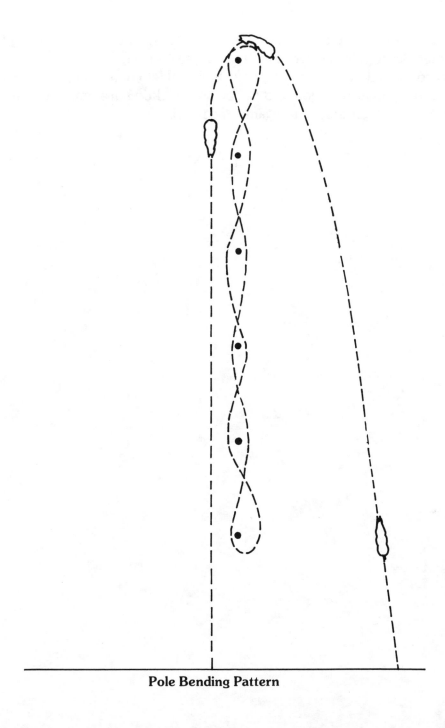

Pole Bending Pattern

This body English will help the horse know when to make his lead change. Don't wait until you are on the pole to change your body position and lead. Do it between poles, not at the pole. If you change too late you will end up hitting the pole or going wide and hitting the next pole.

The horse should not be rubber necked when pole bending. He needs to arc his body around the pole without letting his neck and head get out of position.

It's best to ride with two hands so you can position his nose but don't over do the head pulls. By keeping your hands close to the swells and use a backward side pull you will direct his nose without pulling it out of position.

Many shapes and sizes of horses make top barrel horses. It is the same with pole bending

323

horses. You need athletic ability and desire along with training and conditioning to have a top horse. Always remember to ride in balance with the horse and help him do it right.

Don't over train for speed. Don't beat on your horse. Help him to enjoy the event and enjoy working for you. If he knows he is going to get beat or kicked hard coming home, even if he is doing his best, he is going to get tired of the game and rebel.

CHAPTER TWENTY-ONE
Training, Fitting and Showing the Halter Horse

Choosing A Horse

It is just as important to have a horse trained for showing at halter as it is for the performance events. It also may take as much time and effort to train him for halter.

It takes a top horse to catch the judge's eye and go on to place high in the class. There are many good horses around and many good showmen. To win, you are going to have to put it all together right. The first thing you need is a horse with conformation that can win. The rest is up to you.

In today's shows, the Quarter Horse, Appaloosa and Paint are pretty much judged the same. It takes Quarter Horse conformation of the middle-of-the-road type horse to win. The short, heavily muscled horse is a thing of the past in the show ring. If he doesn't show a little hot blood and some size, he just doesn't have a chance. Go back to the section "Conformation" and study the structure that a good horse should have. Remember the old saying, "No legs, no horse". Horses with attractive color or chrome (white markings) will stand out and can be seen by the judge easier than the solid bay or brown horses. White face markings can make a head look much more attractive.

Geldings are possibly the easiest to show because they aren't worried about breeding or being bred. If you pick a stallion, you are going to have to put more work into handling him and keeping him exercised. You just have to put up with mares in heat. Sucking colts are the worst to train and show because they have a short attention span and they are always thinking of their mothers. Yearlings are not as bad, but two- and three-year-olds are old enough to work with and get something through to them.

4-H showmen should work with older horses that are settled in their ways and will be more trustworthy and ready to cooperate with the young showman.

Show Horse Care

Once you have picked the horse to be shown, the work starts. First, have the horse wormed and have his manure checked to make sure he is clean of worms. Then check the manure every two months to make sure he stays clean. Feed from feeders that are off the ground and open to the air. Keep the stall clean daily so there won't be manure on the ground for your horse to pick worm eggs out of.

Have his teeth checked for loose baby teeth that need to be pulled or molars that need to be floated. This can stop a horse from gaining weight. If you are going to show, you have to have your horse ready to gain weight.

If the horse has some foot problems, have a good shoer come and work on him. Remember, you can change the set of the bone somewhat from birth to one year old. After that, the bones are set so don't let a shoer try to correct the leg position. All he can do is trim or shoe the horse so he looks as good a possible. Flares can be taken off and angles maintained that will make the horse look balanced and symmetrical.

Have your veterinarian give your show horse his complete set of shots for your area. Make sure flu and tetanus vaccines are included in the series of shots.

Some showmen feed a lot of vitamin and mineral supplements. It is good to have the vet check the horse's blood and see if he needs anything special. A vitamin B-12 shot could help him start off with a little boost. If you balance a good ration using high-quality alfalfa, oats, Calf Manna, and possibly a little sweet feed and wheat bran, you shouldn't need more than free choice mineral salt. A lot of money can be wasted on vitamin and mineral supplements.

Once he is eating well and gaining flesh, you need an exercise program to put the weight in the right places and keep the belly down. Some horses put on a belly easy, while others never do, even without an exercise program. If at all possible, pony the show horse at a trot for thirty minutes to an hour a day. A treadmill can also be used quite adequately. This will have to be built up gradually, but at a trot the horse will muscle up and also heat up so the hair will shed and the skin will be cleansed from the sweating. Use clear water and Absorbine as a bath after the workout if the horse is wet. Be sure to walk him and cool him out good before putting him up. It is best to use a hot walker or a longe line sparingly to exercise the horse because he will start flipping his front feet out to the sides.

Longeing

To longe a horse you need a longe line, about twenty-five feet long, and a whip. A fifty-foot round corral is really nice to have, but you can longe a horse almost anywhere, once he is accustomed to being longed.

The problem with longeing is that the handler generally pulls the head as the horse travels in the circle. This will cause the horse to drop the inside shoulder and throw the outside hip out. The horse will flip his feet to the outside as he makes the tight turns. This is unnatural and starts the horse in a poor way of traveling.

If you have the facility, it is much better to turn the horse loose and work him with a whip in a fifty-foot round corral. Under these conditions the horse will travel with his head and shoulders in a proper position.

If you must longe your horse, you should train him to relax and work on the longe line without pulling on the line. Start by using a round or rectangular corral with a fifty-foot opening. Have a helper take hold of the longe line next to the horse as if he were leading the horse. You stand in the center with the end of the line. Now have the helper lead the horse on the inside of the circle around you on a walk and trot in both directions. This will show the horse just what it is he is supposed to do. If he has an idea of what you are asking, he will be much more at ease once he is on his own.

Shorten the line to about ten feet and step towards the horse's hip. Place your whip horizontal across his tail and move him forward. Drive him around with your whip, as you control his head, holding him in a circle while feeding him line. You can walk or trot yourself in a small circle to the inside and behind the movement of the horse. If he doesn't want to go, encourage him with your whip. Just tap him with the whip. You don't want to scare him or he will try to run away from you.

Have your helper stand on the open side, if you use a rectangular corral, so the horse won't have a place to run away from you. If he tries to cut in towards you, step out behind him and drive him again, using a little more whip.

Let him get a little tired and ready to stop. Say "whoa" and step towards the fence in front of him to cut him off. Don't pull on his head or he will start stopping on an angle. Make him stop on his own just from the word "whoa". He will do it right.

Once he is stopped, say "come here" and tug on the line. Soon he will walk to you when you stop him and say "come here". Pet him and let him rest a moment. This will carry over to the corral. You will find him coming to you when you go to catch him if you just say "come here".

Use the words "walk", "trot", "lope", "whoa", and "come here" when you longe the horse. He will learn these words and work off them while you are riding, also.

**Get behind and
drive him into
the circle.**

Control his speed

**Make him stop
and come to you
on command.**

On the first few rides a colt may get scared and start to buck. By saying "whoa", the colt may stop in his tracks and just stand there.

When you are riding and the horse wants to break from a walk to a trot, the word "walk" can be used to let him know what gait you want. If you have taught him that word on the longe line, he will respond properly.

Don't think you can do all your training on a longe line. Use it sparingly, for there is no substitute for riding him.

Training the Halter Horse

Each day when you lead the show horse out of his stall, pull his blanket and put a pair of hobbles on his front legs. Drop the halter rope and go to grooming him. If he wants to fool around, put the rope come-along halter on him and give him a few jerks on that and say "Whoa" and let him know you expect him to stand still. Spend plenty of time brushing. Use your hands for a finished rub-down. This will bring the oil out in his hair and make him shine. After his exercise and when he is cooled out, work on his halter training.

The first thing you need to teach him is to walk at your side with your shoulder at his throat latch, not behind or ahead of you. Next, encourage him to trot beside you. If you have problems,

Move along the wall with the whip out of sight of the horse. Tap as needed.

use one of the three aids mentioned in the "Halter Breaking" section to encourage him to move forward. Generally, the whip is the best choice. Kiss or cluck as you move him into the trot. This is a cue for him to trot. He must learn this cue and respect it. Say "Whoa" to stop him each and every time you pull him to a stop. Teach him to turn right with his hind feet in one place and his front feet walking around. You will always want to turn to the right in a show when presenting your horse to the judge.

While teaching the above actions, you should also add the back and the stationary positioning. Here again you want to use verbal commands to aid in teaching the horse these actions.

One thing to emphasize here is that voice commands can greatly aid in training the horse. Unpublished research indicates the horse responds more to voice than touch or sight. You may recall the old work teams that functioned by voice commands only. Commands were used such as "Gee" and "Haw", "Back", and a cluck for ahead. Try to reinforce your physical cues with voice commands and you will find the horse learning quicker. Your voice can provide punishment and reward. The horse will also learn the tone of your voice. You can quiet him down or hype him up by the tone you use.

The next problem to solve is positioning your horse's feet so he is able to stand squarely on all fours on command. This is probably the most difficult thing to teach a horse because it is not in his nature to stand at attention. You seldom see a horse naturally standing square. He will generally have the weight off one back foot and the back feet will be unevenly positioned. By touching his front foot you will cause him to shift his weight onto the other three feet. This will cause him to distribute the weight on the back feet. Now you're going to ask him to come to attention and hold that position until you tell him different. That is hard for even a well-trained horse.

Start with the back feet. You have less control over the back feet than the front, so position the right back foot and build your position around it. By moving the horse's head with the lead shank to his right, you can make him move his left back foot up, or by moving the head to the left you can make him move it back a little. Don't back him up to position his back feet. This will cause him to turn his toes out and bring his hocks in. Don't worry about his front feet until you have the back feet parked.

If the right foot needs to be moved back, go over to that side of the horse and touch him right above the hoof with your toe and say "Move it". Move to whichever side you want to back and move the foot in this manner. If you want him to move his foot forward, turn the head slightly to the right to move the left foot forward and left to move the right foot forward. You do this slow and easy. If you get in a hurry you will have him moving his back feet and you will have to start over.

Don't try to teach your horse too much too fast. For the first few days get him walking and trotting beside you and teach him to stop square. You may have to get a little tough with the horse to make him give you his undivided attention, but then reward him with a pat on the neck or a kind word. Work on making him come to a stop and plant his right hind foot, then you set his left hind. Don't worry about the front feet for a few days, just work on the back feet.

Horses get nervous just like people. They can even have ulcers. You must realize you have to get them to relax as much as you can. Make the lesson as short as possible to get the job done then let him relax. Now that he will walk, trot, stop and set his back feet for you, the next step is to teach him to position his front feet without moving the back ones. Remember, never lose your temper and kick the horse in the leg. All you need to do is touch the foot with a pointer stick just above the hoof and he will move the foot back. Use the halter to stop the movement or regulate the length of step. Once the horse learns your pointer cue, all you will have to do is point your finger at the foot you want him to move and he will move it.

Some trainers use a pointer with a nail sticking out of the end. They point it at the foot to be moved and touch the nail to the ankle. Soon, just pointing the finger can make the horse move his foot back. If he is resting a back foot touch the front foot on that side so he will square his weight.

Using the hobbles when grooming will teach your horse to stand with both front feet even when you're working with him. This will help when you get him squared up and want him to stand. Don't ask him to stand more than a minute or two at first. Then build it up to five or even ten minutes.

You will want his ears at attention when the judge is going to look at him in line, so teach him to pay attention to you. Kiss easy to him to make him lift his ears and listen. He will only stay that way for a very short time, so don't try to keep him alert when the judge is way down the line. Watch to see when the judge is just about through with the horse next to you and then get your horse alert and make sure he is square. If you fiddle with him all during the class, your horse will lose interest and get irritated with your prodding. For this reason, don't pick at him continually during his training. If he looks pretty good and is standing still, leave him alone.

Grooming For The Show

Grooming your horse for a show will do almost as much to help him win as the training. You can have a beautiful coat and finish on a horse and not clean up the long hair on his face and he won't be impressive. It's just like taking a man that needs a haircut and shave, putting him in a $400 suit and sending him out to look for a job.

Take a candle and singe the long hair under the horse's jaw and throat latch. Be careful not to get the candle too close and burn the horse. Sometimes there will be some on down his neck. If you start using the clippers, you will find there is no place to stop and soon you have a mess.

You can pluck or cut the long hair around the horse's eyes. Be sure to use round nose scissors. His muzzle should be shaved with a safety razor. The ears should be clipped with small animal clippers. The mane should have a bridle path cut in it starting at the flat bone between the horse's ears and coming back the length of the horse's ear. It can be cut longer depending on the horse's neck and throat latch. If the horse has a thick throat latch, cut a longer bridle path to make the impression of a narrower neck. If the horse is a little lacking in the neck, cut a shorter bridle path to give the neck more body.

Shorten the mane by pulling to the length desired. This can be done by taking hold of a few of the longer hairs. With the other hand, push the surrounding hairs up, separating those to be pulled. Pull these hairs and go on to other long ones. Continue this process until you have the proper length.

If the mane is still thick, thin it by pulling the underneath hair in the same manner described above. Never cut it. By cutting, you may thin part of the mane, but the root area will still be full. This will make it difficult to get the rest to lie down properly.

Once it is thinned, you can use a mane trimmer to cut the very ends of the mane to a uniform length, if desired.

The foretop should be shortened and thinned so it will make the head look shorter and broader. The day of the show, put a towel or other type of neck wrap on to hold the mane down until you're ready to go in the arena, it will stay laying better.

The tail can be of any length desired. The AQHA Handbook still recommends the tail to be of hock length. The new show style is to have the tail to the ground. This may hide crooked legs and help prevent tail switching but it distorts the full stifle look we are seeking.

To pull the tail, take hold of the tail at the length you wish it to be. Use a metal curry and draw the curry down the tail to your hand and then exit the tail (wear a glove on the hand holding the tail.) By maintaining pressure on the curry as you come down the tail, you will pull some hairs from the roots. As you reach your hand and exit, you will cut the hair at that length. It will take a number of passes before you get through that hair you took hold of.

Once the length is obtained, you can lift the tail up and pull out strands at the top working to the bottom so the tail tapers when it is held up. This can also be done in the same manner as described above.

The finishing touches can be done with your hands. Pull the hairs at the top of the tail from the side and under the sides. Pull these until the tail sets in the crease of the rump without looking like a whisk broom. There should be no short hairs hanging down at the tail head when you hold the tail up. This will make the hips and stifle look broader.

The hair at the top of the hoof should be cut even with the top of the hoof and the fetlock hair should be trimmed so there is no long hair hanging.

330

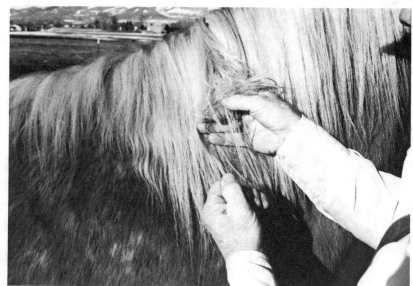

Pull a
few hairs
at a time.

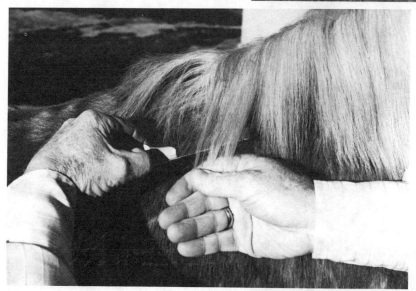

Once the
mane is shortened,
use the mane
trimmer for
a finished look.

There is a
difference.

Hold the tail
at the length
you wish to
end up with.

Start the
curry comb
down through
the tail and exit
at your hand.

Pull the long
upper hairs
in the same
manner.

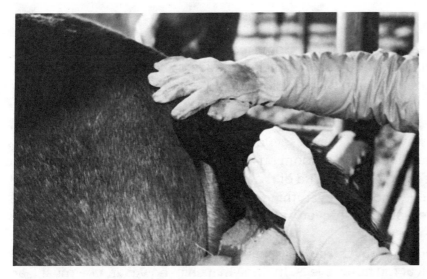

Pull the short side hairs out by hand so the tail will fit down in the rump crease.

Some trainers don't believe in washing the horse the day of the show because it may make the hair look dry and curly. Most do wash the horse the day of the show because it is so hard to keep a horse clean in a stall, especially an Appaloosa or a Paint with a lot of white.

When you wash him, use a lanolin soap that will not be harsh on the hair. Be sure to rinse all the soap out of the hair so you won't irritate the skin. Some trainers don't like to use a metal scraper because they feel it dulls the hair. A discarded fan belt can be used as a water remover.

When the hair is almost dry, you can apply a hair conditioner such as Dazzle over his entire body. Then brush it in with a clean brush as the hair is drying. Put a clean sheet on the horse and leave it there until it is just about time for your class, then pull it and brush him some more. Use your hands and rub him good so the oil will be up in the hair and he will look his best.

If you have a horse with a white mane or tail, you may want to use a blueing or bleach in a bucket of water as a rinse to whiten them. You can use corn starch or talcum powder on white legs to white them up, too.

Use hoof black or black liquid shoe polish to cover the hooves of the Quarter Horses and Paints, but a clear hoof polish should be used on the Appaloosas. Make sure the hooves have been cleaned and picked underneath.

Take some vaseline or baby oil or even better a sun screen lotion and smooth a fine coating around the eyes and muzzle. This will make them look shiny and clean. Use some hand lotion or hair set lotion and smooth down the mane and tail. Now your horse is groomed for the show.

If your horse has a refined head, use a small, refined halter. If he is a little large in the head, use a thicker halter so the head won't look large in comparison to the halter. Be sure the halter fits snug, whatever the width. To get more control, you can snap the chain on the right side of the halter after going through the left side of the halter and under the chin. If you don't need this control, run the chain through the bottom ring, double it and snap it back by the strap. This will shorten it so you won't have your hand on the chain.

Today, most halters are silver mounted. The judge is not supposed to be judging silver, but some do. It may help catch the judge's eye, but it really should not be necessary if you have the best horse.

It will help if you take your show horse to a few fairgrounds and work on your showing lessons. You can even take him to a few small shows just for the training. He needs to get used to the other horses and all the noise that goes with a show. Don't expect perfection out of him the first time or two because he is going to have to get used to the whole experience.

Showmanship

You should be dressed like a horseman, not a dude. Some judges like showmen in suits, but it is your performance they should be judging. Look neat and clean and like a horseman.

If you enter your class either first or last, you will be able to be seen better because you are not just one of the crowd. It is not always possible to be first or last, so be sure to give yourself plenty of room between you and the horse in front of you. You might tell the fellow coming in behind you that your horse kicks, so he better stay back. This will set you apart from the crowd, also.

When you line up, make sure you have plenty of room on each side of you. If the horse next to you won't stand still, you may have to move to the end of the line so you can have some room and your horse will be calm. It's like love and war, everything's fair when you are showing. You're trying for the blue ribbon, so give your horse every change you can to win it. Winning isn't everything, but losing isn't anything.

In a Halter class, if your horse doesn't travel true, you may want to trot a little crooked to the judge so he won't get a straight look at the horse's legs. In Showmanship, however, you must lead your horse straight to the judge. In this class the horse's legs are not judged for straightness.

If the horse is wide in the hind legs, you can back him up a step before you square him and he will stand closer. If he's close in the hocks in a Halter class, you could go around behind and push his hocks out and it would turn his toes in. His feet would hold his hocks out, but generally this is too obvious and should be omitted.

Remember, you are showing your horse to the judge, not the audience so watch the judge with one eye and know when he's going to be looking at your horse. After the placing is set, accept it, whether you win or lose and remember, it's just one man's opinion.

Showmanship at halter is different in as much as you, the showman, are being judged as well as your horse. You must present yourself as well as you do your horse. In a Showmanship class you should not touch the horse or speak to the horse so the judge can hear you. You have to be showing all the time you are in the arena and keep your horse alert and square. Smile, but don't talk. Keep your excess lead strap figure-eighted in your left hand and hold it at your belt or slightly above. The right hand will hold the lead about where the chain begins, but never on the chain because it is dangerous. Hold the right hand about the same height as the nose band on the halter. If you hold it too high, you will raise the horse's head out of position.

You should lead the horse from the left and put him in line and set him up. As the judge is coming down the line it is not necessary to keep the horse between you and the judge. This has been a procedure in past years but it now is changing so that you move to a position where you can see the judge at all times. As the judge approaches your horse from the rear left, wait until the judge is at the horse's shoulder before you move to the right front position. As the judge passes the horse's head moving to the right, you should move back to the left front. As he walks down the right side you can move back to the right side when the judge passes the shoulder of the horse.

When your horse is lined up head to tail, stay on the left side until the judge starts to approach your horse. Then move on the opposite side of the judge when he is standing from the shoulders forward. Then stay on the same side of the horse as the judge when the judge is from the shoulders back to the tail.

As a showman you should keep your attention on the judge, the horse's feet and his ears. Make sure your horse is set up properly. Get his attention as the judge approaches, watch the judge and move as he moves around your horse. If you are showing an old show horse that will stay squared up, you will have part of the battle won. You still can't ignore your horse or he may stand with a hip down when you're not paying attention. Always be alert and be in command.

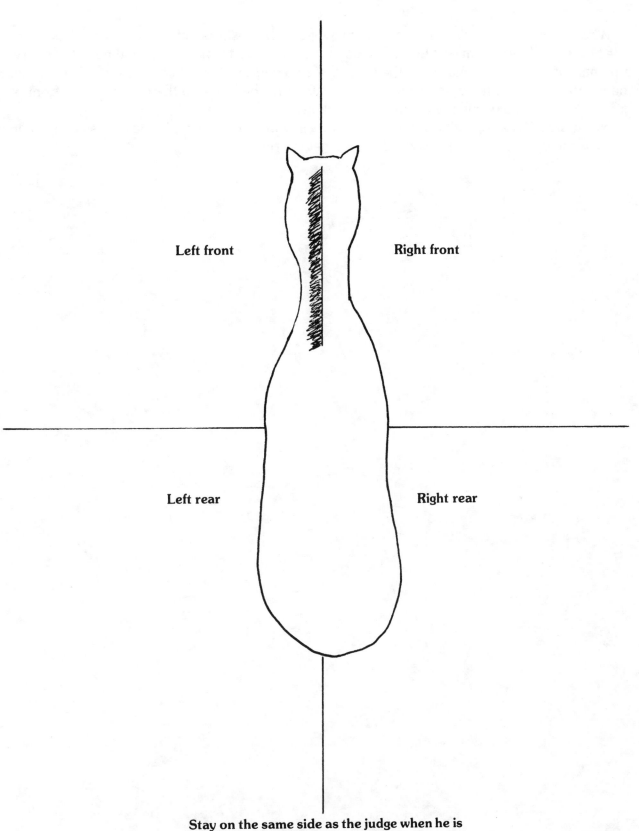

Left front

Right front

Left rear

Right rear

Stay on the same side as the judge when he is behind the shoulders. Be on the opposite side of the judge when he is in front of the shoulders.

When you lead towards the judge, know whether he has requested the contestants to square the horses up before him or if he wishes you to just turn and trot back. If you need to square him up, make it quick, but square and then stand at a 45-degree angle to your horse. Your toe should be pointed toward the horse's front feet. Always turn the horse to the right when in front of the judge. You can make half a left turn to get back in line.

Never stop showing until you have the ribbon in your hand. Some judges will switch you in the placing line-up if you stop showing before you get the ribbon.

FOUR POSITIONS OF NEW STYLE
Using the same horse

X = Judge
● = Showman

No. 1   No. 2   No. 3   No. 4

Using The Positions In A Class

PATTERN 1

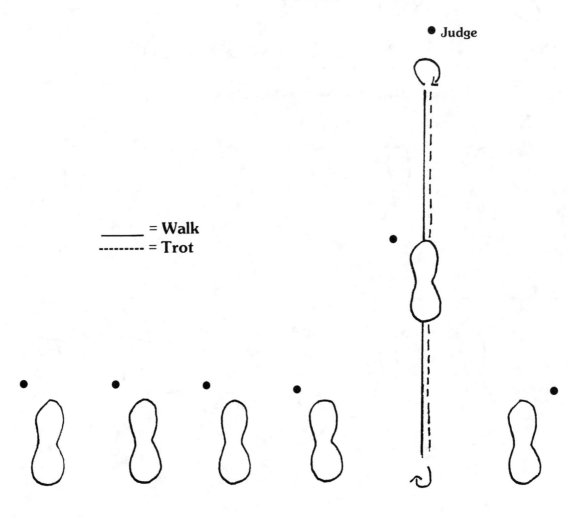

PATTERN 2

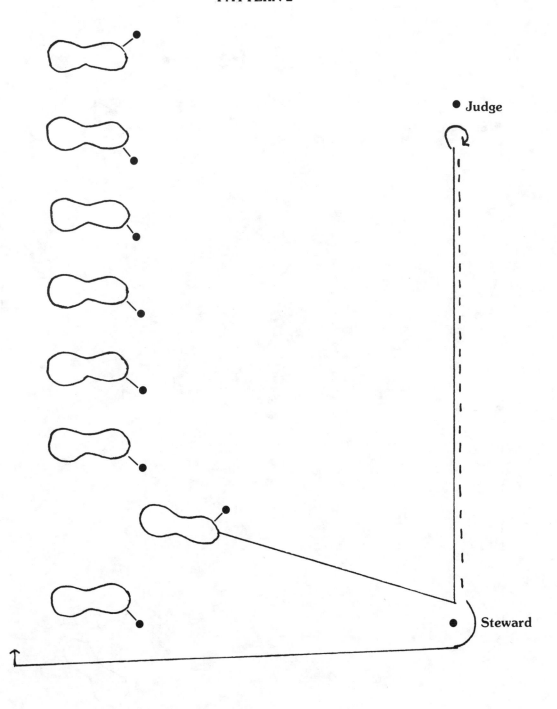

——————— = Walk
— — — — = Trot

339

PATTERN 3

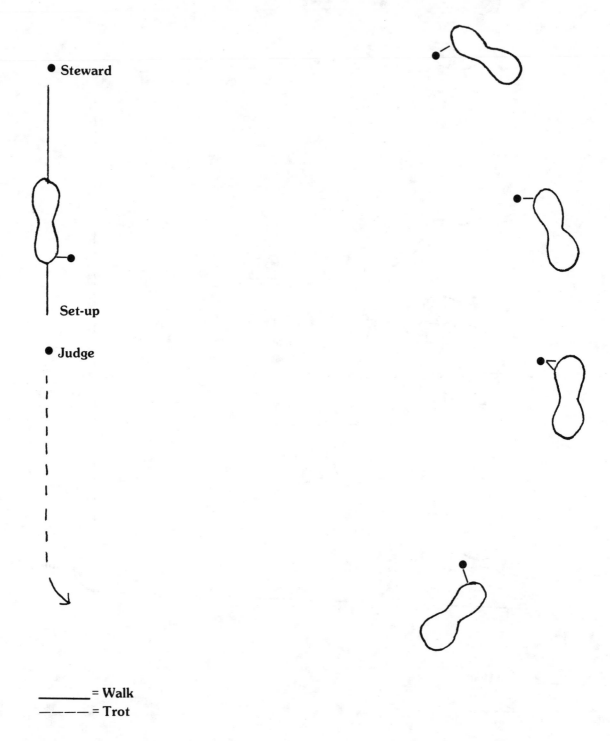

Steward

Set-up

Judge

_____ = Walk
– – – – – = Trot

340

CONCLUSION

The great General Xenophon wrote the golden rule dealing with horses. "Never approach the horse in anger. Anger is so devoid of forethought that it will often drive a man to do things, which in a calmer mood, he will regret. Thus, when a horse is shy of any object and refuse to approach it, you must teach him that there is nothing to be alarmed at, particularly if he be a plunky animal; or, failing that, touch the formidable object yourself, and then gently lead the horse up to it. The opposite plan of forcing the frightened creature by blows only intensifies its fear, the horse mentally associates the pain he suffers at such a moment with the object of suspicion which he naturally regards as its cause."

How many times have we been told this? Think of how many horsemen through the ages must have heard or read this. Will we ever learn from history or do we have to try to establish all truths for ourselves. We are always looking to the new writers for new ideas and how to solve old problems. Xenophon told us many of these answers in 365 B.C. Xenophon learned much of his knowledge from reading Simons dissertation on the subject in years before him. You ask how far back does this go? It is known that horses were domesticated by 1700 B.C., but many believe they were used as far back as 3000 B.C.

Upon realizing this, one understands how little we know about horses or horsemanship. As long as you keep searching for knowledge you will progress. As soon as you think you have enough, that's when everyone else knows how little you really have.

"Mac"

341

About The Author

J'Wayne McArthur is Horsemanship Program Director at Utah State University in Logan, Utah. He came to that position in 1969. Mac, as he is called by his students, teaches horsemanship, colt breaking, judging, packing, roping and shoeing.

Mac has been involved in most all aspects of the horse industry. Owning mares and stallions he has been involved in the breeding aspects. He has been buying, training and selling horses most all his life. He has shown halter and performance horses including cutting and roping horses. Mac even owned one race horse until he realized that was the sport of kings.

The Quarter Horse has always been his favorite horse to use. The color breeds, however, have made him the most money. Though, he always wanted his color breeds to have that Quarter Horse conformation.

Mac has a Master of Science Degree in Agricultural Economics from Utah State University. This has helped in the marketing of hundreds of horses he has owned. He has provided the horse and tack for the horsemanship program at his own cost while he has directed the program. To do this he has had to apply the marketing and judging principles he teaches as well as making sure the horses received proper training to make them more saleable. He practices the four marketing principles discussed in this book.

Mac has worked as a Vocational Agricultural teacher in Lyman, Wyoming, a Research Scientist in the Economic Research Service, U.S. Department of Agriculture and President of a research corporation doing domestic and foreign studies. Still his greatest love is working with horses and teaching.

Over the past fifteen years Mac has published many articles in national horse magazines including **The Western Horseman, Quarter Horse Journal, Hoofs and Horns and The Appaloosa News**. Presently he is writing weekly horse columns for the **Herald Journal** in Logan, Utah, and the **Post Register** in Idaho Falls, Idaho. He has a bi-monthly column in the **Farmers Stockman** magazine in Utah, Idaho, Washington, Oregon, Montana and Nevada, as well as a monthly column in **The Horse Times** magazine and **The Grainews** magazine of Winnepeg, Canada.

During the summer Mac travels around the Western states putting on horse clinics, giving talks and judging horse shows. In 1986 and 1987 he was asked to be a participant at the Cowboy Poetry Gathering at Elko, Nevada. Some of his poems were included in the book, **Cowboy Poetry from Utah, an Anthology,** by Carol A. Edison.

Mac has also just completed the book **The Cowboy Life, *in Short Stories and Poems,*** a 96 page book of fun stories of fact and fiction built around his life working with horses and horse people.